CW00607197

Property Rights, Indigenous People
and the Developing World

Property Rights, Indigenous People and the Developing World

Issues from Aboriginal Entitlement to Intellectual Ownership Rights

By

David Lea

LEIDEN • BOSTON
2008

This book is printed on acid-free paper.

Library of Congress Cataloging-in-Publication Data

Lea, David, 1940-
  Property rights, indigenous people and the developing world : issues from aboriginal
entitlement to intellectual ownership rights / By David Lea.
    p. cm.
  Includes bibliographical references and index.
  ISBN 978-90-04-16694-3 (hardback : alk. paper) 1. Indigenous peoples--Legal status, laws, etc.
2. Right of property. 3. Land titles. 4. Intellectual property (International law) I. Title.

  K3248.L36L43 2008
  346.04'2--dc22
                                                                              2008018215

ISBN: 978 90 04 16694 3

Copyright 2008 by Koninklijke Brill NV, Leiden, The Netherlands.
Koninklijke Brill NV incorporates the imprints Brill, Hotei Publishing,
IDC Publishers, Martinus Nijhoff Publishers and VSP.

PRINTED IN THE NETHERLANDS

Contents

Acknowledgement ix
Introduction 1

Chapter One. Aboriginal Entitlement and Conservative Theory 13
  Henry Reynolds and Aboriginal Title 16
  James Tully and Amerindian Land Claims 18
  Kymlicka and the Customary Context of Choice 23
  'Control Rights' and 'Income Rights' 26
  Conclusion 29

Chapter Two. Individual autonomy, Group self-determination and the
  Assimilation of Indigenous Cultures 31
  Introduction 31
  Protection and Empowerment of the Local Community 35
  Aboriginal Empowerment and Incorporated Groups 38
  Aggregates and Collectivities 43
  Political Organization and Culture 47
  Conclusion 48

Chapter Three. Shareholder Wealth Maximization, Multinational
  Corporations and the Developing World 51
  Shareholder Wealth Maximization 53
  The Justification of SWM 54
  The Contractarian Legal Model and Shareholder Wealth Maximization . 56
  Ethical and Legal Implications of Contractarian and Communitarian
    Theory 57
  Stakeholder Theory 59
  Economic Realities and Managerialism 62
  Performativity Indexing 68
  Agency theory and Managerial expertise 69

Chapter Four. Tully and de Soto on Uniformity and Diversity 77
  James Tully and Modern Constitutionalism 78
  De Soto and the Mystery of Capitalism 81
  Differences Between Western and Customary Ownership in Melanesia
    and Elsewhere 83

Differing Concepts of Ownership and the Transformation of Traditional
    Cultures.. 87
Conclusion 91

Chapter Five. Customary Land Tenure and Communal Holdings 95
The Communal Nature of Customary Land Tenure..................... 97
The Nature of Customary Land Tenure................................. 100
Forests and Pastures... 103
Agricultural Land... 105
Advantages and disadvantages of Western forms of Private Ownership... 108
Control and Income Ownership 111
The Relation Between Income Rights and Future Development 112
Voluntary Association and Development............................... 113
Enclosure and the issue of Individuating and defining Income Rights.... 115
Purchase and Sale of Land... 117

Chapter Six. Custom as Law 121
Legal versus Customary Property rights 128
Summary 130

Chapter Seven. Papua New Guinea and the Legal Methods for
    Maintaining Customary Land Tenure.................................. 131
The Bougainville Crisis.. 132
The Southern Highlands 135
The Forestry Sector 142
Possible Solution.. 149
Conclusion 152

Chapter Eight. Customary Land Tenure in Fiji: A Questionable Colonial
    Legacy 153
Jamestown and Plymouth 153
Contrasts with events in Fiji.. 155
Later Developments in Fijian Land Tenure 158
Fiji Today 159
Conclusion 164

Chapter Nine. The Expansion and Restructuring of Intellectual Property
    and Its Implications for the Developing World 167
Western Formal Property 167
IP as Income Rights 170
Global Implications 182

Taxation as slavery 193
Conclusion 195

Chapter Ten. The Myth of Free Markets: Intellectual Property, the IT
    Industry, and Market Freedoms in the Global Arena 201
    Intellectual Property Rights and Stallman's Criticisms 207
    Intellectual Property and market freedom 211
    The Global Arena 213
    Summary 216
    Conclusion 217

Chapter Eleven. From the Wright Brothers to Microsoft: Issues in the
    Moral Grounding of Intellectual Property Rights 219
    Locke's Theory of the Moral Basis of Property 222
    Control and Income Ownership 225
    Monopolistic Control of Products and Income 226
    Microsoft and Market Dominance 231
    Conclusion 237
    Appendix 240

Chapter Twelve. A Delicate Balance: The Right to Health Care, IP Rights
    in Pharmaceuticals and TRIPS Compliance 241
    The Fairness Argument 242
    IP Rights and Innovation 243
    Countervailing Moral Arguments 244
    Shared Responsibilities 246
    Pharma Lobbying, legal challenges and the TRIPS Agreement 248
    Determining the Effect of the Implementation of the TRIPS Agreement
        in India 253
    Conclusion 255

Chapter Thirteen. Rights and Genetic Material in Agriculture and Human
    Research: Two forms of Biopiracy? 261
    Agribusiness and the Patenting of Genetic material 262
    The expansion of IP rights, the TRIPS Agreement and Farmers' Rights.. 265
    The Effect of IP on Agricultural Research 269
    Intellectual property and the Human Genome 273
    Conclusion 275

Bibliography 281

Index 293

Acknowledgement

I would like to acknowledge the following Journals in which some of the material first appeared and their permission to reuse this material in a larger work.

Chapter One: "Aboriginal Rights and Conservative Theory," from *Journal of Applied Philosophy* 15, no 1 (1998): 1–13. Blackwells Publishing.

Chapter Seven: "Papua New Guinea and the legal methods for Maintaining Customary Land Tenure," from "The PNG forestry industry, incorporated entities, and environmental protection," *Pacific Economic Bulletin* 20, no 1 (2005): 168–177. Asia Pacific Press.

Chapter Nine: "The Expansion and Restructuring of Intellectual Property and Its Implications for the Developing World," from *Ethical theory and Moral Practice*, vol. 11, no 1 (Feb.2008): 37–60. Springer-Verlag Publishing.

Chapter Eleven: "From the Wright Brothers to Microsoft: Issues in the Moral Grounding of Intellectual Property Rights" from *Business Ethics Quarterly* 16, no. 4 (2006): 579–598. Philosophy Documentation Center.

Introduction

Property Rights, Indigenous People and the Developing World: Issues from Aboriginal Entitlement to Intellectual Ownership Rights

In his inaugural address of 1949, President Truman announced the Point Four Program of development aid and subsequently the United States saw itself as initiating a policy to aid the efforts of the peoples of economically underdeveloped areas to develop their resources and improve their living conditions. This idealized political model was paralleled by intellectual theory realized in the so called the sociology of modernization. This view held central prominence up until the mid-1960s. So called modernization theory saw the causes of under-development, in general, to rest within these societies. It was theorized that if the so called third world were to develop, attention would have to be paid to internal societal characteristics, which would need to be adjusted to bring about a greater fit with industrialization and modernity. However, 1970s and 1980s underdevelopment theory, also called at times dependency theory, strongly challenged this earlier view. Whereas modernization theory had highlighted the positive aspects of development: the diffusion of values, cultures, technology, capital and expertise; underdevelopment theory stresses the undesirable elements and the imbalance of transfer or exchange. Underdevelopment theory, or dependency theory as originally articulated by Gunder Frank, Immanuel Wallerstein and Samir Amin, has been summarized in the following points:

1. Development and underdevelopment are essentially aspects of the same economic process, and the former has been able to occur by increasing the latter.
2. The development of potentially underdeveloped countries is thereby blocked by the capitalist system.
3. All societies whether they possess a colonial history or not, are all incorporated into the capitalist system.
4. The system is maintained through exchange based on asymmetrical power relationships, which allow the developed nations to maintain an advantage over the others in terms of trade.

5. The world is divided into two main groups, those who have economic power, the developed, the North, the centre, the West or the metropoles and their polar opposites. There are also the partially developed or the semi periphery regions that are exploited by the centres but in turn exploit their own peripheries.
6. The transnational companies, in particular, are commonly regarded as the main agents of the neo-colonialism in that they are a vital mechanism in the transfer of surplus from the periphery to the semi-periphery or the centre.
7. Development requires that the links between the underdeveloped and the capitalist centres be broken or weakened, Usually these thinkers advocate a combination of self-reliance and socialism as the substantial answer. The long-term solution is said to be a non-exploitative socialist world system.[1]

However, third world countries that appeared to follow the solution proposed by dependency theorists, and attempted to escape the cycle of poverty by severing links with the developed world and instituting self-reliant socialist regimes did not meet with spectacular success. Socialist regimes like Tanzania were spectacular failures, with Tanzania becoming—what it had not been in 1960—one of the poorest nations in the world. Throughout sub-Sahara Africa the heavy involvement of governments in the economy proved to be an economic disaster giving further evidence of the inappropriateness of the solution. In the South Pacific, most significantly in Papua New Guinea, the pre-independent Michael Somare government in December 1972, adopted "eight aims" based on Tanzania's official goals. But these goals were eventually given up in preference for capitalist economy based on close relations with multinational developers.

Given this history, development theory's solution, centrally planned economies, dominated by government, came under strong attack. Some argued that autonomy and state planning are not appropriate in the developing world. Academically the Right has argued that central planning in the Third World has led inefficient and corrupt governments to interfere with free trade with disastrous results. Stretched to carry out even the "essential" functions of government they have failed. They often seem anxious to plan but are unable to govern.[2] All too often they accept the apparatus, symbols and rhetoric of planning but lack the discipline and forethought to carry it through.[3] The consensus among these critics is that planning should be confined to oiling the wheels of the market.

---

[1] David Harrison, *The Sociology of Modernization and Development* (London: Unwin Hyman, 1988): 29–32.
[2] P. Bauer, *Reality and Rhetoric: Studies in the economics of Development* (London: Weidenfeld Nicholson, 1984).
[3] I.M.D. Little, *Economic Development: Theory, Policy and International Relations* (New York: Basic Books, 1982).

At the same time the analysis itself which posits an essential dependency relation between the developed and developing worlds has also been questioned. For example, development theory as applied to Papua New Guinea, particularly in the text published by Amarshi et al., certainly suffered some very strong criticism along these lines.[4] Some argued that foreign ownership in PNG declined after independence with increases in ownership by the PNG government and private citizens. It was claimed that, far from being subservient to foreign interests, the state exhibited a marked degree of autonomy.[5] Similarly, others rejected the idea that the local bourgeoisie is subject to international capital and saw the emergence of an indigenous class of capital who, since independence, have taken over agricultural large holdings, processing factories, trading firms and other commercial operations in competition with the prior dominance of settler and international capital.[6] Another probably summed up the general criticism in finding the version of dependency theory presented by Amashi et al., "crude" and simplistic, and the alternate proposed, the "rhetoric" of local self reliance and autonomy, too vague for practical implementation, even when proposed by the early Somare government.[7]

The following work essentially offers an analysis of moral justification of the institution and claims of ownership as well as specific property issues that confront indigenous peoples and generally the people we associate with the developing and less developed worlds. However, as the text develops we reintroduce themes that are central to dependency theory that emphasize the potentially exploitive trade relations between the developed and developing world. We argue that the concept of internationally contrived dependency has gained renewed application in a contemporary context which has seen the expansion and continuing redefinition of intellectual property rights. The concept of intellectual property has in recent years been extended to include relatively novel phenomena such as computer software and subject matter previously immune to such claims, such as laws of nature and mathematical formulae; living organisms; genetic material; processes that are not necessarily non-obvious; and techniques that are already in the public domain. But equally important, the implementation of the TRIPS (Trade Related Aspects of Intellectual Property) agreement has sought to give the instruments of intellectual

[4]   A. Amarshi, K. Good, and R. Mortimer, *Development and Dependency: the Political Economy of Papua New Guinea*, (Melbourne: Oxford University Press, 1979).
[5]   R. Garnaut, "The Neo-Marxist Paradigm in Papua New Guinea", *Social Stratification in Papua New Guinea*, ed. R. May, (Canberra: Research School of Pacific Studies, 1984).
[6]   S. MacWilliams & Thompson, H., 1992. *The Political Economy of Papua New* Guinea, (Woolongong: Journal of Contemporary Asia Publishers, 1992).
[7]   R. Stewart, "Autonomy, Dependency, and the State of Papua New Guinea" in R. May ed., *Social Stratification in Papua New Guinea*, (Canberra: Research School of Pacific Studies, 1984).

property—the majority of which have been generated in the developed world—a global application.

As I mentioned in the seven point summary, dependency theory posits a system in which asymmetrical power relations exist between the developing and developed nations based on economic power that allows the former to exploit the latter. Transnational companies are said to be the main agents that effect the transfer of the 'surplus' to the developed world. Certainly the implementation of an intellectual property regime with a global reach appears designed to realize an asymmetrical relationship between the technologically advanced and the less technologically developed. The IP regime, promoted by multinational companies, insures that the latter pay the former for access to these technological systems. The technology once created can often be replicated cheaply ensuring that greater compensation 'surplus' will continue to flow to the more advanced. Moreover, in the case of payments over licensing agreements, often little is exchanged and forthcoming beyond the exercise of a monopolistic power to grant consent to the use of processes subject to these monopolistic rights. The superior wealth of the developed world guarantees the effective enforcement of these revenue claims.

However, one should note that there exists the claim that reference to developed nations should not necessarily mean a reference to hegemonic states in the spirit of hegemonic stability theory. It is argued that the correct view understands the developed world, not as a collection of autonomous individual nations, but as representative of the transnational capitalist class.[8] For example, although one can say that US trade negotiators were instrumental in pushing the TRIPS agreement through the WTO with the assistance of European and Japanese negotiators, in reality the national identity of the negotiators is irrelevant in so far as they are representative of a transnational capitalist class with a common interest. This interpretation assumes that the interests of the developed industrial nations don't significantly differ from the interests of their capitalist classes, the individual wealthy capitalists and multinational corporations, and moreover, this class within a given nation has interests that generally overlap with the interests of similar classes in other developed countries. With increased globalization of trade, the importance of the multinational company has grown in terms of influence over national government policy, an influence, which is often not confined to a particular national location. However, it still remains that head offices are invariably found within the countries of the developed world with the greatest concentration in the United States. To certain degree, therefore, the hegemonic goals of US foreign policy must also be seen as an important motivational component that drives international policy to promote these commercial interests.

---

[8]   D.G. Richards, *Intellectual Property Rights and Global Capitalism: the Political Economy of the TRIPs Agreement* (Amonk New York: M.E. Sharpe, 2004).

Our initial starting point is indigenous land claims and the principles that have been utilized to further land ownership claims. This first chapter is important because it serves to introduce the distinctions between "special" and "general rights", "income" and "control rights" that will become central to moral issues raised when a given property claim is asserted. Having discussed the moral grounding and viability of indigenous ownership and territorial claims we go on to discuss the fact that the legal instruments that have been introduced to empower indigenous groups economically have often failed to preserve customary values in so far as they introduced structures of ownership based on Western values and principles of interaction. I specifically refer to the introduction of the legally incorporated body as a vehicle to represent communal property interests in Australia, the United States and Papua New Guinea. We proceed to outline James Tully's position, which argues, that Western governments especially the United States and Canada should recognize a fiduciary duty to maintain parallel systems embodying different institutions, including ownership, in the interests of maintaining cultural integrity. But we also point out, following the work of Hernando de Soto, that sanctioning distinct institutions with distinct modes of acquisition within a single political entity, as advocated by Tully, undermines the Western liberal notion of ownership, which demands formal uniformity of application, which according to de Soto, is the basis of the capitalist system and its global success.

Having outlined de Soto's argument, we proceed to consider what his recommendations would mean within the social, economic and political realities of developing states. Recognizing that one of the serious challenges that face Pacific nations in the twenty first century is that of sustainable development, we go on to consider the frequently mooted proposal to replace the diverse customary systems of land and property in the South Pacific with more formalized Western systems of private ownership. Among the issues addressed we include: the nature of customary land tenure in the Pacific, the viability of custom as law, the effects of the cash economy on customary distributive mechanisms and the advantages and possible disadvantages of organizing property rights in line with Western formal ownership. In considering these issues our emphasis will be concentrated on social and political realities in contemporary Papua New Guinea and Fiji.

But although it would seem that indigenous peoples and those in the developing world should embrace the Western system of ownership in order to be financially empowered, there are also dangers, both economic as well as cultural. We point to the expansion of intellectual property rights. We demonstrate that intellectual property rights are significantly different from other forms of property and therefore the usual and accepted moral arguments that underpin our acceptance of personal property are not readily accessible to the promoters of intellectual property. In other words, natural rights arguments that we associate with authoritative thinkers such as John Locke cannot function as the basis for the rights claimed by holders of so called intellectual property. At the same time we seek to demonstrate that the push to give the institution of intellectual property a global reach through international accords such as the TRIPS agreement ultimately works to the disadvantage of the developing world and the indigenous peoples of the world while further advantaging the interests of the developed. These issues, one argues, reinvigorate an analysis that points to the exploitative dependency relationship which is being imposed globally through the intellectual property regime. In the following pages I will summarize more specifically the content of each chapter.

As mentioned above, in the first chapter I turn attention to the issue of indigenous land claims and the justification which is utilized to ground these land claims. This obviously concerns an overall justification of the mode of acquisition. We argue for an interpretation which regards the property right as a "general right", one which all individuals possess. This is proposed in contrast to the view that property is a "special right", a right which flows out of special relationships based on contingent events. We argue that the property right should be regarded as a general right, and that it follows that the accepted modes of acquisition can be qualified and modified to effect a distribution that confirms to general principles of justice. A significant part of this discussion considers an argument for parallel jurisdictions in which indigenous institutions exist within nation states in harmony with the more recently established Western institutions. James Tully has advanced this view as a solution to the conflict between indigenous and Western rights. However, we argue that this approach really fails to answer the fundamental problem concerning the extent and appropriateness of the original aboriginal ownership claims. We also point out that indigenous land claims are often justified by reference to contingent facts, but we argue that these claims also have to be justified according to certain general principles of justice. We suggest that Kymlicka's emphasis on the cultural context of choice and its importance for individual autonomy would provide a general principle, which can be utilized both to justify and limit land claims, where necessary. We also suggest that this principle may be used to justify commercial rights over resources, which may thus include rights that were not part of the original traditional bundle of property rights, as exercised by indigenous people. The inclusion of the latter, would be contrary to Tully emphasis on maintaining the original aboriginal institutions, but we point out that autonomy entails a degree of group economic self sufficiency, which requires the necessary means to access financial resources.

In the second chapter, we go on discuss the difficulties inherent in attempting to preserve traditional communities in which the cultural context of choice is maintained. This is especially the case for indigenous communities within Western societies that must deal with the exigencies of economic survival. In this instance, the community may either have to depend upon the financial support from the non-indigenous government, in which case financial dependency poses a potential threat to the community's self determination, or attempt to become financially independent. If either route is followed, the members may have to adopt behavioural patterns, which are antithetical to traditional forms of life. Moreover, this move may foster social divisions that fracture the community as it becomes divided between those who successfully adopt the Western economic culture and those who cling to a traditional way of life. This, of course, is related to the fact that the legal instruments that have been introduced to empower indigenous groups economically have often failed to preserve customary values and introduced structures of ownership based Western values and principles of interaction. I specifically refer to the introduction of the legally incorporated body as a vehicle to represent communal property interests in Australia, the United States and Papua New Guinea. Rather than strengthening the traditional community, this institution creates an additional tangible cultural dissonance as the corporation, an organization based on choice and initiative, is imposed on another organization, the indigenous community, based on traditional kinship relationships and customary obligation.

Having discussed efforts to introduce the Western model of the corporate body to represent communal land holding interests in certain traditional societies, in the third chapter we go on to consider this distinguishing feature of Western systems of ownership, the legal entity, which we refer to as the corporate body, or the corporation. Corporate ownership of assets represents a form of ownership, which has no parallel in traditional societies. Essentially this is because the corporate body or the corporation is regarded as a separate legal entity apart from its membership. A traditional community, for example, which in a traditional society might exercise ownership rights, is not usually regarded, ether in customary law or by its own members, as a separate legal entity that can be entirely divorced and separated from its past, present or future membership. Thus one needs to appreciate this modern economic arrangement through a closer comparison with the traditional community and customary forms of communal ownership. In the latter system ownership, management and beneficial interest can all be identified as belonging to a single unified group, the community. But in the modern large limited company, these different roles are associated with separate and distinct groups, for example, those who own shares in the company are most often distinguished from the managers that control and run the company. The fact that a corporation is functionally structured into distinct and separate groups rather than a single unified entity necessarily creates a plurality of interests. Because it is assumed these groups are rationally coordinated to discharge a beneficial function the issue is what is the nature of the benefit and to whom is it owed? There are two competing views of corporate responsibility: the principle of shareholder wealth maximization and stakeholder model. We go on to discuss these two views and ultimately consider the implications for indigenous peoples, and the developing world in general, especially given the current context, which has seen the ever increasing empowerment of the multinational corporation.

In the fourth chapter in this series on issues relating to indigenous ownership rights we take a further look at the implications of maintaining parallel systems embodying different institutions including ownership. Following the work of Hernando de Soto, we point out that the notion of sanctioning distinct institutions with distinct modes of acquisition within a single political entity, as advocated by Tully, undermines the Western liberal notion ownership, which is, according to de Soto, the basis of the capitalist system and its success. De Soto argues that the Western system of ownership provides a unified system of principles that allow for an identification of property interests, which is independent of parochial arrangements, shifting political alliance and local customary practice. This allows for intra-national and transnational transactions of property, which interconnect with the global economy which is driving the process of wealth generation. By creating distinct enclaves that are independent of these Western institutions one is obviating the possibility of membership and participation in the global economy and benefiting from its activities. De Soto has stated the case cogently and it is important to keep his ideas in mind when one advocates securing traditional customary institutions especially those relating to property and its varied modes of acquisition that differ fundamentally from the Western paradigm. At the same time, one recognizes the value in maintaining distinct cultural communities rather than homogenous groupings, yet one must acknowledge the dangers and avoid fostering enclaves, which are merely impoverished dysfunctional backwaters.

In the following chapters we study relevant issues to be addressed when de Soto's proposals are applied within the so called third world. In conducting this inquiry we consider issues and controversies involving the formalization of property relations and the privatization of property within the customary land tenure systems of the South Pacific, with particular emphasis on Papua New Guinea and Fiji. In the fifth chapter we discuss the meaning of customary land tenure and communal holdings. Although it is readily assumed that customary land tenure means communal rights rather than individual private exclusive rights, this is a matter that is far from clear—in fact, in the third chapter, even we, for simplicities sake, assume the distinction is fairly clear. However, it is demonstrative that customary systems include important aspects of both community rights and exclusive individual private rights, and it is important to distinguish the extent to which both apply.

In the sixth chapter, we consider carefully the meaning of custom and the capacity of custom to function as law. This is a crucial issue given de Soto's argument that wealth generation depends on property rights protected by unambiguous formal rules with universal application. According de Soto, the

Western system of legal property rights can satisfy this condition, but we have to decide whether a customary system based on an oral tradition can also support significant wealth generation. In the seventh chapter we consider a number of cases in which different mechanisms have used to distribute revenue from large development projects in Papua New Guinea. After consideration of the cases we argue that individual income rights should be assigned in order to facilitate an efficient and just distribution of revenue.

In the eighth chapter we turn our attention to the Fijian land tenure system. As we have seen, customary communal ownership is often endowed with significance and central value in the cultural lives of many indigenous peoples of the South Pacific. This is especially true in Fiji as well as Papua New Guinea. In Fiji legal mechanisms and bureaucratic institutions, some dating back to the nineteenth century, were introduced to protect an alleged customary system. In this chapter we seek to demonstrate that it is often the case that the mechanisms work to create something radically different and non-customary, which is the unavoidable legacy of the colonial rather than the pre-colonial era.

Having discussed the matters associated with indigenous and non Western institutions relating to personal property and land tenure, we go on to consider an apparently radically different issue, intellectual property. If we ignore some very significant cultural issues, it would appear the under developed countries and indigenous peoples have much to gain by embracing the Western system of ownership rights and thereby ensuring a greater participation in global capitalism and its benefits. However, in chapter nine we argue that one needs to proceed with caution in making the recommendation. We argue that the capitalist system of ownership is being restructured through the expansion of IP rights. This has strong implications for the developing world and its acceptance of the modern system of Western property, given the direction in which the institution of ownership is being redefined by IP rights. We explain and demonstrate through reference to various examples, how the broadening of the scope of IP rights, which provides the foundation for the application of income rights, is ultimately working to the disadvantage of the third world countries that are struggling to join and benefit from the global economy. Moreover while the meaning of IP rights is being stretched to cover phenomena, which were previously exempt, Western IP rights have been given a global reach through TRIPS (Trade Related Aspects of Intellectual Property Agreement) and so called TRIPS plus agreements.

Intellectual property rights are sometimes thought to be an expression of market freedom In the tenth chapter we discuss the various meanings of market freedom and inquire into the alleged underlying values that justify and animate these freedoms. One often associates John Stuart Mill with the defense of the market based on issues of personal freedom and we begin by considering J. S. Mill's ideas as expressed in *On Liberty*. We also make reference to the ideas of Robert

Nozick and Richard Stallman, creator of the free software movement, and argue that IP rights, while projected as embodiments of free trade, are actually forms of policing, interference and intervention.

In the eleventh chapter we consider a number of specific arguments that have been utilized to support the proposition that intellectual property (IP) rights as applied to software have a moral basis. Undeniably, ownership rights were first applied to chattels and land and so we begin by considering the moral basis of these rights. We then consider if these arguments make moral sense when they are extended to intellectual phenomenon. We identify two principal moral defenses: one based on utilitarian concerns relating to human welfare, the other appeals to issues of individual autonomy and private control. We argue that both fail to provide a moral defense of IP applied to software. We also go on to mention the possible alternatives to proprietary software.

In the twelfth chapter we discuss the moral issues relevant to the controversies that surround IP rights and their use by the pharmaceutical industry. We consider the arguments utilized to support and attack pharmaceutical patent protection. In the course of this chapter we argue that moral considerations relating to the right to health care impose obligations on the pharmaceutical companies that cannot be avoided by asserting the necessity to exercise intellectual property rights, maximize profits and recover R&D costs. Having made this point we go on to discuss the impending crisis in the health care occasioned by the insistence that Indian pharmaceutical industry be TRIPS compliant.

In the final chapter we focus on the application of IP rights to genetic material. We specifically consider the use of such rights in fields of agricultural and human research. We draw attention to the expansion and increased use of these rights within both fields, which threaten deleterious results for both the developing and developed world. With respect to the former issue we specifically focus on the patenting of seeds. The patenting of seeds has implications for the traditional farmer's right to save, plant, share, sell and exchange seeds. We go on to discuss associated issues such as "biopiracy", the vitiation of publicly funded research institutions, monopoly control of the food system by giant agribusiness, loss of biodiversity, ecological risks from genetically engineered seeds, and ultimately loss of sovereignty not only for the local farming community but also for the developing nation itself. In the final section of the chapter I briefly discuss the human genome project and the human genome diversity project and issues related to the patenting of human genes. Ultimately people in the developing world may well feel profound resentment over the patenting of seeds and patenting human genetic material. We point out that with respect to both cases, that which is essential for existence (agricultural produce) and essentially part of individual existence (genetic makeup) appear to have been illegitimately appropriated by Western corporations. Western legal authorities defend the appropriation of genetic material and associated forms of traditional knowledge as Western intellectual property through reliance on a labor theory of acquisition, which has its philosophical origins in the political philosophy of John Locke. Finally, we argue that the apparent legitimization of these forms of acquisition can only be achieved by an extrapolation beyond Locke's intent and an ellipsis that renders Locke's labor theory both incoherent and inconsistent.

Chapter One

Aboriginal Entitlement and Conservative Theory

Aboriginal land rights are becoming an increasingly contentious issue world wide. However this paper argues against an oversimplified solution of the issue by reliance on the notion of custom and customary rights. In the South Pacific indigenous land issues are central to many of the social problems and the complexities of development. However, indigenous land issues generate different sets of problems in different countries. Indigenous land issues in Papua New Guinea are different from those in Australia and are different again from those in Fiji and Tonga, not to mention those in Chiapas, and Alaska. For example, in Australia the issue is one of reclaiming aboriginal rights due to an initial colonial policy, which refused to recognise customary ownership and regarded Australia as 'Terra Nullius'. In Papua New Guinea the independent indigenous government has run out of crown land for the development of schools, hospitals and aid stations as 97% of the land remains locked up in customary communal ownership. In Fiji 83% of the land remains in the hands of 50% of the population, the indigenous customary owners, while the other 50%, Indian non-indigenous Fijians, hang on to an uncertain economic future because of lack of secure access to land. All these problems are different and cannot be universally and successfully resolved by reference to the 'priority' of customary entitlement.

It can be argued that Western debate about property rights and their relation to the state's authority neatly divides between conservative and liberal or leftist positions. The conservative position, historically derived from the writings of John Locke and more recently defended by modern writers such as Robert Nozick, understands property rights as historical entitlements which generate moral claims (natural rights) independently of convention and social agreement. First of all, these rights make normative claims upon the structures of society and the state, constraining them to recognise and protect these rights. Secondly, because conservatives believe these historical property entitlements necessarily include rights to use, possess, destroy, transfer and gain income from property, it follows that the state cannot limit these rights without compromising the moral integrity of the individual and his property. Richard Epstein, for example, in his influential attack on government regulation of property, has argued that ownership is necessarily a unified bundle of rights and anything less than the full bundle should not be seen as ownership at all.[1]

In contrast, liberals and leftists reject these two central points which summarise the conservative theory. Liberals and leftists maintain that all property rights in any society are a matter of convention in the sense that they are derived from the social context and the rules of justice and distribution adopted by that society. First, it is part of the liberal faith that the state is entrusted to define rules of distributive justice and ensure that convention properly corresponds to the former understanding.[2] Among other things, many liberals and leftists believe that a major component of the economic structures of the state must reflect policies which direct the distribution of goods and resources towards equality.[3] Secondly, because rights to use, possess, destroy, transfer and gain income from property, are not independently established moral givens but reflect conventions shaped by society, the state can regulate or limit these rights to correct a distributive pattern (and further goals of equality or liberty etc.) without undermining the integrity of ownership.[4]

Thus, ontic interpretations of property rights are imbedded in the beliefs which reflect the state's moral jurisdiction over these rights. These different understandings of the 'institution of property' also generate different perspectives on the issue of acquisition. Liberals have often found the moral justification of individual acquisition to be problematic. Famous contemporary evidence of this liberal thinking is to be found in John Rawls' *Theory of Justice* in which he rejects entitlement according to merit as unjust because such a distribution ultimately rests on a contingent lottery of opportunities, talents and personal characteristics. Historically liberals have been unprepared to countenance property relations and resource distribution resulting from unconnected contingent events. If property entitlement is to be justified, distribution must be controlled by general principles projected to some universal human interest. Further evidence of liberal abhorrence for entitlement tied to contingencies is manifest in Jeremy Waldron's analysis of property rights. Waldron has argued that liberals who support property rights lean towards a Hegelian belief that owning property contributes immensely to the ethical development of the individual person. Following Hart, Waldron argues that a right to property, which promotes some basic human interest (ethical development) which everyone is said to have, is a general right.[5] A general right is

---

[1] Richard Epstein, *Takings: Private Property and Eminent Domain* (Cambridge Mass.: Harvard University, 1985).

[2] John Christman, *The Myth of Property* (New York: Oxford University Press, 1994), 126.

[3] *Ibid.*, 148.

[4] *Ibid.*, 6.

[5] Jeremy Waldron, *The Right to Private Property* (Oxford: Clarendon Press, 1988), 3.

one which all men capable of choice possess.[6] Waldron holds that a general right-based argument for private property establishes a duty to see to it that everyone becomes a property owner—an argument against inequality.[7] On the other hand, with reference to what we have called the Lockean-Nozick approach, the interest which commands respect is one which people have on account of what they happened to have done or what has happened to them. Property rights are alleged to be special rights which arise out of special relationships based on contingent events, either transactions between individuals or particular states of affairs which define acts of original acquisition.[8] Since these events create special rights for certain individuals which bind the rest of society (rights *in rem*) without their consent, Waldron believes that these rights cannot be morally justified without some argument for implicit societal consent.[9]

It is noteworthy that much of recent liberal scholarship aimed at empowering aboriginal peoples, and supporting their land rights, has often unwittingly embraced the conservative Lockean-Nozickian tradition based on contingencies, rather than the tradition of left-leaning-thinkers like Rawls and Waldron. (By 'liberals' I mean generally those who are open to the interests and aspirations of other individuals and groups distinct from the dominant group.) My argument is that many of the 'liberal' supporters of aboriginal land rights tend to view property rights as contingently determined historical entitlements which are established independently of the state's authority. This, in fact, also represents the view of the conservative supporters of untrammelled capitalism. Secondly, there seems to be a remarkable degree of silence concerning the bundle of rights which are

---

[6] *Ibid.*, 113.

[7] *Ibid.*, 4.

[8] Cristi Renato, "Waldron on special rights *in rem*," *Dialogue*, 23, 2 (1994): 183–190, has argued that the idea of a special right *in rem* is an oxymoron. However, it remains that Waldron's distinction does capture the idea that conservatives are prepared to countenance resource distribution resulting from unconnected contingent events rather than controlled by general principles projected to some universal human interests.

[9] Waldron, *op. cit.*, 268–273. Waldron points out that the liberal tradition believes that there must be some consensus with respect to societal and political arrangements including systems of distribution. He mentions Rawls, for example, who believes that justice demands hypothetical consent. Even Locke ultimately held that there are some institutions like absolute monarchy which justice rules out because a whole people could not possibly agree to it; and also Kant who held that justice denies those arrangements which no rational person could agree to. The liberal position, therefore, holds that the incidence of ownership cannot be justified by contingent events alone, but is only justifiable when it is seen to promote some further interest which all members possess, and often it is understood as an interest which is capable of eliciting consensus for the institution, e.g. basic subsistence, ethical development, autonomous control of personal affairs etc. Accordingly the state possesses the authority to regulate and determine property rights to ensure that they further these more fundamental interests.

derived from these acts of original acquisition. This is to say that one finds little effort to articulate elements of commonality and difference between rights derived from customary ownership and those associated with the modern liberal institution of ownership. This may lead one to the assumption that supporters of aboriginal land rights agree with the conservative view that all the recognised components of modern liberal ownership, from the right to use, to the right to income, are acquired in the initial events associated with historical entitlement. It is my argument in this paper that basing aboriginal land claims solely on customary historical entitlement results in too close an alignment with a conservative ideology which has been used to support unrestrained capitalism. Furthermore, I argue in the later sections of this paper that customary 'rights' actually fall short of the modern liberal concept of ownership. This means that justification of aboriginal claims to the additional rights belonging to the liberal notion of property, needs to be based on something other than custom and the contingencies of historical entitlement.

Henry Reynolds and Aboriginal Title

As an example, let us turn to Henry Reynolds and his arguments supporting aboriginal land tenure in Australia. Over the last decades Reynolds has meticulously documented the historical events which resulted in dispossession of aboriginal land in Australia. The evidence of injustice which Reynolds documents is overwhelming. But, *pace* Reynolds, his theoretical analysis evinces shades of conservative thinking. In *The Law of the Land*, Reynolds mentions John Locke and the *Two Treatises of Government* as influencing European attitudes to indigenous land rights in Australia and providing a rationale for this dispossession. Reynolds criticises both Locke's theory and its application to the Australian context; however, this does not prevent Reynolds from utilizing what has been called the Lockean-Nozickian approach to legitimate aboriginal claims. In one respect, Reynolds, like other writers, believes that Locke's account has been utilized to deny aboriginal land claims. According to Locke, mixing of one's labour with the soil, through agriculture, endowed rights to personal ownership. Reynolds cannot accept this account of original acquisition because lack of aboriginal inclination towards agriculture would have rendered them propertyless according to Locke's understanding of original acquisition of unowned objects.[10] But, he argues, English law, as applied in Britain, was, in fact, flexible enough to recognise very different forms of property, for example, tenure over uncultivated land used exclusively for hunt-

---

[10] Henry Reynolds, *The Law of the Land* (New York: Penguin Books, 1992), 25, 26.

ing and fishing, and in many cases local customary tenure.[11]There is, therefore, no reason to deny the justice of aboriginal original acquisition through occupancy and customary use of the land even if these uses were non-agricultural, argues Reynolds. Thus, Reynold's dispute with Locke is over the manner and mode by which property is originally acquired, but otherwise there is no inconsistency with the Locke-Nozick view that these contingently acquired rights, created independently of the state, cannot be abrogated by the organisation of the state and the European form of civil society.

One sees this more clearly in Reynolds' argument for entitlement based on the antiquity of Aboriginal occupation and their sophisticated systems of land usage and tenure. Reynolds approves Justice Brennan's statement (in the Mabo decision) that "…the fallacy of equating sovereignty and beneficial ownership of land gives rise to the notion that native title is extinguished by the acquisition of Sovereignty".[12] For Reynolds this means that the erroneous doctrine of '*Terra Nullius*' was generated by conflating the two distinct notions and believing that because aborigines either did not have recognised sovereignty over their territories or lost it to the British, they had no proprietary interest in these lands.

Reynolds' analysis unearths the train of reasoning which in part was used to generate the doctrine of 'Terra Nullius', but a total rejection of this reasoning could also amount to a denial of the liberal view that civil society, together with the state, confirms and legitimates the conventions which create property rights. Conversely, rejection of the liberal position gives us something approaching the essentialities of the traditional Lockean-Nozickian view, a view in which property rights are ontically independent and distinct from the sovereign state, and generate a normative claim which binds both the respect and protections of the state. Moreover, alignment with conservative analysis might also imply that these customary rights constitute indefeasible normative demands which the state cannot regulate and limit in accordance with the prescriptions of distributive justice. Also, as a related point, one might well wonder whether Reynolds also embraces the position taken by Richard Epstein and Robert Nozick which understands that ownership implies the full bundle of liberal property rights—including a right to income from transfer—none of which can be limited without denying ownership. In short, does the notion of customary entitlement imply the liberal concept of ownership or something else?

Thus, while Reynolds' view of aboriginal land-claims apparently conforms to the commonly accepted Locke-Nozick paradigm, Reynolds criticises certain specific elements in Locke's theory. Though Reynolds agrees that acts associated with original acquisition of holdings trump the authority of the state, he rejects the

---

[11] *Ibid.*, 20.
[12] *Ibid.*, 187.

Lockean account of original acquisition. But his analysis leaves it unclear whether the full liberal concept of ownership applies to acts of customary communal acquisition.

James Tully and Amerindian Land Claims

Let us take a look at another approach to aboriginal land claims. In North America, the Lockean scholar, James Tully, has defended indigenous land claims against the Canadian and US states but in a manner which appears to avoid consistency with a conservative Lockean-Nozickian tradition. Indeed, in previous work on Locke's political philosophy, Tully pushed for a revisionist reading in which the formation of state and the institution of civil society rightfully dissolves holdings acquired in the state of nature, empowering the state to substitute conventions of ownership projected towards the public good. *A-priori*, Tully's communitarian-leaning interpretations of Locke went even further and seemed to deny that natural rights could ever attach to land, whether in the state of nature or in civil society:

> A property in something is the completion of man's natural right to the means necessary to preserve and comfort himself and others. It is a paramount and remarkable feature of this initial claim right that it is not to the earth itself but to the manmade products useful to man's life.[13]

Thus, it would be rather cavalier to attribute to Tully the traditional Lockean interpretation while Tully clearly denies that Locke ever actually maintained the ascribed views.

Tully's earlier work on Locke required the rejection of land entitlements as antecedently created constraints on the state's authority. Contrary to Reynolds, Tully conflates sovereignty and beneficial title to land. Tully argues that aboriginal societies were nations with independent systems of property, traditions of thought and international customary law developed over centuries of use.[14] Aboriginal property rights, therefore, were already enshrined within indigenous customary law and sanctioned by these sovereign nations. Tully asserts that Indian nationhood was recognised by the European powers as evidenced by negotiating processes and treaties. Tully states: "Negotiations cannot extinguish the status of Aboriginal societies as nations with independent systems of property and traditions of

---

[13] James Tully, *A Discourse on Property: John Locke and his Adversaries* (Cambridge: Cambridge University Press, 1980), 122.

[14] James Tully, "Aboriginal property and Western theory: rediscovering a Middle Ground," *Social Philosophy and Policy* 11, (1994): 153–180, 178; see also "Rediscovering America: the two Treatises and Aboriginal rights," in G.A. Rogers ed., *Locke's Philosophy: Content and context* (Oxford: Clarendon Press, 1994), 165–196.

thought, any more than negotiations can extinguish the equal status of the U.S. and Canada".[15] Furthermore, and most importantly, he maintains they did not lose this sovereignty but remained independent nations under the fiduciary protection of the North American states.[16]

Tully's view on aboriginal land rights is thereby consistent with his previous work on Locke. Unlike Reynolds, he puts more emphasis on the organisation of aboriginals into sovereign nation states. Aboriginal land tenure does not constrain the state because these holdings were legitimately acquired independently of and prior to the existence of the state; rather they represent inviolable claims against the North American states because they reflect the sovereign territories of extant independent nations within their borders. Trenching upon Indian land implies denial of ownership, but only because these conventions are grounded in a more fundamental notion of national sovereignty.

Moreover, Tully concludes that North American states continue to have fiduciary obligations to respect and recognise the jurisdiction of these Indian nations, even though they have since breached the original understandings. Tully sees linkage between the subsequent breach of trust and the emergence of modern constitutionalism.[17] Modern constitutionalism is seen as the intellectual legacy of writers such as Hobbes, Bodin and Locke. The constitutions generated by their ideas call for seamless legal uniformity and centralized authority rather than the ancient acceptance of parallel jurisdictions in which ethnic variation generated diverse jural systems, social political structures and greater local autonomy. Tully argues that the language of modern constitutionalism has come to be authoritative and designed to exclude or assimilate cultural diversity and to justify uniformity.[18] In contrast, he states that:

> An ancient constitution is multiform, an 'assemblage' as Bolingbroke puts it, whereas a modern constitution is uniform. Because it is the incorporation of varied local customs, an ancient constitution is a motley of overlapping legal and political jurisdictions, a kind of *jus gentium* 'common' to many customary jurisdictions, as in the Roman Republic or the common law of England.[19]

---

[15] *Ibid.*

[16] See also Bruce Morito, "Aboriginal Right: A Conciliatory Concept," *Journal of Applied Philosophy* 13, 2 (1996): 123–140, who also argues that fairness demands upholding the original fiduciary arrangement for the mutual protection of the well being of diverse cultures. Morito concludes that this means that Amerindians are independent of European law. He argues that imposing European based legal procedure onto negotiations and treaty signing was itself a denial of the common ground that existed between nations.

[17] James Tully *Strange Multiplicity: Constitutionalism in the Age of Diversity* (New York: Cambridge University Press, 1996).

[18] *Ibid.*, 58.

[19] *Ibid.*, 66.

According to Tully the latter institutions were the paradigm of the ancient constitution prior to the Peace of Westphalia in 1648. They made room for custom. For example, customary forms of ownership, institutions and laws differed from locale and jurisdiction yet were preserved within the blanket protection of the ancient constitution. Tully uses the analogue of an ancient city to explain such a constitution. The ancient city unites within a single territory the co-existence of old eccentric streets and new geometric thoroughfares, modern business areas, and diverse ethnic neighborhoods with different traditions and folkways.[20] In contrast, the modern constitution refuses to accept varied local customs and seeks a procrustean solution in which all communities and institutions are flattened and subsumed under uniform laws and subject to one national system of institutionalized legal and political authority.[21]

In the case of the aboriginal peoples of North America, the upshot of this reasoning led to the abrogation of the original commitments as stated in the Royal Proclamation of 1763 and the U.S. Supreme Court decisions of John Marshall. Rectification of this state of affairs entails the reinstitution of a constitutional accord which reflects the original understandings between the Amerindians and the Europeans, an understanding which guaranteed the co-existence of both cultures within a fiduciary relationship. Recognition of this accord means that neither the European nor the Indian system of integrated law, custom and thought is held to be superior, both continue to exist and apply contiguously, receiving mutual respect and necessary operational protections. This recognition requires the rejection of modern constitutionalism with its authoritative and exclusionary features which deny the distinct territorial jurisdictions of indigenous peoples.

This argument for ancient rather than modern constitutionalism is persuasive in many respects and appears to give us moral grounds for affirming the historical entitlements of aboriginals on grounds other than contingent facts relating to original, or in any case, earlier occupation. In part, Tully argues a return to earlier commitments while at the same time he extols these earlier virtues of ancient constitutionalism rather than the modern constitutional preference for inflexible uniformity. He maintains that a constitution of equal citizens which treated people identically did not necessarily treat them equitably; justice could only be realised where difference is recognised, protected and respected. In order to realise these ends, one must preserve rather than destroy the jurisdiction of ethnic groups with respect to social organisation, language, kinship, leadership, property and territorial control.

---

[20] *Ibid.*, 112.
[21] *Ibid.*, 66.

This all sounds convincing enough until we look more closely at the issue of property rights and land claims. Different forms of social organisation, language, leadership and property relations can theoretically be accommodated within a sufficient territory by recognising different social modalities where long established ethnic jurisdictions co-exist. In Switzerland, for example, we find a unified state consisting of different cantons within which different languages and traditions flourish. But this solution only partially touches the problem of aboriginal land tenure where the issue is not established claims but establishing claims, given the passage of time in which these claims have gone unrecognised.

One begins to see this when one attends closely to the different facets of the Aboriginal land issue. The problem is not entirely whether customary forms of ownership and devolution should apply over aboriginal territory (though this is a very important component of the disagreement) but rather the identification and bounding of the relevant territory. Aboriginal land claims often intertwine two issues: 1) the physical extent of the territory or territorial boundaries claimed by a specific group; 2) the jural system of property relations which will apply within that territory; i.e., whether customary indigenous law applies or the real property law of Western society. Now answering the second question may not necessarily give us answers to the first question. The state may assent to the application of customary law within tribe x's jurisdiction but have profound differences with tribe x as to the extent of that territorial jurisdiction. Furthermore, there is no reason to assume that a given indigenous group is equally interested in both issues. Tribe x may be indifferent as to whether customary or Western law applies so long as a given territory is recognised as belonging to them. Tully's promotion of indigenous autonomy which allows that the ethnic group may determine its own laws within its own legitimate territorial jurisdiction, still begs the issue as to legitimate boundaries of that jurisdiction.

But, of course, different systems of ownership determine different modes of acquisition. A reconfirmed version of the ancient constitution would tend to recognise property relations and customary modes of acquisition, rather than subsume both under a universal system. If we accept that the indigenous system recognised forms of acquisition different from the Western, then the temporal priority of the indigenous system entails that territories which the Europeans viewed as empty or waste land may have already had recognised indigenous owners, owners who had gained these rights through customary modes. Tully and Reynolds, among a great many others, take this approach, although Tully offers the more sophisticated articulation through his attack on modern constitutionalism.[22]

---

[22] See for example: Herman Lebovics, "The uses of America in Locke's Second Treatise of Government," *Journal of the History of Ideas* 47, 4 (Oct–Dec 1986): 567–581; Thomas

In many respects, Tully's particular approach seems to offer us a return to general principles for aboriginal entitlement; i.e., ancient constitutionalism and the universal value of preserving original communities. But I would argue that falling back on these arguments does not extrude one from the Locke-Nozick model which recognises ownership of resources to be founded on contingent events: in this case Tully's analysis still depends upon priority of entitlement associated with earlier territorial occupation, rather than legitimisation through a consensus-based conception of justice. Tully would remark, of course, that there is no ultimate transcultural concept of justice but rather conceptions of justice according to ethnic groupings. Since indigenous people, no doubt, acquired their holdings through modes of acquisition conforming to non-Western indigenous forms of justice, these holdings must be preserved in accordance with ancient constitutionalism, and respected by Westerners who may entertain different notions of distributive justice.

The problem with this approach, as I see it, is that acceptance of customary modes of acquisition is not entirely symmetrical with acceptance of other customary arrangements, notwithstanding the value of ethnic diversity. There is a dimension to issues of property which is missing from other forms of social interaction and arrangement. To apply custom to issues of property and territorial acquisition, as we would to issues of marriage, kinship, institutional arrangement, choice of political leadership etc., ignores the fact that the latter really only affect those who aspire to the ethnic membership. Non-members will remain unaffected unless they join or move within the jurisdiction of the ethnic group. This is all to say that acceptance of a given customary property claim, especially with respect to extensive areas of land, has social consequences greater than those associated with recognition of other customary institutions; e.g., kinship relations, forms of leadership, forms of devolution, language preferences etc. Unlike these arrangements, customary property claims have a profound effect on non-members, and as Tully himself pointed out, Locke, in the Two *Treatises of Government*, stated that it is precisely the conventions of ownership which require some form of consent from the rest of society and, therefore *a fortiori*, not merely

---

Flanagan, "The agricultural argument and original Appropriation: Indian lands and political philosophy," *Canadian Journal of Political Science* XXII, 3 (Sept 1989): 589–602; Barbara Arneil, "John Locke, natural law and colonialism," *History of Political Thought* 13, 4 (1992): 587–603; James Tully, "Rediscovering America: The Two Treatises and Aboriginal rights"; Marilyn Holly "The persons of nature versus the Power Pyramid: Locke, land and American Indians," *International Studies in Philosophy* XXVI, 1, (1994): 14–31; Mary. Caldbick, "Wild woods and uncultivated waste: aboriginal versus Lockean views of land Ownership," unpublished paper presented to the Canadian Political Science Association (St Catherines: 1996).

one's ethnic group.[23] Again, it was remarked, in the Notes section of the *Harvard Law Review*, that the configuration of property law determines the organisation of power over economic resources and concerns not only levels of personal material welfare but also the individual liberty of other members of society.[24] Among other things, property relations generate relationships of power and vulnerability which structure levels of personal liberty throughout society.

Given these reasons, *inter alia*, liberals have traditionally argued that the state must have the authority to determine holdings in accordance with distributive justice. If we acknowledge this, then it is insufficient to argue, notwithstanding matters of custom, that the accidents of history associated with the prior occupation by one group, rather than another, assure the justice of the claim and the ensuing arrangement. This would involve a conservative preference which bases a given distribution on contingent events, rather than the liberal reliance on controlling general principles based on a transcultural universal interest. Following the liberal route means abandoning commitments to maintain the accidents of historical entitlement. Contrary to Nozick, commitment to acceptable levels of liberty does mean effecting certain end states which tend to conditions of equality.

Kymlicka and the Customary Context of Choice

A more convincing approach remains that of Will Kymlicka who has sought to promote the customs and claims of ethnic communities, through reliance on theoretically transcultural liberal principles. As have Tully, Joseph Raz, Avishai Margalit, and Vernon van Dyke, among others, Kymlicka argued for the devolution of state powers to members of cultural groups so that they might maintain the integrity of their cultures, customs, norms and languages which

---

[23] John Locke, *Two Treatises of Government*, in P. Lazlett ed., (Cambridge: Cambridge University Press, 1967) 2:45. "...Several Communities settled the Bounds of their distinct Territories, and by Laws within themselves regulated the Properties of the private Men of their society, and so by Compact and Agreement. settled the Property, which Labour and Industry began..."

[24] Notes *Harvard Law Review*, 107 (1993): 859–876,860. The authors in the *Harvard Law Review* Notes reject the tendency in modern liberal thought to assert the lexical priority of liberty over distributive justice and point out that relative levels of liberty are determined by relationships of power and vulnerability that "pervade and partially determine the actual choices available". This is all to say that acceptance of a given customary property claim especially with respect to extensive areas of land, has social consequences greater than those associated with recognition of other customary institutions, e.g. kinship relations, forms of leadership, forms of devolution, language rights etc. This is because this recognition profoundly affects the configuration of wealth, power and relative liberty through relations which reverberate throughout society and the state.

compose their way of life.[25] Kymlicka has questioned the liberal tendency to articulate principles of justice premised on the 'bi-polarity' of the individual on the one hand, and the state on the other. Kymlicka has maintained that cultural communities, particularly 'indigenous peoples', ought to be accorded special protections of the law so that their culture is not undermined in so far as an attenuated cultural structure damages the individuals who live within it. Yet Kymlicka specifically equates this personal damage with undermining the liberal value of autonomy.[26] Selecting autonomy as the central concern of liberal discourse, Kymlicka asserts that the range of choice which allows us to be autonomous is undermined when one's cultural community is in peril.

Kymlicka emphasises the fragility of the cultural community and the dependence of the individual on a 'cultural context of choice'. Kymlicka reasons that autonomy depends upon a viable cultural community which can offer a range of culturally sanctioned and societally reinforced options. He believes that threats to the autonomy of ethnic individuals justify empowering cultural groupings in order to maintain traditional culture.[27] Kymlicka's two examples are Canadian Indians and French Canadians, 'national minorities' who, he claims, face these threats.[28]

But more specifically, it is also the case that Kymlicka has offered only qualified support to special indigenous land rights based on native title. In fact, he pronounces that the extent of land reserved for indigenous peoples could exceed the point where it is no longer necessary to provide reasonable cultural protection for them, and they begin to benefit from conditions of unequal opportunity.[29]

---

[25] See Will Kymlicka, "Individual and community rights," in J. Baker ed., *Group Rights* (Toronto: University of Toronto Press, 1994); Will Kymlicka, *Liberalism, Community and Culture* (Oxford: Clarendon Press, 1989); Avishai Margalit & Joseph Raz, "National Self-Determination," *The Journal of Philosophy* 87, 9 (Sept 1990): 439–461; Avishai Margalit & Moshe Halbertal, "Liberalism and the right to Culture," *Social Research* 61, 3 (1990): 491–510; Vernon Van Dyke, "Justice as fairness; for groups?" *American Political Science Review* 62, (1975): 607–614.

[26] Kymlicka, 1989, *Ibid.*, 170.

[27] *Ibid.*

[28] Kymiicka's argument for cultural protection on the basis of individual autonomy, in itself, provides no reason why one would give priority to the culture of the indigenous community over that of non-indigenous communities. But in point of fact, he distinguishes between 'national minorities' or self-governing, territorially concentrated cultures which have been incorporated into the larger state through conquest and colonization, and 'ethnic groups'. The latter groups have voluntarily become part of the larger state through immigration. Kymlicka accords rights of self government to 'national minorities' while denying these rights to 'ethnic groups' on the principle that the latter consented to join the more numerous group whereas the former did not.

[29] Will Kymlicka, *Multicultural Citizenship* (Oxford: Oxford University Press, 1996), 110.

He says that justice would then require that the holdings of indigenous people be subject to redistributive taxation.

For our purposes, the important point about Kymlicka's approach is the fact that it offers statement of a general principle, which is theoretically based on a universal human interest. This analysis justifies a general right to property, rather than a special right founded on contingent events. It is, therefore, consistent with the liberal tradition rather than conservative approach. This is important because liberals who wish to uphold the government's right to limit and regulate the prerogatives and advantages of the accumulators of capital and property, and at the same time uphold the rights of the victims of capitalist expansion, especially indigenous people and ethnic communities, cannot coherently maintain both positions on the basis of historical entitlement. The contemporary liberal tradition has argued that circumstance, luck, temporal priority, opportune placement, and transactions alone should not give anyone an inviolable right to control and dispose of property. This is the reasoning which has been used to justify the dissolution of trusts and monopolies and restraint of trade legislation, as well as welfarist programmes to redistribute income in accordance with distributive justice. It diminishes the credibility of liberal reasoning if one agrees (without introducing further relevant qualification) that aboriginal rights based on contingent events associated with earlier occupation and the temporal priority of the groups' customs, are sufficient to generate inviolable rights to territory, yet one refuses to recognise the inviolability of the capitalist's rights based on contingent events associated with commercial transactions, inheritance and even priority of temporal and spatial placing.

Furthermore, Tully's preference for respecting the property and ownership claims established in accordance with a given customary system gives no rationale for 1) limiting these customary property claims which overly advantage a particular indigenous group; 2) deciding between conflicting claims promoted by members of synchronically established, but different customary systems. With reference to the first point, we have already seen that Kymlicka's justification of land claims on the basis of the liberal tradition of autonomy would only license claims in so far as they are necessary to protect and maintain a given 'context of choice'. Land claims then become unjustifiable where the territory claimed is no longer necessary to maintain a particular life style and simply advances economic positioning and power relations. This is important, for conflicts between indigenous land claims and those of non-indigenous people do not always occur in first world contexts, where we nearly always begin with the assumption that indigenous is synonymous with disadvantaged. While we often have this first world paradigm before us, conflicts also have arisen in third world countries like Fiji, where the indigenous people possess extensive ownership rights originally based on custom, and non-indigenous Fijians, especially Fijian Indians, are legally precluded from acquiring significant land holdings. This state of affairs endows indigenous Fijians with overwhelming political and economic advantages. Although to date they have yet to exploit their full economic potentialities, their political hegemony continues. Arguably there is a point, one would say, where egalitarian considerations should take precedence over local custom, or where a primary concern with respect to distributive justice should be the promotion of minimal levels of personal well-being and liberty of citizenry. Again, the advantage of Kymlicka's approach, which ties indigenous land claims to general liberal principles like autonomy, is that it offers a criterion by which to limit claims when these claims begin to disadvantage other members of society.

On the other hand, Tully's multicultural constitutionalism offers us no guidance or principle by which to distinguish and limit different jurisdictions in cases of conflicting and overlapping group claims and interests in which no group evidences temporal priority. Again, the problem is not so much the recognition of value and validity of ethnic and community forms of life, as distinguishing general principles which both groups might recognize as legitimate. Tully's multicultural constitutionalism satisfies the former interest but not the latter. Tully's preference for the multi-cultural mosaic will not tell us which claim or interest is to be preferred or how we might harmonise competing claims. Kymlicka's concern with autonomy does offer a rationale for determining and limiting claims which do not leave sufficient territory necessary for other groups to maintain their 'context of choice' or which ascribe to a particular group overwhelming power over economic resources. This is important, because in reality, the lexical ordering which distinguishes between rights associated with liberty and distributive justice cannot be maintained. The capacity to be autonomous depends upon possession of sufficient resources to resist the economic power of others.

'Control Rights' and 'Income Rights'

We have argued that property in the communal land base ought to be recognised as integral to the 'cultural context of choice' rather than deriving entitlement from custom and ultimately the accidents of history. But if we accept that a certain territory forms a necessary land base for a given cultural context of choice, there remains the further issue of the nature of rights acquired. The conservative view has been that full-blown property rights, including rights to use, possess, destroy, transfer and gain income from property, are originally acquired independently of the state and require the respect and protection of the state. This is the view, popularised by Richard Epstein, which sees any diminution of the whole bundle to be a fundamental violation of the right to property. Property therefore logically implies nothing less than the acquisition of the entire bundle of rights.

However, others, such as John Christman, have argued that the concept of ownership does not hang together in a seamless package of rights. Christman argues that ownership should be bifurcated, giving us two separate notions: 1) 'control ownership'; and 2) 'income ownership'.[30] The first refers to the power to use and consume something and involves having the ultimate authority over access to the item. The second refers to the right to exchange the holding with other willing parties and keep the proceeds from such trades. The right to income includes the natural return from trades, i.e. rent, interest and profits.[31] Unlike Bruce Ackerman, who believes that control rights and income rights are incompatible perspectives on ownership, Christman maintains they represent two different modes of ownership.[32] Nevertheless, the two are separable, he claims, and one mode need not entail the other. Christman refers to both psychological and historical evidence to confirm this view.

Christman's remarks raise the issue of whether or not customary rights, associated with a given territory, should be seen as encompassing both control ownership and income ownership. It is fairly obvious that if these customary ownership claims have meaning, they must have included the necessary rights of access, use and exclusion. But it is far less clear that they included rights of income, especially those associated with economic rent.[33] In indigenous societies land was often said to be inalienable, thus it could not be exchanged, sold or given away. This is because the people and their land were often said to be inseparable. However, Christman is not simply distinguishing rights of exchange from rights of control, for he is saying that the right "...to use, possess, consume, destroy and alienate one's property manifesting primary fundamental control (control rights)—can be meaningfully distinguished from the right to transfer title conditional upon receipt of goods in trade and the right to increased welfare and income from so doing..."[34] Furthermore, Christman has in mind benefits which are of a monetary character and which are determined by market forces, for he says that unlike control rights, income rights are unequally conditional, "...for while the right to income from trade or rent of an asset is itself fixed, the content

---

[30] Christman, *op. cit.*, 128.

[31] See *Ibid.*, 31, 130, 169. He states that income rights include not only rights to alienate one's holdings, and exchange goods but to all the economic rent which is available from those trades. Since a full right to income gives owners rights to all flows from market transactions, such transactions afford owners the right to economic rent.

[32] *Ibid.*, 143.

[33] *Ibid.*, 31. Economic rent is any income from the trade of some good (factor) which is over and above the amount necessary to motivate the person controlling the factor to trade where the surplus. is due to the fixed supply of the factor (its scarcity).

[34] *Ibid.*, 131.

of that right, is not since this depends upon market factors over which one has no control or presumptive claim."[35]

The right to income is, therefore, one which could only exist in a cash-driven economy where relative scarcity and market factors will determine a fluctuating flow of welfare and benefit from the exchange of holdings. Consequently, income rights with respect to land could only exist in a non-indigenous context and can not be normally enlisted as customary ownership rights. Certainly customary land as it existed in pre-colonial places like Australia, Papua New Guinea, Fiji and Tasmania was not rented or sold or exchanged to gain increased levels of welfare or a continuing flow of monetary benefits, though in the colonial and post-colonial period customary land was and is being used in such a way.

The last observation raises several questions. The first is whether or not the state is under an obligation to recognise income rights when ascribed to customary land, where such rights were not included in the original bundle of customary rights. If we adhere to the strict meaning of customary rights it is clear that in many cases income rights would not be recognised as rights belonging to indigenous land tenure. But, often liberal writers, and even courts, do not make it clear that something other than customary rights are at issue when income rights are ascribed to these land claims. Again I would argue that a tacit assumption that these rights are logically continuous with the original customary claim (as well as the usually recognised rights to exclusive use and occupation) will also unwittingly strengthen the agenda of a conservative faction wishing to argue that any regulation or diminution of the individual's right to trade and exchange for maximum benefit will be viewed as an attack upon ownership. Again, liberals cannot afford to manufacture arguments on an *ad hoc* basis. It is blatantly inconsistent to maintain that regulations which perhaps aim at environmental protection, but which adversely affect the income derived from a certain piece of property, do not amount to a fundamental denial of ownership, while, with respect to indigenous customary rights, implicitly accepting Epstein's view that ownership must always include the right to derive income from the property claimed.

There is a further reason for being hesitant in hastily connecting customary ownership claims with the right to income. Supporting customary laws and folkways is about preserving customary forms of life and the communities which embody these forms of life. Impacting customary rights with the non-customary will have quite the opposite result. This underlines the wisdom of Kymlicka's remark that land claims should only be recognised in so far as they promote a given 'context of choice' and not to give undue economic advantage. One can be fairly sure that when land is utilised as a commercial commodity, in exchange or

---

[35] *Ibid.*

rent, customary interests will no longer be operative, and it would be fraudulent to acquire such land on the pretext of custom with the motivation of commercial transaction. My point is that one may argue that limiting non-customary uses, like the exercise of what Christman calls the 'right to income', is, in fact, justified not from a narrow juristic point of view, but because the exercise of these rights may hasten the dissolution of the customary forms of life which bind indigenous communities. On the other hand, the liberal principle of autonomy would license the inclusion of income rights if we regard a certain minimum command of resources as necessary for the exercise of liberty and autonomous decision-making. I believe that given the reality of the monetary societies in which many indigenous people find themselves, this is a realistic assessment.

But Christman understands 'control rights' as determinants of autonomy, whereas 'income rights' are less directly related to issues of autonomous behaviour, because of the unpredictability of market forces.[36] I don't believe this is quite correct, notwithstanding the issue of predictability. Income rights are a significant factor in structuring the relative bargaining power of agents in a modern economic context even if these relationships are, from time to time, susceptible to the instabilities of the market. The capacity to be autonomous has to be a function of one's relative bargaining power. As the editors in the *Harvard Law Review* have pointed out, ownership and levels of personal liberty are not unconnected, because property rights determine relationships of power and vulnerability. The contradiction then arises. In order to be sufficiently autonomous in many traditional cultures, 'the cultural context of choice' must be protected against incursions from Western capitalist systems and incorporation of behavioural forms which are adapted to and consistent with income generating functions. But it is also apparent that the more these societies become integrated into the realities of the modern market economy, the more vulnerable they become, and susceptible to loss of liberty and autonomy if their membership is not in control of sufficient income-generating rights, or cannot utilise resources to protect themselves.

In reality, if autonomy is the central value to be protected, indigenous land claims should be honoured in so far as they are necessary to maintain the traditional 'cultural context of choice' and at the same time to allow sufficient territory and resources necessary for the effective exercise of 'income rights'. Regardless of the strength of the traditional customary claim these claims should still be limited where they begin to effect undue economic advantages which disadvantage and undermine the liberty of other individuals and groups.

---

[36] *Ibid.*, 164.

Conclusion

My conclusion is that indigenous claims to land can be better supported by appeal to Kymlicka's arguments for a cultural context of choice, rather than arguments like those of Tully and Reynolds which theoretically parallel the conservative Locke-Nozick tradition. Kymlicka's reasons avoid the latter tradition through emphasis on the trans cultural liberal principle of autonomy and the necessary protection of the indigenous land base. Furthermore, Kymlicka's approach gives good reasons for limiting historical entitlement to accord with principles of distributive justice where extensive territory is not necessary to the viability of ethnic existence and the individual 'context of choice'. In addition, the protection of autonomy offers a rationale for incorporating non-customary 'income generating rights' into customary ownership in order to maintain the relative bargaining power of the indigenous community. On the other hand, if we base aboriginal land claims on principles of customary historical entitlement which necessarily share certain of the central elements of the Locke-Nozick tradition, we imply an ontic and moral priority to property relations which is greater than the state's authority to regulate in the interests of individual well-being and general equality. The identification with the Locke-Nozick tradition is to be resisted by all those who are not in sympathy with untrammelled capitalism.

Chapter Two

Individual autonomy, Group self-determination and the Assimilation of Indigenous Cultures

Introduction

For many, the solution to the crisis and survival of the community has centred on special group rights aimed at both the protection of these groups and their empowerment. This philosophy has served as powerful rationale for policies designed to enhance the potential self-determination of indigenous communities, communities which in the past have suffered extensive cultural destruction from settlers and colonists.

But one needs to appreciate these developments within their historical context. In the 1970s Ronald Dworkin wrote a definitive work, *Taking Rights Seriously*, in which he contrasted liberal commitment to individual rights with utilitarian calculations associated with economic rationalism and policy driven initiatives aimed at general social welfare.[1] In this text Dworkin argued that, a commitment to the protection of individual rights distinguishes liberal society as one which is willing to suffer the disadvantages to policy and economic rationalism in order to preserve the freedom and dignity of the individual. Dworkin argued that it may well be the case that greater levels of general welfare might be achieved by imposing a seamless uniformity which disregards individual rights, however, this would compromise the liberal philosophy of Western society which values the dignity and freedom of the individual.

It is from this philosophical perspective that Dworkin went on to defend tolerance and restraint with respect to the actions of dissenting individuals and groups who may offend the general mainstream of society. Since Dworkin's work appeared after the bitter winding down of United States involvement in the Vietnam conflict in which allegations of civil disobedience and disloyalty frequently surfaced, his statements were extremely apposite. At the time it was frequently claimed by those who supported United States and Western

---

[1]   R. Dworkin, *Taking Rights Seriously* (London: Duckworth, 1977).

military involvement, that the actions of a minority of dissenters were undermining the efforts of the troops and thereby damaging to the best interests of society. On this basis many argued that these dissenting individuals should be suppressed. Dworkin's defence of individual rights served to remind people that any such policy contradicted the rationale the West gave for entering the conflict, which was to oppose totalitarian states. Dworkin argued that toleration was the price society would have to pay if it were really to distinguish itself from its enemies and remain a polity and a society which accorded real dignity and respect to the individual and dissenting minorities.

Until the 1980s the liberal political philosophy of people like Dworkin and John Rawls dominated academia and was widely regarded as an authoritative and convincing presentation of the superior justice of liberal democratic societies.[2] Liberals like Dworkin and Rawls forcefully demonstrated how liberal societies achieved individual justice and justice for minorities through the institution of equal individual rights. But in the 1980s their arguments began to be questioned. A powerful movement sometimes called communitarian or culturist began to gain force and stress the value of community.[3] They questioned the liberal tendency to articulate principles of justice premised on the 'bi-polarity' of the individual on the one hand and the State on the other. They often argued that justice must go beyond the idea of equal rights for all citizens and provide special rights for communities and cultural groupings in order for cultural communities to survive and endure potentially overwhelming threats to their traditions. The political philosophers who initially criticised liberalism argued that an undue emphasis on the importance of the individual was contrary to the lived experience of human life. Communitarians argued that liberal philosophy, which based its systems of justice on the pre-eminent liberty of the individual, projected a notion of the self which conveyed 'radically unengaged individuality.' This 'liberal self' represented the so-called 'thin view of the self,' a deracinated self which was disengaged from culture and community and accordingly suffered the modern diseases of alienation and anomie. These thinkers believed that emphasis on equal individual rights fails to protect and even undermines communities and cultural groups because these policies do not allow for cultural difference or officially recognise its possibility. Some suggested that the notion of citizenship should be redefined in a manner to incorporate difference so that cultural communities

---

[2] John Rawls, *A Theory of Justice* (Oxford: Oxford University Press, 1971).
[3] Vernon van Dyke, "Justice as Fairness for Groups?" American Political Science Review 69, (1975): 607–614; Michael Sandel, *Liberalism and the Limits of Justice* (Cambridge: Cambridge University Press, 1982) Avishai Margalit & Joseph Raz, "National Self-determination," *The Journal of Philosophy* 87, (1990) 439–461.

could gain collective rights like trade unions and corporations. It is in this context in which we observe the ascendancy of special group rights for indigenous communities.

One might mention that these intellectual shifts were not simply played out within the academic community. This alteration in perspective was also evident in a changing public policy toward indigenous groups, reflected in real administrative and policy rearrangement. One commentator on Aboriginal affairs notes that in the 1950s and 1960s institutional reform in Australia centered on exclusionary policies with respect to indigenous Australians. This initial period of institutional reform was based upon the unproblematic and uncontested ideology of equal individual rights for indigenous and other Australians. However, there began a second wave of institutional reform beginning in the 1970s through into the 1990s which has been more about group rights, especially with respect to land rights.[4]

In North America one can perceive a similar trend. In the United States, the *General Allotment Act* of 1887 (called the Dawes Act, after its principal senatorial sponsor) brought wide scale private ownership of land to Indians.[5] This emphasis on individual private rights was part of a grander scheme of assimilation and Christianity.[6] This process was abandoned by the government in 1934. In the 1950s the so called termination policy was introduced that sought to terminate Indian tribes with ensuing loss of Indian status and reversion of tribal reservations to private or government ownership. The goal again was assimilation in which Indians would possess the same equal rights and status as other American citizens.[7] However, The US government in the latter half of the twentieth century abandoned these policies. "Self-determination" is a term that has been used to describe the most recent era of federal Indian policy. Instead of breaking up the land base and membership of Indian tribes and terminating the relationship between the tribes, its members, and the federal government, the United States now seeks to promote Native self-government and economic self-sufficiency while maintaining the "… Federal Government's unique and continuing relationship with a responsibility to the Indian people…"[8] In Canada one notes a similar

---

[4] N. Pearson and W. Sanders, "Indigenous Peoples and Reshaping Australian Institutions: Two Perspectives," AEPR Discussion Paper No. 102, (Canberra: Centre for Aboriginal Economic Policy Research, ANU, 1995).

[5] Fred Mc Chesney, "Government as Defender of Property Rights: Indian Lands, Ethnic Externalities and Bureaucratic Budgets," *The Journal of Legal Studies* 19, 2 (June 1990): 297–335, 301.

[6] *Ibid.*, 302.

[7] J.F. Walsh, "Settling the Alaska Native Claims Settlement Act," *Stanford Law Review* 38, 1 (Nov. 1985): 227–263, 231.

[8] Bart K. Garber, "1991 Balancing Individual and Group Rights after ANCSA," *Alaska Native News* 2, (January 1985): 21–30, 25.

movement away from a policy of assimilation and equal rights for indigenous peoples towards a reinstatement of Indian status in the latter part of the twentieth century and thereby a renewed recognition of special group rights for indigenous peoples.

But this growing tide of 'communitarian' thinking and public policy centered on group rights has not been without its critics. Liberals remained skeptical as to how community rather than the individual could serve as the moral basis for a reworked 'communitarian' vision of justice. Many liberals were uneasy with this articulation because it appeared to reintroduce a cultural relativism, which denied the universal application of the core liberal values and by implication the preeminence of liberal notions of justice, which had been central to Western liberal democracies. Indeed it was feared that communitarian philosophy would reopen the door to restrictions on individual liberty, promoted in favour of conformity and group solidarity.

The most successful effort to reconcile the apparent irreconcilable clash of liberal and communitarian values was to be found in the political philosophy of Will Kymlicka.[9] Communitarians argued that we can only understand the individual and the exercise of freedom of choice, by viewing the human agent within the context of his community and his cultural traditions. These are the circumstances in which individuals realise moral choices and live out their individual lives, and therefore rather than emphasising the value of the individual to the exclusion of the community, we ought to reaffirm the value of the community and extend the protections necessary for its survival. Kymlicka points out that theoretically there is no inherent conflict between valuing the individual and protecting the community. Underlining individual autonomy as the central value of liberal society, he claims that a viable community is essential for providing a cultural context of choice in which autonomy is possible. He argues that autonomy depends upon a range of choices, and these choices are embedded in a particular cultural context. The cultural community maintains a particular cultural context; when the cultural community is undermined, shocks to individual identity also undermine autonomous decision-making. The context in which the individual would have traditionally realised his identity is weakened or obliterated. The traditional ends, from which the individual would have chosen to mould his life, have been removed, and the individual suffers disorientation, purposelessness and alienation associated with the disintegration of the cultural context. Kymlicka draws our attention to Canadian Indians and French Canadians, groups who, he thinks, face threats to their continuity and whose individuals suffer the anomie and other forms of social disorientation associated with the above phenomena.

---

[9]   Will Kymlicka, *Liberalism, Community and Culture*, (Oxford: Oxford Clarendon Press, 1989) and *Multicultural Citizenship* (Oxford: Oxford University Press, 1996).

Kymlicka claims that, far from being an interest antithetical to liberal values, the community and the protections of its traditions are essential if the core liberal value of autonomy is to be a reality.

Kymlicka's formulation thus brings together two concepts, that of autonomy with respect to individual agency, and autonomy as applied to the group. In short the argument put forth is that the latter is necessary and supportive of the former. These two distinct ideas are often blurred in the simple demand for the self-determination of indigenous groups, as Stephen Schecter observes. "Self determination is a concept that manages to combine individual and collective rights without mentioning either. It has a better press than collective rights, since the self makes us think of the individual."[10]

In the following pages I wish to point out that these two forms of autonomy may well prove to be antithetical in practice. I mean this not in the more familiar sense in which liberals fear that prioritising the rights of the collectives may license the suppression of individual choice and associated freedoms, but in another sense in which the successful survival of the community may inevitably mean the unconscious adoption of assimilationist forms of behaviour. In short I wish to point out that there is an economic component embedded in the issue of autonomy. Ultimately economic realities may entail that the survival of traditional communities in pluralistic market economies of Western states requires the incorporation of behavioural forms which are antithetical to traditional forms of life. In short the survival of the group as a self-determining entity may result in the obviation of the original cultural context, which is conceived to be necessary to individual autonomy, according to Kymlicka.

Protection and Empowerment of the Local Community

Kymlicka has specified practical measures which should be instituted to ensure a measure of local autonomy and effect cultural protection for indigenous minorities within larger political entities.[11] These are:

- special representation at the Federal level through special group representational rights;
- devolution of authority over issues relevant to local culture to smaller political units, especially issues of immigration, education, resource development, language and family law;

---

[10] Christine Fletcher, "Federalism and Civil Societies", *Federalism Studies* 14, (1999): 97–121, 107.
[11] Will Kymlicka, *op. cit.*, *Multicultural Citizenship*, 1996.

– polyethnic rights which protect special religious and cultural practices through the funding of special programs which would otherwise not be protected through the market.

In general terms, the goal of these recommendations is to establish indigenous communities as self determining political entities within the pluralistic state, placing limits on the central authority of the state. Often advocates of greater autonomy for Aboriginal groups envision a form of federalism where sub-national groups claim some form of territorial jurisdiction in which traditions and distinct cultures can flourish within a greater political entity. In some cases this involves the creation of new territories such as Nunavuk in Canada, lesser forms of indigenous self government in the United States or establishing inalienable freehold land rights in some Australian States and the Northern Territory of Australia.[12] Of course at the extreme we have the demand for wholesale secession.

But the issue is at the same time both political and economic. In order for indigenous people to be self determining they need to have the necessary political right to realize this goal. The above political arrangements indicate some of the possibilities. Political re-arrangements are intended to create a potential self-sufficiency which minimizes and restricts the areas in which the group will be subject to the political will of the central government, usually representative of the dominant majority culture. However, political self-sufficiency would also require an important component of economic self-sufficiency. Legislating the framework for the realization of a degree of political autonomy does not guarantee the achievement of conditions of self-determination and autonomy. In addition to political empowerment there needs to be economic empowerment. Reflection indicates that autonomy and self-sufficiency are also a function of relative bargaining power. As the editors in a recent *Harvard Law Review* have pointed out, ownership and levels of personal liberty are not unconnected because property rights determine relationships of power and vulnerability. In this vein, the editors reject the tendency in modern liberal thought to assert the lexical priority of liberty over distributive justice and point out that relative levels of liberty are determined by relationships of power and vulnerability that pervade and partially determine the actual choices available.[13]

Aboriginal communities which find themselves within modern Western states have not only been politically weakened, they have also been economically disadvantaged. For example, the economic vulnerability of Aboriginal communities in Australia was underlined by Frank Brennan in *One Land, One Nation: Mabo—*

---

[12] Christine Fletcher, "Does Federalism Safeguard Indigenous Rights,", Discussion Paper 14, (Darwin: North Australia Research Unit, Darwin, 1999), 10.

[13] Notes, *Harvard Law Review* 107, (1993): 859–876, 860.

Towards 2001. Brennan points out that despite growing demands by Aborigines to manage their own affairs there is a tension between the right of an Aboriginal community to do its own thing on its own terms on its lands, and the notion of public accountability for the expenditure of funds approved by Parliament.[14] He points out that, given the financial poverty of these communities, they are all but totally dependent on the receipt of government funds. This means that for most of these communities, the financing of education, training, health and welfare must come from outside the community, which means from the government.

General conditions of economic disempowerment can be seen to undermine the specific areas in which indigenous communities have been making tangible political gains. W. Sanders in his recent work on local governments and indigenous Australians observes that a major dilemma or problem facing discrete predominantly Aboriginal or Torres Strait Islander communities in sparsely settled areas, who have achieved local government status, is their rather 'weak independent financial capacity'. On the other hand, non-Aboriginal local government communities have traditionally been able to carve out a degree of autonomy from Commonwealth and State authority, through the collection of rates, an option which is not available to poorer Aboriginal and Torres Strait Island communities.[15] Furthermore on the issue of greater regional autonomy for the Torres Strait Islanders through a proposed Torres Strait Regional Assembly, a 1997 Report of Inquiry on greater autonomy tied greater financial autonomy (through grant block funding from the State and Commonwealth Governments) to the ability of Islanders to increase their involvement in local industry—particularly the commercial fisheries.[16]

Even if we feel that the federal government has a responsibility to supply this funding with no strings attached, the autonomy of the indigenous community cannot be assured, insofar as it is dependent on the good will of the donor, and the

---

[14] Frank Brennan, *One Land, One Nation: Mabo—Towards 2001* (Brisbane: University of Queensland Press, 1995).

[15] W. Sanders, "Local Governments and Indigenous Australians: Developments and Dilemmas in Contrasting Power to Sell, Lease, and Dispose of Customary Land Otherwise Than to Natives in Accordance with Custom, and a Contract Circumstances," CAEPR Discussion Paper No. 84 (Canberra: Centre for Aboriginal Economic Policy Research, ANU, 1995). Sanders notes that predominantly Aboriginal or Torres Strait Island Communities have gone furthest to becoming local governments in sparsely settled areas of Queensland and the Northern Territory, pages 17–20.

[16] W.S. Arthur, "Towards A Comprehensive Regional Agreement: Torres Strait," CAEPR Discussion Paper No. 147 (Canberra: Centre for Aboriginal Economic Policy Research, ANU, 1997), 15.

inevitable demands of accountability. As we know, Aboriginal self-determination has been put forth on the grounds that it is necessary to preserve the distinct values and cultural difference. It becomes highly imaginable that if the Aboriginal community decides to spend government funds in ways conflicting with the dominant group, the funding would cease. Being autonomous means being empowered to make one's own choices regardless of what other groups or the dominant group think of the choices.

Aboriginal Empowerment and Incorporated Groups

A number of policies designed to empower indigenous people economically have introduced corporate bodies for holding and managing communal assets especially land. In the following discussion I make reference to the Australian *Native Title Act*, the US *Alaskan Native Claims Settlement Act* (ANCSA) and the Papua New Guinean *Land Groups Incorporation Act*; all of which employ the incorporation model for indigenous land holding. In Australia, the Native Title Act 1993, was drafted to give effect to the Supreme Court decision of Mabo v State of Queensland 1992, which recognised a form of customary land title, which Aborigines possess. Until the Mabo case Australian law under the doctrine of *Terra Nullius* did not recognize the existence of Aboriginal interests in land. Under the *Native Title Act*, the Aboriginal registration of land title requires that there exist an incorporated body under the *Aboriginal Councils and Association Act* 1976 (ACAA). In the North American context, the *Alaska Native Claims Settlement Act* (ANCSA) in 1971 granted Native title to nearly forty million acres of Alaska and provided one billion dollars in direct compensation in exchange for extinguishment of Native claims to Alaska lands based on aboriginal use and occupancy. The ANSCA also established a system of Native corporations, each organized under Alaskan law to insure the best use of the land and to distribute financial compensation among the Natives.[17] In 1974 the year before independence the *Land Groups Incorporation Act* was introduced in Papua New Guinea providing for the legal recognition of traditional groups and their incorporation for purposes of acquiring, holding, disposing and managing land.[18] Although the latter is not intended to empower a cultural community against a dominant majority culture, it is intended to offer economic and management control to communities exhibiting indigenous forms of collective ownership.

---

[17] J.F. Walsh, *op. cit.*, "Settling the Alaska Native Claims Settlement Act," 227.

[18] *Land Groups Incorporation Act*, (1974) ch. 147, s. 1 (e). This was enacted by the PNG Legislative Assembly a year after power was transferred from the Australian Commonwealth Parliament to the PNG Legislative and a year before official independence in 1975.

Having mentioned these three policies it should be said that the three incorporation models are not identical in structure. For example, the US legislation does provide for individual shares in native corporations and the alienation of shares, whereas the others do not. Also the PNG legislation does place serious restrictions on land dealings. Papua New Guinea legislation provides that all dealings with respect to customary land between customary owners and non-citizens are void and unenforceable.[19] In order to avoid this result the customary owners can lease their land to the government who then lease it back. But nevertheless, what is significant is that all three prescribe some form of the Western corporate structure as the appropriate form of land holding.

Many, of course, believe Western corporate bodies have important affinities with communal forms of land owning and therefore are appropriate vehicles for controlling and holding traditional lands. For example, Canadian academics, Michael Trebilcock and Jack Knetch, (engaged by the Papua New Guinea Institute of National Affairs) argued that the importance of individualization of land tenure to support enhanced economic productivity is easily exaggerated. They state that "Even in developed economies, most major economic resources are owned by groups, whether corporations, cooperatives, insurance companies, pension funds, mutual funds etc."[20] Nevertheless dissimilarities also need to be highlighted.

But, experience in Papua New Guinea indicates that the empowerment of the group representatives or leaders may not necessarily empower the group or promote its interests and well-being. This point is illustrated by the fact that the landowner companies, which are assuming a negotiating role in areas such as forestry, are often not entrepreneurial enterprises in the true sense of the word. They are more accurately seen as brokers or middlemen interposed between the foreign interest and the customary landowners. Given this reality, the interests of those managing the Landowner Company may not coincide with the best interests of the traditional customary owners. For example, it has been demonstrated that landowner companies which sprang up in Manus Province in the 1980s actually frustrated the Province's efforts to manage the timber harvest on a sustainable basis.[21] Against the Province's wishes they interposed themselves into negotiating

---

[19] Revised laws of Papua New Guinea, *Land Act of Papua New Guinea*, (1982), ch. 185, s. 73. Subject to Sections 15 and 15A, a native has no power to sell, lease, dispose of customary land otherwise than to natives in accordance with custom, and a contract or agreement made by him to do so is void.

[20] Michael Trebilcock and Jack Knetch, "Land Policy and Economic Development in Papua New Guinea," *Melanesian Law Journal* 9, 1&2 (1981): 102–115, 105.

[21] Rodney Taylor, "Sustained Yield Forest Management in Papua New Guinea," *Resources, Development, and Politics in the Pacific Islands*, in Stephen Henningham & R.J. May ed., (Bathurst: Crawford Home Press, 1992): 129–144.

roles with foreign logging interests and effected deals which exceeded sustainable quotas of timber. As these landowner companies seldom offer their own expertise, management, capital or labour to the enterprise, they can best be described as opportunistic middlemen rather than entrepreneurial associations, an impression which is further strengthened by the fact that these associations are most often led by a small elite of the more literate westernised tribesmen rather than organisations with the full participatory involvement of the greater community.[22]

The Papua New Guinea experience indicates that organisational structures such as the modern corporation, or trusteeship arrangements (which are also essential to the internal relations of the corporation) have not been successful vehicles for the economic mobilisation of indigenous people. There are two reasons. First, because they are Western organisational models, they are foreign to the traditions of the indigenous communities. Second, successful adaptation to such an organisational structure requires adoption of Western thinking and behavioural models. This means that only the most Westernised and educated members of the community can understand and avail themselves of the opportunities. This then creates a division within the community between the traditional membership and their minority Westernised counterparts who are able to participate and take advantage of the economic possibilities. Those who remain attuned to a traditional lifestyle find themselves alienated from the processes and decision-making procedures designed for economic empowerment. At the same time enrichment will flow to the minority who have adapted their behaviour to these Western organisational models designed for wealth generation. Consequently, the community as a whole is not empowered, but often divided because only a minority acquire the economic advantages. In general, rather than working to preserve the traditional community, these strategies tend to create divisions between those who are integrated into the cash economy and the economic market and those whose lives adhere to indigenous traditions. Gradually this becomes a division between the have and the havenots. The result, as in the Bougainville crisis, can lead to the fracturing of the community into warring generations, thus destroying its social fabric.[23]

---

[22] *Ibid.*, 141. The author points out that the so called landowner companies which sprang up on Manus Province to deal with the foreign timber interests failed to satisfy the legitimate reasons for their formation which include: 1) bringing customary land and associated rights under corporate title, the by use of the *Land Groups Incorporation Act*; 2) forming a business for the carrying out of forestry and spin off enterprises; 3) managing funds accruing from the enterprise for community development projects. In reality they simply operated as middlemen between logging interest and customary owners.

[23] C. Filer, "The Bougainville Rebellion, the Mining Industry and the Process of Social Disintegration", in *The Bougainville Crisis* in R J. May and M. Sprigs eds., (Bathurst: Crawford House Press, 1990).

Similarly in Alaska, the hereditary chief of the Ahtna and Tanaina Athabascan peoples and elected chief of the Chickaloon Athabascan village, decries the creation of Indian corporations for the financial management of Indian lands. He states, "ANCSA is an experiment gone awry. There are a whole lot of attorneys, accountants, administrators and consulting carpetbaggers who have retired as multimillionaires and the people have still not received what they were promised."[24]

A study published by Australian National University (ANU), does a thorough job distinguishing significant areas of the incorporation process which are at variance with Aboriginal customary law. In discussing prescribed bodies under the *Australian Native Title Act*, the study makes the general point that the holders of Native Title in Aboriginal law are a social community with a distinct political structure which is not embodied in the Western concept of an incorporated body.[25] It is pointed out that the rules and mechanisms for regulating a corporation are inappropriate for governing a social community in possession of a discrete territory.

Similarly in Alaska Indian leaders have highlighted significant differences between ANCSA corporations and the traditional tribal system. One leader explicitly states, "There are a lot of differences between a tribal system and a corporation. Corporations are responsible to outside entities, whereas tribes are responsible to the people." The leader goes on to explain that tribes are matrilineal communities with clan systems and traditional Native values. "The people run the tribes," he argues, "Corporations are run by people who control media and have enough money to mail out proxies."[26] Others have explained that Indian Tribal property is a form of 'ownership in common'; it is not analogous to tenancy in common, however, or other collective forms of ownership known to Anglo-American private property law because an individual tribal member has no alienable or inheritable interest in the communal holding. Rather, tribal property interests are held in common for the benefit of all living members of the tribe, a class whose composition continually changes as a result of births, deaths, and other factors. The manner in which a tribe chooses to use its property can be controlled by individual tribal members only to the extent that the members participate in the governmental processes of the tribe.[27]

---

[24] Dave Stephenson, "Tribalizing Alaska's Native Corporations," *Indian Country Today* (June 3, 2003) http://www.indiancountry.com/content.cfm?id=1054648796.

[25] Patrick Sullivan, "A Sacred Land, A Sovereign People, An Aboriginal Corporation: Prescribed Bodies and the Native Title Act," NARU Report Series No. 3, (Darwin: North Australia Research Unit, 1997).

[26] Dave Stephenson, *op. cit.*

[27] Quoted by Bart K. Garber, *op. cit.*, 28.

The ANU study of Australian aboriginal corporate bodies highlights in detail the incompatibility between aboriginal customary law and the provisions of the *Aboriginal Councils and Association Act*, which requires incorporated bodies. For example, the simple provision requiring that the incorporated body claiming under the Act keep a register of its members, is already incompatible with the full exercise of common law Native Title holder rights because customary law does not keep lists. According to customary law, title holders are determined by relationships and processes. In contrast, the possession and exercise of title under the Aboriginal Councils and Association Act 1976, requires application and registration.[28] If the application of and exercise of rights is dependent on corporate bodies then some title holders will be missed and unable to exercise their rights, since no list can be entirely conclusive, it argues. On this point it is interesting to note that when the Papua New Guinea government in July 1995 pushed for a policy of land registration following structural adjustment recommendations from the International Monetary Fund, there were violent protests. Eventually the government abandoned the policy in the face of strikes by students and soldiers. I suspect that much of this hostility was also based on the fact that Melanesian customary law operates informally and flexibly and cannot easily reduce entitlement to a comprehensive list. An Australian National University researcher, Glen Banks, gave a graphic illustration of the flexibility of kinship systems, and their application to land entitlement, in his study of compensation claims related to the Porgera Mine in Enga Province.[29]

Furthermore, the Act provides that the Registrar is required to refuse incorporation if the rules of the corporation 'are inequitable,' or do not make sufficient provision (as required by section 58b) to give the members effective control over the running of the association.[30] The study argues that this provision allows for inappropriate assimilationist measures to be inflicted on groups who are required to incorporate. Again, we see that a form of organization which is intended to empower the community in order to protect cultural difference, could actually be used to enforce conformity through the discretionary powers of the Registrar. Furthermore, it is pointed out that the Registrar usually prefers that the method

---

[28] *Ibid.*
[29] Glen Banks, "Compensation for Mining: Benefit or Time Bomb—The Porgera Case," *Resources, Nations and Indigenous Peoples*, in. R. Howatt, J. Connel, & P. Hirsh ed., (Melbourne: Oxford University Press 1995), especially page three. He states "Land ownership in Porgera consists of a series of rights which an individual may claim through either parent (a system of cognatic descent)." This has allowed a large number of kin who were born and living outside Porgera to move in and occupy land to which they do not have full ownership rights, although they can only do so with the permission of the landowners themselves. This group is referred to by the Ipili (the local tribe) as epo atene, 'those who have come' or 'invited guests.'
[30] *Ibid.*

of decision making at meetings be by voting and that the method of appointment to the governing committee be by election.[31] Again the study suggests that this procedure may be contrary to customary law. Also section 49B governs office holding by persons with criminal convictions, which may contravene rights under customary law.[32] The conclusion reached is that the *Aboriginal Councils and Association Act 1976* is weighted to the mainstream Australian interpretation of corporate accountability and produces Aboriginal corporations that are distinct from and differently structured in comparison to the communities they are supposed to embody.[33] Finally it states: "What is required is a social and political structure that will unite once more the system of custom with the fact of land holding. The assumption that native title is a property right bearing with it no political rights, and that it therefore need only be administered by a corporation established by the general law, is manifestly contradictory. A parallel political and legal system necessarily exists side-by-side with the mainstream European—based law, it is from this that native title derives in the first place. Of course, it will vary from place to place."[34]

Aggregates and Collectivities

The ANU study does a significant job in demonstrating variation between the provisions of the incorporating act and customary indigenous law. My particular criticism of the suggested policies for Aboriginal empowerment is that they overlook important characteristics of the organisational structure of communities and the special characteristics of indigenous communities. What I intend to demonstrate is that there is not simply rule conflict between indigenous customary law and Western law, as embodied in the modern company, but rather that there are fundamental functional differences between communities and modern economic organisations. Furthermore the introduction of the latter into traditional societies may undermine the cultural cohesion of the community.

Self-determination for indigenous communities has become associated with the notion of group rights. However, a group is a generic term and we need to know the special features of groups to which we ought to ascribe rights. We might begin by noting that a community is obviously a group of people, but we need to ask ourselves what exactly makes a group a community. Some writers have suggested that we distinguish between aggregates and collectivities, collectivities

---

[31] *Ibid.*, 21.
[32] *Ibid.*, 22.
[33] *Ibid.*, 16.
[34] *Ibid.*, 25.

are said to be 'self collecting' in the sense that the members engage in rule following activity. Sometimes the rules are said to be formal as in the case of the rules of incorporation, or of nation's constitution, while in other cases they may be more informal as in the case of the rules uniting a tribe or a village.[35] To this point this analysis is fairly simple and persuasive. Emphasis on recognition of a common set of rules allows us to distinguish groups which are clearly accidental aggregates from more meaningful collectives like corporations, nations and communities. Groups, such as all the people who are presently crossing main street, or all the people currently at Bondi Beach, or all the left handed baseball players, are clearly accidental aggregates in this sense, and no one would be interested in ascribing them a set of special group rights.

It is suggested that we might further distinguish between self collecting groups, consisting of those in which membership is based on will or choice and those in which membership is based on recognition of some significant commonality. Falling into the former class we find clubs, teams, corporations, and governments, while within the latter class we might find families, communities, clans, tribes and societies. In a related point one writer has made the following observation:

> In traditional societies, we would expect values to be based more on recognition than on choice, with the result that the collective and individual identity and well-being would be less open to volition than, in say liberal individualistic societies. This, I claim marks the major difference between native communities and our own.[36]

Another commentator makes similar observations:

> Members of the (indigenous) community are expected to participate in communally orientated functions, and to respect the authority of the community and its traditions and values; withdrawal from participation is equated with withdrawal from the community, since membership can mean nothing other than participation.[37]

Drawing from the above analysis and these accounts, the point I wish to make is that membership in a traditional indigenous community is not one of choice (as it is with many communities), but rather is marked by community orientated obligations rather than individualistic forms of freedom of association and choice. The fact that membership in a traditional indigenous community has not usually been a matter of choice would seem almost too obvious to mention, but this

---

[35] Michael McDonald, "Collective Rights and Tyranny," *University of Ottawa Quarterly* 56 (1986): 115–125, 120.

[36] Michael McDonald, "Indian Status: Colonialism or Sexism?" *Canadian Community Law Journal* 9 (1986). 23–47, 42; See also Darlene Johnston, "Native Rights as Collective Rights: A Question of Group Self-Preservation," in W. Kymlicka ed., *The Rights of Minority Cultures*, (Oxford: Oxford University Press, 1995).

[37] Frances Svensson, "Liberal Democracy and Group Rights: The Legacy of Individualism and Its Impact on American Indian Tribes," *Political Studies* 27, (1979), 431.

fact is important in a comparison of communities with economic organisations. Within the economic realm the most important vehicle for the production and distribution of wealth in Western society, for almost three hundred years, has been the corporation. The modern corporation and its predecessor, the joint stock venture, have historically been organisations whose membership is voluntary. One is not usually born into a corporation, one creates, joins or chooses to be associated with a corporation. This is to say that corporations are highly voluntary in character, in contrast to traditional indigenous communities which are far less so.

Returning to the observation in the first of the above quotes, it is usually accepted that there is a higher level of choice and voluntary association in Western cultures than is found in traditional cultures. Frank Brennan, in his work on Aboriginal self-determination, observes that in contemporary Aboriginal society there is often a tension between the demands of custom or Aboriginal law, and the freedom of choice which is found in the white man's culture.[38] He claims that younger Aborigines often complain that following traditional Aboriginal law should be a matter of choice, or that they should have the same freedom of choice as members of the dominant white society. While choice and voluntary association may be more prominent in the dominant Western culture context, from the perspective of economic organisation they are fundamental. Similarly, another researcher notes the differences in cultural outlook between members of Aboriginal communities and the young Aborigines who work cattle stations in the Kimberleys. The latter are often far more closely linked to the global commercial culture and the aspirations for world wide rodeo fame, money etc, than the traditions of the aboriginal community.[39]

Francis Fukuyama has argued that there is a high correlation between the presence of voluntary associations, and societies that have generated significant economic wealth. With reference to the United States he states:

> ...most serious social observers have noted in the past that the United States historically has possessed many strong and important communal structures that give its civil society dynamism and resilience. To a greater degree than many other Western societies, the United States historically has a dense and complex network of voluntary organizations: churches, professional societies, charitable institutions, private schools, universities, and of course a very strong business sector.[40]

---

[38] F. Brennan, *op. cit.*, note 11, 196.
[39] Richard Davis, *Black Spurs: Aboriginal Pastoralists in the Kimberleys*, draft paper presented at the North Australia Research Unit, Australian National University, Darwin, Dec, 1, 1999.
[40] F. Fukuyama, *Trust: The Social Virtues and the Creation of Prosperity* (London: Penguin Books, 1995). 50.

Fukuyama argues that these are associations, which flourish in the intermediate realm between the family and the state, and are found most often in economically successful nations like the United States and Japan. Following this line of thought, my point is that modern economic collectivities are organised according to the principle of voluntary association and therefore, it is not surprising that societies which encourage these values are also economically successful.

These facts underlie the incongruous situation in which legislation seeks to empower and preserve one organisational structure, which is based on authority, tradition and conformity to custom, by superimposing a different form of organisational structure, based on the dynamics of choice and voluntary association, typical of the dominant culture. From the earlier discussion of incorporated land holding groups, it is evident that those who may be successfully adapted to a traditional organisation and its customary rules, laws, and life style, may be entirely unadaptable to the dynamics of a voluntary organisation like a incorporated body. Sullivan has done an excellent job documenting specific areas of conflict between specific provisions of the *Aboriginal Councils and Associations Act* on prescribed corporate bodies, and customary Aboriginal law. My argument is that not only will one find specific rule conflict, but moreover, there are profound structural dissimilarities between the two organizations, not in the least is the fact that in one organisation, membership and participation is based on choice and initiative, while in the other, membership and participation are based on traditional relationships and custom. Ultimately I agree with Sullivan's conclusion that the former cannot represent the latter and adequately meet its needs and expectations.

But this does not mean that the issue is easily reconcilable by making the organisational structures fit the traditional mould. The dilemma will persist, with respect to the issue of autonomy or self-determination and its resolution. In order to be sufficiently autonomous within a traditional culture, 'the cultural context of choice' must be protected against incursions from the dominant culture and Western Capitalist systems. But it is apparent that societies ineluctably placed within the context and realities of the modern market economy, are economically vulnerable. This means they are susceptible to loss of self-determination (autonomy) if their membership is not in control of sufficient income generating rights or cannot utilise resources to protect the community. In order to protect themselves economically they will have to form income generating organisations and these collectivities will necessarily vary from the dynamics and structures inherent in traditional community organisations, in part by the very nature of their voluntary character, as we have mentioned. At the same time, as members of a traditional community form financial organisations and initiate corporate bodies and associations, the more they will find themselves assimilating to the dominant culture and assuming behavioural forms and values which are adapted to, and consistent with, income generating functions, and inconsistent with custom and tradition.

Political Organization and Culture

This sketchy analysis of economic organisations and voluntarism can also be applied to political life. In Western societies, the facts of membership and association by choice also apply to political life. The division of labour inherent in Western society means that livelihood and position are to a greater degree a matter of choice. This also applies to the role of governing. One usually chooses to join the government or run for office—it is a career decision. In traditional societies leadership is often a matter of inheritance or it is bestowed through customs and tradition. The usual recommendations for political empowerment, e.g., special representation at the federal level, and greater autonomy at the local level again, may undermine the cultural context insofar as these proposals often embody forms of procedure and processes which are foreign to indigenous traditions. For example, proposals for representation at the federal level often envision some form of popular election which may be at variance with customary procedures for selecting leaders. The act of 'running for office' would certainly have been a behavioural form unknown to traditional societies. Likewise, greater autonomy and self-government at the local level, often mean the institution of councils to draft bylaws and other forms of municipal legislation, as in the Canadian *Indian Act*. Similarly in the Australian experience, one commentator has noted that local governments drawn from Aboriginal and Torres Strait Island communities face both financial hurdles and structures that are simply State government imposed.[41]

But perhaps the overall point which this chapter makes is that the introduction of the incorporation model for land holding effectively separates the economic activities with respect to the traditional land base from indigenous political institutions. This development is obviously contrary to cultural tradition and customary practice. In Alaska the ANCSA can be viewed as damaging to tribal political self-determination in that it denuded Native governments of their traditional lands in the name of economic self-determination by placing them under the control of newly created Indian corporations. This has created the obvious conflict between tribal self government and the drive for economic self sufficiency. In Australia the imposition of the Western corporate model has similarly intervened to remove traditional lands from the Aboriginal traditions and customary forms of political control. The success of the capitalist system, as we shall see in a later chapter, is in part due to the capacity to distinguish the political and the economic as distinct spheres. But the traditional communities regard these activities as part of a single holistic enterprise in which the community through its political traditions manages its land base to coordinate its productive activities to sustain and benefit itself.

---

[41] Sanders, *op. cit.*, 22.

Conclusion

My conclusion is that if the survival of indigenous communities as distinct cultural enclaves is guided by a policy which aims for autonomy and self-determination, it is difficult to avoid the economic imperative which links self-determination with a degree of financial self-sufficiency. The political autonomy of the community may depend on an effective command of financial resources. This means that members of these communities must be capable of engaging in income earning pursuits and otherwise participating in the modern, growing global market economy, either on an individual basis or in concert with other community members through viable economic organisation. This means the formation of corporations and financial associations which actually work commercially and which are more than symbolic vehicles for the political ascendancy of particular individuals. However, the more successfully the community becomes integrated into the economic mainstream, the more irrelevant the traditional cultural context may become. One Canadian commentator, for example, has attacked Kymlicka's argument for greater rights and protections for Quebec, complaining that the Quebec cultural context is no longer a significant determinate of behaviour within the province. "In Quebec, as in most other places, people turn for guidance not to in group ideals of their ethnic group but to the beliefs of their religious community, to the consumerist standards of market society, to the meritocratic standards of the corporations they belong to, to the media and so on."[42] Obviously, Aboriginal societies, unlike the Quebecois, have a non-Western religious culture, but the other points will apply equally. As traditional communities become integrated into the modern market economy, it is unavoidable that their values and choices will become determined by a dominant economic culture even if the presence is subtle. Margaret Rodman, in her observations on cash cropping in Vanuatu, remarks that the course of differentiation is proceeding very slowly. This, she says, allows the illusion to persist that the inequalities between ordinary people and wealthy landowners are fundamentally no different from the inequalities between ordinary men and those of rank in the past.[43]

This is the dilemma facing any argument based on the protection of cultural communities through empowerment and self-determination. The subtle assimilationist pressures can be an ineluctable consequent of engagement in economic self sufficiency and associated political strategies like the legal struggle for special group rights. Bruce Morito, a Canadian Indian and professional philosopher, has

---

[42] Brian Walker, "Culturist Dilemmas: On Some Convergences between Kymlicka and the New French Right," draft presentation at the CPSA Annual Meeting 1995, Montreal, June 2, 1995.

[43] Margaret Rodman, *Masters of Tradition: Consequences of Customary Land Tenure in Longana Vanuatu* (Vancouver: University of BC Press, 1987).

argued that fairness demands a fiduciary arrangement for the mutual protection of the well being of diverse cultures. Rather than competing in the market place and legal arena, indigenous peoples should maintain their independence from European law, he argues. In short, by competing in these arenas, indigenous peoples unwittingly adapt the values and strategies of these Western institutions, and the culture, which underlies these forms of life.[44]

Following this line of thought it might be safer for Aboriginal communities to demand greater fiduciary responsibility on the part of government, rather than to press for self-determination. But the danger is that the central government may issue countervailing demands for greater economic self-sufficiency on the part of the indigenous communities, as in the recommendations of the aforementioned Report on Torres Strait Island Regional Autonomy.[45] However, in North America, for example, the Lockean scholar James Tully has argued that native Indians represent sovereign independent nations under the fiduciary protection of the North American States, the United States and Canada.[46] Tully argues that the original understanding based on treaty and negotiation recognised the co-existence of both Amerindian and European cultures within a fiduciary relationship requiring mutual respect and necessary operational protections. In Australia the *Terre Nullius* principle justified an original refusal to recognise indigenous title in Australia. Now indigenous communities can reasonably make a request for the assumption of increased fiduciary responsibilities on the part of the Commonwealth, based on the facts of dispossession, based on the recent repudiation of the Terre Nullius principle. This strategy can then provide a moral basis for justifying continuing government financing of poorer indigenous communities that wish to maintain a traditional lifestyle, independent of the mainstream of the market economy. This would involve the recognition that territory (the Australian Continent) can never be held absolutely by the modern settler state, but in part, is held in trust for the beneficiaries, the dispossessed indigenous people who possessed and possess the original common law title.

---

[44] Bruce Morito, "Aboriginal Right: A Conciliatory Concept," *Journal of Applied Philosophy* 13, 2 (1996).123–140.

[45] Arthur, *op. cit.*

[46] James Tully, *Strange Multiplicity: Constitutionalism in the Age of Diversity* (New York: Cambridge University Press, 1996), 66.

Chapter Three

Shareholder Wealth Maximization, Multinational Corporations and the Developing World

In the modern capitalist system corporations have become the driving force behind trade and commerce. Much of the wealth in Western societies is owned by corporations as well as private individuals. At the same time much of the wealth of private individuals is realized in various forms of property interest in corporations, often held as corporate bonds or corporate equity. In the last chapter we touched upon difficulties involved in introducing the corporate form of ownership as an appropriate model for the definition of property rights within traditional indigenous communities. In order to understand the issue in greater depth, one needs to appreciate the essential difference between the values that animate a traditional community and the objectives and values, which are embraced by the modern corporation. Because there is considerable controversy as to the primary responsibilities of the commercial organization these issues will be discussed in relative detail. However, it is important to establish initially in general terms the values which traditional indigenous communities tend to uphold in terms of individual interests, community interests and land itself, the principal property asset and means of production. In this respect I will refer to the Melanesian context, however, there exists considerable evidence that the essential elements can also be found in other indigenous communities.[1]

In contrast to the accepted Western ideology, traditional Melanesian societies have promoted the pre-eminence of community values over individual preferences. Ethical rules tend to correspond to this primary value.[2] Moreover, Melanesian identification with the community is intimately and inextricably linked with

---

1   See for example R. Crocombe, *Land Tenure in the Pacific* (Suva: University of the South Pacific, 1987). C.K. Omari, "Traditional African land Ethics," in R. Engel and I.G. Engel, eds., *Ethics of Environment and Development: Global Challenge and International Response* (London: Belhaven Press, 1990): 167–175; on the North American Indians see, for example, W. Cragg, A. Wellington and A.J. Greenbaum, *Canadian Issues in Environmental Ethics* (Toronto: Broadview Press, 1997).

2   E. Mantovani, "Traditional Values and Ethics," in S. Stratigos and P. Hughes eds., *Ethics of Development: The Pacific in the Twentieth Century* (Port Moresby: UPNG Press, 1987): 102–111.

a parallel identification with the communal land holding. A leading authority asserts that the lynch pin of the Melanesian group, which assured the continuity of community life and history, was the land holding. The community land holding provided the locus for the community's cultural activities: political, military and social.[3]

Accordingly as land through generations was held by force of arms through social groupings, the fundamental ownership of land is by groups of some sort or other. The important constant was the group owned, and individual used the land. "Individual land usage rights did not remove the reality that the group was the basis for ownership and the basis for the defense of these rights."[4]

We have discussed efforts to introduce the Western model of the corporate body to represent communal land holding interests in certain traditional societies. Certainly a distinguishing feature of Western systems of ownership is the legal entity we refer to as the corporate body, or the corporation, and moreover, corporate ownership of assets represents a form of ownership, which has no parallel in traditional societies. Essentially this is because the corporate body or the corporation is regarded as a separate legal entity apart from its membership. A traditional community, for example, which in a traditional society might exercise ownership rights, is not usually regarded, ether in customary law or by its own members, as a separate legal entity that can be entirely divorced and separated from its past, present or future membership. Because the corporation is regarded as a separate legal entity apart from its participating membership of financial investors, managers, employees, customers and directorate, the modern corporation possesses a unique structure not to be found in other systems. Accordingly, in large limited companies management of corporate assets and ownership interests are distinguished and these roles are associated with different groups of individuals.[5] Indeed the legal view regards corporate assets as the property of the corporation and not its investors.

One needs to appreciate this arrangement through a comparison with traditional community and customary forms of communal ownership. In the latter system ownership, management and beneficial interest can all be identified as belonging to a single unified group, the community. But in the modern large limited company, different roles and functions are associated with separate and distinct groups, for example, those who own shares in the company are most often

---

3   A.P. Power, "Resources Development in East Sepic Province," in C. Thirwell and P. Hughes eds. *Ethics of Development: Choices in Development Planning* (Port Moresby: UPNG Press, 1988): 56–70.

4   *Ibid.*, 58.

5   See A.A. Berle, G.C. Means, *The Modern Corporation and Private Property* (New York: Macmillan, 1932).

distinguished from the managers that control and run the company, as we noted. Moreover when we speak of beneficial interest, matters become somewhat more complex. In the traditional community issues are simpler and it is assumed that the community owns and manages its holdings for its own beneficial interest. The products of community labor are intended for the consumption and enjoyment of its membership. But in the case of the modern corporation, the products of the corporation's activities are not intended for the consumption and enjoyment of any of its members but rather are intended for its customers that are not usually regarded as part of the corporation.

As mentioned, the law regards the limited company as a legal person distinct from its membership but the term 'corporation' actually designates different groups of individuals joined together in a single productive enterprise. Since the products of these corporate activities are not usually intended for the membership it becomes relevant to ask what is the primary objective that unites the disparate groups within the corporation in order that they may realize some form of mutual benefit.

Shareholder Wealth Maximization

The principle of shareholder wealth maximization holds that a maximum return to shareholders is and ought to be the objective of all corporate activity.[6] From a financial management perspective this means maximizing the price of a firm's common stock. In pursuing this objective, managers consider the risk and timing associated with expected earnings per share in order to maximize the price of the firm's common stock. When this is properly executed management will also have maximized the future stream of dividends and capital gains that accrue to its shareholders. The most defensible form of shareholder wealth maximization (SWM) looks to long-term rather than short-term maximization.

The maximization of shareholder wealth is described as the 'monotonic' view of the purpose of the corporation and therefore of the responsibilities of its managers. It is monotonic because it focuses on the interests of a single group, the shareholders, to the exclusion of other groups that may be affected by the activities of the firm or that could benefit from the activities of the firm. It is for this reason that the principle of shareholder wealth maximization is controversial. Economic, legal, and moral considerations have been used both to defend and criticize the view that the firm should be managed so as to maximize the interests of a single group, namely the shareholders.

---

[6]   G.D. Smith, "The Shareholder Primacy Norm," *Journal of Corporate Law* 23, (1998): 277–283.

The Justification of SWM

Historically, from a legal perspective, the corporation was regarded during the nineteenth century as an instrument of public policy with a social responsibility. These social concerns gave way to the idea of managing the firm for the shareholders' profits. Legal theorists began to regard stock ownership as no different from other forms of private property.[7] The corporation was viewed as owned by its shareholders. This legal model is entirely consistent with SWM. The directors' role is to manage the property of the owners, the shareholders. As stewards of the shareholders' interests, their sole responsibility must be to the shareholders, and promoting the interests of other groups would be a misuse of the property entrusted to them.[8] Insofar as private property plays such a powerful role in the American ethos, the argument for shareholder wealth maximization, based on the value ascribed to private ownership, has had profound appeal.

At the same time, property rights are viewed as the foundation of a capital-driven economic system, and the principle of shareholder wealth maximization also makes sense from the perspective of economic efficiency. The shareholders, as the owners of the corporation, purchase stock because they are looking for financial return. In most cases, shareholders elect directors who then hire mangers to run the company on a day-to-day basis. Since managers are supposed to be working in the interests of shareholders, it follows that they should follow policies that enhance shareholder value. Property rights are deemed essential to the workings of the system, and the resulting outcomes are at the same time beneficial to society. Profits are indicative of the fact that an organization has transformed a set of inputs into a productive output of goods or services that have a higher value than the original inputs. Thus, when SWM is properly pursued, the financial benefits are alleged to include the following: efficient low cost businesses that produce high quality goods and services at the lowest possible prices; products and goods that consumers need and want: new technologies, new products and new jobs; courteous service, adequate stocks of merchandise, and well located establishments.

But one could underline that corporations often have a diversified class of investors with financial claims not only from shareholders but also from bondholders and other holders of corporate debt. Why is it not more economically efficient to focus on this diversity of financial claimants? It is claimed that SWM remains a more economically efficient *modus operandi* because the maximization of shareholder value requires the initial satisfaction of the financial claims of other

---

[7]   A.A. Berle, G.C. Means, *op. cit.*

[8]   Milton Friedman, "The Social Responsibility of Business is to Increase its Profits," *New York Times Magazine*, (September 13, 1970), 32.

investors and interests in order to secure a profitable return. SWM is therefore not inconsistent with the satisfaction of the claims of other investors.

Moreover, defenders of the principle of shareholder wealth maximization or shareholder primacy hold that it is not merely consistent with but that it also promotes the interests of all non-shareholders who have financial interests in the firm, such as bondholders, and other secured and unsecured creditors. Shareholders are less risk adverse than non-shareholders, whereas managing the firm on behalf of interests other than shareholders can lead to greater risk aversion. This will occur if the firm is managed in the interest of its fixed claimants. Fixed claimants, such as bondholders, refer to those financial interests to whom the firm has pledged a fixed rate of return or sum which cannot be varied regardless of the firm's financial success or lack of success. In contrast, residual claimants are only guaranteed a return after all fixed financial claims have been satisfied, and the amount of the return, if any, will vary according to the financial success of the company. In this situation, bondholders, for example, base decisions on the bankruptcy risk on a firm's cash flows, not the firm's value-maximizing potential from free cash flows. The result may well be that the company fails to invest in new opportunities for growth, innovative products, new technologies or markets, which in the long run may undermine the capacity to remain competitive. It is argued that shareholders have a greater incentive to induce firms to engage in activities that other claimants such as bondholders may regard as excessively risky. Shareholders, thus push the managers of the corporation to operate at levels beyond those sufficient to satisfy the interests of fixed claimants. However, it is also true that it is the shareholders who bear the greater loss from excessive risk taking if the firm does badly, because, in any case, other claimants have a guaranteed fixed rate of return. At the same time it is argued that in maximizing shareholder wealth, managers seek to increase market share (in so far as this is compatible with long term profits), which will increases the size of the pie that is available to all participants in the corporate enterprise. In this way the success of the company will offer greater security for fixed claimants by ensuring that the firm is in a better position to cover possible future losses and thereby maintain its commitments to its fixed claimants.

Defenders of SWM also argue that attempting to maximize in more than one dimension at the same time may well be excessively difficult unless the multiplicity of objectives can be reduced to an overall monotonic purpose. The resulting loss of direction from pursuing multiple objectives can mean an equally fatal loss of competitiveness. Moreover, managing the firm for a variety of interests including fixed and residual claimants means a diversity of goals in which overall performance cannot be accurately assessed. In contrast, the principle of shareholder value offers an unambiguous standard, which is measurable and observable.

The Contractarian Legal Model and Shareholder Wealth Maximization

The earlier legal view of the corporation as a form of property that is subject to ownership rights has given way to a contractarian model, which sees the corporation as a nexus of contracts. This alternative model envisions the corporation as offering an umbrella that allows private parties to contract with one another more efficiently than they could in a market by limiting the transaction costs. This view avoids the ontological issues that result when one regards the corporation as a thing that could possibly be owned. In any case, regarding the corporation and its assets as being owned by the shareholders is highly misleading insofar as shareholders usually have no right to manage these assets or unlimited access to information and records relating to these assets. The corporation is therefore more accurately viewed as a device that operates as a nexus for all contracts that various individuals have voluntarily entered into for mutual benefit. Although theoretically the activities of the corporation could be done by individuals through individual contract in a market outside the corporate structure, the costs associated with enlisting cooperation would be significant. As R.H. Coase argued in 1937, the law in effect offers a standardized form of contract or a set of default rules that facilitate private ordering.[9] This legal entity, which is actually a legal fiction, allows those with money and resources to contract with those of managerial skill but little money, to forge a mutually advantageous cooperative enterprise. Moreover, those with labor to sell but lacking monetary resources or managerial skill, can negotiate with the managers acting as agents of the corporation to form employment contracts.

However, according to contractarians, interpreting the corporation as a nexus of contracts, rather than a form of property that is owned, does not invalidate the principle of shareholder wealth maximization. The contractarian perspective describes the corporation as being composed of explicit and implicit contracts held by shareholders and non-shareholders. The interests of non-shareholders such as employees, suppliers, bondholders, communities, and customers are protected by contract, law, and regulation. Shareholders are said to be entitled to the firm's residual cash flow. However the management's obligation to realize and promote this residual cash flow is open-ended because there are no sets of specified actions that can be enforced to realize this objective. In other words, management has a legal obligation to create a healthy residual cash flow but there are no terms that specify particular actions for achieving this goal. But in order to give greater definition to the relationship that embodies this particular understanding, the legal system creates a fiduciary duty to maximize shareholder wealth. This fiduciary

---

[9]   R.H. Coase, "The Nature of the Firm," *Economica*, 4, (1937): 386–405.

duty fills the gaps that arise in terms of management's unspecified or imperfect obligations to maximize shareholder wealth.

Moreover, agency theory supplements the contractarian position and adds weight to the view that the purpose of the firm is the maximization of shareholder wealth.[10] Agency problems arise because contracts are not costlessly written and enforced. Agency costs include the costs of structuring, monitoring, and bonding a set contracts among agents with conflicting interests, plus the residual loss incurred when the cost of full enforcement of contracts exceeds the benefits. It is argued that the necessity of a corporate structure in which ownership and control are separated entails that only the residual claimants can provide appropriate monitoring.[11] It follows that the agency costs inherent in a team organization, such as the firm, are controlled and maximization of output occurs when income rights are assigned to the residual claimants.

Ethical and Legal Implications of Contractarian and Communitarian Theory

We have considered the economic and legal rationales that justify SWM We will now proceed to consider a normative critique of shareholder wealth maximization. The nexus of contracts view of the corporation also has an underlying idealogical basis that embodies a particular moral perspective. We have discussed the view of the corporation as an economic and financial arrangement with an objective of shareholder wealth maximization. However, we have not considered whether this particular governance relationship is and ought to be a product of individual choice. Those who advocate shareholder wealth maximization argue that we should leave it up to the various participants in corporate activity to specify respective rights and obligations through contract, rather than legally imposing relationships. According to this view shareholders bargain and secure from management a commitment to a fiduciary duty to direct the corporation so as to maximize shareholder wealth. This is an open-ended responsibility because it is not realistically possible to specify in detail what exactly is to be done to fulfill this fiduciary duty. On the other hand, other participants in the corporate enterprise contract with the agents of the corporation for more specific rights in return for the particular services provided. Accordingly non-shareholders are free to protect

---

[10] E.F. Fama and M.C. Jensen, "Agency Problems and Residual Claims," *Journal of Law and Economics* 26, 2 (1983): 327–349; M.C. Jensen and W.H. Meckling. "Theory of the firm: managerial, behaviour, agency costs and ownership structure," *Journal of Financial Economics*, 3 (1976): 303–360.

[11] A.A. Alchian and Demsetz, "Production, information costs, and economic organization," *American Economic Review*, 62 (1972): 777–795.

themselves through contracts by bargaining for whatever protections they deem necessary to protect interests that may be threatened by the pursuit of shareholder wealth maximization. For example, workers could bargain for protections against a policy of employment at will or seek other legal protections.

The communitarian view stands in contrast to this contractarian position.[12] While contractarians advocate that the law should play a minimal role in structuring relationships, communitarians argue that the law must intervene to prevent harmful externalities that may result from the single-minded promotion of shareholder wealth maximization. For example, factories may be closed down and workers laid off in order to protect profits, but at the same time this may significantly damage the local community, which depends on this income and indeed may have invested in infrastructure that supports the corporate enterprise. Communities may find it difficult to foresee such events and contract to protect their interests from uncompensated losses. At the same time, public goods that are often essential to the communities in which corporations operate are difficult to secure through the market.

An important difference between the communitarian and contractarian positions is their focus. Communitarians tend to highlight the undeniable social effects of corporate activity, seeing corporations as institutions that have a profound affect on those who are outside the corporation. Accordingly, it is appropriate that the state intervene to enhance the social environment and minimize the deleterious effects of market activity. On the other hand, contractarians focus on the internal relationships. They see the corporation as an organization constituted by private contracts that have been voluntarily entered into. This difference in emphasis sheds light on the important ideological differences that also manifest contrasting and opposing moral values.

Contractarians see society as constituted by autonomous citizens who ought to be free to make the choices that shape their destiny without intervention from outside authority, so long as they are not actively harming other individuals. Governments should not dictate matters involving the type of agreements we make, our individual economic behavior or the redistribution of wealth. Contractual arrangements are a way in which we express this autonomy and freedom. The latter, they claim, form an important foundational value for our social existence. Communitarians, in contrast, emphasize social interdependence and the fact that individual persons and corporate persons derive many benefits from life in society that have no contractual basis. On this rationale, it is

---

[12] David Millon, "Communitarians, Contractarians and the Crisis in Corporate Law," *Washington and Lee Law Review*, 50, 4 (1993): 1373–1380. David Millon, "Communitarianism in Corporate Law: Foundations and Law Reform Strategies," in L. E. Mitchell ed., *Progressive Corporate Law* (Boulder CO.: Westview Press, 1995).

appropriate that the state intervene in order to structure relationships that reflect this interdependence and protect constituencies such as workers and the local community from the deleterious effects of unregulated shareholder wealth maximization. Although contractarians claim that non-shareholders can always enter into contractual relations to protect their interests from harmful externalities, communitarians point out that unequal distribution of wealth produces inequality of bargaining power. In many cases, non-shareholders lack the resources to bargain and negotiate effectively to protect their interests. In reality, non-shareholder protection from the externalities of shareholder wealth maximization depends upon people's capability and willingness to pay for contractual guarantees. Communitarians argue that it is unrealistic to believe that unskilled workers have the resources to buy lay-off protection from the shareholders or their agents. Ultimately, the existence of contractual relations alone does not ensure that arrangements are fair to all parties or even reflect the individual contributions that are made to the greater social body.

Stakeholder Theory

Many, who see a moral dimension to business activities that extends beyond mere contractual obligations and the single minded pursuit of making money for shareholders, propose a stakeholder approach to business activities. Stakeholder theory emphasizes that managers are also moral agents who are responsible to a wide array of groups for their actions. Much of the ground breaking work is associated with R. Edward Freeman.[13] A stakeholder is broadly defined as any individual or group who can affect, or is affected by the achievement of the organization's objectives. If one fails to recognize these responsibilities to other groups, it becomes easy to rationalize a questionable practice that potentially harms non-shareholder stakeholders, such as workers or suppliers, to whom managers supposedly have no moral obligation, in order to realize increased profitability.

The stakeholder theory of corporate responsibility is a developing response to the view that a firm should be run in such a way as to maximize the wealth of the shareholders. The stakeholder approach argues that it is not only those with a financial claim on the institution who are worthy of consideration but

[13] R.E. Freeman, *Strategic Management: a Stakeholder Approach* (Boston: Pitman, 1984); W.M. Evan, and R.E. Freeman, "A Stakeholder theory for of the Modern Corporation: Kantian Capitalism," In T. Beauchamp and N. Bowie eds., *Ethical theory and Business*, 4th edition. (Englewood Cliffs N.J.: Prentice Hall, 1993); R.E. Freeman, A.C. Wicks, and B. Parmar, "Stakeholder theory and The Corporate Objective revisited," *Organization Science*, 15, 3 (2004): 364–369.

that there is a multiplicity of groups with a stake in the operations of the firm, all of whom merit consideration in managerial decision-making. The word "stakeholder" first appeared in usage in 1963 in an internal memorandum of the Stanford Research Institute and has since become a prominent concept in corporate and academic communities.[14] The theory, which is clearly designed to extend the ethical responsibility of the firm, is an alternative to the monotonic fiduciary model offered by the property rights and contractual approaches. According to stakeholder theory a person who holds a stake in the activities of an organization, a "stakeholder", is entitled to consideration in some ways similar to shareholders.

Stakeholder theory has also apparently been reflected in changes to the law, especially in the United States. In the 1990s, many jurisdictions in the United States passed so called "other constituencies legislation" and determined that the directors should consider not only the profit margin in their decisions but also the interests of the employees and the general public. These statutes have been enacted by at least 25 US states.[15] The typical non-shareholder constituency statute authorizes (but does not require) a director of a corporation, in considering its best interests, to consider the interests of persons (often referred to as stakeholders) other than shareholders, and frequently also consider generalized factors such as local and national economies, societal considerations, and any other factors deemed by the directors to be pertinent. The various non-shareholder constituencies may be seen to include employees, customers, creditors, suppliers and communities in whom the corporation has facilities. However, while some have hailed "other constituencies legislation" as rejecting shareholder primacy, many are far more cautious. It has been pointed out that there is little meaningful case law relating to these statutes and so they still stand in need of interpretation. The American Bar Association's Committee on Corporate laws recommends that constituency statutes be interpreted according to relatively recent Delaware precedent. This precedent states that Courts should not allow consideration of non-shareholder interests without relating such considerations in an appropriate fashion to shareholder welfare. Moreover, constituency statutes apply only to a narrow range of decisions, which essentially involve change of control, i.e. takeovers. This means that the range of situations in which boards have the right to consider other constituencies is rather limited. It can therefore be argued that these statutes are really not pro-stakeholder but in fact are designed to entrench management.

---

[14] T. Ambler, and A. Wilson, "Problems of Stakeholder Theory." *Business Ethics: A European Review* 4, 1 (1995): 30–35.
[15] J. Nesteruk, "Law and the Virtues: a Review Article," *Business Ethics Quarterly*, 5, 2 (1995): 361–369.

Again, many of the arguments used to support SWM can be utilized to reject the stakeholder model of corporate responsibility. As we pointed out earlier, defenders of SWM would argue that adopting strategies in accordance with the stakeholder view, which means acknowledging the interests of multiple constituencies in addition to fixed and residual financial claimants, may well result in increased indecision and confusion. Satisfying a diversity of interests may well be difficult unless the multiplicity of objectives can be reduced to an overall monotonic purpose. Loss of competitiveness may well follow. As said before, it is not easy to manage on behalf of multiple constituencies when their goals come into conflict and it may not be socially desirable to give managers unlimited liberty to make choices between competing interests. In contrast, the principle of shareholder value offers an unambiguous standard, which is measurable and observable.[16]

Finally, if the law intervenes and seeks to enforce the stakeholder model, for example, by requiring investors take on increased liabilities with respect to employees, forgoing employment at-will, or giving the employees the right to buy the business at less than market value, any benefit to employees might well be short lived. Investors cannot be compelled to supply capital to the corporation. Shareholders may demand a higher price for capital and thus increase the firms' cost of capital with damaging financial consequences for non-shareholder constituencies. On the other hand investors may simply look to other forms of investment if the monotonic principle is abandoned and shareholder interests are compromised, resulting in insufficient monetary returns. Alternatively, potential shareholders could invest in real estate, gold, Treasury bonds or shares in overseas Japanese corporations, to mention a few examples.[17]

Those who disagree with these points and promote the stakeholder model may well insist and argue that emphasizing the principle of shareholder wealth maximization fails to appreciate entrepreneurial risk in the wider, richer context of joint stakeholder relationships. In addition, emphasizing a single responsibility to make money for shareholders fosters a myopic world view in which managers fail to see themselves as moral agents who are responsible to a wide variety of groups for their actions. In the long run, this monotonic approach may well work to the disadvantage of the shareholder's interests. However, defenders of shareholder value maximization argue that that their position does not encompass the exploitation or alienation of the firm's other constituencies. Strategies that do not take into account the morally acceptable relationships with other stakeholders including affects on the local community, are incompatible with long-term,

[16] A.K. Sundaram, A.C. Inkpen, "The Corporate Objective revisited," *Organization Science* 15, 3 (2004): 350–363.
[17] Ian Maitland, "Distributive Justice in Firms: Do the Rules of Corporate Governance Matter?" *Business Ethics Quarterly*, 11, 1 (2001): 129–145.

shareholder value creation. In this manner, shareholder wealth maximization can be interpreted as an inclusive principle that does not deny that these other interests exist and must be acknowledged in the decision making process. Ultimately, both those who advocate shareholder value and those who advocate the multi-fiduciary stakeholder approach can make reasonable claims that their preferred approach enhances the interests of all related constituencies. One concludes that the monotonic and the pluralistic approaches only become clearly distinguishable in those cases in which managers of a firm, following ethical principles, decide to benefit a particular non-shareholder group in circumstances that negatively affect both short-term and long-term shareholder wealth creation.

Economic Realities and Managerialism

Having provided the competing arguments for both the shareholder wealth maximization and stakeholder approaches to corporate responsibility, and their under-girding ideologies, it is worthwhile stepping back and assessing current realities. My first observation is that the stakeholder theory of corporate responsibility is destined to remain largely theoretical rather than a practical reality. Secondly, I would point out that even shareholder wealth maximization and its modest commitment to the inclusive interests of shareholders are, within large corporations, seriously threatened by managerial imperatives.

However, let us move to the first point. Despite the frequent recourse to stakeholder discourse found in both academic and commercial literature it still remains that primacy is largely accorded to shareholder wealth maximization. Stakeholder theory attempts to reassert, *inter alia*, the importance of the community and the satisfaction of customer needs, but the economy is so structured that business will continue to focus on profit and the bottom line. In the modern contractarian based system, other stakeholder groups really cannot rely on additional concern unless they have bargained for certain specific benefits and they may well be in no position to do so, as we explained earlier.

However, this is not to say that the modern corporation is always lacking in good will. For example, in Papua New Guinea much of the development and infrastructure in remote rural areas is provided by multinational corporations and not government, especially in areas subject to mining and resource development. In many cases the multinational corporation has taken on the role of government providing health care, educational institutions and transportations systems.[18] This is the positive side of commercial enterprise in which we observe the company

---

[18]   David Lea, "The Corporation, Public Responsibility, and Distributive Justice in the Third World," *Business Ethics: A European Review* 8, 3 (July, 1999): 151–162.

assuming responsibilities for its stakeholders in ways which we might associate with a responsible government body. However, having said that, consequences are not always so felicitous when corporations take on the roles we associate with political governance. In the United States and elsewhere in the developed world, large multinational corporations have come to exert so much influence over government policy that it is impossible to distinguish public policy from corporate interests. This is far from a good thing given the realities in the capitalist economy in which a firm's success and even survival require it to focus on the bottom line rather than community or customer interests. Ultimately despite all the theoretical emphasis on stakeholder theory, the diversity of groups affected by the company's activities will usually have to rely on government for the benefits and protections that cannot be secured through commercial relationships. However, it is difficult to see how these benefits and protections will be forthcoming if government policy is dominated by profit seeking commercial bodies.

In the United States, for example, local communities have suffered much from outsourcing, employee layoffs, plant closures and business relocation. But in many cases these developments are simply responses to commercial realities and the vicissitudes of the market. Given the structure of the capitalist enterprise it is simply unrealistic to expect companies to operate at a loss in order to ensure benefits to non-shareholder stakeholder groups, unless supported financially and otherwise by government or philanthropic private individuals. This is all to say that stakeholders that are profoundly affected by a company's activities cannot reliably expect certain protections and benefits unless government is prepared to step in and provide guarantees. Ultimately this will not happen in a state of affairs in which government is entirely driven and controlled by commercial and corporate interests. Moreover, when governments become captured by powerful commercial interests, these interests become reflected in both internal administrative policy and in international relationships.

As the most significant wealth generating aspects of trade and commerce assume an increasingly global orientation, relationships between the developed and developing world are becoming fashioned to reflect the interests of powerful commercial organizations in the developed world. The people and communities in the developing world find themselves in the position of stakeholders in relation to these multinational corporations. Their ultimate protection must come from their own governing bodies but their governments now find themselves under pressure from the developing world to implement policies that reflect commercial interests in the developed world rather than those their own citizens. Despite recommendations that developing countries fashion their systems of ownership to harmonize with Western systems in order to enjoy the benefits of global wealth generation, they also need to be aware that they may be forced to enter into relationships that reflect the interests of these powerful commercial enterprises. In the final chapters I will explain how governments in the developed world are being driven by powerful multinational business interests to force developing countries to implement intellectual property rules that will increase the flow of profits to Western investors while disadvantaging individuals, communities and industries in the developing world.

Our second point centred on the growing importance of managerial imperatives. As we have stated, the modern corporation is understood as an organization that allows those with money and resources to contract with those of managerial skill but little money, to forge a mutually advantageous cooperative enterprise. However, what has become noticeable in the last decades has been growth in the power, authority and wealth of the managerial class. This organizational structure in which authority and control are extended to a distinct managerial class has in fact been exported beyond the commercial world of corporate enterprise. 'Managerialism' as a term has been frequently applied to the so called reforms that in recent decades have swept through prominent Western institutions from the government civil service to the education systems. One researcher explains that the discourse of managerialism or corporate mangerialism appropriates private sector models of administration to the public sector. The proponents of managerialism claim to restructure bureaucratic organizations for greater efficiency and economy. These claims have been linked to the belief that the public sector is inefficient and, wasteful, and, thus not giving value for money because of the absence of an automatic disciplining mechanism.[19]

One also needs to realize that there are underlying problems in advocating the corporate structure as a model for organizational relationships, whether for an indigenous community, the institutions of political governance or a modern educational institution such as a university. While the model has been hailed for its efficiency, it must be appreciated that it also imposes forms of social interaction that foster alienation rather than social integration. I believe that performativity measurement and agency theory, which have been utilized to understand the supposed successful dynamics of group interaction within the corporate milieu, provide the key to understanding certain problematic values and practices effected through the imposition of the corporate model.

As mentioned, R.H. Coase argued that the corporation is merely a creation of the law in which the law in effect offers a standardized form of contract or a set of default rules that facilitate private ordering.[20] This legal entity, which is actually a legal fiction, allows those with money and resources to contract with those of managerial skill but little money, to forge a mutually advantageous

---

[19] Judy Szekeres, "General Staff Experiences in the Corporate University," *Journal of Higher Education Policy and Management* 28, 2 (July 2006): 133–145,136.

[20] R.H. Coase, *op. cit.*

cooperative enterprise. Moreover, those with labor to sell but lacking monetary resources or managerial skill, can negotiate with the managers acting as agents of the corporation to form employment contracts. This understanding of the corporation helps to explain the importance of agency theory. Agency problems are said to arise because contracts are not costlessly written and enforced. Agency costs include the costs of structuring, monitoring, and bonding a set contracts among agents with conflicting interests, plus the residual loss incurred when the cost of full enforcement of contracts exceeds the benefits. Business organizations are supposed to be input-output systems. A firm, therefore combines inputs with a view to maximizing outputs. In order to monitor the situation properly both inputs and outputs must be measurable, it is claimed. As Alchian and Demetz explain, "If the economic organization meters poorly, with rewards and productivity only loosely correlated, then productivity will be smaller; but if the economic organization meters well productivity will be greater."[21] Within the commercial arena this process is relatively straightforward in so far as the balance sheet, found in the financial statement, tells one, in monetary figures, the financial inputs (annual expenses), which are then measured against the outputs or the financial revenue. In other words you have an output, a product, e.g., a vehicle, a dishwasher, a house etc, which can be assigned a relatively straight forward value in money terms. For example, a worker whose output is 10 sewing machines a week at a value of $500 per machine can be said to have an output with a numerical monetary value of $5,000.

This is the model of human organization that is presumed to advance efficiency, whether applied to an indigenous land holding or a university system. When applied to a given institution the organization is viewed purely in economic terms, a decidedly narrow perspective.[22] An indigenous community uses its land holdings for a variety of purposes, both religious and cultural as well as to produce beneficial outputs for survival and enjoyment. Also a government agency does not necessarily provide a measurable monetary output but seeks to discharge a particular public function. If we look at universities for example we observe that they are designed to perform two functions: create original research and impart leaning or knowledge to the students. Neither of these 'products' can be reduced to a monetary value to which one could easily assign an exchange value. A professor whose output is two scholarly articles per year, 6 courses, and work on four committees engages in activities that are to some extent incommensurate and not easily reducible to simple measurable monetary quantification.

---

[21] A.A.A. Alchian and H. Demetz, "Production, Information Costs and Economic Organization," *Journal of law and Economics*, 26, 2 (1972): 777–795,779.

[22] B. Easton, *The Whimpering of the State* (Auckland: Auckland University Press, 1999).

But aside from the fact that the quantification issue is problematic, the rationale that applies to the firm does not necessarily apply to a communal land holding, a government institution or a university. Standard management texts tell us that the purpose of the firm and the duties of the management are shareholder wealth maximization; in other words, the raison d'etre of corporation and its organization is the realization of a profitable return for its investors. However, an indigenous community, a government agency or a university from their inceptions were not intended as commercial organizations with the purpose of enriching investors. The pervasive economic approach that intrinsically structures relationships may well lead to distortions and inappropriate forms of interaction. According to this economic model, a traditional communal land holding is necessarily viewed as an input whose value needs to be maximized through metering and productivity indexing. However, are members of the indigenous community to be viewed as agents of the community whose activities must be monitored, metered and disciplined? Similarly universities are intended to promote knowledge and truth through investigation and teaching. Wealth supposedly was to be used to support these activities and not to create greater monetary wealth from the original outlay of lesser monetary value. Even today, universities are usually classified as charitable institutions, which means that they are not designed to enrich a class of non-participatory investors that are largely extrinsic to the activities of the organization.

Agency theory, although it makes some sense as applied to the commercial corporation does not make much sense beyond this context. Agency theory assumes that self interested individuals will have tendencies to promote their own interests contrary to the interests of the organization. Since the ultimate purpose of the commercial organization is to enhance the interests of the investors it is understandable that other members of the organization may promote their interests at the expense of shareholder wealth maximization. Agency theory tells us that it is important that the agents of the corporation be monitored and constantly disciplined so that purposes of the organization are realized. i.e., promoting the interests of the shareholders class. However, an indigenous community, a government body or a university is not an organization in which the interests of its members need to be constantly controlled and disciplined in order that the interests of another class extrinsic to the organization may receive maximum benefit, in terms of increased material wealth. Within an indigenous community or even a university context it has been traditionally assumed that the interests of its principal members are identical with the interests and purposes of the organization. For example, within the university the interests of the students are identified with learning and not some other personal agenda, which would contrary to the acquisition of knowledge. Likewise the faculty's interests are to be identified with the activities they were expected to perform, research and teaching, Agency issues should not arise in the same way they do within a corporation because of none of the groups that make up the university could be viewed as acting on behalf of, or as agents for some other group that they should seek to benefit at the expense of their particular interests and personal agenda. An indigenous community is expected to manage its own communal land base so as to benefit its membership and not to achieve a level of productivity that enriches an extrinsic group of investors. In the case of a university it might be argued that the faculty and the university have a responsibility to the wider community of stakeholders analogous to the corporation's responsibility to its shareholders, however this statement is little more than a play on words. The university enriches the wider community through its cultural activities: the additions to learning and knowledge, and the education of knowledgeable and learned students. The Faculty, for example, through its own research activities benefits itself as it benefits the university and the wider community. We will discuss this issue in more detail when we later refer to MacIntyre's distinction between the goods internal to practices and the goods external to practices. The point is that an indigenous community or a university does not, as one expects from the commercial organization, produce a product or products that can be assigned a measurable monetary value that directly translates into an increase in the material wealth of its external beneficiaries—in the case of the corporation, its shareholders.

However, it might be argued one of the characteristics of Western university institutions since their inception in the Middle ages is the fact that they are corporate bodies. Thus Bologna, usually recognised as the first university, was a corporation of students (*universitas scholarium*), while Oxford and Paris were corporations of masters. Indeed it has been argued the corporation was undoubtedly one of the factors that allowed the West to forge ahead of Islam's centre's of learning.[23] Muslim religious education was privately organized and set up as a charitable trust without interference from any authority or power. But in the West, it is argued, incorporation allowed Westerns to make the charitable trust dynamic. We observe that by the late eleventh century academics were using new developments in civil and canon law to form a *universitas* or corporation (the actual term for an academic university was *studium generale*) in a similar manner to the craft guilds also appearing at this time. This may be the case because incorporation allowed for greater self regulating and independence from the civil authorities. Because of conflict between burghers and students and the censorship of leading intellectuals by the Church, Abelard and others formed the *Universitas*, modelled on the mediaeval guild, a large-scale, self-regulating, permanent institution of higher education. Modern concepts of a lifetime progression of apprentice to craftsman, journeyer and eventually to widely-recognized master and grandmaster

---

[23] George Makdisi, *The Rise of the Colleges* (Edinburgh: Edinburgh University Press, 1981).

began to emerge. I would argue that incorporation allowed the first universities to become autonomous as is the case with other self regulating professional bodies; in other words, regulation and discipline are imposed by the practitioners themselves, the faculty, and not externally imposed. However, with the modern university, we are witnessing the introduction of the modern corporate structure in which a 'managerial' class with an alleged managerial expertise that is different from that of researchers and teachers has the primary authority and the responsibility for imposing discipline.

Performativity Indexing

We have seen that the managerial ideology, which has become all pervasive, advocates mechanisms of control that seek to engender patterns of behaviour that are most efficiently orientated to economic productivity—so called performativity indexing is indicative of this approach. Performativity indexing is closely associated with the concepts of Quality control and Quality assurance originally finding application in the manufacturing industry. Quality control is concerned with testing products to see whether or not they meet specification. Quality assurance is concerned with ensuring that the productive processes are such that defective products are not produced so that the need for extensive quality control mechanisms at the end point of production is not pressing. This crude industrial model has been superimposed on diverse organizations from the civil service to the institutions of education. While as we have seen, indigenous people have been urged to adapt the corporate model as a vehicle to represent community interests, it is also the case that the attendant over-emphasis on economic productivity may well undermine traditional practices and harmonious relations between individuals and the environment. Universities have undoubtedly suffered much damage to their traditions through the imposition of this model. Members of education institutions have been expected to shift focus from education processes to outputs and leaning outcomes.[24] A new Zealand researcher observed in 1994 that after a decade of neo-liberal reform New Zealand no less than Britain had became preoccupied with performativity, i.e., with what is produced observed and measured.[25] One researcher describes universities as becoming captivated by performance indicators. It is observed that though content or how the index is derived and efforts to improve performance indicators can be critiqued, their

---

[24] John Codd, "Teachers as Managed Professionals, in the Global education industry: The New Zealand Experience," *Education Review* 57, 2 (May 2005): 193–206, 195.

[25] S.J. Ball, *Education Reform: A Critique and Post-structural Approach*, (Buckingham: Open University Press, 1994).

use cannot be questioned.[26] This effort to measure performance is supposed to make faculty more accountable. While the alleged benefits of the exercise remain controversial, the only hard empirical evidence is to be found in the incremental jump in the number of reports and accompanying charts, graphs, numbers, and committees that have to generate this paper work and this so called data. In many cases much of what is recorded is found to be redundant and doubts exist as to whether it is actually read.

One can argue that this reporting and measuring exercise is counter productive in that it obviously diverts resources from productive activities, actual research and teaching preparation to unproductive activity. In *Discipline and Punish* Foucault observes that one of the techniques of control and discipline involves the activity of reporting on oneself and recording one's activities and self evaluation.[27] Through this mechanism the subject learns to monitor and discipline oneself, a form of internal surveillance and control that is far more efficient than external forms of surveillance that can never entirely succeed to be omnipresent. One may well ask why should there exist this necessity to achieve a high level of control. The answer of course lies an attitude of management that on an intellectual level finds expression in so called agency theory.

Agency theory and Managerial expertise

The managerial class conceives of its proper function as one of ordering human inputs so as to achieve a maximized output. It assumes that the personnel, which it must supervise, are prone to interests and tendencies, which are antithetical to this purpose and therefore must be directed and channeled so that proclivities are minimized. John Codd notes that the restructuring and subsequent reforms in New Zealand in the 1980s and 90s undermined the professionalism of teachers who were repositioned as state workers and seen to be motivated by self interest with propensities for opportunism and provider capture.[28] As the researcher observes,

> Within such a culture, the teacher becomes a managed profession who is expected to have specified competencies, to be extrinsically motivated within a contractual relationship, and to produce what performance indicators can measure.[29]

As we have indicated in the previous section, managerial activities that have been associated with the imposition of performativity indexing, very possibly lead to

---

[26] Currie, *op. cit.*, 20.
[27] Michel Foucault, *The Birth of the Prison System*, trans. Sheridan, A. (New York: Vintage Books, 1979).
[28] Codd, *op. cit.*, 201.
[29] *Ibid.*, 202.

a misapplication of resources as individuals spend their time writing, compiling, and analyzing reports about their activities rather than engaging in these proper activities, research, teaching and teaching preparation. But moreover another consequent noted by some is the climate of distrust that is ineluctably part of this culture. Agency theory already assumes that individuals are prone and tend to behave in ways contrary to the purposes of the organization.[30] Thus individuals cannot be trusted to further organizational goals unless constantly monitored and disciplined by management. Some have observed that this atmosphere fosters mutual distrust and moreover those who are systematically not trusted may eventually become untrustworthy.[31]

Trust is a relational concept and the distrust one experiences may well be reciprocated. A climate of distrust may actually contribute to the creation of individuals who cannot be trusted. In contrast, trust actually enhances responsibility because individuals sense that they are valued and trusted, and as a result, freely internalize motivations embodying commitment to the organization and a sense of loyalty and accountability. The individual derives his sense of well being from this context which is also associated with the feeling that one is autonomous rather than controlled.

Alastair MacIntyre, the dominant thinker in the field of virtue ethics, has elucidated the relationship between the virtues, standards of practice and personal self interest. In speaking of the virtues and the achievement of the goods internal to certain cultural practices, MacIntyre explains that the virtues are to be understood as those dispositions, which will not only sustain practices but enable us to achieve the goods internal to practices. At the same time the virtues also serve to sustain the practitioner in the relevant kind of quest for the good.[32] He states that an institution such as a university or farm is the bearer of a tradition of practices.[33] Virtues enable their possessors to pursue their own good and the good of the tradition of which they are bearers through cultivating virtues that sustain these practices.[34] In contrast managerialism posits that the interests of the institution's employees are antithetical to the organization's good, but as MacIntyre points out the goods internal to the practices of the university, for example, learning and the achievement of knowledge, also coincide with the good of the student or professional practitioner. The achievement of these goods is dependent on self cultivation of certain virtues—commitment to an ideal, truthfulness etc.,—which

[30] *Ibid.*
[31] T. Hazeldine, *Taking New Zealand Seriously* (Auckland: Harpers Collins, 1998).
[32] Alistair MacIntrye, *After Virtue: A Study in Moral Theory*, 2nd edition (London: Duckworth, 1985), 219.
[33] *Ibid.*, 222.
[34] *Ibid.*, 223.

cannot be realized through the imposition of eternal controls. MacIntyre makes it clear that achieving goods internal to a particular practice is always in tension with the pursuit of external goods. Institutions tend to be primarily preoccupied with the pursuit of external goods, acquiring money and other material goods.[35] The institution ultimately corrupts when the institution's practitioners become over concerned or preoccupied with achievement of these external goods. Without a doubt this is what we are seeing as Universities attempt to impose a regime based on the pursuit of the external goods on the activities and practices of university faculty that should be focused on the achievement of the internal goods of traditional practice. One may assert similar sentiments with respect to an indigenous community and its relations with the land holding. The community inherits a tradition of customs and practices, which it if followed promote the goal of the individual interest and that of the community. Preoccupation with external goods such as economic wealth and output may well undermine the relations and practices that hold the community together and protect the land holding.

However, despite the popularity of so called managerialism, over-reliance on managerial expertise has been associated with notable and spectacular commercial disasters. This organizational arrangement in which investors place control in the hands of managers has provoked criticism almost from inception and even from Adam Smith the father of modern economic capitalism. Smith distrusted Joint Stock Ventures and the separation between management and financial commitment and felt that there would be tendency toward negligence and carelessness when individuals control money and resources that are not their own.[36] Smith preferred the traditional entrepreneur who combined both the roles of financier and organizer in a single individual. Smith's misgivings had already found significant basis in the South Sea Bubble of 1720, a spectacular fraud in which the managers of other peoples money and assets misled investors and misrepresented the company's activities until reality finally revealed the entire investment had been squandered and speculated away. Moreover, management's fiduciary relations with its investors continues to be fraught with tensions. Most recently the Enron bankruptcy in the United States that brought down America's seventh largest company and its oldest accounting firm continues to haunt and remind us that excessive trust and over-reliance placed on the activities of the managerial class, can be fatal.

We have, of course, already seen the argument that agency costs inherent in a team organization, such as the firm, are controlled, and maximization of output occurs when the residual claimants provide the ultimate monitoring because this activity converges with their own essential interests. This is supposed to

---

[35] *Ibid.*, 194.
[36] Adam Smith, *The Wealth of Nations* (New York: Random House, 1776), 800.

happen because the rights assigned to the residual claimants ensure maximum efficiency through reduced agency costs. It is argued that the necessity of a corporate structure in which ownership and control are separated entails that only the residual claimants can provide appropriate monitoring.[37] In a situation in which ownership and control are separated, it is the residual claimants, the shareholders, who are supposed to provide proper monitoring of the other agents of the corporation, the managers and employees, because shareholders have no interest in shirking their responsibility. However, in reality, with numerous and diverse shareholders, as was the case with Enron, together with the usual lack of access to company records on a routine basis, it is all too easy to hide facts from investors while management enriches itself at the expense of the company and its investors. It is worth noting that most recently, John Bogle, formerly an important figure in American finance, has argued that managerial self interest, not owner self interest, now lies at the heart of capitalism at the expense of owners and other stakeholders such as customers.[38] He argues that the system of checks and balances that is supposed to fill the principal agent gap is not working, and the powers of the CEO are virtually unfettered. The latest round of business scandals can be traced to this phenomenon, he says.

Aside form outright fraud and illegal misappropriation of resources, the growing power of the managerial class has meant a disproportionate distribution of benefits and compensation within the legal framework of the corporation, at the expense of shareholders and other stakeholders. John Bogle states that driven by mega—grants of stock options the total pay of the average American CEO soared from 42 times that of the average worker in 1980 to 280 times in 2004.[39] This development can hardly be seen to be in the interests of shareholder wealth maximization for as Bogle amply illustrates massive rewards have been forthcoming regardless of the performance of the CEO. Bogle argues that over the past century we have moved away from what he calls *owners' capitalism*, in which the greater rewards went to the investors, to *managers' capitalism* in which the rewards of investment are acquired by those who were intended to manage the enterprise in the interests of the investors. He enumerates a number of factors that have contributed to this trend. Among these he includes the fact that boards of directors that are supposed to provide independent oversight of the CEO and the managers are preponderantly drawn from the managerial class. Another factor is the failure of the public servants to impose the necessary standards and rules through their legislative and regulatory powers. This has resulted in the proliferation of lax accounting practices that have exposed investors to great risks and accordingly the disempowerment

---

[37] Fama and Jensen, *op. cit.*
[38] John Bogle, *The Battle for the Soul of Capitalism* (New Haven: Yale University Press, 2005).
[39] *Ibid.*, XX.

of the shareholders in the face of the growing power of private managers and their ability to enrich themselves. In turn this has been possible because private managers have been able to control public servants through lobbying practices.[40]

Although it has become fashionable to view the corporation as a nexus of contracts in which the rights and liabilities of all parties have been freely agreed upon, the reality, at least in America, is one in which there exists significant inequality of bargaining power. In effect, shareholders, the presumed beneficiaries of corporate enterprise, have little or less than marginal control over the interlocking power grid of private management and boards of directors. In America, for example, unlike the UK and Australia, shareholders usually cannot vote directors off the board, ask for votes on resolutions at annual meetings, many of which are binding on the board, or receive an advisory vote each year on top executive compensation. This has exposed investors to grave risks as the CEO and senior management compensation reaches unrealistic levels. At the same time, a climate of speculation has replaced a commitment to long term corporate value fueled in part by generous stock options that are not recorded as an expense in corporate earnings statements and a public that has been conditioned to focus on volatile share prices and the short term valuation of their capital investment. This over emphasis on short term results, published quarterly returns, and the share price has encouraged management to embrace dubious accounting practices that have mislead the public and investors, as well as costs due to increased transactions that seek to capture these illusive short term, speculative gains.

Moreover, as the corporate model becomes exported beyond the world of commerce, one also finds a similar disproportionate rewarding of the managerial class. As universities come under the spell of public choice theorists and the assumed superiority of private sector approaches to management, a great deal of money is expended on salaries and ancillary costs at the senior and middle management levels. The administration designed to serve the academic function of the university has succeeded in having that function made secondary to managerial imperatives.[41] In one study a professor from Florida State argued that the salaries of administrators are enormous comparatively speaking. While the salaries of administrators are in the top 10 percent, the faculty is in the bottom 25 percent nationally. Staff at Australian universities also reported rising salaries for administrators and the growth of corporate managerial tendencies.[42]

One concludes that at least in commercial affairs in America the balance of power firmly favors management over investors, to an extent in which the power

[40] *Ibid.*, 39.
[41] Jan Currie, "Globalization Practices and the Professoriate in Anglo-Pacific and North American Universities," *Comparative Education Review* 42, 1 (Feb. 1998): 15–29, 26.
[42] *Ibid.*, 26.

of the principal manager is virtually unfettered. We have remarked that Bogle enumerates a number of factors that have contributed to this trend. Among these he includes the fact that boards of directors that are supposed to provide independent oversight of the CEO and the managers are preponderantly drawn from the managerial class. Another factor is the failure of the public servants to impose the necessary standards and rules through their legislative and regulatory powers. This has resulted in the proliferation of lax accounting practices that have exposed investors to great risks and accordingly the disempowerment of the shareholders in the face of the growing power of private managers and their ability to enrich themselves. In turn this has been possible because private managers have been able to control public servants through lobbying practices.[43] Bogle argues that the situation must be redressed through the active participation of government. Bogle cites the American patriot Alexander Hamilton who felt that enhancing the role of government promotes market success.[44] The existence of government, Bogle argues, is not antithetical to successful commercial enterprise; it can enhance "market dynamism" and foster more equitable competition. As well as strengthening the regulations governing accounting practice, government should work to remove the archaic proxy rules that limit the power of shareholders, while at the same time working to reverse the investment community's focus on short term stock prices and refocus on long term intrinsic corporate values.

One can argue that the extreme to be avoided is the current situation in America in which the corporate world seems to be virtually hostage to the interests of management rather than those of the investors. This reality underlines the fact that great care must be taken to limit the powers of management in situations in which the corporate model is introduced into non-Western societies. In chapter two we saw that the imposition of the corporate model of organization in Papua New Guinea, Alaska and Australia has provoked a great deal of dissatisfaction. In many cases the people reported little or no benefit but with great frequency complained that those holding executive and influential positions within the formal organization acquired disproportionate benefits. Certainly if relatively sophisticated investors in the developed world, especially in the United States find it difficult to control the self enriching tendencies of management, it will be significantly if not impossibly difficult for commercially unsophisticated tribal people to control the self interested tendencies of management. However, as Bogle points out, it is imperative that government authorities impose standards that compel management to observe their fiduciary duties towards their investors. We have argued that the similarities between a traditional tribal community and Western corporation are merely superficial and an examination of structure and

---

[43] *Bogle op. cit.,* 39.
[44] *Ibid.,* 225.

tendencies indicates that the latter cannot be introduced to discharge the functions of the former without great care, if we are to avoid malefic consequences. We have also pointed out that introducing the corporate structure in non commercial contexts may foster inappropriate forms of personal interaction and even a climate of distrust because of the received notion that management must impose complete control over the non-management membership in order to achieve results. In cases in which the corporate model has been introduced into non-commercial organizations we have observed unwelcome consequences such as the undermining of professionalism, personal self-worth and harmonious cooperative interaction.

Ultimately within the context of a community, the corporate model cannot be used as vehicle to capture and preserve traditional customs and relationships. Nevertheless in certain cases indigenous people within the developed world, and those in the developing world, may seek to create larger scale economic enterprises. In these instances, it will no doubt be necessary to introduce the corporate model to organize their resources including their human resources. The foregoing analysis is meant to draw attention to problematic tendencies and issues which need to be addressed when one initiates this form of commercial enterprise. Great care must be taken not to over-empower the management, as in America where corporations now appear to be designed to satisfy the financial interests of management. Secondly one must be ever on guard to limit profit taking and especially short term money making where these activities threaten traditional values and valued customs.

Chapter Four

Tully and de Soto on Uniformity and Diversity

In the first chapter we discussed the moral basis of legitimate entitlement and argued for a system in which entitlement to property is linked to a general right rather than a special right, based on factual contingencies. Following Kymlicka we argued that for indigenous people and others it is morally preferable to found land claims and other ownership rights on the general principle of personal autonomy rather than historical events. In the second chapter we discussed matters related to the issues of autonomy on individual and collective levels. We underlined the difficulties associated with maintaining the autonomy of indigenous groups facing the economic and political realities posed by the dominant groups. Towards the end of the chapter we suggested that Tully's conviction that sees dominant groups having fiduciary duties that entail moral responsibilities for indigenous peoples may well offer a viable solution to the problem posed by the fact that financial weakness tends to undermine capacity for autonomy.

This solution again reinstates Tully's advocacy of parallel jurisdictions in which the minority indigenous communities maintain their legal systems and traditions while receiving the necessary support from the dominant group according to certain fiduciary duties entailed from earlier historical events. In the first chapter we discussed Tully's argument that "modern constitutionalism" is behind the Western world's intolerance of indigenous customs and legal systems and policies of assimilation. The modem constitution, he says, refuses to accept varied local customs, and reifies relations as it pushes to have communities and institutions homogenized and subsumed under uniform laws and subject to one national system of institutionalized legal and political authority. He claims that the influence of the modem constitutionalism is evident in the treatment of the aboriginal peoples of North America, and the abrogation of the original commitments as stated in the Royal Proclamation of 1763 and the U.S. Supreme Court decisions of John Marshall. James Tully sees the 'ancient constitution' as an 'assemblage' that, as Bolingbroke put it, incorporated a motley of overlapping legal and political jurisdictions. The ancient constitution tolerated and even respected custom.[1] For example, customary forms of ownership, institutions and

---

[1] James Tully, *Strange Multiplicity: Constitutionalism in the Age of Diversity* (New York: Cambridge University Press, 1996), 66.

laws differed from locale and jurisdiction, yet were preserved within the blanket protection of the ancient constitution.

Hernando de Soto, the Peruvian economist, gives us a very different perspective on the motley of overlapping jurisdictions and argues that diversity of systems, customs and rules with respect to property has conspired to maintain the entrenched poverty of the developing world. He argues that it is the unified, codified and integrated systems of the West that have allowed these societies to mobilize capital to escape the endemic widespread poverty of the pre-capitalist age. The West, he says, transformed property from 'dead' to 'live capital'—(to use de Soto's terminology). When this occurs in the developing world, people will be able to play a part in the increasing global economy and begin to acquire access to the world's wealth that at the moment appears locked away in the developed world. Otherwise the peoples of the developing world remain trapped in "…the grubby basement of the pre-capitalist world." The last statement brings to mind Plato's simile of the "cave". In the course of this chapter I seek to compare and evaluate the competing claims of Tully and de Soto.

In the 1980s and the 1990s, we saw a rise in the 'communitarian' or 'culturist' reaction to traditional liberal approaches to governance. Writers such as Will Kymlicka, Joseph Raz, Avishai Margalit, and Vernon Van Dyke, for example, argued for the devolution of state powers to members of cultural groups so they might maintain the integrity of their cultures, customs, norms and languages which compose their way of life. Communitarian and so called culturist critiques of liberal theory questioned the liberal tendency to articulate principles of justice premised on the 'bi-polarity' of the individual on the one hand and the state on the other. Moreover, many pointed to the inheritance of Hobbes and Bodin, which called for strong central governments to impose sovereignty on local political groups, communities and cultures. It was claimed that this failure to recognize the importance of community had generated a very much-devalued notion of liberal justice.

James Tully and Modern Constitutionalism

In the late 1990s James Tully gave the communitarian/multicultural debate an additional historical context locating this rejection of diversity in community and culture in the historical shift from 'ancient' to 'modern constitutionalism'. Tully demonstrates this through reference to the plight of the Amerindians, who are seen as victims of the new constitutionalism. Tully strongly feels that mistreatment of these indigenous peoples is traceable to attitudes of governance which fail to respect difference, and the alternatives to homogeneity. These attitudes have led North American states to breach the original understandings and accords between the settlers and indigenous, that respected the autonomy of these two distinct groups. He argues that North American states continue to have fiduciary obligations requiring respect and recognition for the jurisdiction of these original Indian nations, even though agreements and treaties have since been breached.

As mentioned earlier, Tully sees the overlapping of various legal and political jurisdictions, as in the Roman Republic or the common law of England, providing the paradigm of the ancient constitution prior to the Peace of Westphalia in 1648. The contemporary dominance of 'modern constitutionalism,' alleges Tully, is the intellectual legacy of writers such as Hobbes, Bodin and Locke. The common theme is the centralization of authority and the exclusion of diversity.[2] Accordingly, the modern constitution demands seamless legal uniformity and abhors a multiplicity of local jurisdictions with their diverse jural systems, social political structures and decentralized authority; Tully argues that the language of modern constitutionalism has come to be authoritative and designed to exclude or assimilate cultural diversity and to justify uniformity.[3]

Whereas these modern systems are antithetical to local custom and refuse to recognize its authority, the ancient constitution made room for custom. For example, customary forms of ownership, institutions and laws differed from locale and jurisdiction, yet were preserved within the blanket protection of the ancient constitution. Tully uses the analogue of an ancient city to explore the meaning of this form of constitution. The ancient city unites within a single territory the coexistence of old eccentric streets and new geometric thoroughfares, modern business areas, and diverse ethnic neighbourhoods with different traditions and folkways.[4] In contrast, the modem constitution refuses to accept varied local customs and seeks a procrustean solution in which all communities and institutions are flattened and subsumed under uniform laws and subject to one national system of institutionalized legal and political authority.[5]

The adoption of 'modern constitutionalism' was disastrous for the aboriginal peoples of North America, claims Tully, as the original commitments as stated in the Royal Proclamation of 1763 and the U.S. Supreme Court decisions of John Marshall were abandoned. Reconciliation of present realities demands restitution of a constitutional accord that embodies these original understandings between the Amerindians and the Europeans. The original accords effectively guaranteed the co-existence of both cultures within a fiduciary relationship. This co-existence involved recognition that neither the European nor the Indian system of integrated law, custom and thought is held to be superior. Both were to continue and exist contiguously in a relationship that guaranteed mutual respect and the necessary operational protections. Modern constitutionalism's preference for inflexible

---

2   *Ibid.*
3   *Ibid.*, 58.
4   *Ibid.*, 122.
5   *Ibid.*, p. 66.

uniformity has meant a constitution of equal citizens who theoretically are treated identically, but not necessarily equitably. In actuality, identical treatment has justified the abrogation of earlier accords and the refusal to accept cultural and legal diversity, entailing the ultimate denial of equitable treatment, as distinct cultural communities are pushed to assimilate within one dominant system.

Tully argues for a reinstatement of virtues of ancient constitutionalism and accordingly a return to prior commitments. For Tully justice can only be realised where difference is recognised, protected and respected. In order to realise these ends, one must preserve rather than destroy the jurisdiction of ethnic groups with respect to social organisation, language, kinship, leadership, property and territorial control. Tully's work represents a significant part of the growing antipathy towards uniformity and the universalising tendencies of the modern organization, which, he believes, underwrite a loss of local empowerment. In this respect his thinking and that of the communitarians is consistent with contemporary disenchantment with, not to mention resistance to globalization. Globalization, or the tendency to international uniformity in culture and increasing integration into a global system of economics and power, appears to promote an analogous universalising conformity across borders, while centralizing economic if not political power and control in certain trans-national corporations.[6] Just as localities are losing their diversity and distinctness within the nation state to become increasingly subject to the metropoles, so too nation states, especially the peripheral developing states, appear to be captured by a concatenation of global culture and global economics, which is also robbing them of their autonomy and transferring authority to the multinational conglomerates usually centred in the most developed capitalist states. The tension created by this trend has become evident, as violent as well as intellectual resistance has expressed itself most recently in mass demonstrations against the World Trade Organization in Seattle and Melbourne, and in Quebec during economic summits. There are thus two issues. The first is the dissemination of a uniform culture and a uniformity of social organization across nations and across international borders. The second is the loss of local political autonomy by communities and indigenous peoples both within the nation state and by developing nations throughout the international community. In other words, there is a perception that the most disadvantaged class, consisting of aboriginal communities, and nation states which have been recently formed from aboriginal peoples, has been made worse off by these tendencies. Following Rawlsian principles of justice, it would appear that we are under obligation to protect and reaffirm diversity and redress the shift of power which has been transferred away from local cultural communities and

---

6   See Saskla Sassen, *Globalization and its Discontents* (New York: New Press, 1998) and Eleonore Koafman and Gillian Youngs, *Globalization: Theory and Practice* (New York: Pinter, 1996).

'peripheral states'. In interpreting this imperative, it would seem we are bound to promote local cultural diversity across a spectrum of human behaviour including legal procedures, customary law, folkways, social and political organization etc. It is felt that this reaffirmation of local law and custom will necessarily mean a realignment of power that transfers autonomy back to peripheral nation states, and local communities and diverse peoples within the nation state.

However, the issue I raise in this chapter, in light of de Soto's researches, is whether such a programme is both feasible and desirable. Specifically can it be said with authority that promoting diversity will improve the position of indigenous peoples and peripheral states formed from indigenous groups? I would argue that it may not, if local diversity is encouraged with respect to land and property rights in general, which are key aspects of the programme.

With respect to indigenous peoples especially, land rights, of course, have been one of the most contentious issues, the loss of which is often associated with the erosion of autonomy and political sovereignty. In the face of this loss or perceived loss, indigenous people and others often assert the sovereignty of local custom and customary local law over modern property law and the unified codified systems of European law. The apparent advantage of this approach for indigenous peoples is that it adds force to territorial and land ownership claims which appear to be denied by modern property law. Certainly, James Tully in North America and Henry Reynolds in Australia have forcefully put this position.[7]

De Soto and the Mystery of Capitalism

But while this approach appears persuasive, there exist significant problems that need to be addressed. Most recently Hernando de Soto has tackled the thorny issue of third world poverty and offered a novel analysis that links significant levels of poverty with a diversity of local ownership systems which resist universal application. Relying on meticulously researched statistics he convincingly demonstrates that societies and nation states which accept a diversity of local customary arrangements and do not unify, formalize and codify rules with respect to ownership, are incapable of generating significant wealth to allow escape from the cycle of poverty.[8] While others have linked third world poverty to a diverse aetiology of capital flight, 'Dutch disease', lack of 'trust', moral failure, exploitation by the Northern 'Metropoles' through contrived dependency etc., de

---

7   Tully, *op. cit.*; Henry Reynolds, *The Law of the Land* (New York: Penguin Books, 1992).
8   Hernando De Soto, *The Mystery of Capital: Why Capitalism Triumphs in the West and Fails Everywhere Else* (Sydney: Random House, 2000).

Soto offers a relatively simple explanation that neither condemns nor criticizes. De Soto perceives the causes of continuing economic failure in the lack of system that would unify a diversity of local arrangements into a codified, universally recognized and registered form of land tenure. De Soto makes the telling point that until ownership is universalised and formalized, and registration is realized, a diversity of locally recognized arrangements prevents customary forms of ownership from generating capital which can function in the process of wealth generation. The difference between the successful capitalist states and the impoverished developing world is not so much in the intrinsic value of what is possessed, but in the fact that what is owned in the developed world can function as 'live capital', whereas most of what is possessed in the third world is unformalized 'dead capital', that is to say, it is not recognized as a genuine asset by the market and its lending institutions. In this condition it cannot be the subject of collateral or transfer. Formalization and registration, he argues, allow one to focus on the assets' economic potential, enabling it to be used to stimulate lending and productivity. This allows property to be transformed from 'dead' to 'live capital'.

If de Soto is correct, then encouraging a diversity of cultural approaches and a diversity of local cultural systems, especially with respect to land ownership, will in fact fail to empower groups against universalizing forces that appear to be transferring control from localities to the political and economic centres (whether they are international or within the nation state). If de Soto is correct, this policy, if pursued, will condemn these societies to a continuing marginal existence that maintains the economic hegemony of the developed states, and isolated pockets of third world elites, within the poverty-stricken third world states. It will ensure that those outside the system, or the 'bell jar' to use de Soto's metaphor, will be denied access to the benefits of global capitalism; and this will work to maintain the perceived dominance of the capitalist states and the third world elites, who have embraced capitalist values. Far from transferring power back to the politically and economically disadvantaged, a diversity of cultural systems, especially with respect to land tenure, maintains this status quo of disempowerment and poverty. If anything there is certainly some hard-headed logic in de Soto's position. Clearly the capacity to be autonomous is often a function of one's relative bargaining power. Ownership and levels of personal liberty are not unconnected because wealth determines relationships of power and vulnerability.[9] If we look at the situation with romantic eyes, it is certainly true that most would prefer to see local folkways

---

[9] See Notes, *Harvard Law Review*, 107 (1993): 859–876, 860 in which the authors reject the tendency in modern. liberal to emphasis the lexical priority of liberty over distributive justice and point out that relative levels of liberty are determined by relationships of power and vulnerability that pervade and partially determine the actual choices available.

continue, customary procedures maintained, dying languages preserved, and so on, rather than observe all ground down to uniformity. On the other hand, it is important to recognize the realities of wealth generation and the exigencies faced by many poor and indigenous peoples. Although much of the analysis of this chapter is devoted to ownership issues relating to land, de Soto's analysis applies to any form of property, chattels as well as immovables like real estate and land. In Melanesia, because much of the country has existed with virtual Stone Age economies, the principal means of production has been land. However, there are also more advanced third world countries in South America, Asia and Africa that have been semi-industrialized for some generations, yet despite the presence of valuable assets and more sophisticated means of production, they have been sentenced to poverty because holdings are wedded to inadequate and unformalized systems of ownership. The purpose of this chapter is to illustrate the appropriateness of de Soto's arguments by applying them to the Melanesian context where the most pressing issue is the economic mobilization of land; and in so doing demonstrate why wealth generation has proved to be such an elusive goal in Melanesia.

Within the South Pacific, for example, there has existed a belief since the days of Rousseau and de Bougainville, that the indigenous peoples have enjoyed something described as subsistence wealth. But the reality may be very different. Some note that with population growth, urban drift etc., the days of subsistence affluence, if they ever existed, are past for most Pacific Islanders and the only option left is to grow on the basis of trade and specialization. This will not be possible without increased economic mobilization of land.[10]

Differences Between Western and Customary Ownership in Melanesia and Elsewhere

According to de Soto, Western forms of property possess distinct characteristics, which allow for successful capitalism. Among other things this means: a recorded representation of the economically and socially useful aspects of the asset; a single system of integrated information rather than dispersed data; orientation to individual rather than group accountability; a fungible system in which property is capable of being divided, combined and moulded to suit economic potentialities; a network of connections with both the government and the private sector; record-keeping systems which protect not only the security of ownership but

---

[10] S. Chand and R. Duncan, "Resolving property issues as a precondition for growth: access to land in the Pacific islands," *The Governance of Common Property in the Pacific Region*, Ed. Larmour, P. (Canberra: National Centre of Development Studies, ANU, 2000) pp. 33–46.

more importantly the security of transactions.[11] The systems of ownership that
people devise may be diverse but they must share these central features with
Western systems in order to be integrated into the increasingly global economy.
However, it should be mentioned that de Soto's work does not represent a unique
attempt to highlight the central features of the modern liberal notion of ownership.
Forty years ago, A.M. Honore definitively listed the essential components of
the modern liberal ownership right. He listed eleven "incidents", or rights and
limitations that define ownership in the modern Western sense of the term.[12]
However, the significance of de Soto's work lies in his ability to convey a heightened
understanding by contrasting Western and non-Western systems of ownership. In
doing so he attempts to explain the interrelation between systems of ownership and
economic success, and the continuing lack of success of the so-called developing
world.

To appreciate de Soto's observations, one needs to take a hard look at the
concrete social and economic reality associated with a diversity of local property
relations. De Soto's point is that not only must property be unified and registered
but it must also be individuated. It is only through individual forms of ownership
that accountability and responsibility can be achieved[13] For de Soto individual
forms of ownership evolved in the West with the integration of all property systems
under one formal property law. This, he claims, shifted the legitimacy of the rights
of owners from the politicized context of local communities to the impersonal
context of law. This, he says, created individuals from masses by transforming
people with property interests into accountable individuals. The price paid
meant that the individual lost the anonymity afforded by group membership and
became more identifiable and accountable. But with accountability, individuals
gained access to financing through loans and mortgages and at the same time
found themselves unrestricted by group politics and free to explore avenues for
developing their interests and generating surplus value. But if property cannot be
subject to seizure on loan default, it cannot serve as collateral and be mortgaged
to finance development. It cannot be live capital or an asset that has a functional
role in a market economy.

With respect to Tully's observations, this means that unformalized property
is untouched by dynamic features of modern law. H.L.A. Hart has pointed out
that the law consists of a subset of dynamic rules that allow for the creation of
obligations and rights through promises, commitments, contracts and so on.[14] But

---

[11] De Soto, *op. cit.*, 42–54.
[12] A.M. Honore, "Ownership", *Oxford Essays in Jurisprudence*, ed. A.G. Guest (London: Oxford University Press, 1961), 107–147.
[13] De Soto, *op. cit.*, 46–48.
[14] H.L.A. Hart, *The Concept of Law* (Oxford: Clarendon Press, 1964), 192.

so long as property remains unformalized, it remains subject to local politics and this dynamic aspect of law is necessarily frustrated. In these situations, owners are far less free to contract and transact and thereby create new rights and liabilities with respect to ownership. Because individuals are unable to avail themselves of this dynamic aspect that allows disposal of property, they cannot readily participate in the global market. Tully, as we have said, argues for the promotion of local cultural diversity across a spectrum of human behaviour including legal procedures, customary law, folkways, social and political organization etc. He argues that this reaffirmation of local law and custom will necessarily mean a realignment of power that transfers autonomy back to peripheral nation states, and local communities and diverse peoples within the nation state. However, in reality, individuals and societies may ultimately find their autonomy severely constricted as they are denied opportunities to transact and generate wealth. Without access to wealth, dependency will be heightened as nations are pushed to secure offshore loans and grants to maintain basic infrastructure and provide basic collective goods like education, basic health care, adequate transportation systems, and so on.

A diversity of cultural approaches towards property poses especially acute problems with respect to land development and mobilization. Moreover, the fact that in many indigenous societies land is collectively owned has further militated against economic mobilization. Although we often speak of a diversity of local customs and rules with respect to indigenous land tenure, there do remain certain general features that apply almost universally. Whether we are speaking of the Tanzanians, Papua New Guineans, Fijians, or even Amerindians, it is felt that the group holds land and that it is not subject to purchase or sale. In Papua New Guinea and Fiji, legislation restricts the purchase or sale of customary land, and it cannot be subject to forfeiture in cases of loan or mortgage default. Often, as in Papua New Guinea, these customary arrangements are wholly unregistered, which means that customary owned land can never function as a 'live' financial asset, one that could serve as collateral for a loan and thereby become subject to economic development. Since 97% of the land mass is under customary ownership, economic stagnation is an ineluctable reality.

Moving back from group interests to individual interests, the individual caught in the customary system is not free to initiate any project with respect to property without first mobilizing politically, and gaining consent from the greater political/social community, the reputed owners. The point is that even if collective ownership were properly registered one would face the inherent transaction costs and uncertainties in decision-making associated with collective ownership by groups. Hume, for example, compared the ease with which two individuals can agree on plans with the difficulty of mobilizing larger groups. He notes with respect to larger groups: "But it is very difficult, and indeed impossible, that a thousand persons would agree in any such action; it being difficult for them to concert so complicated a design, and still more difficult for them to execute; while each seeks a pretext to free himself of the trouble and expense and would lay the whole burden to others."[15]

Of course, throughout the Pacific and Africa, post-colonial nations have clung to collective forms of land tenure inherited from pre-colonial times. In Kenya and Uganda, for example, the government sought to individuate title but in the end customary collective forms of tenure prevailed over official policy. It has been argued that experience in Uganda and Kenya, indicates that custom continued to persist and largely nullified programs of registration of individual holdings.[16] In Tanzania, in accordance with socialist ideals, the government sought to bureaucratize and formalize legally traditional forms of local collective ownership for purposes of land mobilization. One commentator observed that this policy really meant that the machinery of the state had penetrated the local organization at the village level, unavoidably vitiating traditional forms of local control and achieving little real development.[17] Indeed the Tanzanian socialist experiment has apparently achieved one of the poorest economies in the world, something it was not during the immediate postcolonial period.

The point by now should be obvious. An individual, with an unspecified interest in a collectively owned area of land, is certainly not free to ask the bank for a loan or mortgage on the basis of his interest, because he/she does not bear sole responsibility and accountability for that land. Lending is the principal manner in which the money supply legitimately expands, thereby stimulating economic growth and the expansion of local markets. The largest part of the money supply, deposits in banks, comes into existence when people and firms borrow money.[18] Furthermore, borrowing and productivity are intimately linked.

---

[15] D. Hume, *A Treatise on Human Nature* (Dent, London, 1911 [1740]), 239.
[16] P. Larmour, "Policy transfer and reversal: customary land registration from Africa to the Pacific, unpublished paper," (Canberra: National Centre For Development Studies, ANU, 2000), 47.
[17] C.K. Omari, *Strategy for Rural Development: The Tanzania Experiment* (Kampala: East African Bureau, 1976). The 1967 Arusha Declaration and the 1975 Village Act sought to re-emphasize communal ownership of the means of production, land. In Tanzania each village was to establish a governing council consisting of 25 members elected from among the villagers of the same unit and from these members five different committees were established. One of these committees was to be responsible for the production and distribution of resources. Despite the elaborate plan for collective control at the village level and the fact that Tanzania is reputed to be the most 'aided' country in Africa, it remains one of the poorer countries in the world.
[18] John Kenneth Galbraith, *Money: Whence it Came, Where it Went* (Boston: Houghton Mifflin, 1975), 209.

"Without borrowing and deposit creation there is no effect on prices, and through prices on production."[19]

This means, of course, that owners have to bite the bullet and allow the mortgagee to seize the property on loan default. The latter statement, of course, sounds harsh and perhaps culturally insensitive to the feelings of numerous indigenous peoples who affirm a special relationship with the land that militates against any form of permanent alienation. However, the sentiment of security derived from a sense of inalienable possession and immunity against seizure on loan default, may obversely conceal a reality of marginal existence and continuing disconnection from the sources of wealth generation. In a word, security of indefeasible possession is false security, which condemns societies to continuing impoverishment. De Soto remarks with respect to the 'owners' of extralegal property that is unregistered and consequently cannot be subject to seizure,

> Because they have no property to lose, they are taken seriously as contracting parties only by their immediate family and neighbours. People with nothing to lose are trapped in the grubby basement of the pre-capitalist world.[20]

Although to this point analysis has been concentrated on the plight of developing states with a predominant indigenous population, the above remarks equally apply to Amerindians. Indigenous peoples in North America have been confined to reserves or reservations, which are protected areas. This means that property cannot be conveyed and cannot be mortgaged. Thus land cannot be developed because it can never serve as capital in the market economy. This is one of the principal reasons why modern Amerindians often appear to be unconnected to mainstream North American society. Effectively, many are untouched by the opportunities and risks experienced by North Americans who participate directly in the economic system.

Ultimately, there is no question that national and international communities should be prepared to tolerate a diversity of cultures, customs, and customary legal systems, but de Soto's point with respect to property is that any system of property relations must bring together the central features of the modern Western system, if the owners are to be beneficiaries of the processes of wealth generation.

Differing Concepts of Ownership and the Transformation of Traditional Cultures

There is indeed in de Soto a certain reverberation of language that is reminiscent of the Platonic tradition. De Soto speaks of people utilizing non-Western or

---

[19] *Ibid.*
[20] De Soto *op. cit.*, 48.

extra-legal systems of property as trapped in the grubby basement of the pre-capitalist world. To many readers this may suggest the famous 'cave' of Book VII of the *Republic* in which the unintellectual materialists were chained. Moreover, he speaks of those whose property is unformalized as being fixated on the material qualities of the property object, whereas those whose property has been formalized are freed from the material substrate and focused on the intellectual qualities associated with its economic and transactional potentialities. In other words, they have transcended the material sphere and are freed from the "grubby basement of the pre-capitalist world." In their emancipated state they now gaze upon the formal rather than material qualities of their property, qualities associated with 'live capital' rather than dead material things.

De Soto's book strongly implies that for certain people, especially indigenous peoples, there must be some form of revolution in the way in which they look upon ownership. There is no doubt that de Soto has convincingly stated the economic advantages of such a revolution. There is, of course, the social cost and the obvious question as to whether they can maintain tradition and cultural diversity in the face of such a revolution. One ponders, for example, the intricate record keeping that is needed to sustain modern Western forms of property. De Soto points out that public record keepers administer the files that contain all the economically useful descriptions of assets, whether land, buildings, chattels, ships, industries, mines or aeroplanes. But at the same time, he notes that many private services have evolved to assist in fixing, moving and tracking representations. These include escrow and closings organizations, abstractors, appraisers, title and fidelity insurance firms, mortgage brokers, trust service and private custodians of documents. According to de Soto, these entities give security to transactions, so that assets may move easily and efficiently through the system.[21] One reflects that the institutional and organizational structure which is necessary to the Western formal system of property representation entails axiomatically that Western forms of property mean Western societies. An indigenous society cannot simply decide to institute a Western formal system, it must also create the agencies, institutions, and organizations endemic to Western capitalism which allow dead capital to be become live capital through the meticulous recording and tracking of assets and transactions. Also one should point out that in order to institute these changes there might well have to be a fundamental cultural shift in attitudes towards, if not modification of, the very concept of 'entitlement'. Here we are speaking of the very validification of property claims and the implications with respect to the notion of 'ownership'. Honore pronounced in his famous essay on ownership: "There are in fact good reasons why the commonest modes of

---

[21] *Ibid.*, 53.

original acquisition (making and taking) and of derivative acquisition (consent and debt) should be recognized. If these are thought to be morally satisfactory, we have arrived at a justification of the adoption of a legal system of certain modes of acquisition. What we have not found is a justification for the institution of ownership."[22]

Our point is that the processes and procedures by which entitlements are recognized and verified have definite implications as to the very nature of the institution of ownership. One assumes that Western and indigenous societies hold common notions of entitlement, or ownership, but that what differs is the procedure by which entitlement is verified. In the West questions of title are usually settled by a process in which one refers to relevant legislation, legal codes and published records. In indigenous societies we assume that there exist similar legal codes which are embedded in tradition and that records are located in oral history rather than in record-keeping filing systems. One surmises therefore that a transition from an indigenous system to a Western system would not require any major social adjustment; we merely have to make the oral tradition explicit and record the information in statutes and registries.

However, one researcher who made a study of the people of the Haeapugua Basin in Papua New Guinea notes that it may well be the case that principles of land tenure carefully elicited and codified by legal anthropologists are more accurately described as rhetorical positions deployed in specific political contexts. It is his view that orators in land disputes, in appealing to different and contradictory principles of land tenure, or any other aspect of social life, are simply drawing upon a wide range of cultural norms and precedents, as these contribute to their position in a particular debate. He says that there is a processual nature of Melanesian land ownership, which suffers considerably in the translation to legal code. This is more than evident in the role played by recognition and acknowledgement in determining land rights. There are, he says, no clear-cut distinctions between users and owners, while ancestral claims also count. Many land disputes revolve around just this form of conundrum, but it is not through the application of hard and fast rules that disputes are resolved. Rather, those involved in the dispute arrive at solutions that are likely to receive broad consensus. He concludes that ultimately recognition of a claim derives from negotiated consensus over a general observance of norms and principles in the dispute process rather than the rigorous application of norms in the form of a code.[23]

---

[22] Honore, *op. cit.*, 139.
[23] C. Ballard, "It's the Land Stupid! The moral economy of resource ownership in Papua New Guinea," *The Governance of Common Property in the Pacific Region*, Ed. Larmour, P. (Canberra: National Centre of Development Studies, ANU, 1997), 47–65, 50–52.

Of course, this is just the sort of thing de Soto is talking about when he speaks of freeing people from reliance on neighbourhood relationships and local arrangements to protect property rights. Recognition of rights that depends on consensus entails a wholly politicized interest. Transforming people with property interests into accountable individuals meant that property relationships would be fixed and recognized nationally and internationally rather than merely locally. And as de Soto observes, in Western countries where property information is standardized and universally available, what owners can do with their assets benefits from the collective imagination of a larger network of people. In the non-Western context, what people can do with their property is limited to the imagination of the owners and their acquaintances.

Transforming non-western forms of ownership into western forms means that the fluidity of traditional indigenous property relations can no longer apply. Clearly in the Melanesian context, as described by the above researcher, and probably in most cultures dependent on oral traditions, one's property interest is merely provisional in the sense that future social and political developments may well mean a loss of that interest. Ultimately one's property right, far from being fixed and recorded for posterity in some collective memory, must be continually revalidated through community consensus. For example, disuse of land may signify a loss of property right. But how much disuse and for what period? No doubt there is no hard and fast answer (as we would expect to find in a Western legal code and as the researcher suggests); ultimately these issues would have to be settled within the community taking into account a range of variables including the current political climate. For example, most Melanesian societies have a "big man." If the "big man" doesn't like you and he argues hard and persuasively against your claim you may well lose the right.[24] Similarly, in other traditional societies, hereditary chiefs or more structured feudal hierarchies provide governance. In all these systems individual rights may be virtually unprotected or derived from the will of the political authorities.

Of course, on a national or international level it is difficult to deal with a system of rights which is so dependent on local social and political arrangements, rather than one that is independent of these contingencies and valid in perpetuity. This is precisely the problem that de Soto outlines. On the other hand, traditional societies may definitely prefer property rights, which are flexible and which may be varied, cancelled, and even recreated in response to the changing social and political landscape of the community. This would be a right which must be continually revalidated through community consensus. At the same time ownership, in this context, may definitely lack two essential incidents which, Honore holds, define

---

[24] Experiences from the organizational context of PNG, indicate the so called "big man" as one who can mould and shape group consensus.

the modern liberal institution of ownership: the right to security and the absence of term. The right to security ensures immunity from expropriation and the absence of term refers to the characteristic by which the temporal length of one's ownership continues for an indeterminate period.[25]

But I suspect this is why there has been within Papua New Guinea continual resistance to official attempts to register customary land. In 1995 the government was forced to withdraw its plans for land registration in the face of violent protests from students and the military. Most recently in June 2001, four people were killed, including two students, in demonstrations against land registration and privatization. The customary property right is closely associated with notions of local control of community affairs through consensus. Once it becomes fixed in the records of a central land registry, it may well gain a life that is independent of and immune from local control and variation.

Conclusion

When one puts the case in these terms, it certainly appears that the Western system of property relations promotes conditions decried by communitarians and culturists, among them loss of local control and autonomy, and the undermining of custom and traditional folkways. If justice requires not only justice for individuals but for groups then the argument can be made that de Soto's proposals are unjust to groups seeking to maintain their cultural integrity. However, the sense of local autonomy may be short lived if following local traditions and customs means impoverishment and economic dependence. Also de Soto notes that collective forms of property are not independent of the vicissitudes of local politics. Moreover, if the famous remark of Tip O'Neill (Former Democratic whip in the US House of Representatives) is accurate, and "All politics is local" these recommendations may also free land rights from interference from the higher political levels. For example, there is a perception in Papua New Guinea that many national politicians (members of the National Parliament) prefer the current unregistered form of customary ownership because it allows them scope for manipulating outcomes to suit their interests. National politicians in PNG are simply the "big men" operating in the national arena, but their power base is a constituency of villages and clans who view them in these terms and await the benefits of their political activities. One of the qualities of the big man is his ability to mould and shape group consensus, and of course these qualities are applied on the local level. If land ownership were freed from politics, then this would severely

---

[25] Honore, *op. cit.*, pp. 107–147.

restrict the ability of national politicians to involve themselves in land issues and mould outcomes favourable to their political interests.

I make this point because while on the one hand unregistered customary land tenure may appear to protect and promote local control and autonomy, on the other hand these rights are left exposed to the contingencies of local and regional politics (and in some cases national politics). Ultimately the romantic perception that sees customary land tenure as an informal bastion safeguarding local autonomy and interests, may miss the concealed reality in which unformalized interests are far more vulnerable to exogenous political machinations and unconstrained local politics. While Tully may reject the intellectual inheritance of Hobbes and Locke, certainly part of that inheritance, as found in the political philosophy of Locke, sought to entrench property rights constitutionally and thereby protect them from the political machinations and arrangements of the majority. In the recommended separation of powers adopted by modern liberal democracies, matters involving property rights ultimately fell within the jurisdiction of the judiciary, thereby providing protection from the political branch of government. In the politics of diversity, which Tully recommends, non-Western forms of property are often vague, uncertain and undefined, and ultimately redefined through the continuing tussles between competing political interests. Part of the success of modern Western forms of property has been the ability to define and fix property rights, so that they gain an independence and protection from the changing contours of political struggle. A quick embrace of the politics of diversity may well plunge property relations back to a pre-Lockean stage in which the rights of the individual are virtually at the mercy of the contingencies of politics and group decision-making. Ultimately the issue may not be one of deciding between competing liberal and communitarian values, but of recognizing that de-emphasis on individual rights in favour of the group does not necessarily empower the community or group. Abandoning a commitment to individual rights may simply provide greater licence to ambitious individuals within the group without any group benefit or structural strengthening. And from a utilitarian prospective it must be recognized that part of the economic success of Western economies is linked to this ability to separate individual ownership from the vicissitudes of the political arena, and thereby achieve a level of stability that allows for successful trade and commerce.

Finally, Tully's promotion of parallel jurisdictions may work to diversify the loci of power, but will not necessarily empower the individual or distinct cultural communities if the reality is impoverishment and denial of access to wealth. In the developing nations spiralling dependency characterized by deficit financing, overseas grants, structural adjustment programs, and growing indebtedness are recipes for loss of autonomy and vitiated independence. Similarly, indigenous enclaves following a diversity of laws and customs with respect to property, within both North America and Australia, may well ensure the necessity for the continuing financial support from the dominant group. The necessity for external financial support signals an inability to manage self-development that does not have implicit or explicit approval from the financial source. Moreover, regardless of the good intentions of the financially dominant group where parallel jurisdictions are locked in relations of financial dependence, the interests and autonomy of the indigenous group will always be in unequal struggle with the interests of the dominant group.[26]

---

[26] The fact that financial health and the capacity for autonomy are closely linked is becoming increasingly recognized. For example, it has been pointed out that in Australia, non-Aboriginal local government communities have traditionally been able to carve out a degree of autonomy from Commonwealth and State authority, through the collection of rates, an option not available to poorer Aboriginal and Torres Strait Island communities. Furthermore on the issue of greater regional autonomy for the Torres Strait Islanders, through a proposed Torres Strait Island Regional Assembly, a 1997 Report of Inquiry tied greater financial autonomy (through grant block funding from the State and Commonwealth Governments) to the ability of Islanders to increase their involvement in local industry—particularly fisheries. These facts illustrate my point, which is that financial dependence means that the direction of future development may well be dictated by the external financial source, unless these communities find a way to become self supporting.

Chapter Five

Customary Land Tenure and Communal Holdings

At this point we proceed to consider the possible application of de Soto's recommendations within the social, economic and political realities of developing states. Recognizing that one of the serious challenges that face Pacific nations in the twenty first century is that of sustainable development, in subsequent chapters we consider the frequently mooted proposal to replace the diverse customary systems of land and property in the South Pacific with more formalized Western systems of private ownership. In this chapter we discuss the meaning of customary land tenure and communal holdings. Although it is readily assumed that customary land tenure means communal rights rather than individual private exclusive rights, this is a matter that is far from clear, even though in the third chapter we assumed for simplicities sake that the distinction is fairly clear. Nevertheless, it is demonstrative that customary systems include important aspects of both community rights and exclusive individual private rights. Therefore, it is important to distinguish the contexts in which inclusive communal rights apply and those in which exclusive individual rights apply.

One notes that many Pacific Island nations, in the decades since independence, have generally failed to experience hoped for gains in material welfare and economic development. A fairly recent United Nations Human Development Report named four Pacific Island countries in which living standards fell in the decade between 1990 and 2001.[1] The countries mentioned were the Solomon Islands, Vanuatu, the Marshall Islands and the Federated States of Micronesia. A 2003 UN report rated Papua New Guinea, undoubtedly the island nation richest in natural resources, as number 132 out of 173 countries according to its 'Human Development Indicator'.[2] This rating was even lower than that of the Solomon Islands where in July 2003, deteriorating conditions of security and order resulted in Australia committing 2000 troops to restore stability.

Although some believe that South Pacific nations enjoy 'subsistence affluence', others argue that this picture is not consistent with the realities of high population growth, rapidly monetising economies, rural-urban migration, the trading of

---

[1] *PNG Post Courier* (July 11, 2003), 11.
[2] Mike Manning, "Mid year review of the economy," *PNG Post Courier* (July 18, 2003), 11.

future consumption for present consumption and the problem of land degradation.[3] Current population growth rates suggest that reasonably high sustainable subsistence levels are not possible with increasing population density. From these observations, one researcher concludes that the days of 'subsistence affluence' (if any) are past for most Pacific Island nations; and the feasible economic option for these nations is to grow on the basis of trade and specialization in areas of their comparative advantage. The link between population density and declining living standards can be broken via trade and productivity growth. But this growth can only be realized through the mobilization of land and the promotion of land based investments such as agriculture and infrastructure development.[4]

Concerns such as these have led to a growing interest in issues involving customary land tenure that include the mobilization, and economic development of lands subject to traditional systems of tenure.[5] This means that the vast areas of land currently under customary and communal tenure need to be organized in such a way as to encourage efficient use and enhance the inflow of technology and capital.

In the Pacific Island nations the status of, and relationship between customary and alienated land differs considerably. The following survey is indicative. In some: notably Papua New Guinea, the Solomon Islands and Western Samoa, dual systems of customary and alienated land (freehold) persist after independence (although in PNG 97% remains under customary control). This contrasts with Fiji, which attempted to freeze and register customary land tenure principles in the nineteenth century, although the state proceeded to arrogate to itself certain powers to effect arrangements, which could not be met within the customary system, such as the authority to regularize leases. In Vanuatu, the former Anglo-French Condominium, the independent government overthrew the colonial system of land tenure altogether without calling into question "pre-eminence of the state

---

[3]   S. Chand and R. Duncan, "Resolving Property Issues as a Precondition for Growth: Access to Land in the Pacific Islands," in P. Larmour ed., *The Governance of Common Property in the Pacific Region*. National Centre of Development Studies (Canberra: ANU 1997): 33–46.

[4]   *Ibid.*

[5]   M. Trebilcock & J. Knetch, "Land policy and economic development in Papua New Guinea," *Melanesian Law Journal*, 9, 1&2 (1981): 102–115; C. Ballard, "It's the land stupid! The moral economy of resource ownership in Papua New Guinea," in P. Larmour (ed.) *The Governance of Common Property in the Pacific Region*. National Centre of Development Studies (Canberra: ANU, 1997): 47–65; B. Aldridge, *Current Land Situation Report*. Report presented to the Special Parliamentary Committee on Urbanisation and Social Development, Port Moresby (2000) unpublished; L.T. Jones & P.A. McGavin, "Land Mobilization in Papua New Guinea," (Canberra: Asia Pacific Press, 2001); T. Curtin, "Scarcity Amidst Plenty: Economics of Land in Papua New Guinea," *State Society and Governance in Melanesia: Discussion Paper 2003/1* (Canberra: Research School of Pacific and Asian Studies, ANU, 2002): 6–17.

and the market in other respects". This is to say that in Vanuatu all forms of land tenure reverted to customary ownership, effectively abolishing freehold.[6] Elsewhere beyond the South Pacific, South Africa, Senegal, Botswana, Mongolia, Uganda, and Tanzania provide *de jure* recognition of customary rights to land.[7]

In essence many see future economic development in the South Pacific as closely linked with a process whereby Pacific Island nations mobilize and order traditional forms of customary land tenure, so as to make these systems more congruent with non-customary practices of global trade and commerce. Proposals are numerous and diverse. Some recommend the formal incorporation of the true customary landowners;[8] others propose privatisation and individual forms of freehold;[9] others recommend registration of customary interests,[10] while some believe that those with customary interests only require better state protection and guidance in matters of development.[11] With so much said about customary land rights as opposed to Western forms of land ownership it is important to firstly distinguish what is meant when we speak of customary ownership.

When one refers to traditional customary land tenure this is usually interpreted to mean a form of communal rather than individual holding but also a form of ownership in which title and 'incidents', rights and liabilities, are enshrined in custom rather than codified laws. Customary rights and liabilities, it is claimed, are accessed through oral traditions just as property rights in modern Western countries are understood through codified laws.

The Communal Nature of Customary Land Tenure

It should be pointed out that the assumption that property for traditional non-Western societies is primarily communal has some strong opposition, especially

---

[6]   P. Larmour, "Alienated land and independence in Melanesia," *Pacific Studies* 8, 1 (1984): 1–47, 38.

[7]   J. Bruce, "Learning from comparative experience with agrarian reform," International Conference on Land Tenure in the Developing World, University of Capetown, Capetown. South Africa, 27–29 Jan. (1998) (unpublished paper).

[8]   A.P. Power, *Land Group Incorporation*, three volumes, (Port Moresby: Aus Aid, 1999).

[9]   Curtin, *op. cit*; D. Lea, D. "Resolving a complexity of land mobilization issues in Papua New Guinea," *the Pacific Economic Bulletin*, 16, 2 (2001): 36–53.

[10] See for example, M. Trebilcock & J. Knetch, *op. cit*; Loani Henao, "Voluntary registration of customary land," *PNG Post Courier* (July 10, 2003), 18.

[11] R. Kemeata, "Land legislation and practice since independence," in M. Rynkiewich ed., *Land and Churches in Melanesia: Issues and Contexts* (Goroka: Melanesian Institute, 2001) pp. 304–334.

from those of libertarian persuasion. F.A. Hayek, for example, attacks the idea of an 'early state of primitive communism' as a 'myth'. He argues that anthropological evidence indicates that recognition of private property rights preceded even the rise of the most 'primitive cultures'. According to him opinions to the contrary have been inspired by the socialist thinking of our age, which regards belief in private ownership, as ideologically motivated.[12] Somewhat more recently Bruce Benson, another libertarian, cites anthropological studies of the Yurok, Hupa and Karok Indians of Northern California, the Ifugao of Northern Luzon and the Kapauku of West Papua as societies lacking the institutional characteristics of the modern state, but clearly structured by notions of private ownership.[13] With respect to the Kapauku, he states, that there was absolutely no common ownership. He cites Leopold Prospsil who states that "Individual ownership ...is so extensive in the Kamu valley that we find the virgin forests divided into tracts which belong to single individuals. Relatives, husbands and wives do not own anything in common".[14]

It seems for libertarians the controversy over communal versus individual land tenure continues unabated. In 2004 the Australian libertarian think tank, the Centre for Independent Studies, stirred up the waters in a series of articles that provoked a strong response from development theorists. In these articles the Centre for Independent Studies questioning the economic viability of Melanesian customary land tenure.[15] Together they issued a strong demand that customary land in PNG be privatized into individual freehold. James Fingleton, a recognized authority on development issues in the South Pacific, answered with a collection of edited papers in *Privatising Land in the Pacific: A defense of Customary Tenures*.[16] It should also be noted that Fingleton drafted the PNG legislation that sought to preserve customary communal ownership of land through what is designated as an "Incorporated Land Group". (We will have much to say about "Incorporated Land Groups" in subsequent chapters.) Fingleton et al. claim that the Centre for Independent Studies misunderstood or misrepresented either the nature of customary land

---

[12] F.A. Hayek, *Law, Legislation and Liberty*, Vol. 1 *Rules and Order* (Chicago: University of Chicago Press), 108.

[13] B.L. Benson "Enforcement of Private Property Rights in Primitive Societies: law without Government," *The Journal of Libertarian Studies*, IX, 1 (Winter 1989): 1–26.

[14] Leopold Prospsil, *Anthropology of Law: A Comparative Theory* (New York: Harper and Row, 1971), 66.

[15] S. Gorsarevski, H. Hughes and S. Windybank "Is Papua New Guinea Viable?" *Pacific Economic Bulletin* 19, 1 (2004): 134–148; S. Gorsarevski, H. Hughes and S. Windybank "Is Papua New Guinea Viable with Customary Land Tenure?" *Pacific Economic Bulletin* 19, 3 (2004): 133–136.

[16] J. Fingleton *Privatising Land in the Pacific: A defense of customary Tenures: Discussion Paper Number 80 June 2005* (Canberra: Australian Institute).

tenure, and thereby offered straw man type argumentation, or began from false premises about the nature of customary land and derived false conclusions.

In the following pages I wish to concentrate initially on the issues that are raised by Fingleton et al. The issue is one of a subject matter, which often eludes a precise definition. Although there is a great deal of controversy over this issue as we have just seen, the received view holds that customary land tenure implies a system in which land is held by the community rather than the individual. However, Fingleton is at pains to tell us that this does not mean communism, that is, commune, collective or cooperative ownership. In other words, where libertarians, such as those represented by the Centre for Independent Studies, go wrong is in thinking that customary land tenure is the antithesis of individual ownership and therefore antithetical to individual rights. In the words of the summary "In simple terms, customary tenures can be seen as a balance between group and individual rights and obligations with land ownership being held at group level and land use being exercised at the individual or household level."[17] On this view customary land tenure is neither individual nor group holding but some balance of both. But the definition rather than clarifying seems to be blurring the distinction. Certainly, researches have tended to see customary ownership as group ownership, subject to communal rather than individual interests, and the assumed altruism of the system has been its appeal. This is related to the idea frequently mentioned that group ownership provides a safety net, whereas individual title fosters a society of have and have nots with the have nots living in un-escapable abject poverty.

Western forms of private ownership in which individuals hold registered title to specific and defined holdings are often said to foster division and a community divided by the better and the less well off. The perceived evil of private ownership has been with us at least since Plato wrote the *Republic*. Sir Thomas More in *Utopia* expresses the sentiment most forcefully. He states:

> For where everyone tries to get clear title to whatever he can scrape together, then however abundant things are, a few men divide up everything among themselves leaving everyone else in poverty. And it usually happens that each sort deserves the lot of the other, since the one is rapacious, wicked and worthless, and the other is made of simple, modest men who by their daily labor contribute more to the common good than to themselves.[18]

More goes on to recommend the abolition of private property and the equal sharing of resources prevalent in the imagined state of Utopia.

---

[17] *Ibid.*
[18] Thomas More, *Utopia*, C.H. Miller, trans. (New Haven: Yale university Press, 2001), 57.

The Nature of Customary Land Tenure

The question is, if customary tenure cannot be given a distinct definition that can be clearly contrasted with individual private ownership why expend such energy and time in establishing that it is not inferior and even superior to individual forms of ownership? We are told by Fingelton that "…agricultural land in the Pacific Islands is allocated in accordance with a complex but flexible system of rights and obligations at individual, family, clan and tribal levels." But even after stating that land ownership is held at the group level and land use exercised at the individual or household level, even this statement is qualified and we are told that even "…this simplified version is arguable".[19] Customary land tenures, we are told, convey the sense of plural systems and variety with many differences within the alleged class.

It is unclear if the authors are simply celebrating diversity and plurality for its own sake or whether there is some essential group characteristic, which runs through all forms tenure which we label as customary. If it is the former then they are taking a position one would associate with the Canadian philosopher James Tully. What is then bad about modern forms of ownership is that they impose seamless uniformity that does not allow diversity to flourish. Tully argues that what he calls the ancient constitution tolerated and even respected custom. For example, customary forms of ownership, institutions and laws differed from locale and jurisdiction, yet were preserved within the blanket protection of the ancient constitution. The modem constitution, he says, refuses to accept varied local customs, and reifies relations as it pushes to have communities and institutions homogenized and subsumed under uniform laws and subject to one national system of institutionalized legal and political authority.

However, by the tenor of the writings Fingleton et al. are definitely saying more than this. In other words the issue is more than that of uniformity versus diversity, that private Western forms of tenure impose a single unyielding system whereas customary tenure allows a diversity of flexible systems to flourish.

Perhaps a way to unravel the issue is to start by considering what we mean by ownership in general. The right to property or the right to ownership is not a single simple right but a concatenation of rights and liabilities. However, we can simplify and refer to three fundamental rights: the right to use, right to exclude and the right to alienate. Whether we are talking about individual private ownership or customary ownership both forms grant to the individual the right to use and to some extent the right to exclude. Even some pure rarified form of group ownership must parcel out certain exclusive individual rights to use property. At the same

---

[19] Fingleton, *op. cit.*, 4.

time this will also include or extend the right to exclude, for rights to exclusive use are not much use or self contradictory if one doesn't have the right to exclude others. For example John Locke in the *Two Treatises* II: 35 states, "…God, by commanding to subdue gave authority so far to appropriate. And the condition of Humane Life which requires Labour and Materials to work on, necessarily introduces private possessions." One cannot effectively follow God's command, which requires preservation, if others attempt to use the same area on which one is working or if they prevent one from effectively laboring in other ways, for example, direct obstruction. In order to ensure survival we need exclusive use, which entails the right to exclude others. Moreover, the same applies to the fruits of our labor. I will not be able to utilize the products of labor to ensure survival if others are constantly stealing my apples or selling them to their neighbors.

It is really with respect to the third right that of alienation that we begin to see a significant difference between Western and customary forms of ownership. It is usually the case that customary tenure does not allow one to sell or deal land. (However, even universalizing this point can be misleading but in general this is the case).[20] Apart from a presumed ideology which does not contemplate the group alienating and alienating itself from its land, there are almost insurmountable transaction costs to overcome in order to get a group to agree upon disposing a part or the whole of its land. It is obvious that individual ownership effectively wipes out these transaction costs thus allowing for alienation. An additional point which enhances the right of alienation is the fact that the cash economy allows one to define individual interests in monetary values. For example, an individual who is said to have customary ownership rights to a particular tract of land in virtue of his/her membership in a particular group, cannot sell that interest because it has no defined monetary value. In contrast an individual who has a share in a cooperative enterprise such as a corporation, which might hold valuable assets including land, can sell that share of ownership because it has a defined monetary value. In contrast, individual interest gained through customary group ownership only gives one the right to use and this interest has no additional monetary definition. The monetary economy, therefore creates interests in cooperative enterprises that can be given a monetary value which then allows for individual alienation.

There is no doubt that Fingleton et al. are correct in claiming that it is highly misleading to contrast customary and Western forms of tenure through the distinction between group and individual ownership. One needs to remind oneself that there are many forms of group and cooperative ownership in our legal

---

[20] In Fiji at the time prior to session, the individual Fijian chiefs were freely selling land to Europeans, although they later agreed that the land belonged to the people and not to individual chiefs.

system, the most obvious and prominent is the corporation, the central form of economic organization. The difference is that Western forms of ownership can be given monetary definition which allows for divisible interests that individuals can then sell, exchange and transform into other forms of ownership.

The coauthors however do offer counter arguments. Michael Bourke mentions the Lease Lease-back system in PNG which allows for subleasing of land through the government in exchange for rents and royalties. The term of the lease is typically 20 years in the case oil palm plantations or one cropping cycle after which landowners can choose to renew or not.[21] Chris Lightfoot argues in the case of Fiji that although land cannot be transferred as individual freehold, the customary ownership system allows for land to be leased. As he states "Other things being equal, there is unlikely to be any significant difference between the economic values of land held either under lease or individualized freehold."[22] He goes on to say that the further economic benefit derives from the ongoing communal ownership of land, which offers a much higher degree of security for its members.

All this does not really touch the main points. Certainly it is true the so called customary land can now be alienated at least in the form of a lease through certain non-customary institutions—in PNG through a lease lease back arrangement with the Government, in the case of Fiji through the mediation of the Native Land Trust Board. However, these Western style administrative bodies are far from being part of the customary landscape but rather represent something that is as non customary as individual freehold. But this does not mean that customary ownership has been modified so that it now *fully* encompasses right number three, the right to alienate, even if we accept Lightfoot's argument that a long term lease is as good as a sale.

The fact is that notwithstanding the possibility of long term leases on customary land, customary ownership with its underlying group title is a cumbersome vehicle for the realization of the right to alienate. The point is that though usage, and to a certain extent exclusion, can be exercized at the individual level, with customary ownership alienation can only occur at the level of the group. In other words the group must reach a consensus on the question of granting a lease. To forge a consensus on such a matter is always going to be difficult. Moreover, this reality transmogrifies simple land transactions into intense political negotiations with all the attendant woes. Fingleton mentions Bronislaw Malinowski's remark, which denies the communist nature of customary tenure, comparing the organization to a modern joint stock venture.[23] This is in fact quite misleading. Attempting to

---

[21] Fingleton *op. cit.*, 9.
[22] *Ibid.*, 24.
[23] *Ibid.*, ix.

describe the structure of customary ownership in terms of the modern corporation leads us to believe that it is not significantly different from the familiar, Western legal instrument of ownership. However, individual members of corporations or owners have very explicitly defined rights, and their holdings in the cooperate enterprise have a fairly precise monetary value. This means that interests can be sold without reference to the group or group consensus, as we have explained.

The point is that individuals cannot act on their own in terms of exercising the right of alienation. This in turn paralyzes trade commerce and development. Every land transaction every decision to lease must be percolated and strained through a tight mesh of individual, sub group and group interests. This means among other things that it is very difficult to achieve the economies of scale that can be realized on sufficiently large land holdings such as plantations. In this instance entrepreneurs will find it difficult to overcome transaction costs involved in acquiring sufficiently large areas to achieve these economies of scale. Additionally, long term planning is threatened because of lack of security of title because renewal of leases is always uncertain. Despite Lightfoot's claim that a long term lease is as good as freehold, the Fijian sugar industry has been in disarray over the last decade because of the failure to renew leases of customary land, which we document in a later chapter.

Forests and Pastures

R.J. Fisher, another author in Fingleton's text, in "Common Property and Development: Forests and Pastures," argues that contrary to Gosarevski, Hughes and Windybank, communal rights to land are not a barrier to development. He points out, however, that his observations do not address issues relating to agricultural land but apply to various type of group arrangements ('common property') which have been quite effective in forest and pasture management. He says that in fact there is "…sometimes no viable alternative in cases where forests are large and remote from places where people live and where environmental conditions require pastoralists to be mobile and respond flexibly to local grazing conditions".[24]

He also accuses Gosarveski, Hughes and Windybank of simplifying the distinction between individual property rights and what they refer to as "communal ownership". He points out, like Fingeleton, that real tenure systems combine aspects of individual and group rights. For example nomadic pastoralists combine common rights to pastures with individual ownership of livestock, also swidden

---

[24] *Ibid.*, 33.

cultivators in South East Asia manage the overall forest area as a group, but allocate cultivation rights to individual households.

In considering matters relating to forestry, he argues that the size and accessibility of forests often make management by individuals very difficult; for example, in cases where forests consist of moderately large areas remote from settlements, management of separate individual plots is often impractical. The larger and more remote the forest, the more likely this is to be true. In such situations, some form of common property arrangement may be the only viable choice. As has happened in Nepal, division of relatively large areas of forest remote from village and individual households (as is common in Nepal) imposes considerable transaction costs, especially in terms of protection.[25] However, Fisher then tells us that the issues are not those of group versus individual rights in Nepal but that of the government inhibiting development. He says that the formal devolution of rights to communities provided increased security of access for necessary production and some generation of income from the sale of non-timber forest products. At the same time the Forest Department has been very reluctant to allow communities to harvest and sell timber from forests commercially even though many forests are suitable for this purpose. The issue here is not the absence of individual rights but absence of devolution of decision making to either individuals or groups, he claims. In contrast, Tanzania, he claims, has established tradition of *ngitili* (forest enclosures) based on individual rights and sometimes on community rights. The result has been, among other things, increased cash income and the regeneration of the forests. Interestingly enough, Fisher concludes the discussion of forestry with the statement that the absence of control of forests by the poor is probably more an issue than whether that control is exercised through individual or common rights.

I would point out, in light of Fisher's remarks, that some have argued that the passage of the 1991 Forestry Act by the PNG government, amounted to the nationalization of the forestry industry. In other words what is in fact occurring is a form of usurpation of customary authority's traditional role in managing a resource in the best interests of those most directly concerned.[26] Thus, as in Nepal, as described by Fisher, the state has created an "absence of devolution of decision making to either individuals or groups". Similarly in Papua New Guinea, the legislation that apples to customary land from the *Land Groups Incorporation Act* to the 1991 *Forestry Act* has created something that is far from customary. This legislation is supposed to help mobilize development of customary land but only creates unnecessary bureaucratic hurdles that could be easily eschewed through

---

[25] *Ibid.*, 30.
[26] Timothy Curtin, "Forestry and economic development in Papua New Guinea". *South Pacific Journal of Philosophy and Culture*, 8 (2005): 105–117.

the implementation of individual land tenure, which in itself is not particularly foreign to the customary system, which admittedly already encompasses significant individual rights.

In matters relating to pasturing, Fisher goes on to point out the fact that herders in China preferred to maintain commonly held land rather than parcel land into sections as individual land tenure. The issue raised is reminiscent of conflicts between the ranchers and the cattlemen in the nineteenth century American. It is obvious that those who want open spaces for the cattle to roam would be opposed to the individuation of land tenure and the enclosure of individual holdings. The argument does prove that in some cases individual land tenure is not in the interests of a particular group. Land is a finite resource and there is never going to be sufficient land that is 'enough and as good for others' to use Locke's phrase, therefore neither system will satisfy both horticulturists and owners of livestock. It is clear that horticulturists would prefer exclusive access to discrete areas of land while the owners of livestock would desire more open space for grazing. The fact is that the carrying capacity of land is more adversely affected by livestock and therefore there is need for greater space to avoid overgrazing. But given that land is a finite resource we ultimately need some mechanism to balance the needs of both horticulturists and owners of livestock by designating areas that can be used for the exclusive use of each group. Common ownership may be more consistent with the interests of holders of livestock while exclusive individual land tenure would be preferred by horticulturists. Since land is a scarce or limited resource, the fact that a particular form of land tenure may appeal to the interests of one group rather than another is rather inconclusive and does not offer sufficient reason to support either system. There is need for a system that can mediate between the interests of both groups. One might well argue that individual freehold does not incur the same transactions costs and therefore is a more efficient mechanism for achieving the economies of scale necessary for either large plantations or the raising of livestock, while accommodating relatively small holding suitable for horticulture.

Agricultural Land

However, Michael Bourke does address issues relating to agricultural land and questions the theory that economic benefits are greater from freehold rather than customary ownership arguing that in Papua New Guinea much of the plantation sector, where production takes place on alienated and registered land, has performed poorly in recent decades, especially for coffee, cocoa, copra and rubber. On the other hand domestically marketed food, betel nut, vanilla, coffee, cocoa, copra and rubber produced on customary land tenures shows the fastest growing agricultural production. However, it has been shown that Bourke's data indicating rapid growth since 1980 of output of cocoa, coffee, and copra from the smallholders, rather than from plantations operating on alienated land, is misleading. In the 1980s the government adopted a policy of buying out estates with many reverting to bush or to mere subsistence production of food crops. It is therefore not surprising that production on alienated land fell away. The sole exception is oil palm, where large equity holdings of the government provided security against landowner claims and enabled the only significant growth of any agricultural output since 1970.[27]

Additionally, one could mention other factors that no doubt have contributed to the declines in plantation production. For example, the demonstrative break down in law and order in the Papua New Guinean highlands and deterioration of necessary infrastructure such as the transportation road system have militated against large scale production and its economic viability. Certainly in a Hobbesian world of chaos and violence it may be far easier just to grow some simple things in your own back yard, rather than participate in something more complex requiring investment of capital, sophisticated organization etc. Also, secondly, despite the statistics and the bold claim that the agricultural sector has grown rapidly in recent decades, the immediate evidence of this is far from apparent. It still remains that PNG is well down the UN index of human development, as of 2005 PNG ranked 122 out of 162 up from 129 out 174 in 1999.

Aside from the difficulties achieving the economies of scale necessary to make a significantly productive economy, there is a denial or least an absence of opportunity which would enable individuals to improve their own welfare. It may be true that the existence of customary land ensures that individuals have access to land for their various needs and uses, but at the same time, customary owners with interests in land cannot apply those interests and use them as capital. Under customary tenure individual interests cannot be assigned a monetary value, which could then be traded, transferred or conveyed to purchase something of equivalent value. This is to say that individuals have the security of knowing that there is land available for their use but on the other hand, they are trapped because even if they desire to, they are precluded from using their interests and converting them into buying power. De Soto describes such people as living in a pre-capitalist world. They possess holdings and property but none of it can be assigned an economic value that would then allow them to participate meaningfully in the business

---

[27] Timothy Curtin "Scarcity amidst plenty: the economics of land tenure in Papua New Guinea," in T. Curtin, H. Holzknecht, and P. Larmour eds. *Land Registration in Papua New Guinea: Competing Perspectives*. Discussion Paper 2003/1 (Canberra: State Society and Governance in Melanesia, Research School of Pacific and Asian Studies, Australian National University, 2003).

of trade and commerce. This means that they are in effect shut out and cannot benefit from the explosion of the wealth creating activities, which is occurring through global commerce.

Another researcher in Fingleton's text, Mark Mosko, argues strongly to the contrary citing the successful marketing of the areca nut (betel-nut) and pepper-fruit in the Mekeo area of Central Province in Papua New Guinea.[28] He argues that, in fact. the people's continued reliance on customary arrangements for land ownership and use has facilitated agricultural success, not impeded it. He rejects what he calls the alleged 'communal land ownership' conjured up by Gosarevski, Hughes and Windybank. He says that ownership consists in a complex allocation of rights and obligations such that there are several discernible categories of 'owners' and 'users' with corresponding different kinds of rights of ownership and use corresponding to responsibilities of custodianship. For example, there exists one chief who is the nominal owner of the land but who must consult with the chiefs and leaders of the other resident owning clans when major issues involving land arise.[29] All this complexity does not really enlighten us as to how customary arrangements have facilitated agricultural success. However, he does empahsize the flexibility of customary Mekeo land tenure as critical to the economic and social success of the people of the Maipa village and the other villages in Mekeo. Here we may well be touching upon Tully's argument that sees diversity and flexibility of ancient constitutions as the key to local empowerment. Mosko explains that since the boundaries between lands owned and used by different people "…are never permanently fixed and claims to ownership and use are never completely exclusive, villagers have the capacity to allocate their land in accordance with prevailing social values of kinship and morality."[30] Each villager has a guaranteed access to sufficient land for bush resources, houses, subsistence and cash cropping. Any villager, he claims, who has need of more land for entrepreneurial activities such as the areca nut (betel-nut) and pepperfruit production will not be denied access or impeded.

These statements would seem to put into question my assertion that because transaction costs with respect to customary land are high it is extremely difficult to obtain land sufficient to realize the economies of scale necessary for significant levels of trade and commerce. Nevertheless they do indicate the difficulties one would face if one wished to lease land from the Maipa village clansmen. Negotiations would have to begin with the head land owning chief who would then consult with the chiefs and leaders of the other resident owning clans. The

---

[28] Mark Mosko, "Customary land tenure and Agricultural Success: the Mekeo Case" in Fingleton et. al.: 16–21.

[29] *Ibid.*, 20.

[30] *Ibid.*, 21.

advantage of Western forms of ownership lies in the fact that these sorts of transactions can proceed on a one to one basis without excessive consultation and political negotiation. One might argue that individual Mekeo clansman would have no need to negotiate a lease if as Mosko says there exist no impediments that would deny them what they need for successful entrepreneurial activities. However, such a fluid situation would only persist so long as there exists land that is 'enough and as good for others', to use Locke's famous phrase. Even in relatively sparsely populated areas of PNG it is hard to conceive of an ambitious project that would not disadvantage some individuals or group of clansmen leaving them with land that is not 'enough and as good'. In these circumstances, in order for the project to proceed some form of compensation arrangement would have to be worked out. But again the transaction costs under customary land tenure make this difficult. The advantage of non-customary Western tenure is that it clearly defines individual property interests in monetary terms that can transacted, sold or transferred on a individual basis rather than worked out through some negotiated political compact which must receive consensus at the group level.

Advantages and disadvantages of Western forms of Private Ownership

Of course, once we institute well defined individual property rights, which allow for the transfer of interests without group supervision, the argument subsequently takes the form of More's admonition against private ownership. It will lead to have and have nots. On the other hand, Locke made the point that once there is no longer as good and enough for others one must rely on trade and commerce, which becomes possible with the invention of money. To put this in other terms for Pacific Islanders, the cash economy has allowed for a level of trade and development that was not possible in traditional customary society. Realistically in a more developed society one no longer relies on personally grown agricultural produce for basic survival. Indeed as we all know a very significant number of individuals can survive comfortably with no access to land or access to land that is agriculturally insufficient for subsistence survival. This is because in a nation with a sufficiently large market with appropriate transportation and communication systems, individuals can specialize in varied non-agricultural ways, which allows for a diversity products and services. These wealth creating activities enrich society and move it to a level of development beyond that of a purely agricultural based economy. Non-customary systems facilitate this process because they assign a monetary value to individual interests in land that can then be sold or exchanged to allow for the free movement of capital. In effect individuals can decide to forego their interest in land by selling that interest and using the proceeds to fund other entrepreneurial endeavors. Without this mechanism land remains in a near feudal state of affairs in which individuals remain tied to the land without opportunity to utilize their interests to enable them to participate in other non-agrarian based economic activities.

This level of development is only possible if we possess interests including land interests that can be assigned an economic value that allows for transactions and exchange. However, it is of course also necessary as Mosko points out that there exist a transportation system and we might add a communication system that can support a high level of trade and commerce. Cultivation of a specialization, which generates a surplus of goods greater than necessary for personal use is useless if the goods cannot be transported to the areas of demand. This is all to say that land tenure reform is not the entire answer to insufficient economic development. The whole package must be there including the roads and other forms of transportation that allow goods to reach their markets.

Finally one needs to address the claim that deprivation and dispossession will occur if individual registered freehold is introduced. There is really no necessary connection between the two. Sweden, for example has individual freehold yet it is on top of the human development index and Swedish society exists in relative equality. Many other countries in South America and Asia have had individual freehold and exhibit high levels of poverty and inequality. Much depends on the type of nation state which develops and the quality of the government. Governments which exhibit little regard for the common good and which conspire with the wealthy to secure an oppressive domination of their own population will no doubt produce societies marked by impoverished landless peasantry. This then touches upon another aspect of governance that needs adjustment, that is, high levels of government corruption. As in many third world countries individuals in PNG conceive the path to wealth and fortune through government. As a result government officialdom fails to concentrate on good governance, and utilizes political office to enhance personal wealth. So long as the economy fails to offer opportunities for successful entrepreneurial activities, this will continue to be the case. The situation can only be rectified through implementation of the proper infrastructure and an economically viable land tenure system.

To this point we have taken a position, which advocates some form of implementation of Western forms of private ownership in order that economic development can proceed successfully. The important issue is how does one introduce and harmonize this system with existing systems of customary ownership. Having considered the counter arguments to the conclusions reached by the Centre for Independent Studies, I believe that we have yet to establish unambiguously the general outlines of customary ownership in Papua New Guinea and the South Pacific region. From the foregoing, it may well be the case that from one society to another there is a degree of variation in terms of land and chattels either individually or commonly held. Given the plurality of societies in the Pacific or even in Melanesia or Polynesia, we may well find ourselves unable to form any general conclusions. However, to proceed we must reach some agreement on the general outlines of customary forms of land tenure. We can see that the issue is not entirely clear as we have seen strong evidence for the existence individual title as well as various aspects of commonly held property. What is needed is a better understanding of those contexts in which individual rights apply and those in which common or community rights apply. In order to achieve greater clarity on this subject, I believe it is worthwhile at this point revisiting earlier field work and researches conducted by R.G. Ward, formerly professor of Geography at the Australian National University.

R.G. Ward, from his researches throughout the South Pacific, proposes a well defined adumbration of the essential features common to tenure systems in the South Pacific. He states, that, "…there are parts of the village territory to which all must have access; for example, the forested area is a source of timber, firewood, birds or animals for meat or decorations and serves as a reservoir of potential agricultural land. This area is held in the name of the community as a whole. It is not the sole property of any clan, sub-clan, extended or nuclear family or individual. In general any individual or household group can gather from it." [31] Beyond that individual rights generally seem to creep into the picture very much in accordance with Lockean analysis, though in a sense which falls short of Western private forms of ownership. Garden land, through labour, remains the property of the family which cultivates it, but reverts to the community with disuse. He states, "Ultimate ownership rests with the whole village community, but as long as a household continues to use a plot its right to continued use is acknowledged."[32] On the other hand, situations involving a great deal of investment of labour in land improvement, for example, the construction of terraces or associated water reticulation systems, the construction of compost mounds for sweet potato production, the creation of raised beds for taro, or drainage of swamps etc., may result in these areas being held by a household or even the individual in perpetuity. Finally he says that within the village itself house sites may be owned almost in perpetuity by the resident household. [33]

From the above one may reach the conclusion that land held communally does not univocally mean land is held in common to the exclusion of individual rights. It is clear that in most cases there exists a substantial commons, to which no individual or family claims rights but each individual or group is free to make use of and which we can truly say is commonly held. On the other hand, as stated, gardens, house sites, and various improved areas through significant labour can be

[31] R.G. Ward, "Pacific Island Land Tenure: An Overview of Practices and Issues," in D.G. Malcolm & J. Skog eds., *Land, Culture and Development in the Aquatic Continent* (Kihei, Hawaii: Kapallua Pacific Center, 1992): 29–40,30.
[32] *Ibid.*, 31.
[33] *Ibid.*

regarded as family or even individually held to the exclusion of the larger group. One can see that this situation is not unlike that which existed in England prior to enclosure in which substantial areas of commonage existed proximate to forms of individual freehold. But the two situations are not entirely consistent. In England property had become alienable after originally being inheritable. But, on the other hand, transfers of land are not unheard of in the Pacific. Certainly property under communal tenure, when individuated through labour, could also become alienable. In many cases one individual or group may transfer or bestow land on another. In this sense we may interpret that communal tenure does not really diverge greatly from our own. The essential rights to exclude, use and alienate property all seem to be present and in many cases exercised by individuals and not merely groups. The difference now appears to be simply one of degree in that within the Western system commonage is less frequently encountered and the essential rights of ownership are more often exercised by individuals rather than the group. However, we can also certainly see that Western forms of ownership recognize land held in common, for example, public parks and recreation areas are obviously territories belonging to an aggregate, the municipality or whatever, but which individual members are free to use.

Control and Income Ownership

From the above it may well be the case that we have simply been speaking of differences of degree rather than substantive differences between customary communal and Western forms of private ownership. We observe that it is simply wrong to regard this issue in terms of an opposition between exercising rights as a group rather than individually. In order to understand better the real opposition we need to reintroduce the distinction between control ownership and income ownership. The first refers to the power to use, consume, destroy, alienate and involves the ultimate authority over access to the holding, the second refers to the right to exchange the holding with other willing partners and keep the proceeds from such trades. The right to income includes the natural return from trades, that is, rent, interest and profits. "Rights manifesting primary fundamental control (control rights) can be meaningfully distinguished from the rights to transfer title conditional upon receipt of goods in trade and the right to increased welfare and income from so doing..." as we have demonstrated.[34]

The point of the foregoing analysis serves to highlight that the significant difference between customary versus private ownership relates not to simpleminded

---

[34] John Christman, *The Myth of Property* (New York: Oxford University Press, 1994): 131.

opposition between group and individually exercised rights but rather to the presence or addition of income rights in Western systems of ownership. Moreover, income rights presuppose the cash economy in which values are determined by aggregate demand and relative scarcity. Moreover, income rights as we shall see require individual specification.

The Relation Between Income Rights and Future Development

We have said that income rights are not simply a given but rather structured by social arrangements and, to a certain extent, by government regulation. This then becomes the problematic area when we attempt to introduce income rights into a system of non-monetary customary forms of ownership. We have seen that many political analysts and economists regard the economic problems of the Pacific in terms of the necessity to develop. Development means moving beyond activities that allow for mere subsistence to those, which stimulate trade and industry. But in order for this to occur, individuals have to see that there is an incentive and reward that compensates for these renewed efforts. Obviously in a subsistence economy there is little incentive to strive to produce more than the individual or family can consume or barter. A cash economy provides these incentives through the institution of a system that compensates the individual for activities that are significantly different from those which relate to a subsistence existence. Among other things this means specialization, and the introduction of the division of labour. This includes matters of entrepreneurship in which property is developed into a means of production that generates income. In order for this to be a reality the individual has to understand how one acquires significant income rights. This entails a system that recognizes, allows for and defines income rights. This is in fact what is missing in Pacific societies and customary forms of ownership.

For example in customary Pacific societies it may be possible to trade items and perhaps even land but the usual forms of selling land would have been fairly rare. *A-fortiori*, the idea of deriving an income from such activities would have been unimaginable because there could not be a system of income rights that one might associate with the development of productive capacity or the wholesale buying and selling of land. In contrast in the West we are usually aware of the structures, practices and obligations that allow one to acquire income rights. Moreover, income rights above all must be defined in terms of individual entitlements because the very definition of such a right must attach to a given individual or set of individuals. Even if we say that the right to a certain sum of money belongs to group x the issue still remains how is that sum to be divided among the members of the group? Until the distributive mechanism is described the right remains inchoate and undefined. It is the existence of recognized mechanisms that determine the individual's income share in a given enterprise, which distinguishes Western societies from traditional Pacific societies. For example, it is generally accepted that the entrepreneur in a business venture is entitled and only entitled to the surplus income which remains after the workers have been paid a pre-agreed sum for their labour. Although this seems simple and obvious it would not be obvious to one who is unacquainted with the cash economy and the capitalist system.

This also means that property itself must be divisible and fungible and capable of being acquired by individuals and not just groups, if income rights are to be a possibility. This is an inextricable part of the mechanism that allows us to determine an individual share in any given stream of income. If Pacific societies are to develop land, as the economists recommend, enterprising individuals must have some idea of the mechanism they can utilize to derive a personal income from the development, that is, the process necessary to acquire a legal right to an income from a given development. This means there must be some way to individuate the share to which one would be entitled. This would be a defined share that cannot be acquired or appropriated by any other member of the group without the individual's permission. This means at the same time, individual interests must be immune to political machination, one must have secure title.

While one might suggest that a more equitable solution demands that income from developed land should be simply divided equally between all members of the group, this policy fails to avoid the free rider issue. Development entails that someone is actually engaged developing land. It is quite foreseeable that the contributions to the process of development from different individuals will be unequal. An individual would not expend greater effort unless confident there is mechanism that works reasonably to reward this effort. Of course these issues can be worked through a sophisticated system of shares as enshrined in the modern corporation. For example, labour and time expended could be translated into expanded shares and income rights, which include a greater percentage of the revenue.

Voluntary Association and Development

However, acceptance of such a formula cannot be simply assumed. Firstly it would have to be agreed upon by the customary group and the issue is what if consensus cannot be reached, which, of course would stifle initiative. One could presume that some arrangement could always be worked out as happens with most corporate bodies but this outcome is far from necessary. Moreover, one labours under a model of corporate enterprise as known in Western business and legal systems and forgets that these groups are formed as voluntary arrangements and necessarily presuppose that the essential voluntary covenants have already been worked out, otherwise the association or corporate body would not have come into existence. In contrast, customary communal land holding groups in the Pacific are not voluntary arrangements, they are generally formed through ties of genealogy and lineal descent over which one has no control. The descent group is the carrier of value and individual identity—although theoretically one could always opt out. But this all means that they do not exist as a group through some essential acts of voluntary agreement and certainly their status as owners of collectively held property is not created through acts of initial and mutual agreement. In fact there is no need for them voluntarily to agree on anything in order to be owners and holders of collective property, although there may be mutual consent to certain of the customary practices that relate to their communal holdings. Nevertheless even this form of consent is not usually a pre-requisite to their status as land owners. This means that if they cannot agree on how income should be divided from future development of land property etc, nothing profoundly follows from this. The group and its members continue as roughly joint owner of a discrete piece of customary land but obviously minus consent, no development would be possible or at least feasible. In contrast, if individuals, in the Western context, wish to form a corporation, and cannot agree on how shares and dividends are to be calculated to reflect individual contributions in labour, organization and personal property, then the corporate body will never be a reality or if a reality will cease to be so.

It follows therefore that since agreements on individual income rights are not intrinsic or necessary for the existence of the customary communal land holding, any mechanism to determine these rights must be extrinsically introduced. As such it will appear merely arbitrary and non-binding because unconnected to the customs and practices of the community. Let us not forget that in the Western systems any entitlement to a right to income is always worked out in terms of values placed on individual contributions in terms of labour, organization, or personal property. Otherwise no collective undertaking could come into existence. The problem with customary communal holding and matters of development is that of transforming an involuntary association of individuals, yoked together through genealogy, into a voluntary arrangement based on agreements over work, productivity and appropriate rewards. The reason why individual property rights rather than collective property rights facilitate development is because individuals begin with a secure knowledge of their property and therefore they know what they bring to the bargaining table when they seek to enter into a collective enterprise. In contrast, the individual with an interest in customary collectively held property has no idea how to value his interest and no mechanism to withdraw and utilize his interest in other ways if he fails to reach agreement with his/her group. An individual operating within a Western system of private ownership always has a defined interest whether a share in a corporate body, a piece of real estate, or an individual holding in personal property and knows he/she can withdraw, utilize or transfer his holding if the individual cannot reach consensus with the group or collective. The individual within customary collective system is tied to his/her group and the undefined income rights one supposedly holds while at the same time seriously exposed to the local politics of the group.

Enclosure and the issue of Individuating and defining Income Rights

To summarize so far, we can say that income rights presuppose that there exists a mechanism to individuate and define the income share to which each individual is entitled as a participant in the collective enterprise of trade and commerce in an association of individuals called the economic market. Collectively held property cannot support income rights because there exists no mechanism to individuate each owner's share in the collective holding. This highlights the importance of enclosure as it occurred in eighteen century England. By Act of Parliament moors, commons or waste lands were divided, allotted and enclosed throughout England. Although many have seen this as unfair and a hardship to the poor it is also the case these events facilitated the acquisition of income rights in so far as enclosure defined the individual interest in any given area of land. To put it another way, it provided a mechanism by which one may determine the extent and reach of the income rights of any given individual. Obviously, as Christman points out, the content of the right is somewhat uncertain because it is subject to market forces driven by issues such as relative scarcity. But, regardless, enclosure meant the ascription of income rights to identifiable individuals allowing one to affix the individual income entitlements to any revenue that might be generated by land which had been previously commonage.

Customary communally held property, especially land, founders on the issue of income rights because ultimately income must be apportioned in individual shares and group rights provide no answers to this issue. In contrast individual property rights give us a fairly uncontestable indication as to how income generated from market activities is to be distributed and ascribed to individuals. Although from a Marxist perspective one might question the fairness and justice of the mechanism in which distribution is determined by individual ownership rights, at the same time Marxian analysis forcefully demonstrated that in the Western capitalist system wealth distribution is inextricably tied to individual ownership rights. Even Marx recognized the achievements of the system in terms of industrial development and productivity, although he vehemently denied that it could provide the ultimate answer to real human needs. In contrast, because customary communal ownership is founded on group rather than individual rights, it fails to provide a mechanism for determining distribution and frustrates development because without secure identifiable income rights individuals have no motivation to develop holdings in a manner that generates an income through market interaction.

It is often said that in the Pacific, land reform involving the individuating of titles will meet with violent resistance, however, the point is that without these sorts of change issues of development and income distribution remain unresolved. Distribution of society's wealth will always be a contentious issue. Unfortunately the generation of significant wealth at this time in world history requires involvement with capitalist system of trade and commerce. Individuals can only be persuaded to freely engage in these activities if they have a fairly unambiguous understanding of the income rights they gain through participation. As in this system income rights are tied to individual property entitlement, individuals will only participate if they have the opportunity to acquire these entitlements. Certainly one could provide a system of distribution that might appear fairer, for example, one based fundamentally on the equality of all members, but the issue is whether individuals will withdraw from the market if they cannot foresee significant income expansion through participation. As Rawls pointed out rational individuals would probably choose a system with certain inequalities, rather than a system of equality where they are generally worse off.[35]

Previously we have said that the difference between customary communal holding and Western forms of ownership is simply one of degree. Both systems allow for individual rights, the difference being that in the customary system more area tends to be subject to communal or group ownership. Why then if income rights are ultimately dependent on a system of individual rights is it so difficult to apportion income rights in a customary system. After all individuals do possess exclusive rights in many cases to use, manage, exclude others from use, and even alienate their holdings so why do we have a problem? One admits that in these instances there should be little difficulty in attaching income rights to the control rights that individuals already exercise. The problem, however, is that areas in which they exercise these rights are limited, i.e., home sites, gardens and other areas over where individuals have laboured to improve the land, as Ward's researches point out. In other words, their entitlements are limited by the extent of their labouring activities in ways similar to conditions in Locke's state of nature where individual holdings only extend over areas laboured upon and thereby transformed from a natural condition. This leaves significant undeveloped areas, which the group holds in common, which cannot be subject to individual title, and which therefore hold significant difficulties for the ascription of individual income rights.

---

[35] John Rawls, *A theory of Justice* (Cambridge Mass.: Belknap Press, 1971).

Ultimately the problem that customary communal land tenure poses for future development cannot be traced to the allegation that the system fails to recognize individual rights; clearly the system instantiates very significant individual rights as we have seen. The problem is firstly that customary systems do not include income ownership that can be attached to existing interests because these rights are associated with monetary economies. This means there is no mechanism for translating income generated through cooperative undertakings into individual shares and entitlements. In England, as we have seen, enclosure of the commons meant individual rights were extended to commonly held areas thus facilitating individual income rights and future development. The problem of development in the Pacific is therefore also the problem of extending individual rights to include areas beyond areas of immediate cultivation, that is, the translation oft the commons into individual forms of land tenure, areas that Ward claims are held in the name of the community as a whole. Certainly, as far as important development projects are concerned, these are the most relevant areas.

Purchase and Sale of Land

The most significant problem for development is the assignment of individual rights to areas that are held in common, that is, areas which individuals are free to use but which are not subject to exclusive individual rights as explained. Any commitment to develop such areas must be a voluntary undertaking, individuals must be free to commit or withhold their resources. This would also require the option to sell one's holding if one doesn't wish to participate in a collective undertaking, for example, the combination of a number of holdings to create a large rubber plantation in order to realize certain economies of scale. Individuals may not wish to participate directly in such an enterprise but they may still wish to share in the income of such a profitable enterprise and may desire to sell their property in exchange for shares. Voluntary involvement is tied up with the ability to sell one's holding and purchase other assets, and for that to be a reality presupposes defined individual income rights.

It is thus important to create a system which is structured to accommodate these rights and activities and thereby promote voluntary participation in profitable enterprise. But many Pacific countries have resisted this with respect to customary land. In Papua New Guinea Tonga, and Fiji, legislation restricts the purchase or sale of customary land, and it cannot be subject to forfeiture in cases of loan or mortgage default. Even in the Cook Islands where there is significant freehold, land cannot be bought or sold except for public purposes by the government. These restrictions severely limit the possibility of acquiring meaningful individual income rights.

One recognizes that income rights themselves can constitute an asset, apart from the actual physical asset, that can be sold and bought. Moreover, income rights become a fungible asset that can be easily divided and sold as shares or traded for something of equivalent value. De Soto sees this as the uncoupling of the economic features of an asset from its physical state.[36] Income rights in their fungible capacity can, as de Soto points out, allow for an indivisible unit in the real world, such as a factory, to be subdivided into any number of number of portions each representing an income right to a defined share of the profits. He states that "Citizens of advanced nations are thus able to split most of their assets into shares, each of which can be owned by different persons, with different rights to carry out different functions."[37] In contrast communally held property, like land, will remain an indivisible unit because lacking defined income rights, its individual customary owners cannot divide or deal with their presumed economic interest in any profitable way. They have interests and rights in a defined piece of property but there is no way to assign an economic value to these rights. Without defined individual income rights individuals are denied access to the world of trade and commerce in which wealth generation is possible and economic development is realized.

The economic possibilities, which are realized through transactions, as de Soto says, allow for property to be owned by different people who may possess different rights with different functions. For example, because income rights are distinguishable from the physical asset, it is conceivable for one to give up one's control rights, for example, the right of use etc. and retain certain income rights. Obviously the Western legal system allows for this possibility. It is also obvious that legal systems that believe they are protecting customary land tenure by precluding the possibilities of sale of property are in effect denying individuals certain liberty rights, i.e., the possibility that they may trade control rights involving use in favour of certain defined future income rights. What is not appreciated is that under the guise of protecting individuals against disentitlement and dispossession (even though voluntary) they are at the same time denying the possibility of individual income rights that may be utilized to participate in the economic market. This may be interpreted as the denial of wealth creating activities that define what we understand as economic development.

Despite our expressed reservations about the modern corporate structure in which ownership and management are separated, it may well be that development in the Pacific demands some form of corporate structure, in which landowners become the beneficiaries of managerial fiduciary duties in areas that are held in the

---

[36] Hernando de Soto, *The Mystery of Capital: Why Capitalism Triumphs in the West and Fails Everywhere Else* (New York: Bantam Press, 2000).

[37] *Ibid.*, 49.

name of the community as a whole. At this point this may well be appropriate to realize the necessary economic and social 'advancement' (if we may use this term) but customary land tenure does not in any way possess this structure or allow for it. This also applies as we will see in subsequent chapters to the Incorporated land Groups and landowner companies in Papua New Guinea. Communal ownership is not based on a "nexus of contracts", it is based largely on kinship relations, which are not contracted for. However, why can not the customary landowners set up a corporation, distribute shares among themselves, hire managers to develop the land and impose the gap filling fiduciary duties through the legal system? At this point in time there is no legal mechanism that allows them to do this in the PNG land tenure system. This is because there is no mechanism for the distribution of the residual cash flow because this would require that we define the individual shares. Since the only corporate asset is the land this means one would have to define the land interest possessed by each individual. However, since there are by definition no individual income rights in customary communal ownership, appropriate shares cannot be assigned to individuals? If individual interests are not defined and the individuals that make up the group identified through registration, there exists no mechanism for the distribution of residual cash flow, meaning that the inevitable disputes over the distribution of revenue will paralyze the system, as they now do. The only feasible way forward is to abandon informal customary land tenure and introduce individual interests in land, probably through some form of 'tenancy in common' in which individual interests are defined and of necessity registered. (Tenancy in common is different from so called customary or communal tenure in so far as each owner has separate shares, say one fourth in a property, and each owner may deal with his/her share as he/she pleases—the share may be transferred or divided into smaller shares).

Chapter Six

Custom as Law

In this chapter we consider the status of custom as law. Those who regard custom as a functioning system, regard customary ownership as a form of ownership in which title and 'incidents', rights and liabilities, are enshrined in custom rather than codified laws. Customary rights and liabilities, it is claimed, are accessed through oral traditions just as property rights in modern Western countries are understood through codified laws. There seems to be an assumption, therefore, that custom can be relied upon like codified law to provide a set of unambiguous objectively recognized rules that can serve as reliable guides to settle disputes and determine rights.

Often, where the law lacks specificity local custom is supposed to provide the appropriate guidelines. For example, Papua New Guinean legislation found in the *Land Disputes Settlement Act* Ch. No. 45, states under 'Practice and Procedure of Local Land Courts,'

> s. 35, d) subject to Section 40, shall endeavor to do substantial justice between all persons interested, in accordance with the Act and relevant custom. Section 68 enables both a local land court and a Provincial Land Court to determine and apply relevant customs.

Under the *Land Groups Incorporation Act*, Ch No. 147

> The Registrar may recognize as an incorporated land group a group consisting of incorporated land groups, if he is satisfied that
>
> (a) The member groups possess common interests and coherence independently of the proposed recognition and share or are prepared to share common customs; and
>
> (b) The association between groups represents a customary form of organization.

The question one needs to ask is whether custom performs the essential functions we associate with the modern concept of law. There is, as might be expected, a strong tradition in the literature on the South Pacific that answers in the affirmative.[1] Robert Cooter an American legal scholar has stated with reference to

---

[1] A.D. Ward, "Agrarian revolution," *New Guinea Quarterly* 6, (1975): 32–40; R. Cooter, "Kin groups and the common law process, in Papua New Guinea," in P. Larmour ed., *Monograph*

custom in PNG, "…customary law is living law, with the power to adapt, not as a static list of regulations."[2]

However, the situation is less than clear. Some point out that custom may well operate in opposition to the rule of law and perform other roles that frustrate the designs of a formal legal system, including its more dynamic functions. Margaret Rodman in referring to the role of custom or 'kastom', which has been given prominence in the Vanuatuan constitution, emphasizes that the concept has identificatory, regulatory and oppositional capacities.[3] The first refers to the capacity for talking about national identity. Rodman sees the reinstatement of the customary tenure system in Vanuatu as a vehicle for reasserting Vanuatuan national identity while breaking with the colonial past. Similarly, R.G. Ward also mentions that in Fiji and Western Samoa politicians use 'customary land' and associated tenure arrangements as markers differentiating their own people from others.[4] Ward points out that in arguing for the need to maintain traditions, barriers are erected to avoid officially acknowledging the 'existence of, and the need for change.'

Moreover, the capacity of custom to fulfil this identificatory role is due to an inherent ambiguity in its meaning, claims Rodman, in her analysis of Vanutuan customary land tenure.[5] Rodman says that confusingly 'kastom' has more to do with tradition, especially invented tradition, than with custom understood in the sense of a set of habitual cultural practices associated with a particular social existence. 'Kastom' operates in the present to create an ideological myth that encodes a presumed continuing relationship with the past, she argues. Both kastom as an invented tradition, and custom as some set of regular practices, she says, have had and will continue to have powerful impacts on the Anglo-French former colony of Vanuatu.

While custom may have, what she calls, a regulatory capacity, and may act as a force for organizing and controlling individual behaviour; at the same time almost in contradiction she says, it also has the potential to unsettle the state and even undermine its order. In Vanuatu the constitution proclaims that land belongs to

29 *Customary Land Tenure in Papua New Guinea* (Port Moresby: NRI, 1991): 33–49; A. Power "Resources development in the East Sepik Province," in C. Thirwall & P. Hughes eds., *Ethics of Development, Choices in Development Planning*, (Port Moresby: UPNG Press, 1988).

2   R. Cooter, *op. cit.*

3   M. Rodman, "Breathing spaces: customary land tenure in Vanuatu," in R.G. Ward and E. Kingdon eds., *Land, Custom and Practice in the South Pacific* (Melbourne: Cambridge University Press, 1995): 65–109, 66.

4   R.G. Ward, "Changing forms of communal tenure," in P. Larmour ed., *Governance of Common Property in the Pacific Region* (Canberra: National Centre for Development Studies, 1997): 19–32, 30.

5   Rodman, *op. cit.*, 66.

the customary owners, but in a sense, she says, this is an appeal to kastom in its oppositional function. It is an explicit denial of colonial attempts to legislate or regulate land tenure; as she states, the proclamation at the same time created a zone of abandonment. In a sense, the post-colonial government abdicated its authority and accepted highly variable customs and the difficulties of identifying customary owners. The problems of identifying owners and applying the various forms of tenure were glossed over as "kastom", ultimately leaving these matters beyond state control.[6]

The above remarks provide good evidence of the symbolic functions and also the sometimes contradictory responses that reference to custom may evoke. But the overriding issue for us is whether it can be relied upon to effect rule governed behaviour which is supposedly the function a recognizable legal system. Can custom work as a effective mechanism to resolve land disputes and authoritatively identify ownership. We have already referred to remarks of Robert Cooter who defended Papua New Guinean customs (applied to land tenure) as living law not an inflexible or static system as maintained by the well known philosopher of laws, H.L.A. Hart. However, it is worthwhile to re-consider in detail the arguments that Hart actually presented to support his views concerning the distinctness of custom and law. In the *Concept of law*, Hart laboured to give a comprehensive account of the essential characteristics of a legal system that would incorporate and extend the tradition of John Austin and Hans Kelsen among others.[7] In his efforts to elicit a workable concept, Hart necessarily found himself distinguishing law from related phenomena such as custom and ethics, for example.

Hart believed the essential functions of law couldn't be captured by custom independent of formalized legal institutions. Law as distinct from custom exhibits certain emergent features and performs certain roles that are not present in customary practice. Firstly, Hart makes the point that obviously every custom is not a law. For example, the failure to take off one's hat to a lady may be a violation of custom but it is not the breach of any law.[8] Obviously we cannot call custom law if there exist many customs, which are not recognized as legally binding. But this observation raises the further question, specifically what are the characteristics of law that distinguish it from custom, beyond the obvious fact that the law in Western minds, as opposed to mere custom, is usually associated with the institutional authority of the state.[9]

---

[6] *Ibid.*, 67.
[7] J. Austen, *The Province of Jurisprudence Determined* (Cambridge: Cambridge University Press, 1995); Hans Kelsen, *The General Theory of Law and the State*, Anders Wedberg trans. (Cambridge Mass: Harvard University Press, 1945).
[8] H.L.A. Hart, *The Concept of Law* (Oxford: Oxford University Press, 1961), 44.
[9] See for example B.L. Benson "Enforcement of Private Property Rights in Primitive Societies:

The key to understanding the additional dimension that law adds to mere custom is the distinction between primary and secondary rules. He notes that customs and laws are similar in that both consist of, what he calls, primary rules, which are sets of imperatives, which command individuals to do or to refrain from doing something. But, for Hart, the law goes beyond a simple set of prescriptions and proscriptions that dictate behaviour. Hart regards a system of laws as a union of, what he calls, primary and secondary rules. Primary rules concern the actions of individuals; secondary rules on the other hand, refer to the primary rules themselves. Secondary rules consist of rules that govern primary rules. Custom as distinct from law is identical with a given class of primary rules and does not go beyond this to include a set of accompanying secondary rules that govern the application of the set of primary rules, alleges Hart.

What then may we conclude from this? The obvious interpretation is one that finds custom deficient in that it fails to fulfill the essential functions of law. Hart argues that custom is defective in three respects. The first defect is termed the 'defect of uncertainty', the second, the defect of the 'static character', and the third, the 'defect of inefficiency'.[10] the defect of uncertainty refers to the absence of an independent authority to identify the relevant principle. The defect of the 'static character' refers to the lack of a formal procedure for changing or modifying the rules. The 'defect of uncertainty' means the lack of an independent judiciary to adjudicate violations. A society, therefore, that relies on custom alone to govern their activities is deficient in these areas. However, John Hund, a South African philosopher, for example, mentions that "...it is a jurisprudential commonplace that in *The Concept of Law*, Hart presents a notion of "primary rules" which, from an anthropologist's point of view is extremely naive since rarely if ever will there exist a society which might be governed by primary rules alone."[11] Following this line of thought, we might conclude that Hart's analysis really has no or little application to the reality of human society whether in the Pacific or the technically advanced centres of Western civilization. But Hund continues and argues that in fact legal anthropologists do recognize that many societies have existed without secondary rules.[12]

If we go beyond the dismissing jurisprudential commonplace we can begin to see how Hart's distinction between primary and secondary rules can be utilized to

---

law without Government," *The Journal of Libertarian Studies*, IX, 1 (winter 1989): 1–26, who believes customary law effectively functions without the institutions of formal government.

[10] Hart, *op. cit.,* 89–91.

[11] John Hund, "H.L.A. Hart's Contribution to Legal Anthropology," *Journal for The Theory of Social Behaviour* 26, 3 (1996): 275–292.

[12] Hund mentions for example S. Roberts, *Order and Dispute: An Introduction to Legal Anthropology* (London: Pelican Books 1979): 25.

make sense of the relation between custom and law, and the appropriateness of custom in fulfilling the functions of law. As the PNG legislation, stated earlier, seams to indicate, there is an assumption that custom functions as an identifiable set of unwritten rules imbedded in a culturally distinct oral tradition. But this assumption may not find correspondence in reality. With around eight hundred different linguistic groups in Papua New Guinea, for example, cultures can vary significantly throughout the region. In a comparison of the Huli and Kewa tribes of the Southern Highlands with the Engans of Enga Province, a researcher states, "From the accounts of anthropologists who have worked among the Enga it seems that the Enga social structure is more clearly defined, or that the putative rules of Enga social structure are more often observed, than is the case among the Huli and Kewa".[13] This brings us to the crux of the matter. What is meant by custom may not only vary in terms of rule content among various groups—not unsurprisingly—but more seriously, different customs may exhibit varying degrees of reliance on rule-guided behaviour. As is the case with Huli and the Kewa, one may encounter a very loose social structure in which the rules, if they exist at all, are not clearly defined and are readily dispensed with. In other words, any given Pacific society may be far less reliant on a set of putative social rules than is generally believed. Thus, the generalization that presumes that a set of customary rules always operate authoritatively in traditional societies in ways similar to the rule of law in Western society, may be far off mark. Another researcher (Ballard, 1997) notes that recognition of a land claims, again in the southern Highlands derives from negotiated consensus over a general observance of norms and principles in the dispute process rather than the rigorous application of norms in the form of a code. Rules again may not be that important if claims can only be validated through a negotiated group consensus.[14]

This phenomena whereby alleged principles are loosely followed and readily dispensed with is also in evidence traditional societies beyond the Pacific. In a study of the Tswana society of Africa, Comaroff and Roberts find that Tswana law and custom cannot be conceptualized as constituting a system of rules of any sort of *corpus juris* that can be contained in a code, which is used deductively

---

[13] M, MacDonald, "Defeating death and promoting life: Ancestors among the Enga, Huli, and Kewa of Papua New Guinea," in S. Friesen ed., *Ancestors in Post-Contact Religion: Roots, Ruptures and Modernity's Memory* (Cambridge Mass: Harvard University Press, 2001): 73–91,75.

[14] Ballard, C., 1997. "It's the Land, Stupid! The Moral Economy of Resource Ownership in Papua New Guinea," in S. Toft ed. *Compensation for Resource Development in Papua New Guinea*. Boroko: Law Reform Commission of Papua New Guinea (Monograph 6). (Canberra: Australian National University, National Centre for Development Studies, Pacific Policy Paper 25, 1997): 12–16.

to determine legal judgements through the connecting of rules to patterns of fact.[15] From their findings they identify sets of prescriptions that lack internal consistency or organization. Public recognition of marriage, for example, does not require that the couple confirm to any rule or defined procedural or ceremonial formality, but is negotiated over highly ambiguous situations that confer status.

The question remains how do we conceptualize and distinguish the *differentiae*, the essential difference between the use rules by the Enga as opposed to the customs of the Huli, Kewa or Tswana. In all cases these societies could be said to be following their customs, although the systems are intrinsically different. In the former instance we could say that the rules more less conform to our notion of law which is that of a code that can be reasonably effective in guiding and explaining human behaviour; in the latter, the existence of rules seems to provide little guidance or explanation of behaviour. To say that in the latter instances the prescriptions are loosely or inconsistently applied, easily dispensed with etc., leaves unanswered fundamental questions as to why this is the case. It is precisely here where Hart's distinction between primary and secondary rules does have application in distinguishing forms of custom which may approximate our concept of law and those customs which fail to do so. In societies that appear to be governed by rule directed behaviour, embodied in certain traditional customs, we should also find the presence of secondary rules. Hund argues that in contexts where secondary rules don't exist, including international law, which lacks the institutional settings to enforce judgements, and in societies like the Tswana or the Kewa and Huli, the primary rules will appear to be a set of manipuable symbols.[16] These societies will lack the recognized independent formal structures and institutions empowered to determine what the law is and authoritatively identify and punish violations of principles.

Hund cites Fallers who has, for example, argued that societies can be distinguished according to legal and pre-legal status to the degree to which they unify successfully primary and secondary rules.[17] Using Hart's distinction, he asserts that law is a variable which exists in degrees of more or less in different customary systems. Hund cites Fallers as giving authoritative support to the proposition that the primary secondary rules distinction can be usefully employed to distinguish societies, which function according to conventions that resemble recognized Western legal systems.[18] The question is why should this all matter. Roberts and Comaroff, for example, in their study of the Tswana, reject the legal politics dichotomy

---

[15] J. Comaroff and S. Roberts, *Rules and Processes: the Cultural Logic of Dispute in an African Context* (Chicago: University of Chicago Press, 1981).

[16] Hund, *op., cit.*, 288.

[17] Lloyd Fallers, *Law without Precedent* (Chicago: University of Chicago Press, 1969).

[18] Hund, *op., cit.*, 287.

seeing all legal decisions as being the outcome or expression of political realities. This is the view one associates with legal realism. On this account then there is no substantive difference between more sophisticated legal systems with their so called independent judicial institutions and societies such as the Tswana in which the determining political processes are more clearly evident. Roberts sees the notion of an independent judiciary as a Western legal ideology.[19] The fact that Tswana or the Kewa and Huli do not appear to be consistently governed by some set of putative rules, cannot be regarded as particularly significant given that ultimately for all societies the legal is somewhat epiphenomenal and subject to political convenience.

If one wished to dispute this position, one could find oneself driven to defending some form of legal formalism, which might lead us well beyond the scope of this chapter. But surely one might say that the ideal of judicial independence, which formalism proposes has never been entirely achieved nevertheless the goal has been realized imperfectly and perhaps in varying degrees. Clearly in the case of the Tswana, the Kewa or the Huli, politics dominates the prescriptive authority of the rules, however, in many modern Western states, and perhaps with the Enga or Basoga of Uganda political processes have, to a degree, been tamed by the rule of law.[20] Hart's distinction between primary and secondary rules allows us to explain why the latter societies differ from the former and with respect to the latter alerts us to the presence of specialized legal institutions that function to identify and apply primary rules authoritatively and consistently. Bruce Benson, for example, cites anthropological studies of the Yurok, Hupa and Karok Indians of Northern California in which non-relatives of aggrieved parties, extrinsic to the local community (called 'crossers') were hired to adjudicate disputes especially property disputes.[21] The designation of special groups to carry out the adjudication function in accordance with defined principles is direct evidence of secondary rules embodying rules of recognition and adjudication, he argues. Moreover, enforcement of decisions was organized through 'sweat house' groups to which each tribesman belonged. Additionally Benson states "…rules of adjudication imply rules of change because adjudication of disputes often leads to articulation of a new law, or at least, clarification of existing law in the context of an unanticipated circumstances."[22] Benson also makes reference to the Kapauka of West Papua and the role of designated individuals of recognized wealth and

---

[19] S. Roberts, *Order and Discipline: An Introduction to Legal Anthropology* (London: Pelican Books, 1979): 22.

[20] *Ibid.*

[21] Benson, *op. cit.*, 7–10.

[22] *Ibid., 12.*

status, known as *towoni*, who specialized in matters of adjudication.[23] Benson's point is that a customary system can perform the defining functions of law even without the institutional characteristics of a modern nation state, one which implies the existence of government, the professionalization of the production and enforcement of law through a full time paid bureaucracy. One might, however, enquire as to whether consistency, coherence even a certain formal elegance in terms of a set of legal principles is an end in itself that particularly enhances or brings some utility to resolving the messy business of disputatious human interaction, especially in issues of land or property.

Legal versus Customary Property rights

I believe that if we turn to the subject of property rights the answer has to be yes. Hernando de Soto has explained what modern Western property rights mean and how they work.[24] As we have seen he holds that the evolution of Western property, shifted the legitimacy of the rights of owners from the politicized context of local communities to the impersonal context of law. This, he says, created individuals from masses by transforming people with property interests into accountable individuals. It is significant that De Soto's conclusions are not, according to him the outcome of theoretical speculation, but rather the product of extensive research conducted throughout the so called third world. The foci of this research has been relations between poverty, wealth and property rights as studied in venues such as Cairo, Lima Peru, Port-au Prince, Manila etc. as well as the major commercial centres of the West.

De Soto explains that in pre-capitalist societies or those which are beyond the reach of the capitalist system, individuals relied on neighbourhood relationships or local arrangements to protect rights and assets. In this situation they stood very much at the mercy of local political arrangements and contingencies. Lack of legal property, he says, means individuals cannot make profitable contracts with strangers because, in effect, they have no property to lose.

Certainly these descriptions would apply to the Kewa, Huli or Tswana. Without a legal system that defines rights according to a unambiguous code of principles, they cannot be certain of their rights as they are continuously dependent upon a landscape of political maneuver and intrigue. There are in effect no reliable principles that exhibit consistency and coherence and that could be transcribed in a code and applied objectively to settle disputes. In this case conventions or

---

[23] *Ibid., 17.*

[24] Hernando de Soto, *The Mystery of Capital: Why Capitalism Triumphs in the West and Fails Everywhere Else* (New York: Bantam Press, 2000).

customs offer little or no indication as to the rights individuals actually possess. This means two things that they are enslaved to the local politics of the group, and secondly, that outsiders cannot transact with them because there are no rules or principles that can affirm the legal status of their alleged rights. De Soto sees such societies as, in effect, trapped in a pre-legal and pre capitalist world.

As we said, de Soto sees this as significant is because they cannot explore possibilities to generate surplus value from their assets, which requires involvement in an expanded system of exchange, trade and commerce, the basis of wealth generation in the modern world. Associated notions of trust and security allow for distantly linked market interaction. This is never possible if only proximate neighbours and immediate kinsmen can be reasonably assured of one's claims to property and assets. Whether or not we believe that law and politics are ever entirely separable inseparable, De Soto's work does provide strong argument for the proposition that without some significant separation of the legal from the political, modern capitalism would never have been possible. Following a Kantian approach and methodology, he puts forth a convincing argument that the success of modern capitalism is best explained in those societies, which evolved legal systems that formalized property rights. These rights are significantly independent of local politics, so as to allow for their national and international recognition.

This observation, of course, touches on issues of economic development. Mere reference to existing customs, as we sought to show, is an unreliable indicator of the presence of a set of prescriptions that can function reliably to approximate the workings of a legal system. We have seen that some customary conventions do exhibit features we associate with a modern legal system and some fail do so. We related the success or failure to the presence or absence of a union of primary and secondary rules. In situations in which one fails to find a set of customary conventions that function more less in accordance with that of a legal system, i.e., exhibits primary and secondary rules, reference to customs as a way to resolve disputes or identify ownership becomes virtually meaningless. It is meaningless in the sense that outsiders cannot rely on these putative rules in their dealings with the customary owners and the owners themselves cannot rely on the rules to protect themselves against the internal politics of the group. The law in appealing to custom in these circumstances is really abrogating its responsibility and creating in Rodman's words a "Zone of Abandonment," where rules really don't matter. On the other hand, reference to customs will not be meaningless where societies are organized to follow generally a set of coherent rules, which are consistently applied. As we suggested this most probably means the presence of independent institutions or agencies that embody Hart's secondary rules. This all entails that reference to the customary to adjudicate disputes is a risky business, which in some instances may just mean abandoning law for political expediency. It would be far better to codify the customs and formalize alleged customary rules in a published system that can them be applied and identified by relevant legal institutions. The reason this is important is especially relevant in the case of property and the ownership of assets like land. As we have explained De Soto sees legally recognized property as removing one's entitlements and assets from the closed system of social relations that are internal to the group and endowing one's property with an existence that is ascertainable outside the group and thereby a value that is independent of local relations and group politics. Property then has economic value that did not exist before. When property is endowed with this characteristic, it allows the owners to expand their activities beyond mere local and group interaction and participate in trade and commerce which has a national and international reach. There is no need to go much further on this point because as Adam Smith demonstrated over two hundred years ago in *The Wealth of Nations*, the size of the market is the *sine qua non* for specialization, the division of labour and thus the generation of wealth.

Summary

We began this chapter with references to PNG legislation that empowers the courts to settle land disputes and the recognition of land owning groups through reference to local custom. We pointed to an implicit assumption that custom entails rule governed behaviour in which the rules are accessed through reference to an oral rather than a written tradition. We went on to mention H.L.A. Hart's contention that custom lacks the secondary rules that characterize a complete legal system. We remarked upon the skepticism with which Hart's theory has met. However, we went on to argue that Hart's distinction between primary and secondary rules can do useful work in explaining why customary systems exhibit differing degrees of rule guided behaviour, in so far as societies, in which behaviour is more closely organized according to rules, exhibit forms of social organization that embody secondary rules or principles. In the final section of the chapter we argued that rule guided customary systems, which approximate formal legal systems, can be efficacious in settling property and land disputes.

We argued that this is important because formal legal systems allow for property rights to gain independence from local political and informal arrangements. When this occurs assets gain an economic value in which trade and commerce become more viable. As economic development in the countries of the South Pacific is becoming an urgent issue, reliance on informal custom rather than formal law in matters of land tenure will be antithetical to issues of land mobilization and development. At this stage I will not venture into the larger debate as to whether the goal of economic development and integration into the greater global economic community is wholly desirable even if it makes economic sense.

Chapter Seven

Papua New Guinea and the Legal Methods for Maintaining Customary Land Tenure

We pointed out in the first chapter that the principal difference between Western forms of property and traditional customary forms centres on the right to income. The right to monetary income through ownership has been seen as an addition to the basic control rights. We suggested that one would not associate income rights with customary forms of traditional ownership. Christman points out that Western societies structure income rights in different ways so as to achieve differing distribution patterns. For example, income, capital gains and sales tax are often employed in patterning income distribution.

We argued that one of the major difficulties in giving definition to income rights in traditional societies is the persisting underlying assumption that property is communal. Essentially income rights must be individual rights. Obviously, one can grant a specified income share to a group; however, ultimately the group must make arrangements for the income to be shared with the membership. This means it must agree on certain principles or rules for the sharing of the aggregate amount among themselves. When these principles or rules are agreed upon one has defined the income right. Without these rules specifying individual entitlements, the income right remains inchoate and contentless. The corollary is, therefore, that defining ownership solely in terms of group rights effectively renders the income right non-existent.

The obvious rejoinder to the above would be something to the effect that individual groups can create their own solution and determine individual income rights in accordance with their traditions and cultural ways. The problem, as we shall see, is that monetary entitlements were not part of traditional cultures and thus there are no tradition cultural practices to draw upon. A further issue, as we underlined in the last chapter, is that many traditional cultures have not been particularly reliant on rule governed behaviour; and certainly income rights are an area in which entitlements must be precisely defined according to recognized rules if we are to avoid chaos and disputatious behaviour.

In this chapter we shall look at the Papua New Guinea post colonial state, and its success or failure in instituting a system for income distribution based on a recognition of customary forms of ownership. In Papua New Guinea over the decades since independence land registration has been one of the most controversial ownership issues. A system of formal registration was attempted in 1952 when the Native land Commission was established to inquire into the ownership of each tract of unalienated land and record the rights of the traditional owners, but the program was pursued for ten years with little practical result.[1] Again in July 1995, the Chan Government considered, as part of the IMF structural adjustment package, the possibility of registering customary land, but abandoned the idea due to a combined protest of university students and army personnel.

In addition to the issue of registration versus non-registration, there has been the issue of individual versus communal ownership. As we have repeated, it has been the traditional view that in PNG property is held in a form of customary ownership in which the group rather than the individual claims title. However, the colonial government in the 1960s did pursue a policy of substituting individual registered titles (freeholds) for traditional communal forms of land holding, and the replacement of customary law by English real property law.[2] But the legislation intended to implement the plan efficiently was ultimately defeated by the PNG members of the House of Assembly in 1971.[3] Significantly, in 1974 the *Land Groups Incorporation Act* provided for the legal recognition of traditional groups and their incorporation for purposes of acquiring, holding, disposing and managing land.[4] This legislation gave legal substance to the view that in PNG it is the group rather than the individual who is primary in matters of land ownership.

The Act thus recognizes a form of group ownership and provides for group incorporation for purposes of acquiring, holding, disposing and managing but fails to address the issue of income distribution to individual membership. In the following pages we will be concerned with the success or failure of various attempts to distribute benefits based on the assumption of group title. Let us move to some striking if not infamous examples in which distribution to groups has led to problematic behaviour.

The Bougainville Crisis

The Bougainville mine, situated in Papua New Guinea's North Solomons, the Bougainville province of Papua New Guinea, when operating, was one of the

---

[1]   R.W. James, *Land law and Policy in Papua New Guinea* (Port Moresby: PNG Land Reform Commission, 1985).

[2]   *Ibid.*, 45.

[3]   *Ibid.*, 46.

[4]   *Land Groups Incorporation Act*, (1974) Ch. 147, s. 1 (e).

world's largest gold and copper mines. Before its closure it accounted for around 40 per cent of Papua New Guinea's exports, and between 17 and 20 per cent of government revenue. Mining exploration began on Bougainville in the 1960s. Nevertheless, despite the increased wealth that was generated by mine, the presence of the mining company had been a source of resentment among the local people in the Panguna area, where the mine was located. Also many Bougainvilleans, less directly connected to the mining operations, felt strongly about the mine, its operations and consequences. A secessionist movement emerged in the late 1960s fueled in part by opposition to mining development. Whether justified or not many Bougainvilleans believed the development of the mine had taken their land, introduced unacceptable changes altering their way of life, while providing inadequate compensation despite the great wealth it apparently produced. In 1988 increasing opposition of landowners towards the mining company, Bougainville Copper Limited (BCL), ultimately expressed itself in violence. Some of the more militant landowners began a campaign of sabotage and harassment of mine employees. In December of 1988 the mine closed briefly, followed by a curfew in the main towns and the mine area as the authorities sought to contain the conflict.

Events began to escalate in March 1989 as riots broke out in the town of Arawa intially provoked by conflicts between migrant workers from the Papua New Guinea mainland and local Bougainvilleans. These events fueled separatist sentiments on Bougainville and at the same time hardened support for the militant landowners. Significant unrest followed the riots and the Papua New Guinea Defence Force (PNGDF) was sent to support the already increased police forces in maintaining law and order. At the same time, the national and provincial governments attempted to negotiate with the militants. Shortly after, security forces launched a 'full-scale military operation' against the rebels.

Francis Ona, the alleged leader of the rebels published a letter in the media on 12 April 1989. The letter appeared in *Niugini Nius*, one of Papua New Guinea's two daily newspapers, stating the revised demands of the militant group. He demanded compensation of 10 billion Kina (about $US12 billion) for environmental and other damage caused by BCL's operations. (The company claimed that this was more than double the total revenue generated by the company since mining commenced in 1967). He also demanded 50 per cent of all profits, and the withdrawal of security forces. The letter also contained the statement: "We are not part of your country any more ... We belong to the Republic of Bougainville and we are defending our island from foreign exploitation."

The mine closed in May 1989 following continued guerilla activities against the mine installations and employees. With the security situation unimproved, in January 1990 the mine was placed on a 'care and maintenance' basis and the company began to evacuate its employees from Bougainville. Although the national and provincial governments promised increased compensation and development funds to landowners and the provincial government, the militant landowner group rejected the offer and continued its guerilla operations campaign against the mine. In March 1990 a ceasefire was negotiated and the national government began a withdrawal of its security forces.

A blockade of the island by the PNG defense force followed these events resulting in the eventual isolation of the people of Bougainville. Throughout the 1990s Bougainville remained isolated and under embargo from Papua New Guinea, while much of the Island remained under the control of the BRA. During this period the people of Bougainville suffered greatly especially with the reduction of essential services relating to health and education. However, matters have since improved with the signing of the Bougainville Peace Accord in January 2001, which granted significant autonomy to the island. The accord agreed upon states that all government functions be transferred to Bougainville, except for defence, foreign affairs, international shipping and aviation, and the supreme court. Furthermore, the Panguna copper mine, that sparked the violent conflict in Bougainville will not be reopened.

Let us now consider some of the important factors that contributed to the so called Bougainville crisis. As stated, hostilities began with the actions of the disgruntled landowners. Matters become clearer when one identifies the disgruntled landowners. Authoritative research establishes the Bougainville crisis began as an inter-generational struggle over the compensation proceeds from the giant Panguna copper mine.[5] One can trace the initial etiology of these events to an absence of defined income rights. CRA the Australian mining giant and the principal owner of the mine agreed to pay groups regarded as traditional landowners for the use and abuse of their territory resulting from its mining operations. Again we need to emphasize that the approach to income distribution involved working through groups and designated representatives of the 'group'. In the Bougainville case there existed a landowner's association and separate from this a trust fund (The Road Mine Tailings Lease Trust Fund), which was administered by the twelve titleholders who represented the landowning clans and communities. The trustees were to invest the money received from the mine royalties, occupation fees and compensation payments "...for future generations while spending the income for the benefit of the wider community". As it turned out the trustees violated their fiduciary duties and kept the money for themselves.[6] Customary guidelines were lacking or confused because inheritance is usually matrilineal

---

[5]   C. Filer, "The Bougainville Rebellion, the Mining Industry, and the Process of Social Disintegration," in R.J. May and M. Sprigs eds., *The Bougainville Crisis* (Bathhurst: Crawford Press, 1990).

[6]   *Ibid.*, 91.

whereas cash crops have thought to belong to the male line.[7] Thus, the leaders, rather than operate in conditions of confusion in which the dissemination of benefits would lead to controversy, decided instead simply to keep the benefits for themselves. Thus stated, one can see that conventions regarding income rights were really undeveloped and provided insufficient guides to individual entitlements. Lack of clear guidelines and adequate rules, and the attendant absence of moral force, created a situation in which the titleholders felt free to pocket the revenue.

Some libertarians have argued that voluntary cooperative arrangements are only likely to arise when substantial benefits from doing so can by internalized by each individual.[8] Individuals require incentives to become involved in social undertakings and thus they must be able to foresee the resulting individual entitlement from doing so. In other words, they must have a clear idea of income rights should they agree to participate. In the case of the Bougainville titleholders, it is probable they had no conception of the appropriate entitlements associated with management of trust monies. Accordingly, they decided to define the rights in a way most favourable to themselves. The Bougainville case should alert us to the inherent dangers when monetary benefits are introduced into a non-cash economy without sufficient specification of individual rights. Defining individual rights is essential both in motivating individuals to assume social responsibilities and also in controlling self interest in so far as one becomes aware not only of one's own rights but also of the rights of others which one should not violate. In the Bougainville case, the titleholders really had no clue as to the appropriate income rights ascribable to themselves or other individual group members, and therefore may not have had a sense that their actions were compromising the rights of other individual members. But moreover can we even say that there were violations of fundamental principles of distributive justice that make sense independently of a given definition of individual income rights?

The Southern Highlands

If we move ahead in time from the genesis of the Bougainville crisis in the late 1980s we continue to find the failure to define individual income rights undermining efforts to provide an efficient, non-contentious if not equitable or just system of distribution. When in the 1990s Chevron (now Chevron Texaco) decided to develop the lake Kutubu oil fields they faced the familiar issue of distributing

---

[7] *Ibid.*
[8] B.L. Benson "Enforcement of Private Property Rights in Primitive Societies: law without Government," *The Journal of Libertarian Studies*, IX, 1 (winter 1989): 1–26, 8.

compensation payments to land owner groups among the local Foi and the Faso tribes. However instead of working out some formula that would define individual rights and entitlements they stuck to the accepted belief that all rights are fundamentally group rights. Payment would be made to groups but again a group is an abstraction and one needs some representative of the group to actually accept payment. In the Bougainville case the representation was worked out in terms of a principal titleholder, who acted as trustee. The on going Bougainville crisis was offering undeniable evidence that there might be fundamental problems with this model. However, these grave concerns did not prompt Chevron to defenestrate the assumption that income rights should be group rights and payment must be made to some representation of the group. Evidently there was a belief that CRA or BCL got it wrong at Panguna because they settled on the wrong incarnation of group representation. Chevron decided that the proper representation should be the corporate model, one already defined in PNG legislation as an Incorporated Land Group. However, unlike principal titleholders, which are pre-existing living entities awaiting identification, corporate bodies as the legal representation of land owning groups were not yet realities in the socio-economic landscape of the mountainous Southern Highlands. Corporate bodies would have to be created from pre-existing individuals, but not just any set of individuals would be legally acceptable.

The *Incorporated Land Groups Act* specified that a group can be incorporated if

(a) The member groups possess common interests and coherence independently of the proposed recognition and share or are prepared to share common customs; and

(b) The association between groups represents a customary form of organization.

One might think that because the government had passed the above legislation, it would have an institutional apparatus that could put the Act into effect. This is to say there might exist some cadre of officers trained to identify customary owners and sort them into groups on the basis of shared customs. But it was evident the Department of Lands and Physical Planning was totally incapable of implementing the Act. Accordingly, Chevron hired anthropologists and local consultants, including one who had been instrumental in creating the earlier East Sepik Province's legislation on incorporated land groups, to identify and verify customs and customary practices that knit the individuals into customary groups capable of incorporation under the *Incorporated Land Groups Act*.[9] After extensive consultation with landowner elders, the Chevron teams felt the job was fairly well done. Once the proper customary linkage had been allegedly verified,

---

[9]   A.P. Power, "State Neglect a Major Factor," *PNG National* (19/15/01), 19.

Chevron implemented the necessary steps to have the groups legally endowed with corporate personality. It was obviously assumed that appropriate customary group representation would thus be achieved and matters of distribution with minimal contention and reasonable social concord would proceed.

This was hardly the reality, which followed. It became clear that many were not satisfied with their legal grouping regardless of alleged customary linkage. Of course this is understandable. Why should income rights to non-customary monetary benefits be tied to something as nebulous as groupings based on shared customs, which is further exhibited in associations between groups that represent "a customary form of organization". Moreover recognition as a member of incorporated customary land group still gives no indication as to the income rights possessed through membership. Accordingly, individuals in the Southern Highlands began to take matters into their own hands in a manner that parallels Western forms of voluntary initiative. They decided to form their own preferred incorporated land groups. Of course, these newly formed corporate bodies challenged the earlier efforts of Chevron to identify and incorporate customary groups.

The principal consultant in the registration of the original customary land groups reported in the media that incorporated land groups had been split and recreated from existing incorporated land groups, while earlier incorporated land groups had been de-registered. He stated "…more than thirty land groups were de-registered without due process…New land groups were then registered without due process. These amounted to a reconfiguration of the same people into non-customary entities like family groups but with new officials. There were no new people." Family ILGs, he claimed, are contrary to customary groupings and are purely intended to maximize shares to the families.[10]

Tony Power, the principal consultant, attributes the breakdown of the original customary groups to the inadequacy of the government agencies that allowed this to happen. To begin, he claimed, Chevron had to incorporate the landowner groups because the Department of Lands and Physical Planning (DLPP) was totally incapable of implementing the Act. Secondly, DLPP officers allowed themselves to be manipulated by other land owner leaders allowing the registration of nonsense land groups without adequate credentials, while deregistering other land groups against their wishes and without due process. He goes on to mention that a similar problem occurred in the Gulf province of Papua New Guinea in which many of the Kerewo ILGs in a manner contrary to custom sought to maximize benefits by forming family ILGs.

For Power the negligence of the state has resulted in a disaster. He says, "the very Act that was designed to empower landowners has been used by manipulators

---

[10] *Ibid.*

to disenfranchise individual landowners and land groups". The negligence that Power refers to obviously involves the incapacity of the Department of Lands and Physical Planning to implement the Act. Specifically, he claims that it lacks skilled manpower and resources because the Department of Justice has allowed the Land Court Secretariat to run down, thus failing to provide a cadre of well-trained magistrates versed in customary land tenure to manage *The Land Dispute Settlement Act* independently and objectively. (*The Land Disputes Settlement Act Ch.* No. 45, states under "Practice and Procedure of Local Land Courts," s. 35, d) subject to Section 40, states that Local Land Courts shall endeavour to do substantial justice between all persons interested, in accordance with the Act and relevant custom. Section 68 enables both a local land court and a Provincial Land Court to determine and apply relevant customs.)

However, regardless of whether customary groups are properly identified, the existence of group rights with unspecified individual income rights essentially leaves the issue of income distribution problematic. Moreover, representation of the group through a trustee who doesn't understand fiduciary duties or an incorporated body still leaves the issue of distribution unsettled and really fails to move matters ahead. In Western capitalist states corporations are voluntary associations of individuals based on mutual agreements as to individual income rights. In the Western Highland individuals decided that they would not be burdened with a customary grouping determined by criteria not based on voluntary commitment. The subsequent associations they formed, regardless of whether they were based on custom, did represent some form of voluntary engagement of individuals. In these circumstances individual members were actually working to determine a clearer idea of income rights based on the agreements between individuals, rather than follow alignments that were supposed to reflect someone's idea of a customary grouping.

The ongoing publicity of misadventures and battles the between the Foe land groups in the Southern Highland dominated the news in March, 2001. Published reports and announcements emanating from this area indicated that land owners were not reconciled to the group alignment that had been configured through discussions between the consultants and assumed Foe leaders. On March 8, 2001 the *PNG Post Courier* published an advertisement from 109 Foe landowners thanking the government for releasing their equity payments while at the same time demanding an immediate investigation of payment of 600,000 kina to another deregistered incorporated land groups also associated with the Kutubu Oil and Gas Project.[11] The following day the Minister for Petroleum and Energy

---

[11] I believe his examples illustrate my point rather than Power's conclusion. Group rights are always more susceptible to individual opportunism whereas individual rights afford much greater protection. Secondly custom is insufficient protection for individual rights in a situation

attacked the Kutubu landowners, on the second page of the *PNG National* stating that "A handful of greedy and power hungry landowners were on the verge of destroying PNG's petroleum industry".[12] A month later the media reported that payoffs had been made by Foe leaders to influence politicians to recognize groups as genuine landowning groups from among the disputing Foe landowners. At the same time the media cited police reports stating that the "Foe Future Generations Fund" was being recklessly spent by the leadership through hire car, hotel accommodation, aircraft leasing and payoffs to politicians.

Similar events happened in the Gulf province where many of the Kerewo ILGs broke up and formed family ILGs in a similar manner to maximize returns contrary to custom. Although some supporters of income distribution through incorporated land groups admit that many allegedly criminal acts of fraud have been perpetrated on the land owners funds ranging from the drawdown of the Foe Future Generations fund to wrongful payments to the then non-existent Kutubu Development Authority, they continue to maintain that failures in income distribution are due to a form of 'gerrymandering' that fractures custom to capture maximum wealth for certain families. However, what one fails to recognize is that the assumption that custom can function as law to delineate entitlements is misconceived. Indeed, it is rational that many within the groups might attempt to organize into smaller discrete groups, that is, families, and register them to maximize the flow of benefits. Custom may well be no more than a loose arrangement which tends to group families into clans, but so long as group membership is not tied to some independent variable like a registered section of land then it is natural that families and individuals will attempt to define the 'group' in a way that is most favourable to their own interests. Moreover, one could overcome these difficulties by assigning rights to individuals rather than groups. It should be pointed out half facetiously that individuals are irreducible and can't be split into sub-persons or combined to create larger individual persons for that matter.

---

in which capitalist relations of production apply, and rights are primarily applied to groups rather than individuals. The conclusion should not be that the government has to take on a greater supervisory role in the "identification and distribution of landowner and local level government benefits," which in the case of the PNG government, would be simply a case of wishful thinking. The conclusion should be that the state needs to abandon a policy which emphasizes incorporated groups rather than individuals, and which only benefits and recognizes groups, rather than individuals.

12 Power's apparent read on this is that these remarks relate to an act of desperation by the original Foe incorporated land groups which led them to shut down the Mubi Vale station in an attempt to stand up for their rights. This group has been frustrated by the lack of success of their court actions in the face of payouts by DPE and MRDC and the drawdown of the Foe Future Generations Fund, he contends.

Efforts to make individuals adhere to traditional customs in matters of income or income distribution may be seriously misplaced. We have pointed out that firstly income rights in terms of defined shares of monetary income from collective undertakings were unknown in traditional societies. Secondly, conceiving property rights as group rights according to statutory instruments such as the *Land Groups Incorporation Act* leaves the issue of income distribution entirely undetermined. This is why it is not surprising that aggressive individuals simply manipulate these unstructured situations to appropriate what they can with apparent disregard for the interests of others. Regardless, so long as individual income rights remain undefined and unrecognized in favour of recognized group rights, there will continue to be no standards by which to assess disproportionate income distribution. Moreover, determining different customs in myriad of different cases can be a daunting task. PNG, for example, has around 800 different linguistic groups each with distinct customs. It should be understandable that the government has neither the resources nor personnel to undertake the task. Moreover, as we argued, different traditional groups will exhibit varying degrees of rule governed behaviour. In some cases there may be no clearly defined rule or consistent set of rules governing important issues such as marriage or ownership rights, thus rendering any investigation fruitless.

But if we wish to solicit a dissenting view from another source who, like A.P. Power, also worked on the incorporation of Kutubu 'land owners', one should refer to the observations of James Weiner. James Weiner, an anthropologist, worked closely with the Foi and the Faso during the period in which groups were incorporated and when they began to tussle and dispute over distribution rights. He observes that the 1974 *Land Group Incorporation Act* had no effect on the Foi until the discovery of Petroleum, as we have already remarked.[13] As he says the conventions of incorporation were forced upon them in order to deal with the government and Chevron Niugini. As we stated, the customary land group is supposed to be an identifiable group through reference to some set of customs. Section 2 (1) of the Land Groups Incorporation act defines relevant custom in relation to an incorporated land group as a) ...any custom that is binding on the group or all the members; and (b) includes any custom that is referred to in the PNG constitution. However, Weiner points out that the Foi customary group is distinguished by the "porousness and flexibility" of its boundaries. He argues that "porousness and flexibility" are the centrally important feature of the social entity that enabled it to mitigate the intractability of internal disputes and maintain a customary distributive mechanism. He observes that the

---

[13] James Weiner, "The Incorporate Ground: The Contemporary work of Distribution in the Kutubu Oil Project Area, Papua New Guinea," *Working Paper 1998/1* (Canberra: Resource Management in Asia Pacific RSPAS, 1998), 11.

incorporated land group, however, served to rigidify the boundaries of the social entity and thus to destroy porousness and flexibility.

According to Weiner, the act of incorporation contrary to the custom of the customary group had the effect of destroying the central customary feature of the social entity. One thus encounters the ironic circumstance in which the legal construction (the incorporated land group), which was intended for the purpose of preserving the customary nature of the group's relations vis-a-vis property, in fact, destroyed the customary relations between group members. One might think there could be some constitutional challenge to the legislation on these grounds given the actual intent of the legislation is to effect a situation in which Papua New Guinea ways are preserved, as the Constitution requires. In speaking of the *Land Tenure Conversion Act*, for example, Judge J. Doherty states in Meriba Tomakala v. Robin Meriba that the duty of the Land Titles Commission is to guarantee and protect the rights of people under native custom. She emphasizes that "...this is a duty, which was imposed on the Australian Administration when New Guinea was mandated a Trust Territory under the League of Nations in 1921. The Act stresses the importance and need of the Commission to protect people's rights to land and ensure custom is upheld."[14] Now the land Tenure Conversion Act is designed to convert customary title into a fee simple. Certainly if, as interpreted, this Act is required to preserve customary practice in its application, then *a fortiori*, the *Land Groups Incorporation Act* is indisputably subject to the same constraint.

But other oddities surface if we follow Weiner's analysis. The entire concept of a social entity, 'customary land group' sharing common customs designated and distinguished from other groups by common customs, in the Southern Highlands appears meaningless. The Act never defines a group and Weiner speaks of 'clans' although the Act never mentions clans. It is perhaps clear that the interpreters of the Act intend group to refer to clan. But does that make anything clearer. It is obvious that various teams set up by Chevron were entrusted to identify relevant 'clans'. But since the Act never refers to clans one wonders whether the term has any legal authority. The Act speaks of a group but never defines a group and certainly never identifies a group with a clan, but it is obvious that most interpreters of the Act have unjustifiably linked a group with the term 'clan'. Weiner remarks that instead of clans what became relevant were sub-clans. Although this choice of terms may simply appear to be the substitution of one term for another without a significant difference, it is interesting that he goes on to explain why he uses the term sub-clan.

In his analysis of the sub-clan Weiner begins by repeating the familiar motif that as Melanesians, Southern Highlanders understand themselves in terms of

---

[14] Meriba Tomakala v Robin Meriba, *PNG Law Reports* (1994): 10–14, 13.

group related conceptions rather than as individual agents. This conforms to our ongoing analysis in which by comparison, Westerns tend to see themselves as individuals first and secondly as members of groups that they choose to associate with. But at the same time, he remarks, the group (clan) does not exert some overwhelming constraint on individual agency. According to him there exists a history of individuals for one reason or another, disassociating themselves from their customary 'group', or let us say 'clan' but taking with them part of the social unit, usually the immediate family hangers on and sympathizers. In doing so they remove themselves and recreate a smaller version of the social whole from which they have detached themselves. Weiner interpretatively describes the situation as one in which there exist sub-clans without there being clans. He asserts that "… sub-clans are the effective social unit in this part of Papua New Guinea."[15] With respect to bride wealth and land owning units, territorial distinctions are made up to the smallest family units possible. He remarks that other clan members could dispute the effective owners' decisions concerning disposal of land but usually the bigger the local clan, the less successful it was in reaching clan wide agreement as to the disposition of its resources, and the more likely that individual men or sets of brothers would arrogate to themselves effective power of disposal. Weiner asserts "…caution should be exercised in assuming that the clan is by definition a corporate group and that it recognizes or acts upon a commonality of interest."[16] He relates that clansmen were obligated to each other to provide support in bride wealth, ceremonial exchange and dispute but the assumption of commonality of interest is neither a necessary nor sufficient condition for the sense of obligation. The obligation, he claims has more to do with blood kinship or affinity rather than clanship as such.

The Forestry Sector

Having talked about affairs in the Petroleum sector, it is worthwhile to turn one's attention to the matters pertaining to forestry. Forestry represents a significant source of export revenue, and along with exports from mineral and petroleum sectors represents an important share of the annual GDP. It is also the case that developers, the majority of which are foreign based, have discovered the Incorporated Land Group as the preferred vehicle for income distribution. If anything the manipulation of this legal instrument to deny individuals income rights has often been more blatant than within the petroleum industry.

---

[15] Weiner, *op. cit.*, 5.
[16] *Ibid.*, 11.

In the early 1990s the PNG government introduced new legislation to cover the forestry sector following abuses documented by the "The Barnett Inquiry" of the late 80s.[17] The new *Forestry Act*, gazetted in 1992 and implemented from 1993, repealed the previous *Forestry Act* and the *Forestry (Private Dealings) Act*. One of the keys to reform was to form resource owner groups under the *Land Groups Incorporation Act*.[18] These customary groups are supposed to be empowered by the Act to make fundamental decisions about their land without reference to any other group or approval from any other group.[19] They are distinct from landowner companies (formed under the *PNG Companies Act*) that do not have to exhibit a customary relationship between shareholders.[20] According to the new Act, when landowners wish to develop a logging project, they are required to incorporate themselves under the *Land Groups Incorporation Act 1974* (Section 57). It is, however, reported that in most cases when landowners proceed to associate with the logging company they persist in setting up so called landowner companies in particular to receive financial benefits, which accrue to the landowners, under terms and conditions of the Timber Permit.[21]

But from a perusal of the new *Forestry Act*, despite the alleged empowerment of the incorporated land groups, one receives the impression that the forest industry in PNG is governed by a piece of elaborate legislation requiring forest development plans and layers of official approval before one tree can be cut. If you relied on this document as your sole source of information you would come away with the idea that forestry is a closely regulated and monitored industry. The reality is and has been somewhat different.

Despite the new Act coming into force in the early 90s the industry has largely remained the same, although with decreasing productivity.[22] The major players both then and now have been the landowner companies and the foreign logging companies. So called "landowner" companies are characterized by shareholders and management who tend mostly to be part of a group supporting a particular leader such as provincial politician or a national Member of Parliament, who has made contact with, or has been contacted by, an overseas logging company.[23] The landowner company traditionally agitated in the highest circles to be granted a

---

[17] Thomas Barnett, *Commission of inquiry into Aspects of the Forest Industry* (Port Moresby: 1989)

[18] Hartmut Holzknecht, *Policy Reform, Customary Tenure and Stakeholder Clashes in Papua New Guinea's Rainforests*, Rural Development Forestry Network Paper 19c (Regents College London: Rural Development Forestry Network, Overseas Development Institute, 1996), 8.

[19] *Ibid.*, 9.

[20] *Ibid.*

[21] PNG Forestry Review Team, *Individual Project Reports 2003/2004* (Port Moresby: May 2004), 29.

[22] Tim Curtin, "Land Titling and Forestry," (2004) unpublished.

[23] *Holzknecht, op. cit.*, 4.

logging permit. When this was successful, the overseas company was contacted to log and market the timber. Very few of the landowner companies presented financial reports of income to the resource owners or sent annual returns to the Registrar of Companies. It was observed that management officers usually resided in the provincial or national capital leading extravagant lifestyles. At the same time local politicians often become captured in a patron client relation with the foreign logging company, something which has tended to be antithetical to the best interests of the landowners and the industry.[24]

It is reported that logging companies, by linking up with a local leader and groups of supporters, ensure that these people are usually kept happy creating a useful buffer between themselves and the actual resource owners they supposedly represent.[25] Not only does this deprive the resource owners of a participatory role in the project, it also diverts profits through the landowner company to a small minority of individuals. Conflicts between the landowners and the logging company often result in the landowner company executives taking the side of the logging company. They may often be able to enlist the provincial police to arrest or harass the protesting resource owners.

Let us now turn our attention to the performance of the Incorporated Land Groups that are supposed to be empowered by the Act. For example, one might begin by taking a look at the *PNG Review Team Reports*, which consist of audits of forestry projects for compliance with the requirements of policy, the Forestry Act and other regulations and guidelines. To be specific I will refer to 20 reports, which were filed on February 5, 2001, and March 5, 2001.[26] These were submitted to government through the Interagency Forestry Review Committee and the Chief Secretary. They were compiled from areas in 11 provinces across PNG: Western Province, Madang Province, West Sepik Province, East Sepik Province, Oro Province, West New Britain Province, Southern Highlands Province, Milne Bay Province, Gulf Province, East New Britain Province, and Central Province. These reports are indicative of the general failure of custom, operating through the legal mechanism of the Incorporated Land Group and Land Owner Companies, to secure an unambiguous, just, equitable and transparent distribution of benefits.

Each of the twenty reports had a section devoted to land owner issues. In a rather rough form of categorization I identify 5 general types of problems. Only one of the 20 case reports was entirely free of any, or any combination of these problems. The issues were as follows:

---

[24] *Ibid.*, 3.
[25] *Ibid.*, 5.
[26] PNG Forestry Review Team, Individual Project Report Numbers 12–32 (Port Moresby: PNG Forestry Review Team, 5 Feb. -5 Mar. 2001).

1. Bogus or flawed ILGs were found in 3 cases. In one of these cases it was explicitly stated that there was mismatching between the group and land ownership.
2. Membership lists of ILGs and land owners were said to be flawed, incomplete or missing in 3 cases.
3. Confusion, uncertainty and, misrepresentation were evident at the level of interaction between ILGs and land owner companies (LOCs) in four cases. (According to legislative intent, the LOC empowers land owners and ILGs and enables them to enter into commercial arrangements by means of this mechanism.) In one case, for example, there was uncertainty as to which ILGs two competing land owner companies represented. In another case in Western Province the holder of the Timber Authority claimed to be a landowner company but was actually a foreign company through 50% foreign ownership.
4. A proliferation of family based ILGs rather than ILGs that reflect the *true* clan (group) ownership were allegedly found in four cases. (my italics).
5. Finally a miscellaneous set of problems including: insufficient care in the formation of the ILGs, 'unresolved landowner problems', 'confusion and unrealistic expectations', 'conflicting aspirations', 'lack of awareness', and 'unsatisfactory activities' were detected in five cases.

Only one of the twenty case studies alleges a level of acceptable land owner involvement. Significantly, in Central Province in Cloudy Bay, the auditors found both sufficient land owner awareness and 'adequately documented' ILGs.

Generally, the commentators seem to approve of the formation of ILGs to organize land owner interests while reserving their scorn and criticisms for the landowner companies.[27] The question one asks is why if the ILG is deemed a singular positive development is it so singularly ineffective in protecting and promoting landowner interests? Moreover why do landowners still need to form landowner companies, even though they are already supposedly organized along customary lines as ILGs? Moreover, one might take a closer look at the facts, which establish that ILGs have been less than successful in resolving problems besetting the forestry industry, specifically the environment.

With respect to environmental issues, the new Act was intended to ensure that harvesting occurred at sustainable rates in accordance with environmental standards and with adequate consideration for forest and biodiversity conservation.

---

[27] Holzknecht, *op. cit.*; PNG Forestry Review Team 2001; Tony Power, *Village Guide to Land Group Incorporation Report for Resource Owner Involvement Component, Forest management and Planning Project* (Wewak: World Bank/PNG Forest Authority/Groome Ltd., Irvin Enterprises, Pty Ltd., 1995).

All forest resources are to be developed according to a "National Forest Plan" (produced in 1996). Forest Management Agreements (FMAs) are to be drawn up to regulate dealings between the resource owners and the Forest Authority. Environmental plans are to be scrutinized and approved prior to issuing of timber permits. The Act also required National, Development Guidelines (produced in 1993). The two key government institutions are the PNG Forest Authority and the Department of Environment and Conservation. They are supposed to put in place more detailed standards and procedures to give operational effect to the policy. These include: specific Guidelines for (Environmental Plans for) Forest Harvesting Operations produced by the DEC; and the Planning, Monitoring and Control Procedures for Natural Forest Logging Operations Under Timber Permit, produced by the PNGFA; Guidelines for Environmental Motoring and Management Programmes; guidelines for Waste Management Plans etc.[28] And none of this has apparently worked to improve matters but seems simply to have added new bureaucratic layers.

Tim Curtin, former financial advisor to the PNG government and a negotiator in the Bougainville Peace Accord, reports that as of 2002 few FMAs had been granted other than conversions from the former Timber Rights Permits under the old Act, so that for the most part ongoing logging projects were those in operation before 1992.[29] The 2003/2004 PNG Forestry Review Team reports also clearly indicate an ineffectual performance by the institutions empowered by the 1991 Act and the virtual insignificance of the new legislation.[30] The Department of Environment and Conservation is responsible for monitoring and controlling logging company compliance with the terms and conditions of the Environmental Plan and as well as the Waste Management Plan.[31] The DEC also shares a responsibility with the Papua New Guinea Forest Authority to control and monitor compliance with 24 Key standards imposed on the logging companies through the PNGFA's Planing Monitoring and Control Procedures given they have an environmental protection basis.[32] The Reports state succinctly that currently the DEC is non-functional. It is stated that while reports exist there is no evidence that genuine environmental concerns have been satisfied.[33] The reason for inactivity and lack of monitoring is obvious when you consider that nearly all the DEC budget is used for personnel costs and running Head Office, leaving a very small declining amount available for operational activities. In 2004,

---

[28] PNG Forestry Review Team 2004, *op. cit.*, 1.
[29] Curtin, *op. cit.*, 1.
[30] PNG Forestry Review Team 2004, *op. cit.*
[31] *Ibid.*,52.
[32] *Ibid.*, 32.
[33] *Ibid.*, 33.

the budget allocation to DEC's Environmental Protection and Pollution Control Program, responsible for the field work for the monitoring and control purposes was 10, 000 kina (around $3,000 USD).[34]

The PNGFA was set up in 1993 and intended to act independently of the logging companies, and so not to be compromised, to ensure compliance with 24 Key standards. The reports also indicate that over expenditure in areas other than monitoring and support is compromising the core function of monitoring and control.[35] Accordingly there was found to be a lack of sufficient PNGFA staff at the large project sites sufficient to provide proper monitoring. Field based staff lack appropriate equipment to carry out their tasks and are dependent on the support of the logging company for housing, office space, and communications services—so much for independence.[36] Dereliction of other non-environmental responsibilities is also in evidence. For example, the PNGFA does not check the IPA registration of intended recipients of logging companies, thus allowing unregistered landowner companies to receive payments.[37]

To this point we have seen that the new *Forestry Act* has sought to remedy the ills of the industry by requiring the involvement of Incorporated Land Groups and by giving greater responsibility to the government and its institutions even though this has failed in the past. Moreover as will be pointed out later, all the new *Forestry Act* and the recently introduced tax system have achieved is the decline of the industry.[38] (233 million kina were exported in the first half of 1997 down to 80 million kina exports in the first half of 1998).[39] Moreover Curtin suggests that the World Bank and others appear to be interested in stopping logging altogether. On might also point to the New Zealand government which has set up an organization that seeks to persuade South Pacific communities to reject logging operations in favour of other forms of income generating activities such as ecotourism.[40]

But rather than Western governments and financial institutions seeking to destroy the industry, they should seek to improve it. After all Western countries tolerate greater levels of logging in their own countries, which generate valuable income for their own citizens, while apparently denying the right of developing

[34] *Ibid.*, 52.
[35] *Ibid.*, 47.
[36] *Ibid.*, 50.
[37] *Ibid.*, 36.
[38] Curtin, *op. cit.*, 9; PNG Forestry Review Team 2004, *op. cit.*, 11.
[39] Curtin, *op. cit.*, 9.
[40] Mohamed Nizar, & Kevin Clark, "Forestry on Customary-owned Land: Some Experiences from the South Pacific," *Rural Forestry Network Paper 19a*, (Regents College London: Rural Development Forestry Network, Overseas Development Institute, 1996).

countries to gain income form the same activities.[41] If we are really interested raising standards rather than destroying the industry one has to step back and consider the dynamics of wealth-creating organizations in order to develop effective remedies.

On the part of the landowners, we have seen that two of the principal players in the organization of the industry are the Incorporated Land Group and the Landowner Companies. We have argued throughout the text that one of the keys to wealth generation is that of commercial enterprise through voluntary association. But although landowner companies more or less appear to be voluntary associations, this is not the case with the ILG. Clearly the ILG is restricted in terms of eligibility. Individuals must be related by custom in terms of kinship ties, consanguinity etc. Although the customary relation is never clearly defined it certainly presupposes clan or tribal relationships. As such it represents an extended familial relationship and therefore is not a voluntary association. However, leaving all this aside, it is also clear, following Fukuyama's characterization, that both incorporated land groups and the landowner companies belong to wealth-redistributing interest groups rather than the wealth creating organizations. To this stage neither of these organizations has been engaged in the productive activity of logging itself. To put the case bluntly, in the forest industry, wealth is created by cutting down trees and transporting them to their markets—neither group has sullied its hands with this type of activity. In an almost pure sense of the term both represent rent seeking interest groups that are engaged in seeking to capture a portion of the wealth that has been produced by the activities of the logging companies and redistribute it to the membership. In most cases it seems that the leadership of these organizations has been more successful at redistributing the greater portion of the captured wealth to the leadership itself.

Indeed we have in effect at least three wealth-redistributing interest groups: the ILG, the Landowner companies and the government each tussling for a percentage of the wealth derived from the activities of the wealth producing economic organization. Certainly the government, as it steadily scales down its services and increasingly abdicates its responsibility for providing the usual public goods, including the monitoring of logging sites, has come to resemble a mere wealth redistributing interest group narrowly focused on redistributing wealth to its membership, the politicians and well placed government officials. It is not, therefore, unsurprising that we find landowner companies colluding with logging companies to reduce the share paid to landowners and landowner companies or government politicians colluding with logging companies to suppress the voice of the landowners in order to secure greater wealth for themselves.

---

[41] Tim Curtin, "What constitutes illegal logging?" *Pacific Economic Bulletin*, 22, 1 (2007): 125–134.

Possible Solution

One possible solution that I suggest is to eliminate ILGs and Land Owner Companies and then substitute foreign logging companies with domestic logging companies.[42] The latter would be companies created on a voluntary basis and could be sole proprietorships, partnerships or public companies according to the Companies Act. Moreover by requiring that all logging companies be PNG companies, which means owned and managed by PNG nationals, we could avoid many of the messy problems which the PNG Forestry Amendment Act was designed to overcome, but really has not. One of the obvious problems highlighted by the Barnett Report published in the late 1980s that precipitated the legislative reform was irresponsible logging and environmental damage of certain areas. Additionally the Inquiry highlighted the practice of transfer pricing as a means to avoid fair payment to landowner companies, taxes and royalties. It is perhaps out of concern for these issues that World Bank perhaps overreacted and encouraged the government to apply a graduated or progressive excise tax that has severely cut into profits and brought about a decline in forestry. Clearly if no or little logging is going on the alleged abuses must also be reduced, just as you might amputate a limb as a way of curing a rash.

However, I have argued that if the government just scraped the Act altogether, including the necessity for ILGs etc., by requiring that logging companies be owned by PNG nationals one could achieve the same results with much greater benefits. Obviously there would be the same significant decrease in logging perhaps even spectacularly because it would take time to develop and train these companies. With the reduced logging the environmental infringements would also reduce as has been achieved by the current Act and the actions of the World Bank. However, critics might object and say that this would destroy the possibility of an industry altogether because nationals have not yet exhibited an inclination or capacity for managing significant logging operations. One might reply that obviously at present there exists a disincentive to get involved because they can simply form landowner companies, a wealth redistributing interest group which can capture a share of the income from foreign logging firms without actually having to participate in logging. By requiring that logging be done by PNG companies a landowner company would actually have to become engaged in logging if it wanted any form of income from these activities. As for the view that PNG nationals might lack the capacity for such endeavors I think that they are equally as capable as the Fijians, for example, who have formed their own companies to harvest the pine and mahogany plantations. These companies are not supervised or

---

[42] David Lea, "The PNG forestry industry, incorporated entities, and environmental protection," *Pacific Economic Bulletin* 20, 1 (2005): 168–177.

government controlled but created by ordinary Fijian entrepreneurs. The Director of Fiji Pine describes these Fijian run companies as one of the success stories of the industry. George Vuki, General Manager of Fiji Pine in speaking of indigenous forest based companies is quoted as stating "…when you look at some of the Fijian businesses that have come up, some of them have really come up well. It's usually the individual owners who pretty much manage their business well, who are surviving now."[43]

These changes would also avoid the problem of transfer pricing in that there would be little incentive to engage in such practices, especially if one abolished the progressive excise tax that was introduced with the new Forestry Act. The question remains what would be the relationship between the alleged owners of the resource and the PNG logging companies? We suggest that the same rules that apply to logging on freehold land should apply. In short logging should simply occur with the consent of the owner(s) in the same way which the current Act applies to freehold (land which is not subject to customary title). Thus all that would be needed is an agreement between two parties which could be in terms of payments calculated on the basis of the value of the logs harvested or if there is a view to creating forest plantations there could be a long term lease, which unfortunately according to the deplorable state of land tenure transactions in PNG would require the usual lease lease back arrangement through the government. But these moves would avoid the various bureaucratic layers. One could thereby avoid the need for bureaucratic supervision through a Forest Management Agreement, which requires an agreement between customary owners and the Authority to accord with a National Forest plan, which also necessitates the ILG etc., etc. One would also obviate the other inefficiencies associated with the tussles and collusion between the various current rent seeking organizations, the landowner companies and their leaders, the incorporated land groups and their leaders, and the government politicians.

At this point one may well bring up the issue of environmental damage? How will it be controlled if you sweep away the Act *tout court*? The Barnett Inquiry heavily criticized the failure of the government to supervise the industry adequately and thereby contributing to the abuses. Ironically, as Tim Curtin points out, the new *Forestry Act* in response to these observations seeks to cure the alleged abuses by expanding the supervisory role of the government whose institutions have already been judged as inadequate to the task.[44] This all brings to mind the American libertarian Tibor Machan and his attack on the view that

---

[43] Ross Duncan, "Mahogany Dreaming," (Oct. 10, 2004) Program transcript from ABC National Radio, www.abc.net.au/talks/bbing/stories/s1218975.htm.

[44] Curtin, *op. cit.*

environmental protection can be achieved by greater government regulation.[45] Machan excoriated those who hold this opinion arguing that governments have always been closely aligned with powerful economic interests. The idea that government will champion environmental protection over economic interest is woefully misplaced. Certainly Machan's words seem to ring true if we consider the philosophy and actions of the many administrations in Washington, or the government officials observed by Holzknecht, who align themselves with foreign logging companies against the interests of their own citizens.[46] Machan's preferred solution is a development of the common law in which the judiciary rather than the government takes a principled stand against industrial activities that cause damage to persons or the environment through pollution or destructive practice. Whether this is a reliable solution is questionable, given that it rests on the view that the legal and the political are clearly distinguishable. However, these observations are worth keeping in mind and moreover, more government monitoring will obviously be ineffective at best if government lacks competency, and more seriously, expanding the role of government agencies in these circumstances may simply create opportunities for more rent seeking and political corruption. Certainly the government could enact legislation setting environmental standards and then leave it to the courts and judicial system to develop the law and enforce sanctions through the usual litigation processes. On the other hand, the common law could be developed, as Machan suggests, to include tortious liability for actions that pollute or degrade the environment.

My argument is that by scraping the Act altogether, abolishing the punitive excise tax, and insisting that logging companies be PNG owned we will achieve all that the current Act and excise tax have accomplished with certain added benefits. It is clear that all that these measures have tangibly done is secure a reduction in logging because as the 2003/2004 Review Team states, logging is simply no longer profitable.[47] By insisting that the logging companies be PNG owned and managed we will initially achieve the same thing, a similar reduction in logging but hopefully we will also be creating organizations that are actually wealth-creating economic organizations rather than wealth–redistributing interest groups. Certainly this is an improvement over the current situation in which landowners and landowner companies simply wait opportunistically for foreign owned logging companies to express an interest in logging their area. It is said that it is better to show a man how to fish rather than to give him fish because then he has the means to feed himself rather than the insecurity of waiting for others to provide the fish.

---

[45] Tibor Machan, "Pollution, Collectivism and Capitalism," *Journal Des Economists et Etudes Humaines* 2 (1991): 82–102.

[46] Holzknecht, *op. cit.*

[47] PNG Forestry Review Team 2004, *op. cit.*,11.

Moreover insisting on domestically based logging companies will give rise to a multiplier effect as profits generated will be spent within the country (rather than repatriated) thus stimulating other wealth producing activities within the country.

Conclusion

My own conclusion from this and foregoing sections of the chapter, is that the Incorporated Land Group, based on customary lines, is a misconceived legal construction. Although in earlier chapters, we highlighted certain deficiencies in this form of organization in which management and ownership are frequently separated, the fact still remains that in Western jural history a corporation has traditionally been an organization based on voluntary association in which the income rights of individual members are based on contractual arrangement between the members. In contrast, membership in an Incorporated Land Group is not based on voluntary association but on a presumed customary linkage, which is not the product of individual choice. Since the modern corporation, as a voluntary association, includes specific agreements as to individual entitlements, a customary association which is not the product of voluntary agreement, *a fortiori*, is not and cannot be founded on prior agreements as to individual entitlements. In these circumstances, membership in an ILG offers no statement as to individual income rights and remains vague and structure-less with respect to principles of distribution. Whereas in the West, individual income rights are worked out before or in the process of forming or joining the organization, the incorporated land group represents an involuntary inclusion in which a system of income distribution, somewhat like Locke's *tabula rasa*, remains unstructured and awaiting definition. It is the very lack of structure that makes it susceptible to abuse. As much as individuals decry the family ILG of the southern Highlands, these organizations, at the least, may represent agreements among individuals in which the participating membership possesses a more defined understanding of their income rights.

Chapter Eight

Customary Land Tenure in Fiji:
A Questionable Colonial Legacy

As we have said, customary communal ownership is often endowed with significance and central value in the cultural lives of many indigenous peoples of the South Pacific. This is especially true in Fiji as well as Papua New Guinea, for example. The legacy from the colonial era has been one of legislation and bureaucracy designed to preserve what is regarded as customary. It is assumed that these mechanisms work to preserve the 'customary' traditions. In point of fact, it is often the case that the mechanisms work to create something radically different and non-customary, which is the unavoidable legacy of the colonial rather than the pre-colonial era. The postcolonial period is often one of reflection and reexamination as the newly formed political entity struggles to harmonize the colonial legacy with the indigenous culture of the membership. Often the assumed 'customary ownership' systems escape scrutiny because of the very assumptions described. However, it is these systems, which most strongly deserve re-evaluation especially in so far as they are crucial to the contemporary economic and social health of society. In this chapter I argue that the Fijian land tenure system, an inheritance of colonization needs to be reexamined especially in so far as it may be significantly contributory to the Fiji's political and economic problems.

In this chapter we begin with a comparative analysis of the colonial experience in Jamestown and Plymouth colonies in 17th century America because these experiences provide contrasts and parallels with later colonial developments in Fiji. The lessons of Jamestown and Plymouth, I believe, serve to explain, at least in part, why the economic problems of the indigenous Fijians and political turmoil of recent decades will continue if the present ownership structures remain in place.

Jamestown and Plymouth

One can draw some interesting contrasts if one compares the colonial land policies in Jamestown, Virginia and the Plymouth colony in the 17th century, with that of the Fijian colony of the 19th century. The first two were North American colonies consisting exclusively of British settlers. Fiji, however, consisted of a minority of European settlers while the majority were either native Fijian, or later, growing numbers of indentured servants from the Indian subcontinent, who were introduced in the late 1900s.

In 1607 Jamestown, Virginia became the first British colony in the so-called New World. It was financed by a Joint Stock Venture, the Virginia Company formed in London. The colony was far from an immediate success. Of the 104 original colonists all but 38 were dead in the first six months. In 1609 the Virginia Company was reorganized, but again out of the original 500 colonists only 60 were left after six months. The deaths of the colonists have been considered somewhat of a mystery given that the land was and is fertile and game was sufficiently plentiful. Thomas Bethel has advanced an interesting explanation based in the subsequent institution of private property. Originally when the company was set up colonists were designated as indentured servants and expected to toil for seven years and contribute the fruits of their labour to a common store before becoming free men.[1] They did not have a modified interest in the soil or a partial ownership in the returns of their labour. Bethel argues that lacking either an interest in the means of production or the products of their labour, the colonists lacked the incentive to commit themselves to their labour. As a result, idleness and lack of industry led to insufficient productivity and eventual starvation. Sir Thomas Dale, the first Governor, in 1611 took note of the situation and sought to change matters through creating a workable incentive system through the establishment of private property.[2] Each man was given a three-acre plot of land. Subsequent to these events the colony becomes a success as productivity increases.

Bethel moves on to a consideration of the other famous 17th century colony, the Plymouth colony. Founded in 1620 for Pilgrims seeking religious freedom, at the insistence of the investors, the original arrangement required that all accumulated wealth would be common wealth and placed in a common pool as 'common wealth'. There would be no private ownership. At the end of seven years everything would be divided equally between investors and colonists. Even personal habitations would be part of the common wealth and subject to the same division.[3] The investors believed that denial of private ownership ensured that workers would be working for the benefit of everyone including investors.

The Governor, William Bradford, found the community to be suffering from confusion and discontent. Distress and demoralization expressed themselves in an unwillingness to work. Bethel notes from Bradford's written comments that much

[1]   T. Bethel, *The Noblest Triumph: poverty and prosperity through the ages*, (New York: St Martin's Griffin, 1998), 34.
[2]   *Ibid.*, 35.
[3]   *Ibid.*, 38.

of the colonist's discontent stemmed not from the 50% tax on wealth, which was to be returned to the investors, but the fact that the Pilgrims felt themselves to be labouring for other Pilgrims.[4] Bradford proceeded to introduce the conversion of communal land into private property.[5] Bethel notes that when land was converted into private property the colonists became responsible for their own actions and that of their immediate families and not the actions of the whole community. Before the individuation of labor it was assumed that if everyone were to end up with an equal share after seven years of work, everyone would presumably do the same work throughout the seven years. The only problem was how to police this.[6] Here we have the familiar free rider problem—why contribute individually if everyone ultimately ends up with the same share regardless. By dividing property into individual or family sized units the worker would enjoy the fruits of his/her labour. This in turn made the system self-policing as colonists became responsible for their own behaviour. The conversion of collective ownership to a system of private property effected an apparent rejuvenation and Bradford was thus able to turn around the fortunes of the colony.

Contrasts with events in Fiji

In Fiji the land tenure system which continues to this day was instituted by the British in the late nineteen hundreds and alleged to correspond to the traditional Fijian system which was said to reflect a form of communal ownership, which was inalienable. In the late nineteen hundreds all lands not already European owned or likely to be occupied by Fijians were placed under control of the *mataqali*, a Fijian kinship group, which by legislative decree was established as the rightful "landowner" in a virtually new land tenure system which, with minor modifications, exists to this day.[7] This move can be better understood through reference to social conditions in Fiji at the time of cession.

Before the British assumed control of Fiji as a colonial unit, the European planter community was rapidly buying up Fijian land with the purpose of creating sufficient acreage for their plantations. Peter France, in *The Charter of the Land*, reports that at the same time the purchase of extensive holdings was also intended to separate the native Fijians from their customary lands so as to create a pool

---

[4] *Ibid.*, 42.

[5] *Ibid.*, 41.

[6] *Ibid.*, 42.

[7] B.H. Farrell and P.E. Murphy, *Ethnic Attitudes Towards Land in Fiji* (Santa Cruz: University of California Press, 1978), 1.

of available, unemployed labour.[8] European acquisition of customary land was facilitated through sales conducted through the agency of the Fijian chiefs. One version holds that in order to protect Fijians and their lands, Chief Cakobau in the eighteen seventies ceded the entire country to England.[9] But the Fijian historian, Asesela Ravuvu, believes that this interpretation is wrong, rather the chiefs were simply responding to British pressure.[10] But regardless of motivation, one researcher, for example, notes that Cakobau could not have performed such an action without "…believing like his colleagues that the lands of Fiji were vested in the ruling chiefs."[11]

In any event, Peter France documents related disturbing events in Fiji. In December 1879, he reports, the Council of Fijian Chiefs met at Bua and agreed with the colonial government that land should be registered and concluded with an affirmation that "…the true and real ownership of land with us is vested in the *mataqali* alone, nor is it possible for any *mataqali* to alienate the land." This statement as, France makes us understand, is a counterfactual. In precession days the members of the Council were freely alienating land to the Europeans.[12] Although customs would vary there was clear evidence of customs that locate the Supreme Chief as the grantor of land and leave the usufruct only, in the hands of the grantee.[13] It is clear the Chiefs had affirmed a statement, which they must have known highly dubious, partly as a result of politics and political pressure from the colonial government. At the time of cession the presumption of chiefly ownership was clearly in evidence as the Chiefs had been selling land and only subsequently informed the commoners that they had done so.[14] It was well known that the Chiefs treated the land as their own and freely sold habitually transferring commoners from one block of land to another without scruple or effective protest form the commoners according to France.[15] However, the colonial Commission of Inquiry accepted the principle both that according to Fijian custom land was inalienable and that absolute alienation of land was unknown—both of which were contrary to all behavioural evidence.

But these principles suited the pre-conceived notions of the colonial power. Sir Arthur Gordon the first Governor of Fiji saw himself as the protector of Fijian

---

[8] Peter France, *The Charter of the Land* (Melbourne: Oxford University Press, 1969), 107.
[9] B.H. Farrell, "Fijian Land: A Basis for Intercultural Variance," in *Themes of Pacific Lands*, M.C.R. Edgell and B.H. Farrell eds., (Victoria: University of Victoria Press, 1974).
[10] See, however, A. Ravuvu, *The Facade of Democracy* (Suva: Reader Publishing House, 1991), 14, who argues that the Fijian chiefs were pressured into an unconditional surrender.
[11] Farrell, *op. cit.*, 113.
[12] France, *op. cit.*, 113.
[13] *Ibid.*, 116.
[14] *Ibid.*, 123.
[15] *Ibid.*, 157.

traditions and customs even though he apparently never spent much time actually investigating or acquainting himself with the presumed traditions. For the colonial masters such as Gordon, communal ownership and the inalienability became the official orthodoxy.

Sir Arthur Gordon was driven by a diverse set of interests and concerns. It is said that he had become alarmed at the encroachments which Europeans had made on Fijian land; and at the same time he was enamored with the Fijian people and their customs and determined to preserve both. It has also been suggested that Gordon was inclined to preserve the customary system of chiefly rule in order to maintain his control through the agency of existing ruling elites, rather than risk imposing an alternative rule with insufficient resources. In any event, he believed that one policy that might promote these ends would involve the registering of all land according to communal tenure as belonging to the *mataqali*, and rendering it inalienable.

But aside from the issue of Chiefly ownership The Native Lands Commission entrusted to investigate and determine *mataqali* ownership found resistance from certain Fijians who often insisted that title was vested in families rather than the *mataqali*. As events unfolded a later governor Sir E.F. Im Thurn, sought to reverse the official orthodoxy, and promoted the idea of individual title as more congruent with the economic challenges and the integration and survival of the Fijians in the modernizing world economy. But France observes that by this point the official orthodoxy had become too entrenched and eventually he abandoned his efforts to reverse course.[16] It was then left to the Native Lands Commission to push through with the registration of land by identification of the 'true' *mataqali* owners with a defined land interest. The Land Commission persevered with the registration despite the fact that their efforts were often resisted or even ignored by the native Fijians. For many Fijians the *mataqali* was either a vague, fairly meaningless concept or often where more fully comprehensible was not regarded as the locus of land ownership. However, those who did not cooperate, by either failing to identify with *mataqali* membership or the notion of *mataqali* land ownership did eventually conform under threat of being rendered landless. Ultimately the registration of presumed *mataqali* land was complete as most of the Fijian localities managed to identify groups, which satisfied the colonial notion of *mataqali* ownership. France concludes that ultimately "…the tenets of orthodoxy, conceived and propagated by a protectionist colonial administration have become ineradicably absorbed into the Fijian national consciousness where they inhibit economic progress by activating all that is reactionary in the society they were designed to serve."[17]

---

[16]   *Ibid.*, 168.
[17]   *Ibid.*, 174.

Our study of the evolution of the land tenure systems at the colonial settlements of Jamestown and Plymouth offer evidence for the view that institutionalized collective ownership is an imposed construct that appears at variance with a more 'natural' tendency towards individual property. Industry, productivity and survival one might say are the natural ends of human beings and the experiences at Jamestown and Plymouth indicate their absence during the periods in which land and property were held in common. When Sir Thomas Dale the first governor arrived in Jamestown in 1611 he found the colonists to be in an idle state and preoccupied with games of bowls when they should have been working to ensure survival. In order to remedy the situation he introduced private ownership thereby investing individuals with the responsibility and motivation to improve conditions by engaging their individual self-interest.

When one compares the above developments with those in Fiji one recognizes the similarities in so far as the original policy of common ownership was also deemed inappropriate and a reversion to private ownership promoted. However, crucially the original efforts at reversing policy failed and common ownership remains in place to this day. Given the nature of counterfactuals we will, of course, never know if native Fijians would have been better off had Governor E.F. Im Thurn succeeded and instituted private individual forms of ownership. Certainly, however, we can reasonably trace many of Fiji's current problems to the peculiarities of the land tenure system.

Later Developments in Fijian Land Tenure

At this stage further discussion is needed to bring us up to date. When in the late nineteen hundreds the *mataqali* was declared the rightful owner of Fijian lands, the colonial government instituted the Native Lands Commission to register and record *mataqali* boundaries. In the 1940s the colonial administration set up the Native Land Trust Board to administer policy, especially the leasing of inalienable *mataqali* land. The latter powerful bureaucratic institution endures to this day.

Today much of the island economy is still heavily dependent on the production of sugar, which is the major export. It is now, however, the Indians who manage most of the sugar production and who supply their labour. On the whole, the Native Fijians have been disinclined to take on these businesses and where they have, they have failed to be competitive with the Indians, with the exception of some island groups.[18]

---

[18] My source of this information is Mr. Steven Retuva, lecturer in sociology, University of the South Pacific.

The system of land tenure, which was instituted by Sir Arthur Gordon, has, to a degree, obviated the need for Fijians to take on this work, as they can exist on rents and subsistence activities. The renting of land, however, is not an unregulated laissez faire matter between the lessor and lessee. In order to set up their businesses the Indians must rent *mataqali* land; however, by law the Indian tenants do not rent directly from the *mataqali*, but rather rent through the Native Land Trust Board (NLTB). Earlier in the twentieth century non-Fijians, especially Indians were leasing directly from Fijians, though the leases had to be negotiated with the members of the owning *mataqali*, and approved by the Commissioner of Lands. Though in practice there is some divergence, the law now requires that leases be negotiated through the NLTB. One of the functions of the Board is to assess the unimproved value of the land and calculate an appropriate rent that is based on a formula that should not exceed 6% of the unimproved value of the land.[19] The *mataqali* does not get all the rent money paid by the renter as the NLTB absorbs up to 25% of the rent in administrative costs. The NLTB assumes control of the disbursements, and deducts administrative costs. Regulations require that after the NLTB deducts its 25%, the three chiefs of the higher level of the hierarchy get 22.5% (the following percentages go to the three principal chiefs of the landowning group from the remainder of the rent—5 percent to the *traga i taukei*, 10 percent to the *turaga ni qali* and 15 percent to the *turaga ni mataqali*) and the remaining members of the *Mataqali* share 52.5%, even if they have localized away from their original *Mataqali*.[20]

The 30-year leases held by the Indian farmers began to expire from 1996 creating genuine uncertainty. This has been a source of anxiety for the Indians whose access to land depends upon both the will of the indigenous Fijians and the policies of the Native Land Trust Board. We will discuss this later in the paper. On the other hand, some Fijian nationalists have demanded the abolition of the NLTB. as well as return of all control to the grass roots village level.[21] This group emphatically declares the NLTB. to be a vestige of colonial paternalism, which is separating Fijians from achieving higher standards of living through higher, rent revenue and greater autonomy in their own affairs. In expanding on their views some claim that PNG and Vanuatu are better off because of greater grass roots control of land.

---

[19] R.G. Ward, "Land, Law and Custom: Diverging Realities in Fiji," in R.G. Ward and E. Kingdon, eds., *Land, Custom and Practice in the South Pacific* (Melbourne: Cambridge University Press, 2000), 221.

[20] *Ibid.*

[21] See Craig Skehan, "Land of Discontent," *Pacific Islands Monthly* 63, 4 (April 1993): 20–23.

Fiji Today

Until the coups of 1987, Fiji was viewed as a pleasant tourist destination with a relatively harmonious accommodation of two dominant groups, the Indigenous Fijians and the Indian descendents. However, the accord, if it existed at all, was tenuous. The political structures favoured the indigenous Fijians but the Indians were generally more successful economically. But it was an illusion to believe that there existed some implicit yet resolved social contract in which political and economic power were neatly balanced between the two groups. The reality was one in which Fijians experienced growing insecurity in the face of Indian numbers and economic success. This insecurity generated a barely constrained desire for maximum political leverage even if this meant undermining the democratic structures of the state.

The point is, however, that political and economic power in reality are never perfectly divisible or distinguishable. It is inevitable that economic power in many respects can translate into political power. In order to be sustainable political power one must find some support within the economic realities otherwise the reigning political authority must revert to increasingly desperate acts and seek to maintain itself by intrigue, coercion, force and ultimately even *coups d'etat*.

In 1987 the electoral victory of the recently formed multiracial Fiji Labour Party (FLP), over the Fijian-dominated Alliance Party, which had led government since independence in 1970, provoked a political crisis that led to the Pacific's first military coup. Lieutenant Colonel Sitiveni Rabuka, number three in the military, detained the elected government of Tioci Bavadra and created a 16 member Council of Ministers, including himself, eleven Alliance MPs (including a former Prime Minister, the late Ratu Sir Kamisese Mara) and four members of the populist Fijian nationalist Taukei movement. Along the way this action was endorsed by the Great Council of Chiefs, the supreme chiefly body representing Fijian indigenous interests.

One might wonder what this all has to do with land tenure. Essentially the election of the FLP in 1987 was interpreted as a threat to the paramountcy of Fijian interests.[22] One can interpret that among these interests, one would include the protection of Fijian interests in land. The etiology of the crisis may well be traced to the fact that native Fijians have been trapped within an antiquated land tenure system, more suitable to the realities of the late 19th century than modern global capitalism, which in turn contributed to their lack of economic empowerment. The situation as conceived by Im Thurn in which an unsuitable land tenure system acts as a constraint on economic growth may well be the reality in modern

---

[22] R. May, "Weak States, Collapsed States, Broken-Backed States and Kleptocracies: General concepts and Political Realities," *New Pacific Review* (2004), 5.

Fiji. In Jamestown and Plymouth individual motivation and productivity became realities when the communal system was abrogated. In Fiji the continuation of the inalienable communal land holding system had sown a false sense of security which stifled motivation. On the other hand, the Indians without having secure interests in land have been forced to rely on personal productivity, which in turn has pushed them to greater economic success. One could argue that as long as the current system continues, Fijians will find themselves increasingly enmeshed in conditions of economic deprivation. Moreover as the economic imbalance persists Fijians will find themselves drawn to desperate acts within the political arena as coups, dubious political maneuvering, human and civil rights abuses and compromised democratic institutions become unavoidable. The abolition of the current tenure system and the substitution of individual entitlements may well be a necessary if not sufficient condition for enhancing Fijian economic performance, thereby redressing the economic imbalance and obviating the need for desperate grabs for increased political power.

These views have been recently echoed by others.[23] Wolfgang Karper argues that de-emphasizing and dispersing government powers is the best guarantee for avoiding the pitfalls of race based top-heavy politics and coercive intervention. This would equip the population of all racial backgrounds for success in the open global economy of the 21st century, he argues. This means a de-emphasis on the collective power of government while devolving as many as possible of the coordinative tasks of government to private competitive decisions of the market. He argues that giving citizens of all classes secure property rights and enforcing the rule of law for all promotes economic growth and fosters civil and economic freedom. These developments should more effectively control arbitrary political power.[24]

He points out that the current reality in which one finds over coordination by government favours the formation of factions and coalitions in which power and coercion, winners and losers are the name of the game. He says that customary small group ownership similar to the *mataqali* system works well in many parts of the world but on two conditions: 1) the owners must face the full costs and benefits of their decisions when deciding what to do with their assets; 2) they need to have clear internal arrangements for making decisions and sharing benefits and losses. As he says, farmers must be able to mortgage their land, raise credit and become self reliant and entrepreneurial. All that is prevented by the presence of the NLTB, which was instituted under Atlee in the 1940s at the behest of the Fabians.

---

[23] W. Karper, "How to learn Racial Harmony? Fiji would Benefit from a New Game," *Pacific Economic Bulletin* 16, 1 (2001) 136–141; Hahendra Reddy and Padma Lal, "State Land Transfers in Fiji: Issues and Implications," *Pacific Economic Bulletin*, 17, 1 (2002): 146–154.

[24] *Ibid.*, Karper, 137.

It amounts to socialization and part expropriation of tribal land. Full property rights need to be returned to the Fijians if they are going to become self reliant and wealthy. Consistent with our recommendations, he is also of the opinion that the current protections only made some sense in the 19th century.[25] But in the contemporary world these protections become a source of political instability. Fijian land controls turn government into a huge political prize and a focus of discords. Indian sugar farmers want long tenure and low rents. Fijians want government to raise land rental and cut the NLTB's high administrative fees.[26] All this might be best solved by removing opportunistic politicians and apathetic bureaucrats from the equation and letting owners and tenants negotiate directly.

If we return to the narrative of military intervention, we will see how land controls have simply become a political prize and a reality from which there appears no escape. As is well documented elsewhere, Rabuka intervened with a second coup in 1987 when he didn't like the way things were going.[27] However, when matters settled down the Rabuka government authorized drafting a new constitution providing for new elections in 1999. Electoral victory went to the FLP (Fijian Labour Party) led by an Indo-Fijian Mahendra Chaudry. In 2000 this government was overthrown by civilian coup led by businessman George Speight who claimed to represent indigenous Fijian interests. Ultimately Speight and other conspirators were arrested and new elections were held in 2001 returning a Fijian led government headed by Laisenia Qarase, who headed the interim administration following the coup.

Mahendra Reddy and Padma Lal have drawn attention to the fact that the new Fijian led government wasted no time pushing through legislation that extended Fijian interests in lands and *a fortiori* NLTB's control of these interests. On April 13, 2002 a land Bill passed in Parliament increasing indigenous Fijian communal ownership to 86.8 %.[28] The New Peoples Coalition Government pushed through the bill, which called for the transfer of Crown land (Schedule A & B) to the native Fijians. Schedule A lands are those transferred to the Crown, which were previously owned by an extinct *mataqali* and Schedule B lands were those deemed unclaimed or unoccupied according to the Land Commission. The fact that the new Fijian led government that came into power after the putsch took no time tabling the above bills, transferring more (Crown) lands into native title and thus enlarging the authority of the NLTB bureaucracy, provides a striking example of the tendency that Karper says needs reversal.

---

[25] *Ibid.*, 138.

[26] *Ibid.*, 139.

[27] See May *op.cit.*, for the references.

[28] Mahendra Reddy and Padma Lal, "State Land Transfers in Fiji: Issues and Implications," *Pacific Economic Bulletin* 17, 1 (2002): 146–154, 149.

Moreover, the total inappropriateness of the legislation can be appreciated in its unavoidable potential to exaggerate an existing land tenure crisis. The current situation in Fiji is one in which the tenant and landowner communities have been unable to resolve the problems faced by the expiring leases.[29] Generations of sugar farming families are facing the prospect of losing their livelihood and becoming landless overnight. This is because there is little alternative for leaseholders outside the native lands. Economically this is creating problems as 25% of the economically active community get income directly from sugar farming. As things stood prior to the passage of this recent bill, 9.5% was government land, 8.2% is freehold and 82.4% ethnic Fijian.[30] It is now the case that 86.8% is ethnic Fijian owned. Farrell and Murphy in the 1970s reported that only 1.7% of the land is owned by Indians.[31] Mahendra Reddy & Padma Lal observe that the move to transfer state land into communal ownership is in defiance of policies to remove barriers to allow the market to operate more efficiently.[32] The Burns Commission of 1960 ruled there is no moral or legal reason for the government to transfer Crown properties to Fijians.[33] Additionally, NLTB will now administer these lands even though there is general hostility towards adding this bureaucratic layer to the process of land mobilization, while the enlargement of this government bureaucracy flies in the face of our recommendations.

As of 2007, the same land issues dramatically continue to influence political events. On December 5, 2006, after weeks of speculation, the commander of the Republic of Fiji Military Forces, Commodore Voreqe Bainimarama announced that he had overthrown the government of Prime Minister Laisenia Qarase in Fiji's fourth military coup in the past 20 years. On January 4, 2007, the military restored the powers of President Ratu Josefa Iloilo, so that he could swear in an interim government with Bainimarama as PM.

Although in some respect these events followed the pattern of previous Fijian coups, there are significant differences. The two coups in 1987 and 2000 overthrew multiracial governments headed by the Fiji Labour Party (FLP) and reinstated the power of the Melanesian aristocracy, while promoting racial divisions between ordinary Melanesians and the Indo-Fijian population in order garner support from non-aristocratic Melanesians.

The most recent coup, however, overthrew Qarase's right-wing Melanesian chauvinist Soqosoqo Duavata ni Lewenivanua party, and the interim government

---

29 *Ibid.*
30 *Ibid.*, 146.
31 Farrell and Murphy, *op. cit.*, 1.
32 *Ibid.*, 151.
33 Burns Commission, *The Report of the Commission of Inquiry into the Natural Resources and Population Trend of the Colony of Fiji* (Suva: Legislative Council Paper No. 1, 1960).

includes members of the FLP, including party leader Mahendra Chaudhry, who has been given the posts of minister for national planning, public enterprises and sugar reform. Chaudhry held the same post in the government of FLP founder Timoci Bavadra, which was overthrown after a month in office in 1987 by Colonel Sitiveni Rabuka. In May 1999 he became prime minister but was overthrown a year later by failed businessman and adventurer George Speight. Chaudhry was imprisoned during both coups. Unlike the Bavadra and Chaudhry FLP governments, the Qarase government is itself the product of a military coup. Furthermore, the dispute betweem Bainimarama and Qarase is over three anti-democratic laws that the latter was seeking to introduce.

It is significant that two of these laws, the Indigenous Lands Tribunal Bill and the Qoliqoli Bill, would transfer land from state ownership to the NLTB, increasing the amount of land under the control of the NLTB to 90%. On state-owned land, Indo-Fijian smallholders have security of tenure for 30 years and rent is fixed at 6% of the land's unimproved value. NLTB land leases are only guaranteed for two years and rents can be increased. The Qoliqoli Bill would also bring marine resources under the NLTB.

Perhaps in an attempt to echo the healing process followed by South Africa, the third law is the benevolent sounding Reconciliation, Tolerance and Unity Bill. This would release Speight and his supporters, possibly with the intention of bringing them into the government

Conclusion

It has been the argument of this chapter that Fiji has been saddled with an inappropriate system of ownership based on communal title of inalienable land. We contrasted this situation with that of the 17th century North American colonies of Jamestown and Plymouth which initially began under similar systems. In the early American cases, the original system of communal ownership was found to stifle individual motivation and productivity explaining poor performance and certain devastating occurrences such as mass starvation. We mentioned the general state of idleness that was obvious before the ownership rights were individuated. In both cases the changeover to individual title was seen to stimulate individual motivation and responsibility, which led to the increased productivity and the enhanced wealth of the colonies. These early colonial experiments at communal ownership should have served to alert future colonists to the economic dangers and social pit falls of institutionalized communal ownership. In point of fact, we argue the same mistakes were made in Fiji and elsewhere in the South Pacific where the communal ownership systems were legally instituted by colonial regimes. But unlike Jamestown and Plymouth these systems have seldom been over turned and in fact have become increasingly entrenched. If we are looking for an explanation for the economic under-performance among indigenous Fijians certainly the colonial legacy, the institutionalized communal land tenure system, deserves attention. At the same time, economic underperformance helps to explain why Fijians have felt driven to extend their control of the state apparatus sometimes by violent undemocratic means and moreover to enlarge the authority of the state at the expense of the private sector. Undeniably Fijians need the opportunity to be individually motivated if they are to be economically successful rather than relegated to being collectors of rental monies. The accounts of the idleness of the colonists in the 17th century American colonies where communal title was institutionalized should alert us to the possible etiology of a contemporary malaise that afflicts much of the South Pacific. For example a former resident of the Southern Highlands Province of PNG, where institutionalized communal title is also firmly in place, gives a chilling account of the current situation in Mendi, the capital of the Southern Highlands—a Province that should be relatively wealthy due to oil revenues from the Lake Kutubu oil fields.

> On Touchdown at Mendi airstrip hundreds of onlookers came to see those of us arriving on the flight from Port Moresby…In the next few or six days of my stay there I was to see a sad and heart breaking place, not the beautiful Mendi of some time ago. First you could see the swarms of people moving around ever so slowly and a great majority of them lining up along the stonewalls. This scenario was repeated day after day. I was told that almost everyone (with the exception of the too old, too young and the disabled) makes it his or her preoccupation to come to town to wander around aimlessly from the morning to late afternoon. (PNG *Post Courier*, August 4, 2004, 12).

Chapter Nine

The Expansion and Restructuring of Intellectual Property and Its Implications for the Developing World

In this chapter we begin with a reference to the work of Hernando de Soto and his characterization of the Western institution of formal property. We note the linkages that he sees between the institution and successful capitalist enterprise. Therefore, given the appropriateness of his analysis, it would appear to be worthwhile for developing and less developed countries to adjust their systems of ownership to conform more closely to the Western system of formal property. Albeit there will continue to exist the problems relating to cultural adjustment that we have already discussed de Soto is arguing that it makes economic sense to align one's system with the Western model of ownership. However, we go on to point out in this chapter that property relationships within the Western system have become subject to redefinition through the expansion of Intellectual Property (IP) rights in ways that ultimately work to the economic disadvantage of the developing and less developed countries.

Western Formal Property

As we pointed out earlier, in the year 2000, the Peruvian economist, Hernando De Soto published a hugely influential book, *The Mystery of Capital: Why Capitalism Triumphs in the West and Fails Everywhere Else*, that linked the success of modern capitalism with the institution of ownership that is prevalent in Western capitalist economies.[1] De Soto made the point that non-western forms of ownership have remained fixated on the material substrate and have been unable to appreciate the economic and transactional aspects of property interests. The latter are said to be the intellectual qualities of property interests associated with commercial potential. According to de Soto, one of the central aspects of the Western ownership

---

[1] Hernando de Soto, *The Mystery of Capital: Why Capitalism Triumphs in the West and Fails Everywhere Else* (Sydney: Random House, 2000)); See also Thomas Bethel *The Noblest Triumph: Poverty and Prosperity through the Ages* (New York: St Martin's Griffin, 1998).

system is the 'fungible' character of the property interest.[2] De Soto speaks of the uncoupling of the economic factors from the rigid physical state that makes the asset fungible—able to be fashioned to suit almost any transaction. This is accomplished through a system of representations. A representation contains the relevant economic features of assets as found in the records and titles of a formal property system. He states, "Whereas assets such as a factory may be an indivisible unit in the real world, in the conceptual world of formal property representation it can be subdivided into any number of portions."[3] Assets can thus be split into shares, and a single factory can be owned by numerous investors, who can divest themselves of the asset without affecting the physical reality of the asset.

However, an aspect of ownership that de Soto does not mention is the distinction between property rights that are "control rights" and those that are said to be "income rights". We will proceed to argue that one also needs to understand the success of Western formal property in terms of its emphasis on the development of the latter category of rights. Control rights consist of the rights to use, possess, manage, alienate, consume (destroy), and modify the owned asset. The income right refers to the rights to transfer and gain income from goods.[4] Although many regard ownership as including both control and income rights in a seamless unity, John Christman has pointed out that these categories of rights ought to be kept separate in any normative treatment of property because they serve different personal and social functions.[5] Control rights are related to the capacity for autonomous existence, he argues. They function to protect interests that agents have in protecting their environment. The exercise of these rights is not contingently conditional upon the preferences and cooperation of others. If one is the legitimate owner, one can, within the limits of the law, freely exercise one's option to use, modify, manage etc. In contrast, rights to income from trade or rent of an asset cannot be exercised unilaterally. The right to income is dependent on the cooperation of others and so the capacity to exercise this right is contingent upon the other's preferences. Others may refuse to trade, for example, or offer unfavorable terms so that no agreement is reached. This right is a contingent right and the content of the right, its value is always indeterminate. Ultimately these rights have a distributive function because they create entitlements that determine the distribution of goods and services in society.

---

[2]   *Ibid.*, de Soto, 56.

[3]   *Ibid.*, 57.

[4]   John Christman, "Distributive Justice and the Complex Structure of Ownership," *Philosophy and Public Affairs.* 23, 3 (Summer 1994): 225–250 at 231; see also John Christman *The Myth of Property* (New York: Oxford University Press, 1994), 13.

[5]   *Ibid.*, "Distributive Justice and the Complex Structure of Ownership," 246.

Returning to the distinction between Western and non-western forms of ownership, one can say that Western forms of ownership are focused on so called income rights, the economic and commercial potential of assets. Non-western systems are far less developed in terms of income rights and emphasize simple control rights. The subject of the control right is the tangible physical substrate. Income rights are the designated intellectual qualities of property as opposed to the tangible physical characteristics that are the subject of control rights. In contrast to the more tangible aspects of physical property, income, as Christman has pointed out, is indeterminate and depends upon a variety of variables and so cannot be given a precise value. Future income is always a prediction or a calculation based on multifaceted evidence, current patterns of behaviour, and relevant statistics subjected to mathematical application. This is also an essential aspect of the fungible character of modern Western ownership to which de Soto refers. Because income can be assigned a potential numerical value it can be divided, subdivided and efficiently traded and substituted. For example, one buys shares in a company that produces widgets, the value of the shares is a calculation based on the projected future earning capacity of the company, although there is always a significant element of uncertainty. But in any case the shares can then be traded and sold for shares in other companies or other forms of more tangible property, real estate for example.

In many instances of ownership we find both control and income rights bundled together in a single holding. But it is also the case that Western formal property allows for a form of ownership in which control rights that refer to the actual use and management of the physical substrate are disassociated from the income rights that refer to the commercial and economic potential of these assets. De Soto emphasizes the availability of a plethora of recorded information that enhances the transactional character of Western forms of property. He underlines the fact that in Western countries property information is standardized and universally available so that what owners can do with their assets benefits from the collective imagination of a larger network of people.[6] However, equally important is the fact that there exist forms of ownership that do not include control rights and extend only to the category of income rights. This is an aspect of Western ownership that we don't find in the institutions that govern property in traditional cultures. Because this form of ownership does not invest an actual right of physical control, it allows for a multiplicity of owners who can transact and convey their various interests without the possibility of creating conflicting control rights. This development of forms of ownership, which separate control and income rights, is significant in the liberation of capital from its material substrate, allowing it

---

6   De Soto, *op.cit.*, 53.

to move swiftly and unimpeded through world markets to finance a multiplicity of projects, developments, enterprises and undertakings to satisfy a world wide demand for a variety of commodities, products and services. This is indeed an important and special feature of Western ownership that has been crucial to the success of modern capitalism.

It would follow, having characterized the system in these terms, that if the non-developed world and the pockets of indigenous peoples within the developed world (in the US, Canada, Australia etc.) are to participate in these wealth generating activities associated with global capitalism, they must modernize their systems of ownership to harmonize with the Western institution.[7] Given financial wellbeing is not unrelated to the autonomy and independence to which these groups aspire, the adoption of the Western forms of property ownership should be seriously considered. At face value it would appear the under developed countries and indigenous people have nothing to lose by joining the system and participating in the benefits of global capitalism. However, one needs to proceed with care in making the recommendation.[8]

IP as Income Rights

Christman explains that the shaping of income rights serves as a mechanism by which economic rent and other unproduced surpluses are distributed to the population.[9] Christman defines economic rent in these terms: "Economic rent is any income from the trade of some good (factor) which is over and above the amount necessary to motivate the person controlling the factor to trade where the surplus is due to fixed supply of the factor (its scarcity)."[10] Societies structure income rights in different ways to reflect foreseeable distribution consequences—

---

[7]   Some, notably James Tully, *Strange Multiplicity: Constitutionalism in the Age of Diversity* (New York: Cambridge University Press 1996) take an opposing view and argue that indigenous societies need to maintain their traditional institutions if they are to maintain their cultural identity.

[8]   We proceed to argue that income rights are being restructured in a manner that works to the disadvantage of the non-Western world. However, even if this were not occurring it is not actually the case that Western interests allow capital to flow unimpeded through global markets. The rejection of Dubai Ports takeover of six US port facilities by US political interests in 2006 indicates that on occasion the rules of the game will be suspended, nor, post the Iraq invasion, can one discount the possibility that on occasion economic agreements will be forced through military intervention.

[9]   John Christman, *op. cit.*, "Distributive Justice and the Complex Structure of Ownership," 249; John Christman, *The Myth of Property*, 13.

[10] *Ibid.*, *The Myth of Property*, 31.

full income rights amount to allowing bilateral trades without regulation or taxation for purposes of directing the distribution of goods, says Christman. Alternatives to full income rights would involve price regulation, wage controls, capital gains and income taxation. Taxation is therefore a government imposed configuration of income rights that results in a distribution of revenue to the government. We will subsequently argue that multinational companies with first world locations are endeavoring to structure income rights on a global basis to realize a distributional pattern of favorable returns from an analogous form of taxation.

If we scrutinize the intellectual property right, particularly patents and to some extent copyrights, it becomes clear that it gains its primary importance as an income rather than a control right. Control rights generally apply to the physical dimension of an asset, which by definition is irrelevant in the case of intellectual property rights. One might argue that copyright law, providing moral rights for authors, which may not have financial implications, and bootlegging rights, which make it illegal to record and disseminate musical performances without consent— regardless of whether there is a financial right in them (for example, folk music or indigenous music)—are issues of control rather than income. One might also argue that with respect to trademark law, derived from heraldry and common law in commercial marks, one is concerned with the primary right to control the use of the mark. Nevertheless we argue that the IP right is primarily an income right because the purpose is not to exercise control over a particular original expression of creativity that has been translated into a tangible medium or a composition of matter but to control the reproduction and sale of reproductions. In fact revenue rather than reproduction is the central interest. For example, Bill Gates' primary concern when you use a copy of Microsoft Windows is that you have paid the licensing fee. In other words, the copyright that attaches to Microsoft windows functions not so much to control distribution but rather as a mechanism to ensure that revenue is returned to the Microsoft corporation every time one acquires a copy of the software. The idea of control implies a power to limit but indeed in most cases the IP right holder has no desire to restrict dissemination and rationally desires the widest possible dissemination in order to augment potential revenue. In point of fact limiting and controlling distribution is entirely irrelevant for the patent or copyright holder so long as each recipient pays the licensing fee.

One might argue, however, that many third world countries and indigenous peoples are primarily interested in controlling distribution of local knowledge, cultural artifacts, crests and music etc. Again, however, the issue for these people is not so much unauthorized access but the fact that Western corporations have often appropriated local indigenous forms of knowledge and creativity, and subsequently acquired IP rights, which have been the means to acquiring revenue, without acknowledging the contributions of the indigenous peoples or sharing the revenue with them. A recent example, would be the efforts of RiceTec inc., a Texan company, to patent Basmati rice, a form of rice cultivated over centuries on the Indian subcontinent.

On the other hand some still argue that the fact that third world and indigenous people are finding their traditional forms of knowledge and creativity appropriated by Western corporations is indeed an argument for enforcement of IP rights. According to this view one should regard IP in a positive light as instruments that could be utilized to protect the achievements of these people. But as one IP expert has pointed out, the patent system offers protection only when the patentee can afford to enforce his rights, which means the enjoyment of patent rights is not so much a question of invention as it is the possession of exceptional wealth.[11] To put the case bluntly the instruments of IP are legal instruments. Enforcement necessitates the participation of legal experts and lawyers. This necessitates a significant expense which a putative IP right holder must be prepared to assume if he is to benefit from the system. For example, in 1997 the Indian government came to the aid of the poor Indian farmers when RiceTec attempted to patent Basmati rice in the US. Their legal efforts were successful in significantly reducing RiceTec's patent claims by demonstrating that most of the strains of rice under consideration were already cultivated on the subcontinenet. Although successful, the legal exercise was particularly costly for the Indian government. However, more recently, Monsanto, the world's largest genetically modified seed company, has been awarded patents on the wheat used for making chapati—the flat bread staple of northern India. The patents give the US multinational exclusive ownership over Nap Hal, a strain of wheat whose gene sequence makes it particularly suited to producing crisp breads. Another patent, filed in Europe, gives Monsanto rights over the use of Nap Hal wheat to make chapatis, which consist of flour, water and salt. Environmentalists say Nap Hal's qualities are the result of generations of farmers in India who spent years crossbreeding crops and collective, not corporate, efforts should be recognised. However there is little hope of the Indian government intervening to prevent the chapati being patented by Monsanto, because it simply cannot afford the legal fees, having spent hundreds of thousands of dollars fighting a US decision to grant a RiceTec a patent on basmati rice in 1997.

To conclude, the IP right primarily functions as an income right because it is overwhelmingly and increasingly used to establish an exclusive claim to the revenue generated by sales of inventions or artistic creations. Given the primary revenue generating function, the enforcement of an IP right, for example a patent, is equivalent to the enforcement of a set of principles that defines a claim on or a share

---

[11] Stuart Macdonald, "Exploring the Hidden Costs of Patents," in Peter Drahos and Ruth Mayne eds. *Global Intellectual Property Rights: Knowledge, Access and Development* (New York: Palgrave Macmillan, 2002): 13–40, 15.

in potential income to be generated from a possible series of future transactions. Although, we have defined the IP right as an income right as opposed to a control right, in actuality we could in effect call all income rights forms of intellectual property. These rights do not prescribe a physical relationship to an existing tangible asset; rather they represent intellectualized claims that have intellectual rather than tangible reality because they refer to potential future earnings that may or may not materialize.

Generally, one can regard the capitalist system as consisting of a body of knowledge or set of principles that defines entitlement to the income generated from commercial transactions. Capitalism, as already stated, recognizes a form of ownership in which income rights are disassociated from physical control. As stated, corporate shares, which don't usually grant physical control over assets, are reducible to claims on future earnings of the commercial organization, or more properly, a claim to a share of the residual income that may or may not materialize after payment of all fixed financial claims. IP rights are often claimed to be necessary to protect the creators' right to control his inventions or creations; in reality, these rights have reference to rights to income, rather than control rights.

We might mention that Christman believes the distinction between control rights and income rights has significant implications for the Western liberal tradition that frequently relates the central value of individual liberty and autonomy with the protection of property rights.[12] Because of the perceived close association between ownership and individual human agency, this tradition tends to regard property as a natural human right, which acts as constraint upon positive law. However, Christman argues that because our capacity for autonomy depends on control rights rather than income rights, one can only legitimately claim that control rights have a moral basis in the human capacity for autonomous existence.

The expansion of IP rights, which are claim rights to future income, is a more recent development and moreover an extension and re-interpretation of income rights. It is true that trademarks existed in Ancient Rome and the laws of heraldry that control insignia have a Medieval origin, and grants of patents can be traced to 16th century England. However, the various controls over cultural products were not considered property. In this sense we can say that to equate these controls with personal property is a more recent development. Moreover what is especially alarming is the diversity of phenomena that is now claimed as intellectual property together with the astoundingly incremental number of patents and copyrights.

---

[12] See for example, John Locke, *Two treatises of Government*, in P. Lazlett ed. (Cambridge: Cambridge University Press, 1967); R. Nozick, *Anarchy, State and Utopia* (New York: Basic Books, 1974); Jeremy Waldron, *The Right to Property* (Oxford: Clarendon Press, 1988) among others.

IP rights, as we said, now primarily exist to impose legal claims on the future earnings from the sale of a specific product (invention or artistic work) regardless of whether the owner of the IP rights (individual or corporate body) actually produces the product. This is an important difference between IP rights and ownership of shares in a corporation, for example. In the latter instance, the claim to future income from the sales of the product or service is contingent upon the acquisition of a financial interest in the company that actually produces a product or provides a service. In the former case, the IP right holder, the holder of a copyright or patent, doesn't need a financial commitment that represents a property interest in the producer or manufacturer of the product in order to have a financial claim on the income.

One begins to see why IP rights can be extremely lucrative; they can act as both a source of control and a tax upon other agents in the market. While shareholders (in bricks and mortar industries) can also make spectacular profits, they can only claim income rights from organizations in which they have a financial commitment. Holders of IP rights can derive income and assert rights to earnings (through licenses and royalties) from companies without financial, or any other form of participatory investment in these companies. If the holder of an IP right so desires, he or she can avoid the production process and allow or license other companies or individuals to produce their products while sharing income from sales and avoiding operational costs. One begins to see why these IP rights have become strongly defended within certain circles in the business community. IP rights when coupled with a successful innovative product realize a form of capitalist nirvana, in which the mere act of licensing other producers realizes a source of unlimited revenue without assuming any share of the operating costs necessary to generate the revenue. In other words, revenue equals profit without the troublesome necessity to deduct any costs.

Let us at this point consider some concrete examples that exhibit the application of these principles. In the early 1990s IBM discovered the financial importance of exploiting patent licensing and deriving revenue through a near costless exercise. In doing so they set an industry standard. At a time when IBM was in a steep decline, veteran employee and lawyer Marshall Phelps convinced the company to raise the fees it charged others for piggybacking on its ubiquitous technology. *Newsweek* reports that a few years later, after forcing licensing agreements on hardware companies IBM was earning an additional $2 billion a year of almost pure profit from licensing revenue.[13] Licenses are often charged as a cost per unit sold or at a few percent of gross sales (not profit), and this license "tax" can become a major burden when several different organizations claim patent violations. Significantly

---

[13] Brad Stone, (Aug. 2, 2004) *Newsweek*, 35.

the famously litigious Microsoft hired pioneer Phelps after he retired from IBM. In recent years Phelps has accelerated the number of patent applications at Microsoft and played a key role in three massive cross-licensing deals with Sun, Siemens and SAP. In 2004 Bill Gates told Wall Street analysts that patents are "a very important part" of the innovation that will fuel the company's future growth, and predicted it would file 3,000 patent applications next year, up from 1,000 several years ago.

Not surprisingly a new line of business has emerged within the software industry that focuses on obtaining and enforcing software patent rights rather than building and marketing usable software systems. Some companies have the backing of large corporations while others are independently enforcing patents.

Having seen IP rights function as effective income rights that need not represent a financial commitment to the productive process, we also need to note the unparalleled expansion of these rights in recent years. For example, in the field of bio-technology, we observe that in October 1992, the U.S. Patent and Trademark Office awarded to a single company, Agracetus Inc., of Middleton, Wisconsin, a patent for rights to *all forms* of genetically engineered cotton—no matter what techniques or genes are used to create them—prompting the following comment from an industry executive: "It was as if the inventor of the assembly line had won property rights to all mass produced goods, from automobiles to washing machines."[14]

Other disturbing extensions of IP rights have occurred in the field of medicine. Recently researchers from Columbia University and the University of Colorado Health Sciences Center developed a test to measure the level of homocysteine, an amino acid. In research on thousands of people, the investigators learned that a high level of homocysteine is correlated with a vitamin deficiency: low levels of cobalamin or folate. Other tests for homocysteine already existed and were used for a variety of medical disorders. But claiming theirs to be an improvement, the researchers applied for a patent. In their application, they argued that because they were the first to recognize that a high level of homocysteine is connected to a vitamin deficiency, they should be allowed to patent that basic physiological fact. Thus they would be owed a royalty anytime anyone used any test for homocysteine and concluded that an elevated level signified a vitamin deficiency. They received U.S. Patent No. 4,940,658—known as the '658 patent—and later licensed it to a third party Metabolite Laboratories. Another company published the biological fact that high homocysteine levels indicate vitamin deficiency. Metabolite sued for patent infringement. The Federal Circuit court, which heard the case, ruled that the company had induced doctors to infringe the patent by publishing the biological fact that high homocysteine levels indicate vitamin deficiency. The court

---

[14] Julio H. Cole, "Patents and Copyrights: do the Benefits exceed the Costs?" *Journal of Libertarian Studies* 15, 4 (Fall 2001): 79–105, 92–93.

also ruled that the doctors had directly infringed the patent by merely thinking about the physiological relationship. It follows that considering publishing and thinking about a law of nature is actionable under patent law contrary to academic freedom, among other things. The decision has set off a rush to the patent office to assert ownership over other scientific facts and methods of scientific and medical inquiry.[15]

The above developments signal the broadening of the application of intellectual property rights beyond the traditional accepted restraints. In the first example we drew attention to IBM and Microsoft and their vigorous use IP rights to enforce income rights and implement favorable agreements with other companies. This needs to be placed in context. Firstly the extension of patents to cover software has only recently been accepted. However it is impossible to distinguish between software and pure mathematics.[16] Thus, when US intellectual property law decided to grant patents to software it contradicted its own fundamental principle that holds that mathematical formulae and algorithms are not patentable. Moreover, because so many patents have been granted it is doubtful whether many of them really satisfy the non-obvious condition. For example, there are more than 170,000 software patents registered with the U.S. Patent and Trademark Office.[17] Moreover, because programmers use similar, if not identical, software and hardware to deal with common needs, certain ideas are independently conceived over and over again. Many of these ideas are patented and so regardless of independent invention, a programmer anywhere can unknowingly be in violation of an existing patent. (Unlike copyright, independent invention is not a valid defense against claims of patent infringement.) It is universally accepted that defending oneself against a claim of patent infringement can cost millions; it is easer just to pay the royalty so that the claimant will go away. It does not take much imagination to realize the implications of this system of IP rights when given global application. Start up companies and programmers in the developed world and elsewhere are exposed to the threat of being closed down if they fail to pay licensing fees.

Our second example indicates a tendency to grant IP rights with broad scope rather than specific application. In the past authorities have tended to narrow the scope to limit the obvious monopolistic rights and to avoid placing too great a constraint on other researchers. For example, Samuel Morse, the inventor we associate with the Morse code, was granted a patent that gave him the exclusive right to the use of electromagnetic power for communications at a distance.

[15] *The Chronicle of Higher Education: The Chronicle Review* 52, 24 (February 17, 2006): B20.
[16] See Ben Klemens, "Software Patents don't Compute," *IEEE Spectrum* (July 2005): 49–50.
[17] Ben Klemens, "New Legal code: Copyrights should Replace Software Patents," *IEEE Spectrum*, (August 2005): 52–53, 53.

The US Supreme court sensibly decided that a legal claim that preempted electromagnetic power for communications at a distance was too broad, and was not enabled by the specification.[18] It is clear that the modern courts are turning their back on this precedent. As in other fields such as information technology, medicine and biotechnology are also experiencing the extension of patent coverage to subject matter previously regarded as un-patentable. In 2001 the United States Supreme Court decided that sexually reproduced plants are statutorily proper subject matter for full utility patents.[19] This decision created full utility patents, which were previously unavailable, for sexually reproduced plants, including basic food stuffs. The decision means that the plant patent holder has the exclusive right to reproduce the plant sexually, i.e., the right to reproduce through seeds. Reproducing a plant by seed (i.e. sexually) can now be a violation of plant patent. Previous US legislation on Plant patents provided limited protection and the exclusive right only applied to asexually reproducing the plant.[20] To put this decision in perspective one notes that the Supreme Court of Canada in contrast has refused to include the higher life forms as patentable subject matter.[21] However, one should not become too sanguine over the Canadian court's decision. In 2004 the same court held that a farmer had infringed a Monsanto patent on a gene by planting seed that produced plants containing the same gene.

There now exists the justifiable fear that the manipulation of the patent system by Monsanto and few other giant agribusinesses, if not checked, will result in their increasing control of the world's food supply.[22] It is already the case that the newly acquired utility patents have been used to close down experimental farms.[23] But perhaps even more alarming in August 2005 it was reported that the Monsanto Company is seeking wide-ranging control over swine reproduction methods in the form of patents which, if granted, would give the corporation economic rights over any offspring produced using those techniques.[24] Besides production methods, Monsanto's applications seek to claim rights to "pig offspring produced by a method ...," a "pig herd having an increased frequency of a specific... gene...," a "pig population produced by the method...," and a "swine herd produced by a method..." respectively. If accepted, these patents would appear to grant

---

[18] Gregory a. Stobbs 'Patenting Propagated Data Signals: What Hath God Wrought?' *IEEE Communications Magazine*(July 2000): 12–13.

[19] J.E.M A.G. Supply, Inc. v. Pioneer Hi-Bred Int'l Inc. 534 U.S. 124 (2001).

[20] Malla Pollack "Originalism, J.E.M., and the Food Supply or Will the Real Decision Maker Please Stand Up?" *Journal of Environmental Law and Litigation* 19, 2 (2004): 500–538.

[21] *Ibid.*, 520.

[22] *Ibid.*, 500.

[23] *Ibid.*

[24] Jeff Shaw, "Monsanto Looks to Patent Pigs, Breeding Methods," *The NewStandard* (Aug. 18, 2005): 5–7.

Monsanto intellectual property rights to particular farm animals and particular herds of livestock. Previous efforts at patenting life forms have exclusively focused on genetically modified organisms. But Monsanto's new patent claims would give the company rights over pigs that have not been genetically modified, and swine that have merely been produced with certain breeding protocols. One expert stated that there is really nothing new to the breeding processes over which Monsanto is seeking to claim exclusive ownership; rather, the patents attempt to privatize farming techniques already in existence for centuries.[25]

In the final example, drawn from medical research, we observe the extension of patents to cover laws of nature, which previously had been regarded as un-patentable. Again, traditionally it has been felt that patenting laws of nature would have unfavorable consequences in terms of the potentially extensive monopolistic powers and the limitations this would impose on other researchers. However, the legal system is now indicating that it is abandoning these sensible constraints. The above examples are significant because they indicate a disturbing trend in which the number of patents and other forms of IP are accelerating with the objective of extracting income from other producers, researchers and practitioners. Moreover not only has there been a tendency towards broadly defined IP rights but the subject matter is also expanding with intellectual property rights now applied to: laws of nature and mathematical formulae; processes that are **not** necessarily non-obvious; and techniques that are already in the public domain. As IP rights extend their application into areas hitherto untouched, they are creating income rights over areas of productive activity and research that have been traditionally immune to this form of interference. At the same time the expansion of intellectual property rights may be distorting the process of innovation. The focus of research and investigation is no longer innovation that enhances competitiveness, but rather the creation of intellectual property rights that function as effective income rights as an end in itself. This is evidenced by the fact that research that cannot create effective IP rights is often abandoned regardless of potential benefit or usefulness. Accordingly we observe, for example, that the pharmaceutical industry will devote disproportionate research resources to life style enhancing drugs, such as Viagra, rather than concentrate on life threatening tropical illnesses, such as malaria, because the former allow greater possibilities for commercial exploitation.

But although we have argued that patents should not be applied to laws of nature one needs also to recognize that it may well be inherently impossible for the patent system to sustain the distinction between natural products and processes that can be discovered, and artificial products and processes that are invented. Both the constructivist approach, which sees all scientific and technological theory as

---

[25] *Ibid.*

socially constructed and the realist perspective that sees all invented processes as discoveries tend to collapse the distinction between the invented and the naturally occurring. According to the former view everything including laws of nature is a social construction, whereas the latter sees the invented procedure as no more than the discovery of a natural process. The former position supports the belief that all discoveries and innovations are human made artifacts and therefore all are patentable, whereas the latter supports the position that nothing can be patentable because man-made inventions fundamentally rely on naturally occurring processes and principles.[26] Thus, limiting patentability to the invention of non-natural processes cannot be achieved conceptually without resolving these difficult philosophical interpretations of science and technology. Perhaps even more important, the sharp distinction between inventors and discoverers is no longer even tenable within the realities of modern scientific research.[27] As one researcher explains, scientific theories have an intrinsic tendency to generality. "Scientific claims apply not only to the objects we know, but to all entities that could exist within a given field. To test the generality of the laws and to find new ones, we have to create new situations and finally new objects. This is not applied science or technology but an inevitable characteristic of advanced theoretical science."[28]

It has been suggested that a more fruitful approach can be achieved by avoiding the distinction between the natural and non-natural and concentrating on the distinction between product and process patents.[29] A patent can be granted for processes, for products or for both processes and products. A product patent is a patent on the product as such and valid for any process that produces the product. It is important to distinguish so called broad patents from product patents. Product patents extend an additional advantage to the right holder. In the case of broad patents, other processes through which the product might be obtained are to a certain extent suggested. A product patent once granted is valid for both known and all potential yet unknown processes.[30] This finds significant relevance in researches related to biotechnology and genomics, areas which have special application in the fields of health care, agriculture and food production.

---

[26] H. Radder, "Exploiting the Abstract Possibilities: A Critique of the Concept and Practice of Product Patenting," *Journal of Agriculture and Environmental Ethics* 17, 3, (2004): 275–290, 279.

[27] E. Vermeersch, "Ethical Aspect of Genetic Engineering," in S. Sterckx, ed., *Biotechnology, Patents and Morality*, 2nd ed. (Aldershot: Ashgate, 2000): 165–171.

[28] *Ibid.*, 169.

[29] Radder, *op., cit.*

[30] *Ibid.*, 281.

We have witnessed in recent times the commercialization of the agricultural science, which has been accompanied by an increased number of patent applications and grants. Academic researchers and institutions have become active in this area. It is in fact stipulated that the results of US federally sponsored research must be patented for commercial purposes.[31] Numerous product patents have been granted for particular genes of plants, animal and human and for parts of plants and animals. The Agracetus example is a case in point in which product patents were granted, one for all genetically modified cotton for any trait and one for any method of modification.

However, product patents fail to satisfy certain stipulations that are integral to the patent system. The first is disclosure and the second is the stipulation that ideas and concepts in themselves are not patentable. In the application for a patent, disclosure is a necessary condition for the granting of a patent. This means in theory a publicly accessible description. In theory the description should make it possible for a skilled colleague to reproduce the invention, which means that it should be sufficiently detailed so as to enable reproduction. The description allows other individuals and research organizations to build upon the patent holder's research without having to establish the same information independently. But by definition an invention protected by a product patent can never be sufficiently disclosed because this would require foreknowledge of all the different ways in which the product could be produced in the future. This relates to the important point that a product patent once it has been granted is valid for any known or unknown process that may produce the product. This allows the holder rights on conceptual and as yet unknown potential future developments. In effect what is being protected by the claims of the patent is not a concrete technological invention but rather an abstract conceptual or theoretical possibility.[32] Thus, for example, if another innovator discovers a more efficient and perhaps safer method or process for realizing an invention, which is subject to product patent, the innovator will not be free to market the product because it falls under the original patent holder's rights.

There are two moral issues that are raised by these facts. Firstly from a consequentialist utilitarian perspective, patents are supposed to encourage innovation that is socially beneficial. However, in fact product patents stifle innovation. There is no motivation for a researcher to work and spend time enhancing a production process, if the rights to such a process have been potentially anticipated by the original product patent. Secondly, a product patent undermines the moral argument based on merit. Richard M. De George has pointed out that within the economic system of free enterprise those who invest effort and or

---

[31] *Ibid.*, 277.
[32] *Ibid.*

money in the development of ideas that create innovations that are beneficial to others, should have the opportunity to recover the investment and possibly make a profit.[33] It would, therefore, be unfair and unjust for others to take the result, market it as their own, and profit from it without having spent comparable money or time in the development of the product. Thus IPRs are argued to be necessary in order to exclude others from free riding on the investments, labor and ingenuity of the innovator. Because of the crucial distinction between the claims of the patent and the specification of the invention, the holder of a product patent has rights to future discoveries and new creative processes that realize the same product, which ultimately means that the original patent holder is rewarded for the achievements of others, thus undermining the argument that the IPR is justified as a reward for investment and intellectual labor.

What we see therefore is that if the putative IP right holder of a product patent can successfully define the product itself in sufficiently broad terms, he/she will effectively stifle valuable research and potential patent rights of competitors. Projected globally this strategy would also exclude potential competitors from the developing and less developed world. The effect, therefore, would be to carve out a domain of information technology in which an original patent holder retains a form of sovereignty with broad powers. These powers entail the ability to limit the entry of competitors and also claim royalties from those who endeavor to produce the patented product by known or as yet unknown processes.

It should be noted that product patents are particularly relevant to the patenting genetically modified organisms. With respect to the patenting of the products of biotechnology the problem of reproducibility has in the past been a problem within the European context. Theoretically the repetition of the process of making has been a condition that must be met in order to obtain a patent. However, the German Supreme Court decided that product protection is always possible for organisms thus removing the required repetition of the process of making.[34] Product patents apply not only to the original genetically modified organism— thus overcoming the reproducibility objection—but also extend ownership rights to all future organisms reproduced by the natural reproduction. It is in this way that product patents have a revolutionary impact on traditional farming practice. Farmers who sow seeds from genetically modified plants are prevented from selling or using the seeds resulting from the harvest.[35]

Nevertheless, some argue that with both copyrights and patents, the monopoly is considered acceptable on the basis that it extends only for a limited time.

---

[33] Richard De George, "Intellectual Property and Pharmaceutical Drugs: An Ethical Analysis," *Business Ethics Quarterly* 15, 4 (2005): 549–575.

[34] G. Van Overwalle, "From Law to Ethics," in S. Sterckx, ed., *Biotechnology, Patents and Morality*, 2nd ed. (Aldershot: Ashgate, 2000): 197–206, 204.

[35] Radder, *op. cit.*, 281.

However, one also needs to recognize that a combination of ingenuity and legalistic maneuvering on part of groups pushing for stronger IP rights has realized ways to extend the life of the patent and copyrights beyond acceptable limits. For example the TRIPS agreement (Trade Related Aspects of Intellectual Property Agreement) initiated by the World Trade Organization that requires member states to enforce IP rights under the threat of sanctions requires WTO member states to grant patents on all relevant classes of products (including medicines), to provide protections for a minimum of 20 years. Thus a product, which has been patented in one member state gains an additional 20 years of patent life within another member state, when granted a patent in that state. Also with respect to pharmaceuticals, the patent system often generously allows new patent rights to certain new uses, formulations, delivery systems, combinations of existing products, and minor variations of existing chemical entities.[36] Also given the rapidity of technological change, a twenty year patent proves much more than sufficient to for the life of an effective monopoly. With respect to copyright, the original Berne convention, which sought uniformity in copyright laws in 1886, required that most types of work be protected for a period of the life of the author, plus a further fifty years. In recent years the United States and the European Union have changed their laws to increase the term to life of the author plus 70 years. More recently the United States has embarked on a "TRIPS Plus" agenda and is requiring selected countries to adopt its life plus 70 years formulation.[37] This means that education materials and software, for example, remain private property and inaccessible for an additional twenty years. It certainly conveys a misconception to refer to these extended periods of IP protection as a "limited amount of time".

Global Implications

One concludes that the capitalist system of ownership is being restructured through the expansion of IP rights. This has strong implications for the developing world and its acceptance of the modern system of Western property, given the direction in which the institution is being redefined by IP rights. We will proceed to explain how the broadening of the scope of IP rights, which provides the

---

[36] Brook k. Baker, "India's 2005 Patent Act: Death by Patent or Universal Access to Second— and Future—Generation ARVS?" *Health Gap Global Access Project*, Sept 19, 2005 (www. healthgag.org.).

[37] Alan Story, "Copyright, TRIPS and International Educational Agenda," in P. Drahos and R. Mayne eds. *Global Intellectual Property Rights: Knowledge Access and Development*, (New York: Palmgrave Macmillan, 2002): 125–143, 130.

foundation for the application of income rights, is ultimately working to the disadvantage of the third world countries that are struggling to join and benefit from the global economy.

Significantly the US, Europe and Japan have been the leaders in patenting and copyrighting within the information technology, electronic, pharmaceutical, entertainment, medical and bio-technology industries. These are also areas in which these countries have been leading innovators and producers. Over the last two decades these countries especially the US have been pushing for the international recognition of their IP rights and global agreements that sanction countries that do not enforce these rights.

The point is that IP rights, while projected as embodiments of free market activities can also be seen as forms of policing, interference and intervention. As we pointed out copyrights and patents through royalties and licensing agreements act as a tax upon other producers. The reported spectacular profits realized by IBM in the 1990s, 2 billion a year through licensing alone indicate the nature of an extremely lucrative business or system of privileged entitlement that eschews production costs. If we think of this IP tax projected world wide, then one is talking about a multibillion dollar business imposed on the technologically challenged developing world in favor of companies with first world locations. However, the collection of this tax on unauthorized operations that are alleged to make use of IP requires policing and enduring vigilance. Because world wide enforcement from the centres of technological innovation is impossible, there has been movement to manipulate international bodies and agreements between nations to realize the effective enforcement mechanism. Accordingly we have seen the implementation of the TRIPS (Trade Related Aspects of Intellectual Property Agreement) by the World Trade Organization that requires member states to enforce IP rights under the threat of sanctions. Moreover governments are prohibited from ignoring IP rights even in cases in which the welfare of the country is an issue.

It is worthwhile replaying the political and intellectual history that led to the implementation of the TRIPS agreement. As summarized by A.S. Oddi, industry groups (lobbyists) in developed countries, particularly in the United States, persuaded a receptive government that their intellectual property was being "stolen", "pirated" "counterfeited" and "infringed" by unscrupulous people in certain countries and this was to the detriment of intellectual property exporting countries.[38] These industry interests argued that the problem stemmed from inadequate intellectual property protection in these foreign countries. Although the World Intellectual Property Organization presumably had jurisdiction over international intellectual property matters, these interests had become dissatisfied

---

[38] A.S. Oddi, "Nature and Scope of the Agreement: Article: TRIPS _ Natural Rights and a Polite Form of Economic Imperialism," *Vanderbilt Journal of Transnational Law* 29 (1996): 415–429.

with the WIPO's failure to act on their concerns. Evidently the developing countries within the WIPO did not share the same sense of urgency. GATT, General Agreement on Trade and Tariffs, which has since morphed into the WTO, provided a much more satisfactory venue because the leverage of trade and access to markets could be used against developing countries to enforce compliance. The developed countries strategically shifted the issue from the WIPO to the more accommodating GATT with intellectual property now fundamentally acquiring trade-related aspects. In fact, they argued, these aspects were of such importance they could not be left to the domestic policy of individual countries but must be imposed as international minimum standards.

The aim of TRIPS was to secure two things. First a broad and minimal standard of protection across a wide range IPRs, and even more significantly, direct and legal responsibility for the enforcement to fall on the signatories.[39] Developing countries are faced with an unpleasant option either forego the trade advantages of WTO membership, or work on the TRIPS package. With regard to the latter requirement any country that becomes a member of the WTO is subject to monitoring and review systems which oblige the WTO member to inform the relevant authorities of their progress in TRIPS implementation and more significantly, once transitional measures expire, it is possible *in extremis* for a member to be punished for non-compliance following complaint by another. Ultimately failing settlement under the procedures of the Dispute Settlement Body, WTO agreement allows a complaint country to implement trade sanctions where authorized by the DSB.[40]

In order to link IP rights to matters of international world order, groups dominated by multinational corporations employed the rhetoric of natural rights and natural law. According to this linkage IP rights are not "privileges" granted by governments guided by instrumental concerns but rather a recognition of natural rights with universal application that must be respected throughout the world community.[41] The argument is highly suspect because as John Christman points out, income rights, which we identify with IP rights, are unrelated to the issue of human autonomy that founds our belief in natural rights. Also we would argue that the natural rights argument that follows the Lockean property right based on the mixing of labour fails to satisfy in the case of IP rights.[42] Locke of course

---

[39] See Gary Lea, "Digital Millennium or Digital Dominion? The Effect of IPRs in Software on Developing countries," in P. Drahos & R. Mayne eds. *Global Intellectual Property Rights: Knowledge Access and Development*, (New York: Palmgrave Macmillan, 2002): 144–158, 152.

[40] *Ibid.*, 153.

[41] *Ibid.*

[42] Lockean property right—of mixing labour was enshrined in the French patent law of 1791, and the UK patent reform campaign of the 1820s used it as an argument by JR McCulloch. "If anything can be called a man's exclusive property, it is surely that which owes its birth entirely to combinations formed in his own mind, and which, but for his ingenuity, would not

was speaking of the acquisition of physical holdings not intellectual holdings and his argument works well in this context because the claim only extends to the particular product the claimant owner has actually modified and altered through his/her labour. In contrast the IP claimant demands property rights in the products of another's labour according to an allegation that these products resemble the claimant's original products or make use of ideas and techniques which originated with the claimant. Certainly one needs an additional argument, beyond a simple labour theory of original acquisition, to establish that the IP claimant possesses not only a property interest in his/her immediate products but also in the products of another's productive activity, i.e., labour.

Moreover, natural rights have traditionally been defined as having universal application because theoretically they are assumed to be universally recognized by all rational agents. In the case of IP protection for software, in 1984 the Japanese originally proposed *sui generis* protection which featured a short protection period followed by compulsory licensing provisions. At that time the US trade representatives remonstrated with the Japanese demanding that the form of protection should be copyright and that the level of protection should conform to US law. The Japanese subsequently adjusted their policy accordingly.[43] These facts give undeniable evidence that the rhetoric of natural rights fails to reflect the reality in which there is a remarkable absence of universal a-priori recognition or consensual agreement on matters relating to IP. The initial disagreement between the Japanese and Americans and the lack of consensual agreement on these matters firmly indicates that IP issues concern positive rather than natural law. Moreover, the confrontation between the Americans and the Japanese over IP protection gives further indication that the push for global IP rights that conform to American guidelines is not the product of purely judicial considerations relating to international law or accepted legal precedent. Rather the rationale behind the implementation of these rules is clearly political rather than legal. This conclusion is undeniable given a history in which the implementation of these rules has been driven throughout by powerful localized corporate interests that benefit from their imposition on global community. Significantly one notes that when TRIPS was introduced in the following decade it was mandated that software be copyrighted.

---

have existed." Sam Ricketson, *Intellectual Property: Cases, Materials and Commentary* (Sydney: Butterworths, 1994), 563. The Lockean argument was accepted in relation to the justification of copyright. This was seen as a right of return on the labour (Ricketson, 72–73). The labour justification was roundly criticised at the time of the patent reform campaign on the basis that "No inventor can, in fact, have any natural right to prevent another person from making and using the same or similar invention, and therefore the law does not recognise any right or property whatsoever in an invention that is not made subject to a grant by patent." (Hindmarch cited in Ricketson, 563).

43 See Gary Lea, *op. cit.*, 148.

As against the natural right tradition with respect to personal property, we argued in the first chapter property rights are not pre-existing facts or discovered contingencies but rather conventions that society creates and whose legitimacy depends upon societal consent. Ideally, we argued these entitlements should be linked to certain general principles which have overall social consensus. It would be illegitimate to claim that IP rights, which have been established in a particular jurisdiction, have universal application beyond that jurisdiction, which need not be based on the consent of the parties that make up these other political jurisdictions.[44]

Perhaps a more convincing argument for IP is one based on fairness which sees other producers free riding and benefiting from the research and efforts of the inventor and failing to compensate the inventor or innovator in the absence of IP rights. We can begin to answer this argument by considering the meaning of the term 'innovation' that is supposed to found our believe in the IP right.

IP protection is all founded on the very dubious principle that intellectual phenomena can be appropriated as personal property. Intellectual property is a relatively new notion and IP rights are a relatively recent extension of our notion of income rights, i.e., rights to income that flow to the individual in virtue of the fact that one holds a property interest. In the near past, and perhaps still in the East, knowledge or the fruits of creativity (art, design) were and are not regarded as someone's "property". The inventive, creative individual or artist was merely a conduit through which the muse of inspiration or even divine grace flowed. Discoveries, inventions, texts, works of art and music, designs etc., belonged to the community and could usually be replicated freely. Although one must recognize that controls were not entirely absent, since the origins of copyright are in censorship, and the control of dangerous books and heresy, however, what is new is the utilization of the IP as an income generating mechanism which imposes claims on the revenue of other agents.

Recent scholarship also recognizes the anomaly that IP rights represent. Even the most innovative breakthroughs depend ineluctably on knowledge and information contributed over centuries by other human researchers and developers.[45] In other

---

[44] The issue of consent is indeed interesting. Even though many developing countries have agreed to the TRIPS agreement that mandates legislation on IP that largely follows US and EU guidelines there is a strong element of coercion in so far as membership in the WTO is not possible without agreeing to implement the TRIPS guidelines. Initially developing counties that had WTO membership were induced to agree to TRIPS because they were promised increased investment and greater access to Western markets for their agricultural products. Moreover, despite their reservations, the developing countries were also subject to a well organized campaign by the developed countries to push through TRIPS guidelines.

[45] P.H. Werhane and Michael Gorman, "Intellectual Property Rights, Moral Imagination and Access to Life-Enhancing Drugs," *Business Ethics Quarterly* 15, 4 (2005): 595–614.

words the technological advance is never *sui generis*. It is part of a chain of technological advances that reach back in time to the works of countless other inventors and creative individuals. In this sense every innovative contribution belongs to a collective human endeavor in which many individuals have played their part, including support groups, institutions, donors, volunteer subjects etc. For example, the discovery of DNA required centuries of research to become a possibility, it did not simply emerge full blown from the minds of Watson and Crick, without antecedents. The discovery of DNA and years of subsequent research were then necessary to realize the various human genome projects. It makes little sense to regard the latest scientific or technological achievement as exclusively belonging to the efforts of a single individual or particular corporate team of individuals. Without exception every significant intellectual discovery or creation has many ancestral "owners". But it is this erroneous idea of sole responsibility that has been implicitly promoted as the basis of an exclusive entitlement to the income that flows from any productive process that relies on information or knowledge subject to IP rights.

Further examples also underline the inadequacy of this approach. One might draw attention to the controversial pharmaceutical industry, which has also defended its profit taking through the overly simplistic approach of equating the latest scientific advance with sole proprietorship. For example, the drug AZT has been a hugely profitable and very effective drug for HIV. Burroughs Wellcome (now GlaxoSmithKline) claimed the drug as their product, patented it, and has profited from its success. However, the remedy was first synthesized by Dr. Jerome Horwitz at the Detroit Institute of Cancer Research as a cancer drug but never patented because it proved to be ineffective for cancer. It was tested at the National Institutes of Health for efficacy on human subjects after it was rediscovered at Burroughs Wellcome (now GlaxoSmithKline). Other researchers played important roles in first isolating the compound, and testing the drug on other non-human subjects.[46] The point is that a number of individuals and organizations played key roles in the development of this important remedy yet a single organization claims exclusive ownership and therefore income rights to the sales of the drug.

Although, we are arguing that innovation needs to be seen in context and thus requires that we also recognize earlier contributions and therefore contributors other than the patent holder, it is still the case that the patent or copyright holder, in many cases, has done research and work, which has realized a significant advance. If IP rights were not available others would simply free ride on this research and benefit without recognizing or compensating the innovator or inventor.

---

[46] *Ibid.*, p. 601.

The problem with this argument is that it sets up a false dilemma. In other words if we don't have strong IP rights, and a strong patent system for example, then innovators will unfairly be denied their compensation. However, as Richard Stallman has pointed out with respect to software, software programmers can be compensated for their work in a number of ways without having to resort to IP protection.

It is also worth noting that the ascendancy in the authority and emerging dominance of IP rights through TRIPS should be appreciated in the context of earlier developments in the United States. One accepts that the viability and meaningfulness of any system of rights is dependent up the existence of institutions and formal mechanisms designed to enforce a specific system of rights. In 1982 the US Court of Appeals of the Federal Circuit (CAFC) was established as a specialist body to deal with the growing complexity of patents and their subject matter. But the court was also the product of powerful interest groups. A group of large high technology firms and trade associations in the telecommunications, computer and pharmaceutical industries were essentially responsible for the creation of CAFC, believing that a court devoted to patent cases would better represent their interests. This indeed proved to be the case. Between 1982 and 1987, the CAFC upheld 89 percent of district court decisions dealing with patent validity whereas only 30 to 40 percent had been upheld previously.[47] It has been commented that the result has been to increase the value of an American patent.[48]

Moreover the creation of CAFC represents a significant institutional change that gave increased reality and meaning to IP rights. In effect it represented a redistribution of power in favor IP right holder over IP right users. With institutional change we have also seen the development of a vocabulary and discourse that has accompanied the increased enforcement of IP rights. For example, we see IP right infringement commonly referred to as piracy, which originally meant a robbery, kidnapping or violence committed on the sea. Strengthening the mechanism of enforcement has meant a consistent enforcement of these alleged rights with the result that rules that apply to intellectual property become gradually internalized and individuals become persuaded that they are in some sense "natural".[49]

Michel Foucault has made considerable effort to remind us that institutional change and changes in discourse reinforce one another. This can be documented in the appearance of new power relationships. In speaking of the emergence of the modern prison system in the early 19th century, and the resulting illegalities and mechanisms of power, Foucault has commented,

---

[47] Stuart Macdonald, *op. cit.*, 29.
[48] *Ibid.*
[49] See H.L.A. Hart, *The Concept of Law*, (Oxford: Clarendon Press, 1961), 85–92.

That these mechanisms are applied not to transgressions against a 'central' law, but to the apparatus of production—commerce' and industry'—to a whole multiplicity of illegalities, in all their diversity of nature and origin, their specific role in profit and the different ways in which they are dealt with by the punitive mechanisms. And that ultimately what presides over all these mechanisms is not the unitary functioning of an apparatus or an institution, but the necessity of combat and the rules of strategy.[50]

Similarly for our purposes the expansion of the illegalities associated with the use of information technology can be seen as a mechanism to enforce revenue claims and similarly extract commercial profit. Accordingly one researcher notes that the increased scope and scale of patent protection as a result of the creation of CAFC effected a shift in corporate strategy. As an example he mentions the IBM case (already discussed) and also the behaviour of Texas Instruments, a company which once was liberal in its cross-licensing arrangements with competitors but which now is particularly litigious. Its most profitable product line has now been patent royalties and in some years the company's licensing fees exceed its operating income.[51]

One can conclude that having imposed this power structure within the US it became appropriate to impose the relationship globally. The TRIPS agreement can be seen to have its logical antecedents in the creation of CAFC. In any event, this is the intellectual and political history, which has realized the WTO as a tool for the global enforcement of the developed world's Intellectual property rights. At the same time, TRIPS, the enforcement mechanism for IP rights, has been supplemented through various free trade agreements between individual countries.[52]

The reality is that Western forms of property have played a key role in revolution of wealth generation that people such as de Soto regard as the "triumph" of modern capitalism. The less developed world would do well to adopt the system if it wishes to participate. However, at the same time, one needs to be aware that the system is also being tilted in favour of the Western enterprises at the expense of the developing and the undeveloped world. The promotion of intellectual property rights through the push to acquire ever more patents and other instruments of IP coupled with the broadening of these rights to cover areas previously untouched is designed to create an income imbalance in which wealth will continue to drain from the poorer countries to Western localities. In more ancient times the

---

[50] Michel Foucault, *The Birth of the Prison System*, trans. Sheridan, A. (New York: Vintage Books, 1979), 308.

[51] Stuart Macdonald, *op. cit.*, 29.

[52] For example, in 2004 Australia developers of open source software expressed their wariness of the free trade agreement (FTA) struck with the US, saying it would lead to the acceptance of American-style patent and intellectual property laws which, in turn, would cripple the local software industry. See Sam Varghese, *Melbourne Age*, (March 12, 2004), 41.

imperial power would directly impose taxes upon subject peoples and acquire their wealth in this manner. In contemporary times a softer form of imperialism has been introduced. Instead of seizing jurisdiction over physical territory, first world corporations are seizing intellectual territory and claiming title over ideas, natural laws, mathematical algorithms, and even established techniques and processes. In doing so the developed world is demanding that foreign ownership systems conform to its institutions and recognize the established intellectual property interests as having universal application. These developments are empowering first world organizations to impose intellectual property taxes on entities in the third world that are seeking to become productive and participate in this revolution in wealth generation. In these circumstances, third world companies have few options. If they refuse to pay these taxes, and utilize technology, ideas or procedures now subject to IP rights, the countries in which they operate will be heavily sanctioned by the World Trade Organization and excluded from the networks of trade and commerce that that are the source of this global prosperity.

As one authority notes,

> ...there is no recognition that the legacy of colonialism and the power of multi-nationals has, to a significant extent, created the highly unequal world knowledge system...There is a kind of OPEC of knowledge in which a few rich countries have a great deal of control over how and where books are published, the prices of printed materials, and the nature of international exchange of knowledge ...There has, in fact, been relatively little expansion in the number of knowledge producing countries— and the price of entry into the cartel increases as the cost and complexity of knowledge production goes up.[53]

In the first part of this chapter we discussed the expansion of income rights that has been founded on putative IP claims. Increased legal protection of these alleged rights is not driven by a disinterested recognition of legitimate moral claims but by political and economic pressure. One legal scholar has already noted the political dimension to one of the relevant recent decisions of the US Supreme Court.[54] In the later sections we mention that corporate interests have pressured their governments to give these income rights a global reach. The TRIPS agreement that has been implemented by the WTO can be understood as a product of this intense lobbying.[55] The TRIPS agreement seeks global recognition of IP rights and specifically the rights to revenue claimed by certain high tech industries. In 1999 the net surplus of the US companies from the global trade in royalties and

---

[53] P. Altbach, "The Subtle Inequalities of Copyright," in P. Altbach, ed., *Copyright and Development: Inequality in the Exchange* (Chestnut Hill Mass.: Bellagio Publishing, Network Research and Information System, 1995),2–6, 6.

[54] Malla Pollack, *op. cit.*

[55] Oddi, *op. cit.*

licenses was 23 billion. As one author has commented "...the main global function of TRIPS is the protection, expansion and longevity of these massive copyright and patent revenues."[56]

However, it is worth mentioning that earlier before the arrival of TRIPS there had been moves to reduce the commercial barriers to information technology. In the 1970s under the aegis of the United Nations, specifically the UN Conference on Trade and Development (UNCTAD), efforts were initiated to create an international Code on Technological Transfer. This would have, *inter alia*, controlled or eliminated certain practices of royalty pricing and restrictive terms which had hampered the take-up of advanced technologies in developing countries. However progress was ultimately opposed by the hardening of attitudes among developed countries and work stopped in 1985. Matters became worse as developed countries began to rely increasingly on the revenue from intangibles such as services and IPRs, which led to tighter rather than looser controls over trade activities in developing countries.[57]

Nevertheless article seven of TRIPS declares that the protection and enforcement of intellectual property rights should contribute to promotion of technological innovation and the dissemination of technology to the mutual advantage of the users of technological knowledge. Defenders of intellectual property rights and in particular the patent system argue that the granting of a patent represents the outcome of a bargain between the inventor and society by which society grants the inventor certain rights with respect to his/her invention in return for disclosure of whatever he or she has invented. Thus the patent's ideas can be spread for use by all through the publication of details of the invention. In this way, patents provide an alternative to people protecting useful ideas through secrecy. But as one researcher has pointed out, only in theory does the patentee provide society with information concerning the invention. In practice he or she discloses the information required by the patent system, not the information required by society to replicate or develop his/her invention.[58] Ultimately as he says the patent specification is a legal document not a source of information for innovation. For example, statistical evidence indicates that small firms for a variety of reasons find patent specification too limited and of little use as a source of information.[59] The view that patents benefit small firms through the publication of innovation by means of the patent system is illusory. The author states that the same reasoning applies to underdeveloped countries which are supposed to benefit from the TRIPS agreement.

---

[56] Story, *op. cit.*, 131.
[57] Gary Lea, *op. cit.*, 151.
[58] Macdonald. *op. cit.*, 15.
[59] *Ibid.*, 17.

Throughout the text we have discussed the link between inventiveness, economic prosperity and patents. There is therefore no question that the system provides benefits but the issue is who benefits. Often those who reap the benefits from the patent system are not those who incur most costs. Benefits one can say are closely focused and costs are widely distributed. Possession of significant wealth is a pre-requisite for benefit because of expenses and legal fees that must be covered in order to gain a patent. Moreover, the patent system offers protection for the patentee only when the patentee can afford to enforce his/her rights. This means those who can benefit from the system are those possessing exceptional wealth. For those who do not already possess sufficient resources a patent is of little use. For example, under resourced small firms acquire unwanted costs through the system because they find it necessary to conduct a significant percentage of patent searches simply to check for possible patent infringement. It is very much the case that the extension of this system through the mechanism of TRIPS works to the disadvantage of the of the underdeveloped and less wealthy countries in a manner very similar to the way in which it disadvantages small firms within a national economy.[60]

Having stated that promotion of IP rights with universal application adversely affects the non-Western world we should consider the impact in more specific terms. Professor Oddi, writing on the impact of TRIPS, which has transformed patents from domestic privileges to universal entitlements, argues that the greatest effect will be on the newly industrialized countries (NICs).[61] The NICs are said to include countries such as: Brazil, India, Malaysia, Mexico, Singapore, the Republic of Korea and Taiwan for example. He argues that these countries were the basic targets of TRIPS because they had the industrial capacity of replicating foreign technology and were evidently competing effectively with the creators of this technology. The TRIPS agreement reduces access to technology and thus seriously weakens the ability to compete (for NICs) because they are prohibited from replicating products subject to IP rights. Moreover reduced access also prevents them from mastering the technological expertise thus blocking future ability to compete in the area of research and technological innovation. The technological hegemony of the West is thus protected and can be extended indefinitely through the ability to limit access to the latest technology and techniques. Ultimately the implementation of dubious IP rights with universal application is implicitly designed to secure the future for Western companies. One foresees that Western multinational corporations will continue to strive to appropriate the world's intellectual heritage in order to secure a continuous flow of potentially cost free revenue.

---

[60] *Ibid.*, 35.
[61] Oddi, *op. cit.*

With respect to the lesser developed countries (LDCs), which lack the industrial capacity to copy foreign technology, TRIPS ensures an import monopoly in these countries for the exploitation of patented products. Prof. Oddi opines that such a monopoly is not particularly significant for developed countries because consumers in the LDCs lack disposable income. Nevertheless one observes, for example, that the ubiquitous Microsoft software is everywhere in the developing world and the company is turning healthy profits from individual and institutional licenses. Given the spectacular profits that Microsoft has been able to realize it would be naïve to underestimate the costs to poorer countries in acquiring this overpriced software (i.e., revenue that significantly exceeds costs of production).[62] Moreover, Microsoft regards potential revenue from third world sources very seriously. Microsoft has recently excoriated governments of South East Asian countries that have adopted open source software. The multinational software giant has issued a thinly veiled threat claiming that countries that use the opens source system Linux risk sanctions from the WTO for 228 alleged patent violations.[63] Of course, they are referring to US software patents, many of which controversially cover fairly obvious procedures and mathematical algorithms that can be independently conceived.

Finally so called free trade agreements represent another form of Trojan horse which allows US copyright and patent law to be imposed on other nations. For example, in 2004 Australia developers of open source software expressed their wariness of the free trade agreement (FTA) struck with the US, saying it would lead to the acceptance of American-style patent and intellectual property laws which, in turn, would cripple the local software industry.[64]

---

[62] On April 5, 2004 Judges in the US state of Nebraska re-activated a class-action lawsuit against Microsoft Corp. The action claims Microsoft over-charged customers for Windows 98 by setting the cost artificially high, and seeks $425 m in damages. E-mail is likely to form the basis of much evidence in the case, including a 1997 communication reportedly sent by Microsoft group vice president Jeff Raikes to billionaire Warren Buffet, seeking his investment in Microsoft. Raikes told Buffet that some observers had likened Windows to a "toll bridge" adding the company is a "90% + margin business." Buffet did not invest in Microsoft, "US Judges Re-Activate Microsoft Antitrust Case," *ComputerWire*, (March 22, 2004), Issue 4883.

[63] Steve Ballmer, Microsoft's CEO, warned Asian governments they could face patent lawsuits for using the Linux operating system instead of its Windows software. Ballmer stated that Linux violates more than 228 patents, but significantly did not provide any details on the alleged violations, which the Linux community disputes. *The Gulf Today* (November 17, 2004): 23.

[64] Sam Varghese, *Melbourne Age*, (March 12, 2004): 41.

Taxation as slavery

Robert Nozick, as mentioned, was extremely critical of any interference in the market in which the free transfer of holdings was disturbed. He argued that any interference in terms of restricted or coerced transfers is immoral. This includes an imposed system of government taxation, which he views as a coerced transfer. One might recall Robert Nozick's view in *Anarchy, State and Utopia* that taxation, of the redistributive sort in which modern states engage in order to fund the various programs of the bureaucratic welfare state, is morally illegitimate. He argues that it realizes a form of forced labor, for the state so structures the tax system that any time you labor at all, for a certain amount of your labor time you involuntarily work, in effect, for the state. This amount of time that produces the wealth is taken away from you forcibly via taxation. It is for this reason that taxation amounts to partial *slavery*, for in giving every citizen an entitlement to certain benefits (welfare, social security, or whatever), the state in effect gives them an entitlement, a right, to a part of the proceeds of your labor, which produces the taxes that fund the benefits. It follows in such a system that every welfare recipient becomes a partial owner of you (since they have a partial property right in part of you, i.e. in your labor). But, claims Nozick, this is morally wrong because it is inconsistent with the principle of self-ownership, which he believes follows from the dignity and value of the individual.

The various programs of the modern liberal welfare state are thus claimed to be immoral, not simply because they are often alleged to be inefficient and unworkable failures, but because they make slaves of the citizens of such a state. For Nozick slavery is contrary to the fundamental notion of self ownership and an imposed tax on the income from our labour makes us slaves of the government. One can of course object to this equation of slavery and imposed income tax since, obviously, citizens can still choose not to work whereas slaves have no choice. Moreover, to say that any form of income tax equals slavery is somewhat of an overstatement. Much depends upon the burden and its relation to the social benefits that supposedly flow back to the tax payers. It is not simply that income is taken from tax payers without any compensation.[65] However, Nozick's description

---

[65] Government taxation normally funds public goods that are not reliably provided by the market: roads, transportation, health and educational systems, for example, as well as the alleviation of the more impoverished members of the population. Also, with respect to welfare payments to poorer citizens, it is an oversimplification to regard this as a case in which wealthy and productive agents are forced to transfer some of their income to unproductive citizens without compensation. Minimum wage laws, unemployment insurance and welfare payments began to be introduced in the late nineteenth century in order to mitigate the harsher realities flowing from unregulated capitalism. Social commentators such as Karl Marx had predicted that as these trends continued the mass of impoverished unemployed citizens would join

of slavery through enforced taxation better describes the system of IP tax that is being enforced through the WTO. In this case, companies and governments in the developing world are being forced to return a portion of the income to first world countries and, following Nozick's analysis, this means that during a certain period of their hours of operation they are working without remuneration for first world companies that hold IP rights. Moreover there is no pretense that this tax will be indirectly returned to the tax payers through public services in terms of education, health benefits or enhanced security etc. The money received goes directly into the profits of the first world corporations and redistributed as increased salaries for its membership and greater returns for its stockholders, and finally greater personal income and corporate taxes for their governments. In short this is a much truer form of slavery than that described by Nozick in his analysis of the welfare state.

Conclusion

We have argued that IPRs created in the developed world function as a tax on the productive activities of the developing and less developed world. This, one surmises, is the strategy behind much of the push to globalize IPRs through TRIPS and TRIPS plus type arrangements. Having adumbrated the difficulties the developing world is facing with the expansion of IP rights, one might question, however, the degree to which this so called tax on the developing world works to the advantage of the first world and its corporations both financially and innovatively. One can say that there are tangible and less tangible benefits, which occur in different degrees in different industries. Certainly in agribusiness, a strategy aimed at direct, immediate tangible benefits is strikingly evident, as giant conglomerates such as Monsanto push for the global acceptance of genetically modified plants and organisms and claim ownership rights in the seeds and offspring. In order to be competitive small farmers are increasingly under pressure to choose production methods dictated by the biotechnology industry. Because farmers are prohibited from harvesting and using or selling patented seeds, they must purchase their seeds from the industry. Not only will the world's farmers be paying government taxes

---

together to overthrow the established order. In part, the redistribution of wealth that occurs through these forms of taxation is meant to improve the conditions of a significant segment of society that might otherwise turn to various forms of criminality or the more serious forms of political insurrection. It is for this reason that the institutions of the welfare state cannot be painted as a zero sum game. The income earner and more advantaged citizens are compensated for improving conditions for the least advantaged class through greater security for themselves associated with the reduction of political and social unrest.

but they will also be paying taxes to multinational corporations for the privilege of growing produce with privately owned genetic material. Beyond purchasing seed this involves the adoption of an entire package of capital and chemical intensive complementary inputs. Little discretion is left to the individual farmer because the use of these inputs dictates the timing and intensity of the productive process and the farmer increasingly becomes the provider of raw unskilled labor power.[66] The push to globalize this form of control can be seen in the recent legislation in India and Iraq, legislation which undermines the farmer's traditional right to save seed, because the legislation is designed to force farmers to obtain a yearly license for genetically modified (GM) seeds from multinational corporations.[67]

With respect to the software industry, IPRs and especially the increased use of patents to cover fairly simple procedures in software engineering mean that programmers in the developing world can face daunting licensing fees as they struggle to join and participate in the information technology revolution. Although the less developed world is not yet poised to join this revolution, it certainly needs to utilize software to participate in modern commercial enterprise and the revenue derived from licensing their activities is certainly not inconsiderable.

Finally, with respect to the pharmaceutical industry it has been shown that the costs to India from adapting the patents system for pharmaceutical products are greater than the perceived benefits to Western pharmaceutical companies that pushed through the TRIPS agreement that required the implementation of the patent system.[68] In short, it would appear that the Western pharmaceutical companies are not really gaining significant revenue from the developing and less developed worlds to derive profits and cover R&D. However, this does not mean that they have failed to gain any noteworthy advantages. Circumstantial evidence suggests the push to globalize patent protection for pharmaceutical products is not related to a concern for short term or even medium term profit. Patent protection is part of a longer term strategy to maintain future control and dominance in the industry.[69] The TRIPS agreement required that India, the major

[66] D.G. Richards, *Intellectual Property Rights and Global Capitalism: the Political Economy of the TRIPs Agreement.* (Amonk New York: M.E. Sharpe, 2004), 198.
[67] V. Shiva, "The Indian Seed Act And Patent Act: Sowing The Seeds Of Dictatorship," (February 14, 2005) Retrieved November 14, 2006 from www.zmag.org/content/showarticle.cfm?ItemID=7249; St Louis Independent Media, "Monsanto Pawn forbids Iraqis to Save Seeds," (October 2 2006). Retrieved October 15 2006 from www.stlimc.org/newswire/display/2276/index.php.
[68] S. Chaudhuri, P. Goldberg, and P. Jia, "Estimating the Effects of Global Patent Protection in Pharmaceuticals: A Case Study of Quinolones in India,". *American Economic Review*, 96, no. 5, 1477–1491.
[69] Richards, *op. cit.*

producer of generic drugs, implement patent protection for pharmaceuticals by 2005. This poses major difficulties for the generic drug industry. In reality, the large pharmaceutical companies realize that the continued production of generic drugs in the developing world ultimately enhances the wealth and technological expertise of the producers. If this trend is not reversed, the current producers of cheap generic drugs may one day technologically match advanced first world pharmaceutical companies and in doing so compete with them in the lucrative markets where they currently dominate.

One concludes that the motivation behind the realization of IP protection with global application is somewhat mixed. In part it is the desire to extend one's dominance and maintain a monopolistic or oligopolistic global control. In some cases as in agribusiness, the strategy is designed to secure both immediate revenue and long term control as the industry strives to make the producers, the farmers, the captives of patented technology. Similarly, with respect to software and educational resources, which are fundamentally necessary for competitive participation in the world economy, the non-Western world serves as an important revenue source for Western companies. On the other hand, patented medicines do not currently realize significant profits from sales in non-Western markets, and for the foreseeable immediate future, profits will continue to be realized in the richer Western markets. However, this may not always be the case as the emerging economies of India and China develop. Therefore, in this case the strategy may well have a longer term goal, which is to maintain the dominance of the Western pharmaceutical giants in terms of technological capacity in preparation for the anticipated exploitation of future, emerging, potentially lucrative markets.

Ultimately, as public policy, IPRs are granted on the understanding that they provide an incentive for innovation, however, Western corporations have convinced their governments that the incentive would be vitiated if IPRs are not given a global reach. My point is that in fact the agenda actually entertained by the relevant industries strives to stifle foreign innovation, maintain technological hegemony and exploit non-Western organizations and individuals that ineluctably depend on Western technology or even utilize basic concepts and ideas associated with technological processes. Although in some cases, as in the pharmaceutical industry, profit derived from non-Western markets is negligible, a long term strategy may well be in place that is poised to tap these markets as they develop.

One might ask, however, what path should be taken to resolve many of the issues we have mentioned. In other words, how can the IP system be changed or restructured to meet present and future challenges. Firstly, we could say that one needs to recognize that a one shoe fits all systems, which is being imposed through globalized IP rights must be rejected. In other words, different industries may well require different solutions. The following are a few suggestions.

In some cases IP rights might be abolished altogether, for example, with respect to the patenting of life forms. The Chair of the African Group in the Negotiations Surrounding the Convention of Biodiversity (CBA) argues that inappropriateness of the patent system with respect to biological processes is due to the fact that living things are not invented, or inventions.[70] However, this may be a matter of interpretation rather than fact. For example, the German Bundesgerichtshof in the Rote Taube case of 1969 decided that a technical invention can also exist in the systematic application of biological forces of nature.[71] Moreover, we have already seen the difficult philosophical issues that surround the assumed distinction between natural and invented processes. Following Radder and others, it may well be worthwhile simply to prohibit the issuing of product patents. This would not only obviate overly broad patents that constrain other researchers by attaching legal rights to unrealized conceptions and procedures, but would also undercut the patenting of life forms and their offspring. This is because the creator of a generically modified organism would be forced to patent the process rather than the product, which means the patent holder could not claim rights to future GMOs resulting from the natural reproductive process. Among other things, this would safeguard the farmer's traditional right to save and exchange seed and thus reduce threats to biodiversity, a possible consequent of the potential monopolization of the food industry by centralized giant agribusiness.

With respect to software it may also be advisable to reduce the overly commercial character of software engineering through abolition of intellectual property rights as applied to software. Richard Stallman, the principal proponent of 'free software' believes software innovators would continue to invest their creative energies in the production of software, even if the possibilities for profits were vastly reduced, simply because of the desire and commitment to exercise their creative talents.[72] In point of fact he sees copyright and patent law as constraints on the exercise of creative talent, because software engineers are precluded from redeveloping, improving, disseminating, or sharing software that has been copyrighted or patented. Stallman advocates the creation of publicly funded research institutes to provide the necessary software innovation, which the public can access freely or at far less cost.[73]

In other areas, such as pharmaceuticals there may be a need to maintain some aspects of the IP system. Empirical studies appear to support the notion that

[70] Khor, *op. cit.*, 207.
[71] G. Van Overwalle, "From Law to Ethics," in S. Sterckx, ed. *Biotechnology, Patents and Morality*, 2nd ed. (Aldershot: Ashgate, 2000): 197–206, 204.
[72] Stallman, *op. cit.*
[73] *Ibid.*

strong intellectual property rights have a positive relation to innovation in the pharmaceutical industry, which is not the case in the software industry, for example. In the pharmaceutical industry 'spillovers', the capture of intellectual property value by competing firms due to imperfect appropriability, would lead to R&D disincentives.[74] However, at the same time it has to be recognized that these monopolistic powers are only justified to support research and development, not to amass spectacular profits at all costs. The right to health or the right to health care should trump the monopolistic powers granted to the pharmaceuticals through the relevant administrative, legislative and international bodies. Individuals and companies have an obligation to help those in need in circumstances in which the effort does not entail a great expense to themselves, and clearly, a heavy responsibility falls on the pharmaceutical companies. Moreover the TRIPS agreement and other related agreements with respect to drugs should be reversed and the decision to implement patents for pharmaceuticals should be solely in the hands of the country claiming legal jurisdiction. Because the TRIPS agreement in the long term may actually stifle the research potential of industries in the developing world, universally enforced patent rights, applied on a global scale, are potentially antithetical to future R&D.

In point of fact, we argue that patent rights should only be granted where there exists a demonstrative relation between profits that depend on IP protections and the finances necessary to support effective R&D. In markets where profits would not be sufficient or marginally important for the support of effective R&D, IP rights should have no application. Companies such as those in India that can produce lower cost generic drugs (because they don't need to do their own R&D) should then be allowed to be productive and offer their products within markets in which the large firms have little interest, while being precluded from the lucrative markets where patents apply. In effect, we are arguing for the pre-TRIPS situation. This would better secure the mandate of the UN under the Universal Declaration of Human Rights that prescribes the universal the right to health care. At the same time, pharmaceutical multinationals will have to live with the possibility that companies, located in the developing world, will elevate their imitative activities and become effective originators of innovative R&D. When this occurs they will also be able to patent their products and enter the lucrative markets in which IP rights are recognized and generic imitations of patented medicines are prohibited.

---

[74] Levin, *op. cit.*, 427.

Chapter Ten

The Myth of Free Markets: Intellectual Property, the IT Industry, and Market Freedoms in the Global Arena

In March 2004 the European commission (EC) found that Microsoft used its market dominance to compete unfairly and fined the World's number one software company 497 million Euros. Microsoft appealed and the case made its way through the Court of First Instance in Luxembourg before a five judge panel headed by Judge Hubert Legal. In June 2005, the media reported that Legal was in hot water after publishing an article in the French Journal *Concurrences* saying some of the judges' clerks tended to regard themselves as "ayatollahs of free enterprise" and should avoid an impression of "arbitrary power". It was also reported that as a result of the controversy the Court of First Instance President, Bo Vesterdorf, planned to move the case away from the current judge and panel to the court's Grand Chamber, headed by Vesterdorf himself.[1]

The question one should ask is whether dominance in the software industry is an expression of the values we associate with the so called free market. Copyrights, patents and non-disclosure agreements have been instrumental in securing a pre-eminence within the software industry, but are they consistent with the values conjured by the expressions free enterprise and free market?

In the last chapter, following Christman, we argued that because the IP right is an income right a discussion of issues of freedom and autonomy is indeed irrelevant. However, market freedom is conceived as an extension of natural freedom; and thus a right to land or goods is a right not only to the fruits of use but also to the fruits of exchange.[2] The question thus remains, whether the denial of intellectual property rights is denial of the fruits of exchange and therefore a denial of market freedoms. In order to answer this question we must consider the values and freedoms we associate with the usual market activities and decide whether or not IP rights represent a consistent extension of these values.

We will begin by asking what are meant by the market freedoms and inquiring into the alleged underlying values that justify and perhaps animate these freedoms.

---

[1]   *Gulf Today*, June 21, 2005, 23.
[2]   Robert Nozick, *Anarchy, State and Utopia* (New York: Basic Books, 1974).

One often associates John Stuart Mill with the defense of the market based on issues of personal freedom. J. S. Mill, for example, in *On Liberty*, argues that there are three fundamental freedoms governments and the collective must respect: freedom of thought, freedom of lifestyle and freedom of association. The market freedoms are usually identified with freedom of association. However, Mill's thought is not always consistent. Later in the text he refers to the 'free market', but states that the value of the free market does not rest on the principle of liberty. Rather restrictions are wrong because they don't really produce the desired result. Mill does not see commerce as belonging to a sphere of personal control, which should be on principle immune from state control, rather he states that restraints on trade affect that part of conduct that society is competent to restrain.[3] But further in the text his thought takes another turn. He states that the objections to government interference are three when it is not seen to infringe on liberty. First, where there is no one fit to conduct business as those who are so interested in it. This is the objection to the interference of the legislature or the officers of government with the ordinary processes of industry as enlarged upon by political economists. The second objection has relation to individual self development. Although the individual may not be able to do this particular thing so well as the officers of government, he says, it is desirable that it should be done by them as a means to their own mental education, thereby exercising the judgement and giving them a familiar knowledge of the subject with which they deal. The third and most cogent reason for restricting the interference of government is the greater evil of unnecessarily adding to the power to the state. He tells us that regardless of the freedom of the press and constitution of the legislature, if all affairs were managed by a government bureaucracy: "…the railways, the banks, the great joint stock ventures, the universities and the public charities…then the country would never be free other than in name."[4] A little later on he makes some further interesting remarks

> What the French are in military affairs, the Americans are in civil business, let them be left without a government, every body of Americans is able to improvise and to carry on that or any other public business with sufficient amount of order, intelligence and decision. This is what every free people ought to be: and a people capable of this is certain to be free…No bureaucracy can …make such a people as this do or undergo anything they do no like.[5]

Mill's thought conveys the message that the freedom to associate embodied in the market freedoms allows for the realization of an autonomous citizenry rather an immature one dependent on control and direction from authority. Even though

---

[3] John Stuart Mill, *On Liberty*, (New York: The Liberal Arts Press, 1956) 115.
[4] *Ibid.*, 135.
[5] *Ibid.*, 137.

he admits that the market is not inviolable or immune to government control because it does represent a sphere in which the public does have an interest, at the same time, it is preferable that it be maintained free of intervention because it promotes the realization of a free citizenry. Mill's hostility to government controlled commerce, as well as government regulation and interference lay not so much in invisible hand arguments, but from the conviction that these controls rob individuals of responsible agency. In this context we are not speaking about the absolute liberty to do whatever one wishes, or license, but the value of freedom when employed in responsible management of individual affairs. Following Mill's thought it is clear that he had in mind the forms of free enterprise and voluntary association, which were seen in the growth of commercial organizations such as the joint stock ventures. These commercial bodies had powered England's commercial ventures and expanded overseas undertakings even creating, for example, the original North American colonies of Plymouth and Jamestown in the New World.

We remarked earlier in our discussion of groups and collectives that Francis Fukuyama has used the phenomena of voluntary association to explain the remarkable success of modern capitalism.[6] We referred to the fact that he has seized on the element of trust as being the principal trait of the peoples who populate the successful capitalist countries like the United States, Japan and the nations of Western Europe. In exploring this insight he allows that the element of trust is essential in the creation of those voluntary organizations, such as the private university, church groups, news groups, sporting clubs, and the firm etc., which make up civil society that intermediate realm between the family and the state. Economic success, he argues, is dependent on the capacity of individuals to become motivated by trust and move beyond familial interaction and mere reaction to the authority of the state. Voluntary association is not mere social interaction required by family association or political imposition. Voluntary associations give civil society its dynamism and resilience. Countries whose civil societies exhibit these features have also succeeded in creating vibrant and wealth generating economies. Fukuyama's thesis is, of course, that successful economic activity is produced ultimately not through the coercive authority of the state but rather by business organization based on voluntary enterprise. At the same time, societies in which individuals are dominated by family ties to the exclusion of other forms of social commitment exhibit 'amoral familism' to use Banfield's term, which is equally antithetical to successful economic activity.[7]

One may become convinced that societies that are capable of creating these voluntary associations, which are dependent on high degree of trust between

---

[6]   Francis Fukuyama, *Trust: The Social Virtues and the Creation of Prosperity* (New York: Penguin books, 1995).

[7]   Edward Banfield, *The Moral Basis of Backward Society* (Gencoe Ill: Freepress, 1958).

people, not related by consanguinity, will enjoy greater economic prosperity. However, is the mere presence of voluntary association sufficient to ensure wealth creation? Fukuyama points out that not every voluntary association with economic designs is wealth creating. He distinguishes between wealth-creating economic organizations and wealth–redistributing interest groups. His examples of the latter are the mafia, the United Jewish Appeal and the Catholic Church. He states that "...there are societies that are good at producing only interest groups without being able to create effective businesses, in which case sociability will be considered to be an overall liability".[8] He argues that many third world countries only appear to be capable of an excess of this type of organization. He lists an overabundance of "...parasitic employers' groups, labor unions, and community organizers and a dearth of productive corporations".[9]

In any case, in both Instances, Mill and Fukuyama regard the phenomena of socialibility, the freedom expressed in voluntary association without outside intervention as animating successful commercial enterprise. In an important sense voluntary association is seen as instrumental in creating desirable social outcomes. However this is not to so say the market only has instrumental value. Mill sees a society which enjoys these freedoms as intrinsically valuable. This is the case because Mill reasons, following Aristotle, that the enjoyment of these freedoms tends to realize and maximize human happiness not as a consequent or by product but rather, as form of enjoyment indistinguishable from the activity itself. Similarly, Fukuyama may well be seen as celebrating the intrinsic values of societal dynamism and resiliency, which mark a community that engages in the free market, apart from the positive economic results. But in the case of Mill, one should not become confused and see him as championing the value of the individual. One needs to recognize that Mill remains one of the great utilitarian thinkers, and as consistent with this tradition, he is not championing the value of the individual. Clearly his thinking is directed toward the utilitarian end in which the maximized happiness of the aggregate is conceived and achieved through maximized individual liberty and minimal government. One needs to turn to different traditions to find other strains of thought, which link the free market with the value and dignity of the individual.

The religious tradition, of course links the value of the individual with the value of the immortal soul. The Christian philosopher, Jacques Maritain, saw the individual as part of the whole which is society and as part of this whole could be sacrificed for its ends. However, at the same time the individual person surpasses the whole that is society in virtue of the subsistence of his/her spiritual soul. The spiritual soul is destined for union with the transcendent Whole, whereas

---

[8] Fukuyama, op. cit., 158.
[9] *Ibid.*

the particular society in which the person lives, by reason of it not having a spiritual soul, is not destined for union with the transcendent Whole but will die in time. In describing the relation between the individual and society Maritian spoke of the "Creed of Freedom" that lies at the very basis of democracy.[10] According to Maritain, men belonging to very different political and religious backgrounds can and should cooperate in the common good of political life but he did not go on to explore extensively the relation between freedom and the economic market. However, secular thinkers have linked market freedoms with the value of the individual deriving their positions from the Kantian tradition. Kant identifies intrinsic individual value with the freedom of the will. It has been suggested that we can see the influence of Kant in Hegel's *Philosophy of Right*. In this text trade and commerce are viewed as activities inherently associated with modern statehood. For Hegel market activities are not only useful in realizing the material good of the collective, but also guide us to recognize the humanity and worth of other human beings regardless of ethnic or familial origins. In this vein it has been suggested that Hegel understood trade and commerce as important means by which we come to realize Kant's categorical imperative, which requires us to treat the other not merely as means but also as an end.[11]

In contemporary times the relation between the free market and individual worth and dignity has been most prominently advanced by a strain of libertarianism perhaps best represented in the writing of Robert Nozick.[12] On this understanding the locus of moral value can not be coherently identified with the collective and its supposed wellbeing but rather must be associated with concrete individuals and their freedoms and rights. Any social arrangement or political system, if it is to be consistent with the recognized value of the individual, must respect the fundamental rights and freedoms of the individual. Nozick argues that the freedom and autonomy of the individual is protected by certain moral side constraints which are identified with fundamental rights which should not be violated. The side constraints create the space in which the individual can control his destiny, organize his projects and follow his or her prerogatives. Violating the side constraints, which means failing to respect fundamental individual rights, interferes and constrains individual freedom, which is equivalent to a denial of the value and worth of the individual.

---

[10]   Jacques Maritain, *The Person and the Common Good*, trans. John FitzGerald (New York: 1947).
[11]   Rupert Gordon, "Kant's Categorical Imperative and Hegel's Conception of the Economic Market," unpublished paper presented for the Canadian Society of Political Science, St Johns Newfoundland, June 1997.
[12]   Nozick, *op. cit.*

The link between individual value and market freedom is the property right. The right to property protects a sphere of autonomous activity, an area in which one may exercise control over one's personal affairs. Very much in the Lockean sense this right is seen as fundamental to one's personal and human identity. The right to property or the right to ownership is, as we know, not a single simple right but a concatenation of rights and liabilities. However, one can simplify the discussion by mentioning three fundamental rights: the right to use, right to exclude and the right to alienate. Nozick puts emphasis on the third, the right to alienate which we can simply call the right to transfer. Nozick's preoccupation with this particular right is tied to issues of distributive justice and entitlement. Moral entitlement in most cases, he argues, is dependent on the free transfer of owned holdings unless we find ourselves in the more unusual circumstance of discovering and acquiring an un-owned holding. The individual property right represents the linkage to the free market, because individual entitlements can only be just and moral if they are derived from the free transfer of holdings. Conversely a market, which is marred by interference and coerced transfers would be unjust and immoral because this would mean that the right to transfer freely had been denied which in turn means the violation of the moral side constraints (the property right) and the treatment of individuals as less than ends in themselves. The value of the individual entails respect for human liberty embodied in individual property rights, regardless of preferred utilitarian outcomes, which in turn entails a market, which is free and undisturbed by external interference.

It should be underlined that Nozick's defense of market freedoms clearly implies a system of distribution, which is far from uncontroversial. Nozick's moral defense of the free market entails that individuals are fully entitled to all the fruits of market exchange. On this basis any intervention, taxation, for example, that deprives the individual of any part of the received transfer is immoral. Others have sought to dispute this moral entailment as contrary to fundamental issues of distributive justice. David Gautier, for example, believes that moral entitlement to the fruits of exchange does not extend to an amount which exceeds the minimum necessary to induce the individual to transfer the holding or provide the service. Gautier in *Morals By Agreement* argues that the right of the individual to their respective natural endowments does not imply a right to rents non-coercively derived from the sale of their services.[13] But Eric Mack has rightly disputed this position. In this case, as mentioned, rent is by definition a return over and above the cost of supply.[14] But as Mack points out a credible demonstrated willingness to seize services, albeit with payment of social determined no-rent market compensation,

---

[13] David Gautier, *Morals by Agreement* (Oxford: Clarendon Press, 1986).
[14] Eric Mack, "Gautier on Rights and Economic Rent, *Social Philosophy and Policy*" 9, 1 (1992): 171–200.

is essential in practice to sustain the no-rent policy.[15] Such a policy would deprive agents of choice over the disposition of their talents and powers, thus depriving one of the moral authority over the disposal of one's endowments and entitlements. This means Gautier's position does not escape Nozick's criticism of writers such as Rawls, which sees the Rawlsian program of justice as denial of entitlements and market freedoms because implementation would require constant interference in individual freedom of choice in order to secure presumed just outcomes. Similarly Gautier's no-rent compensation policy would, as Mack points out, also require continual intervention in the market to prevent compensation that exceeds the minimum necessary to motivate transfer, thereby vitiating individual choice and personal liberty. One might also mention that tying entitlements to a principle of autonomy and limiting them when they exceed that which is necessary to ensure autonomous agency as recommended by Kymlicka, would also require some intervention in the free market.

Nevertheless, one can say, therefore, that regardless of which of the two defenses of the free market system is adopted, the free market is interpreted to mean an arena of trade and commerce in which individuals come together to interact and transfer and trade freely without external interference or coercion. The value which we attribute to his system of interaction differs according to whether we follow the Mill/Fukuyama or the Nozickian libertarian perspective. According to the former, this system is inherently valuable because it creates a social entity, a community which maximizes free unconstrained unsupervised interaction, allowing for personal development and the expansion of responsible agency, which promotes the greater happiness of the whole. According to the latter, the free market system is valuable because it represents a system which respects individual rights especially property rights thereby safeguarding the dignity and worth of autonomous individuality. This respect entails that individuals are left alone to transfer property freely without interference.

Intellectual Property Rights and Stallman's Criticisms

Unlike physical property rights, intellectual property protects my income or right to potential income by maintaining legal restrictions on the reproduction of the product and transfer of information. Once information and information technology are made subject to intellectual property rights, a unique form of ownership is created that legally restricts the transferee by ensuring he/she receives a title that falls short of full ownership, in so far as the recipient is

---

[15] *Ibid.*, 119.

prevented from alienating the holding by selling or freely disseminating, which is not the case with physical things. This ensures maximum profitability for the originator in so far as each recipient of the information or information technology must represent a monetary return to the originator.[16] The distinction reinforces the fact that intellectual property rights do not protect the personal freedom to make use of the holding, rather, they protect the income that flows from holding title though specifying exclusive control over production and dissemination.

We shall now consider more specifically how intellectual property rights in software affect the freedom of individuals engaged in the production of computer software. It can be said that the move to cyberspace not only relates to technology but also to social restructuring, and political restructuring, through a change in the kinds of relationships that will either improve or disadvantage the well-being of mankind.

At this point in time we should mention Richard Stallman the creator of the GNU project and the principal behind the Free Software Movement. Stallman is interesting because he has been the most prominent and outspoken critic of the use of copyright and patent as applied to software. Stallman relates that in the 1970's it was a bit rare for there to be a community where people shared software.[17] But, in fact, although this was rather an extreme case, Stallman worked in an MIT laboratory in which the entire operating system consisted of software developed by the people in that MIT community, and shared with anybody. He states that the public was welcome to come and take a look, and take away a copy, and do whatever he or she wanted to do. There were no copyright notices on these programs. Cooperation was our way of life, he says. In this context he says there was free software, but there was no free software movement.

Stallman's awakening came when he sought to make improvements on a printer that had been donated to MIT but was unable to do so because he lacked the source code. He heard that somebody at Carnegie Mellon University had a copy of that software. So he visited Carnegie Mellon and introduced himself saying, "Hi, I'm from MIT. Could I have a copy of the printer source code?" He was refused and referred to a non-disclosure agreement with Xerox. He was angry but realized that he was seeing not just an isolated instance, but a social phenomenon that was important and affected a lot of people. He complains that because of a non disclosure agreement the individual had promised to refuse to cooperate with just about the entire population of the Planet Earth.[18]

---

[16] For a fuller discussion of the above points see chapter seven.
[17] Richard Stallman, "Free Software: Freedom and Cooperation," New York University, New York, 29 May 2001. http://www.mirror5.com/events/rms-nyu-2001-transcript.txt.
[18] *Ibid.*, 4.

Stallman saw his community collapse because the operating system he worked on became obsolete and many went their own ways signing up to write commercial software. But when somebody invited him to sign a non-disclosure agreement, his conscience was already sensitized. He states that he remembered how angry he had been, when somebody refused to help him and his lab to solve their problem. He states that he couldn't turn around and do the exact same thing to somebody else that had never done him any harm. Stallman believes that signing a non-disclosure agreement turns one into a predator. According to him, the purpose of science and technology is to develop useful information for humanity to help people live their lives better. If we promise to withhold that information—if we keep it secret—then we are betraying the mission of our field.

Stallman's principles have led him to produce a free software system, which in effect is meant to re-create the sort of software community he had known at MIT. He states that a program is free software for a particular user, if you have the following freedoms:

— First, Freedom Zero is the freedom to run the program for any purpose, any way you like.
— Freedom One is the freedom to help yourself by changing the program to suit your needs.
— Freedom Two is the freedom to help your neighbor by distributing copies of the program.
— And Freedom Three is the freedom to help build your community by publishing an improved version so others can get the benefit of your work.[19]

He enlarges on these freedoms.

Freedom One is the freedom to help yourself by changing the software to suit your needs. This could mean fixing bugs. It could mean adding new features. It could mean porting it to a different computer system. It could mean translating all the error messages into Navajo. Any change you want to make, you should be free to make. Now, if you don't have this freedom, it causes practical, material harm to society. It makes you a prisoner of your software. He refers to the earlier example of the laser printer. The inability to repair software means that we become prisoners of the software.

Freedom Two is the freedom to help your neighbor by distributing copies of the program. He explains that for beings that can think and learn, sharing useful knowledge is a fundamental act of friendship. He argues that when these beings use

---

[19] *Ibid.*, 9.

computers, this act of friendship takes the form of sharing software. Friends share with each other. Friends help each other. This is the nature of friendship. And, in fact, this spirit of goodwill—the spirit of helping your neighbor, voluntarily—is society's most important resource. It makes the difference between a livable society and a dog-eat-dog jungle. Its importance has been recognized by the world's major religions for thousands of years, and they explicitly try to encourage this attitude, he explains.

Freedom Three, he explains, is very important both practically and psycho-socially. If you don't have this freedom, it causes practical material harm, because this community development doesn't happen, and we don't make software which is as powerful and reliable as it could be. At the same time this causes psycho-social harm, which affects the spirit of scientific cooperation—the idea that we're working together to advance human knowledge. He argues that progress in science crucially depends on people being able to work together. IP rights foster a reality in which one often finds each little group of scientists acting as though they are at war with other gangs of scientists and engineers. But ultimately failure to share with each other means they are all held back.[20]

Stallman has created what he calls the GNU General Public License to protect free software. This license embodies what he calls the "copyleft", which states, "You're authorized to distribute copies of this. You're authorized to modify it. You're authorized to distribute modified versions and extended versions." Stallman explains that the "copyleft" uses the existing copyright law, but to achieve a very different goal. There is, however, a condition, which requires that whenever one distributes anything that contains any piece of this program, the whole program must be distributed under these same terms, no more and no less. One can change the program and distribute a modified version, but the people who receive the program must have the same freedoms to modify and distribute modified versions. These freedoms must apply not merely to the original parts of the program that were received as free software, but also to any additional parts that have been added to the free software. In other words, the whole of the program has to be free software.

It should also be pointed out that Stallman has strong counter arguments against the usual criticisms of free software. One such argument holds that free software fails to reward creativity and another holds that it is unreliable because you cannot rely on the type of support offered by large commercial providers such as Microsoft. With regard to the first point, Stallman points out that free software does not mean that the programmer is prohibited from selling free software. In fact Stallman himself survived by selling his GNU software. In reality, however, it does

---

[20]   *Ibid.,* 9–11.

mean that programmers will probably be unable to realize the disproportionate rewards that sometimes result from selling commercial, copyrighted software. Moreover, he says, although programmers deserve to be rewarded for innovation, they actually deserve to be punished for restricting use through IP rights. Finally on the issue of support, he argues that free software does not preclude the possibility of innovative service companies offering their services to fix and modify free software. Indeed, he argues, free software is more reliable than the usual commercial software because all users have access to the source code and therefore are better able to share information about faults in the system.

Intellectual Property and market freedom

From the foregoing one observes a strong reaction to intellectual property rights when applied to software and its effects on what are perceived as the individual freedoms. One might argue that intellectual property rights in this instance structure economic relations in ways that are contrary to the freedom of the market and the alleged justifications for a the free market. Let us reconsider property rights in general. Nozick as we have seen interprets the property right as creating an area or sphere of autonomy in which the individual can exercise his liberty to transfer freely holdings or entitlements, which in turn entails a free market. But intellectual property is information which one is not free to transfer. Of course the creator or innovator possesses this right in the full unrestricted sense but all those who claim title from him/her through transfer are precluded from exercising this right. So called intellectual property fails to realize the full bodied notion of property as applied to physical phenomena and thereby denies the possibility of an important sphere of autonomy in which one exercises the freedom to transfer or freely grant.

Since the property right has been identified as entailed in the definition of human personality, the question is are we treating individual as less than human, as a mere means rather than an end in him or herself by imposing these restrictions. This may not be the case. Certainly we all possess entitlements that we are not free to transfers either by sale or grant, for example, public offices, rights to pensions, entitlements to a place at university etc. Clearly, the right to transfer freely one's entitlements cannot be an indefeasible right which would mean expanding all personal holdings and entitlements into a form of personal property. In any civilized society we see restrictions on this right imposed by the public interest. But at the same time there must be some space for the exercise of the personal property right and the freedoms associated with it. It is for this reason that libertarians such as Nozick endeavor to expand the personal property right at the same time narrowing the public interest, i.e., the area susceptible to government interference and regulation. He does so by limiting the government power to that of a minimal night watchman state. While limiting the role of the state to the protection of individual rights and freedoms, Nozick even questions whether the common good or public interest can be given any meaning at all. But I think one would agree that that is somewhat of an extreme view and most would recognize that we cannot turn all rights and entitlements into a form of personal property, and that with respect to certain entitlements we need to recognize restrictions on the right to transfer based on public or organizational interests.

However Stallman has made the point that intellectual property rights, such as copyrights and non-disclosure agreements, actually defeat the public interest by encouraging people to hoard rather than share information. As seen earlier patents require disclosure but non-disclosure agreements obviously mean a constraint on disclosure. Source and object codes are copyrighted and companies protect against copying by keeping the codes secret. This in turn stifles improvements, inventiveness and creativity. Rather than cooperating to promote the progress of science each working group is sworn to secrecy and proceeds in isolation from other researchers except those committed to the same narrow commercial organizational goals. The free transfer of information is vital to the growth of science, but it would seem that this end is frustrated by intellectual property laws.

Stallman's analysis clearly throws doubt on the idea that restrictions on the transfer of information technology relating to software are justified and therefore represent an acceptable restriction on the liberty of the individual. People such as Stallman and other members of the free software movement argue that we are treating other human beings in ways incompatible with their humanity by placing these restrictions on their activities. It is human to want to share what one has with others especially information whether it is given away or sold, and this is what is being denied. This also has relevance to Mill's idea that the free market is valuable because it creates a community in which engagement with others is voluntary, unrestricted and immune to external interference. For Mill these are the necessary conditions in which individual maturity and self development can be realized thereby creating enhanced social wellbeing and happiness. Stallman obviously sees intellectual property rights as erecting barriers that divide rather then bring the community together and restrict rather than enhance its development. Because important elements like the source code are kept secret, the ways in which one might achieve self development are frustrated. Moreover the community itself is threatened and even impaired by denying the important relations which hold any scientific community together, that is, the sharing of ideas and information. Stallman's own personal history would seem to attest to that. His original community at MIT was destroyed when the operating system they were working on became obsolete project. The GNU project, which he originated and eventually became the familiar GNU Linux software program, was driven by a desire to re-establish that community through the creation of free non-commercial software.

Ultimately intellectual property rights have created a market in software that is far from free but regulated by legal rules and the intrusion of those empowered by the special rules that apply to copyright, non-disclosure agreements and now patents. These restrictions intrude into the creative process and hinder the free flow of information. They create a market of ideas and information technology that is far from free from interference and onerous regulation. Libertarians point out that IP rights create a *de jure* or legally assisted monopoly, which also entails significant costs incurred by society to regulate the market and enforce the privileges that so called intellectual property sanctions. Society also suffers because it must divert scarce resources from important needs to pay the costs for supporting the institutions that license intellectual property and also those that facilitate the prosecution of those that fail to acknowledge the privileges of the patent or copyright holder.[21]

The Global Arena

However when we speak of community we must also mention the global community. Stallman speaks of his experience as member of a community of researchers at MIT, but intellectual property rights have far reaching consequences, which also affect the national and the world community. Information technology can be seen to have promoted the globalization process. People from diverse corners of the globe can share and store vast amounts of information instantaneously. Will Sweet, for example, speaks of IT contributing to a global ecumenism in which individuals from diverse groups come together to recognize certain shared interests and dominant ideas, which at the same time are not inconsistent with a diversity of national, cultural and religious origins.[22] In other words, it is possible to envision a global community that has been fostered and nurtured by developments such as the internet. But at the same time intellectual property rights at least as applied to software are intruding, dividing people and structuring relations in ways, which reflect some of the worst fears about the globalization process. Dependency theorists can point to the Information technology revolution as exacerbating the North South divide in which poor countries are exploited for their resources and

---

21 R.M. Stallman, "GNU Manifesto," in M.D. Ermann & M.S. Shauf eds., *Computers, Ethics and Society* (Oxford: Oxford University Press, 2003): 153–161.

22 Will Sweet, "Globalization, Philosophy and the Model of Ecumenism," *South Pacific Journal of Philosophy and Culture* 4 (2000): 1–18.

cheap labour which in turn enrich the developed world.[23] In order to maintain some semblance of technological parity the developing world must purchase its technology from the developed world. Patent and copyright allow software companies to keep software artificially high which in no way reflects cost of production.[24] Intellectual property rights are increasingly seen as an important tool which supports a system of exchange based on asymmetrical power relationships thus maintaining the trade advantage of technologically developed nations.

These asymmetric relations are even evident in relations between developed countries. So called free trade agreements are one form of Trojan horse which allow US copyright and patent law to be imposed on other nations. For example, in 2004 Australian developers of open source software expressed their wariness of the free trade agreement (FTA) struck with the US, saying it would lead to the acceptance of American-style patent and intellectual property laws which, in turn, would cripple the local software industry.[25] Linux Australia president Pia Smith said Linux and open source were becoming vital parts of the local IT landscape. "Australia has more active Open Source developers than Canada, and dominates the Asia Pacific," she said, quoting data from the Boston Consulting Group. Smith also pointed to the issue of software patents, which were disallowed in Europe. Software was originally copyrighted rather than patented, however, significant judicial decisions in the US have extended the use of patents to software. Although patents require disclosure of the relevant process, information or technique, they can be used to confer monopolistic rights over procedures and process that are readily susceptible to independent discovery or formulation. "The FTA commits Australia to continue allowing increasing numbers of such patents," she said. Linus Torvalds, the creator of the Linux kernel, has pointed out that any non-trivial program will infringe on some patent or the other." Sydney Linux User Group president Jeff Waugh likened software patents to landmines. "Like landmines, they pose a huge threat to the open source community," said Waugh, who is also the manager for the GNOME desktop project. "Stepping on just one of these mines is enough to cripple a project, destroying years of effort donated by the project to the world."[26]

---

[23] For a classic example of 'Dependency Theory' see A. Amarshi, K. Good and R. Mortimer, *Development and Dependency: The Political Economy of Papua New Guinea* (Melbourne: Oxford University Press, 1979).

[24] For example, in a 1997 communication reportedly sent by Microsoft group vice president Jeff Raikes to billionaire Warren Buffet, seeking his investment in Microsoft, Raikes told Buffet that some observers had likened Windows to a 'toll bridge' adding the company is a '90% + margin business'. (Buffet did not invest in Microsoft.) "US Judges Re-Activate Microsoft Antitrust Case," *ComputerWire* (March 22, 2004), Issue 4883.

[25] Sam Varghese, *Melbourne Age*, (March 12, 2004), 41.

[26] *Ibid.*

Essentially large software companies have been able to acquire numerous patents many of which cover some very simple procedures and inventions. The US patent office has been liberally granting such patents. Small open source companies may not realize that some of the procedures they employ may or might infringe some patent granted to one of these larger companies even if they formulated, discovered or derived the process independently. In these circumstances patents can be used as a means to crush the smaller opposition. If sued by one of the large multinationals, they face a difficult dilemma. They usually do not have highly paid lawyers on staff and find it difficult to afford the legal fees to defend their interests. On the other hand, it may be easier just to capitulate and pay the licensing fees. In either case they will add to their operating costs and find it difficult if not impossible to compete.

At the same time some countries, unlike Australia, refuse to get stuck in the game. Iran for example operates entirely on pirated Microsoft software, although to avoid problems they are intent on switching to GNU Linux. On the other hand Microsoft has responded to Iran's refusal to pay by actively translating their programs into Farsi. This, of course, is to discourage them from going over to GNU Linux in which case the game would be virtually lost altogether. Nevertheless, the large software giants haven't given up threatening the users of free or open source software. Many South East Asian governments to avoid the costs of proprietary software are operating on Open Source. Powerful interests are pushing an implicit agenda to bring the legal systems of WTO members into conformity with US intellectual property laws, as discussed extensively in the last chapter. As Peter Singer points out once nations join the WTO they lose significant national sovereignty and run the risk having the organizational trade rules imposed on them.[27] This, of course, will especially true with respect to intellectual property law.[28]

---

[27] Peter Singer, *One World: the Ethics of Globalization* (New Haven: Yale University Press, 2000) 73.

[28] Steve Ballmer, Microsoft's CEO, speaking in Singapore warned Asian governments they could face patent lawsuits for using the Linux operating system instead of its Windows software. Ballmer stated that Linux violates more than 228 patents, but significantly did not provide any details on the alleged violations, which the Linux community disputes. *The Gulf Today* (Friday November 17, 2004), 23. Ballmer went on to warn in the same speech that the World Trade Organization may one day require substantial payment from patent violators. This is an interesting remark and points to the irony that the WTO, the organization that supposedly supports 'free trade', can be vehicle by which companies, governments and individuals will be restricted in the freedom to transact, trade, alienate and share software products. All in this is done in the interests of and to facilitate 'rent seeking' on the part of certain multinational corporations with first world locations.

Summary:

We have explored the reasons the so called free market has been seen as valuable. The tradition closely associated with John Stuart Mill understands the market, which is free of government interference as synonymous with a society marked by a sociability which is the expression of responsible agency. These minimally regulated circumstances allow for the nurturing of a productive human relations and a self-determined citizenry. Accordingly, under these conditions the community or social whole will then achieve the appropriate goal, the maximized level of happiness. On the other hand, following the Kantian tradition as articulated by Robert Nozick, we encounter a defense of the free market based on the pre-eminent value of the human individual rather than the interests and well being of the social whole. This justification does not rely on arguments based on the overall social good but on the rights and freedoms of individuals. On this view the principles of free enterprise and market freedom are understood to serve as protections for individual rights and freedoms that ensure the integrity of the human person.

The foregoing analysis points to significant doubts as to whether intellectual property rights as applied to software can find support from either of these approaches. Stallman's criticism specifically underlines that intellectual property rights actually interfere with and destroy productive interaction and the social fabric that furthers the wellbeing of the community and the progress of science. Aside from frustrating the ends of social interaction, intellectual property rights are counter productive with respect to relations within the software community because they foster a divisive approach, which undermines more harmonious forms of sociability and autonomous agency. Turning from the well being of the community to issues of individual value and freedom one again needs to note the criticism drawn from the free software movement. Nozick as we have seen champions the free market because its principles tend to enlarge and protect individual freedoms. Intellectual property rights, however, are seen to restrict and deny individual freedoms, most specifically the freedom to transfer and share so called intellectual property. In this way they narrow the fundamental right we associate with ownership in a way, which is inconsistent with the value of the individual. Finally, on the global level we have observed intellectual property rights working to create markets that are marked by monopolistic practices that can only disadvantage the general global community by exacerbating conditions in which wealth is concentrated in the developed world. Ultimately those, who equate market dominance with free enterprise and see government efforts to control and regulate the situation as unwarranted interference, are fundamentally mistaken. Dominance in the software market, as we have sought to demonstrate, has been actually built upon the state support of intellectual property laws that intrude into the system of exchange, and impede and frustrate the free trade of ideas and technology.

Conclusion

The point is that IP rights, while projected as embodiments of free trade, are actually forms of policing, interference and intervention. As we pointed out copyrights and patents through royalties and licensing agreements act as a tax upon other producers. The reported spectacular profits realized by IBM in the 1990s, 2 billion a year through licensing, indicate the nature of an extremely lucrative business or system of privileged entitlement that eschews production costs. If we think of this IP tax projected world wide, then one is talking about a multibillion dollar business imposed on the technologically challenged developing world in favor of companies with first world locations. In order to collect this tax on these operations that are alleged to make use of IP in the productive process requires policing and enduring vigilance. Because world wide enforcement from the centres of technological innovation is impossible, it is necessary to use international bodies and agreements between nations as the effective enforcement mechanism. Thus, we have seen the implementation of the TRIPS agreement by the World Trade Organization that requires member states to enforce IP rights under the threat of sanctions.

Chapter Eleven

From the Wright Brothers to Microsoft: Issues in the Moral Grounding of Intellectual Property Rights

Having denied the linkage between intellectual property and the belief in free market values, I wish to explore more extensively additional ethical arguments that could be used to support IP rights in software. This course of investigation will initially lead us to a fuller exploration of the meaning of private ownership and its moral foundations. This will allow us to determine whether the traditional arguments that have been used to defend non-intellectual property have application to intellectual property. We will go on to discuss the possible relationship between IP rights and innovation, including the alleged linkage between research and profits as realized within the software industry. We will also highlight the unique character of software market as resulting from the application of IP rights to software and the consequences in terms of the economic market and utilitarian outcomes. Ultimately, this investigation is intended to determine whether there exist possible utilitarian benefits that result from IP rights, and which might justify the intervention in the market that IP rights in reality represent.

After Orville and Wilbur Wright successfully flew the first powered aircraft, they sought for years to obtain patents that would restrict others from developing or creating their own airplanes. Fortunately the Wright brothers never succeeded. Propelled by the efforts of myriad independent inventors, varied and innovative airline design flourished in an unrestricted environment. Had the Wright brothers been successful, the development of the airplane may have been severely retarded.[1]

In this chapter I am not attempting to reach a final judgment as to the moral basis of intellectual property rights in general, instead I want to offer a more specific treatment of the possible moral basis of intellectual property as applied to computer software. The issue is, indeed, quite controversial. As the above reference to the Wright brothers indicates, there is the question of whether copyright and patent actually impede invention and the creative process. There are the costs to society incurred by arrangements to make people pay for a program and the

---

[1] Peter L. Jakab, Tom D. Crouch, *Visions of a Flying Machine: The Wright Brothers and the Process of Invention* (Washington: Smithsonian History of Aviation Series, 1990).

licensing of copies.[2] Barriers are created by the necessity to conduct extensive searches to determine if a newly created program contains elements that have already been protected by existing patents or copyrights. If a search confirms the existence of pre-existing patents or copyrights, one may have to pay significant fees to license a process that has been patented or draft a copyright claim "…in contorted ways to ensure that its claim does not infringe on others."[3]

Despite critical observations, it is also worth keeping in mind that intellectual property rights are supposed to have a positive function. Patents were created to encourage people to disclose the details of their inventions. Copyrights were created to encourage authorship.[4] For example, Section 8, clause 8, of the United States constitution, specifies that Congress shall have the power "To promote the progress of science and useful arts, by securing for a limited time to authors and inventors the exclusive right to their respective writings and discoveries."

Keeping these issues in mind, I will begin with a criticism of intellectual property rights as applied to software and then proceed to consider the central moral arguments that have been used to support the general institution of ownership rights. John Ladd, for example, strongly believes that ownership rights have been misapplied to intellectual phenomena.[5] Ladd points out that the traditional conception of property comprises three basic elements: the right to exclude, the right to use and the right to dispose or alienate (sell or give away). He argues that these traditional elements are incompatible with intellectual property. This incompatibility he associates with the 'fallacy of location', which occurs when notions consistent with physical property are mistakenly extended to intellectual phenomena.[6] In committing the fallacy of location we erroneously assume that once intellectual property is given or exposed it cannot be retrieved. As he states, "Furthermore, there is no point in retrieving a bit of information that has been taken from you—because you still have it. Bill Gates has lost nothing if someone copies one of his software programs, *except money*."[7] One of the consequences of this assumption is the belief that, as with physical objects, the possession of information or knowledge is a zero sum matter: if one person or party has it, then the other persons or parties automatically cannot have it. It is ridiculous to think about intellectual property in this way, claims Ladd; people may for various

2   R.M. Stallman, "GNU manifesto," in M.D. Ermann & M.S. Shauf eds., *Computers, Ethics and Society* (Oxford: Oxford University Press, 2003): 153–161.
3   D.G. Johnson, *Computer Ethics* 3rd Edition (New Jersey: Prentice Hall, 2001): 143.
4   Stallman, *op. cit.*, 159.
5   J. Ladd, "Ethics and the Computer World," *Cyberethics Social and Moral Issues in the Computer Age* (New York: Prometheus Books, 2000): 44–55, 52.
6   *Ibid.*
7   *Ibid.*

purposes wish to prevent others from possessing a piece of information, but their reason can never be that they could lose their information by sharing it with others.

What Ladd means is that if information is shared and used by others or given away etc., the original possessor has not suffered a *prima facie* loss. On the other hand, if others take possession of my car then I can no longer use it, effectively alienate it, or exclude others from using it—everything is taken out of my hands. This is why we have legal rules prohibiting others from using, removing or alienating our physical possessions without permission. But these prohibitions lose their justification when applied to intellectual holdings (information), as these activities when performed by others with respect to my intellectual property, do not abnegate or undermine my capacity to perform the same activities. For example, I can still use my computer program even if someone else makes a copy and proceeds to make use of the same program.

But others, such as David Pogue, a defender of intellectual property rights as applied to software, argue that the fact that unrestricted access to the same information leaves all the users free to use that information, fails to justify unlimited access to 'intellectual property'. If this were the case, we would have to exonerate credit card fraudsters, such as Kevin Mitnick, on the grounds that they merely copy credit card numbers for personal use while leaving the original owners at liberty to utilize the same cards.[8] But this counter argument, rather than a refutation, serves to underline Ladd's point. So called intellectual property, *per se*, is not lost through others gaining access, but rather what is at issue are the possibilities of related monetary loss (a form of non-intellectual property). Intellectual property laws are not primarily concerned with protecting information *per se* as some special, non-physical, intellectual species of property, rather, they serve to protect existing wealth, possible income and future income by restricting access to and use of information. The question that this necessarily poses is whether the moral grounds that support protection of monetary wealth or income justify the restrictions on access to information and the associated social costs of maintaining these restrictions.

With these thoughts in mind and leaving aside Ladd's skeptical remarks on the very possibility of intellectual property, let us now consider information and information technology as a possible form of non-physical property. In this context, information as property has an additional peculiar aspect, which distinguishes it from the usual forms of ownership associated with tangible assets. This is particularly the case with respect to income and rights to income. One starts with the simple fact that income is generated through the sale or transfer of

8   David Pogue. *Macworld*, San Francisco, 14, Issue 10 (Oct 1997): 190–191, 191.

property. Sam Goldwyn is said to have once remarked that one of the attractions of the film industry is the fact that you could make money without having to lose ownership of the product or production.[9] One could sell the product, by selling tickets to a show or film production, without surrendering overall title. A single film could be sold over and over again without having to repeat the original production process. Analogously, holders of software patents or copyrights sell individually packaged software but retain overall ownership rights that prevent others from copying or reproducing the same software for resale or gift purposes. Like the film industry they in effect sell the same product over and over again yet still retain their ownership rights. The singular feature of intellectual property, which distinguishes it from physical property, is the fact that alienation (sale or transfer without sale) effects something less than a full transfer of title, in so far as the transferee or grantee does not receive the right to alienate the product, that is, pass on the same information to others, e.g., by making copies for distribution. Unlike physical property, significant ownership rights remain vested in the creator because something less than full title is transferred.

Having gained some clarity as to the nature of intellectual property rights, we shall now proceed to consider the moral arguments that are frequently used to support the institution of private ownership. We then consider whether these same arguments make sense or are meaningful when applied to intellectual property in software.

Locke's Theory of the Moral Basis of Property

Many contemporary writers when discussing property issues draw inspiration from John Locke's 17th century work, *Two Treatises of Government*, which offers an extensive exploration of the origins and moral basis of private ownership rights.[10] Ian Maitland, for example, in defending intellectual property rights as applied to patents on prescription drugs, makes reference to Locke's view that one is entitled to that which one has discovered or created. He states,

> A company's (or for that matter anyone's) moral right to the fruits of its discovery is independent of and antecedent to patent law. On the Lockean argument that people are entitled to the fruits of their labor, patent law simply recognizes and gives legal effect to the company's prior moral claims. (Put another way, as a matter of morality, the company would have a right to profit from its discovery even if the law did not

---

[9]   Scott Berg, *Goldwyn* (New York: Alfred Knopf, 1989).
[10]   John Locke, *Two treatises of Government*, P. Lazlett ed., (Cambridge: Cambridge University Press 1967).

enforce the right. If the law failed to guarantee the company's rights to the fruits of its discovery, then the law would be morally at fault.)[11]

Certainly no one disputes the proposition that the creator or discoverer is entitled to enjoy or use his/her creation or discovery or that he or she can transfer it to another and make a profit. However, relying on the authority of Locke's arguments to support intellectual property rights is somewhat risky. In presenting his views on matters of justice and the acquisition of natural rights to property, Locke was referring to non-intellectual physical property. It is certainly questionable whether Locke would have intended or contemplated a form of ownership in which subsequent alienation (sale or direct transfer) effects something less than a full transfer of title in so far as the transferee or grantee is denied the right to alienate, i.e., transfer or sell the same intellectual property (information) to another.

If we look more closely at Locke's argument, which was originally intended to apply to the acquisition of physical property, the role which creative labor plays in the moral argument will become clearer. According to Locke, ownership rights have an origin in our obligations and specifically in the obligation to preserve ourselves and, as best we can, the rest of mankind. ("Every one is bound to preserve himself and not to quit his station willfully; so by the like reason when his own Preservation comes not in competition, ought he, as much as he can, to preserve the rest of mankind…" *Two Treatises* II: 6) In order to preserve ourselves we need to transform nature to ensure our own survival. This is only possible, he argues, if we have access to some part of the earth's surface for exclusive individual use. *Two Treatises* II: 35) "…God, by commanding to subdue gave authority so far to appropriate. And the condition of Humane Life which requires Labour and Materials to work on, necessarily introduces private possessions."

One cannot effectively follow God's command, which requires preservation, if others attempt to use the same area on which one is working or if they prevent one from effectively laboring in other ways, for example, direct obstruction. In order to ensure survival we need exclusive use, which entails the right to exclude others. Moreover, the same applies to the fruits of our labor. I will not be able to utilize the products of labor to ensure survival if others are constantly stealing my apples or selling them to their neighbors.

In the case of land and chattels etc., which are physical entities with a definite location, ownership rights make sense because without them we cannot utilize our possessions. If we cannot utilize that which we have produced and the principal means of production, the land on which it is produced, then we will be unable to satisfy God's command that requires preservation. Through working this land,

---

[11] Ian Maitland, "Priceless Goods: How Should Life-Saving Drugs Be Priced?" *Business Ethics Quarterly* 12, 4 (2002): 451–480, 464.

which we claim through our labor, we preserve ourselves and indirectly the rest of mankind (through the support of the family etc.). On this understanding, labor does not function as the primary justification for ownership, but rather is presented as the appropriate mode of acquisition. The act of laboring does not actually touch the moral basis of the right *per se*. Locke sees labor as defining the extent of the ownership claim in so far as that which one has transformed through labor is no longer part of nature but becomes invested with the self and thereby linked in a relation of ownership with the human subject. Properly understood, labor is introduced to place natural limits on that over which we can claim ownership. We can not claim unlimited areas of the earth's surface as necessary for survival but only that part of the natural world, which has been modified by labor. *Two Treatises* II: 36) "The measure of Property Nature has well set, by the extent of Mens Labour, and the Convenience of Life: No Mans Labour could subdue or appropriate all..."

We can say therefore that the obligation that founds the private ownership right has a strong utilitarian aspect because property is justified as it tends to promote the survival and flourishing of the individual and the human species. However, strictly speaking Locke has only really established a usufructuary right, i.e. the right to use and exclude others from using our holding. But ultimately, with the invention of money, Locke introduces the justification for trade and commerce and by implication the alienation of property as individuals can now acquire gold and silver to trade to ensure survival, rather than simply relying on what they can produce on their own. (*Two Treatises* II: 36). As Locke explains this also allows for the expansion of property rights to include acquiring more than is necessary for immediate use thereby avoiding the *proviso against spoilage*.

Ultimately, despite the reference to obligation rooted in a command of God, modern liberal secular thinkers often dispense with the religious assumptions, and find the arguments meaningful because of their appeal to utilitarian considerations. Private ownership and the attendant rights to use, exclude and transfer are justified because they are understood to be conducive to the survival and flourishing of both the individual and mankind. The act of laboring is really a description of a preferred mode of acquisition opposed to mere taking from another and as necessarily supplementary to the act of discovery. The institution itself finds its moral basis in the utilitarian concern for the survival of the individual and the rest of mankind. H.L.A. Hart, although a legal positivist, has also made this point and defends an attenuated notion of the natural law based on the goal of survival. A natural right to property would then follow from the natural law as necessary to the goal of survival.[12] Hart believes that the natural law makes sense

---

[12] H.L.A. Hart, *The Concept of Law* (Oxford: Oxford University Press, 1961).

as essentially founded on this natural purpose or end and that which frustrates this goal is contrary to the natural law.[13] Though rules may differ widely, they will not be contrary to the survival of organized society and its membership. He argues that viable societies will exhibit rules with the following similarities: forbearances or rules that restrict the use of violence; minimal rules governing the institution of property; dynamic rules allowing one to set obligations through promises and commitments etc.; and the presence of sanctions.[14] Natural law rules, which include universal rules relating to the institution of property, can be interpreted as supporting property rights based on the goal of survival.

Control and Income Ownership

Having discussed the institution and issues relating to utilitarian consequentialism, let us turn to the defense of ownership based on autonomy and individual control rights, which is the approach associated with the Kantian tradition.

To summarize developments to this stage, we have seen that utilitarian issues offer us powerful reasons for acknowledging a moral point to the existence of the institution of ownership as it applies to land and chattels. As we have repeated, ownership includes the most important rights to use, exclude and alienate. However, the peculiarity of information and information technology is that there is really little reason to protect rights to use, exclude and alienate. I still retain capacities to perform these activities even if others have access to and use the same information or information technology, as we have pointed out. But unlike physical property rights, intellectual property protects my income or right to potential income by maintaining legal restrictions on the reproduction of the product and transfer of information. Once information and information technology are made subject to intellectual property rights, a unique form of ownership is created that legally restricts the transferee by ensuring the he/she receives a title that falls short of full ownership, in so far as the recipient is prevented from selling or freely disseminating this holding. This ensures maximum profitability for the originator in so far as each recipient of the information or information technology must represent a monetary return to the originator. But at the same time, these restrictions raise issues relating to personal freedom, which do not apply when we speak of non-intellectual property.

Robert Nozick's *Anarchy, State and Utopia* represents the most influential contemporary attempt to ground property rights in Kantian principles that eschew the utilitarian approach and emphasize the centrality of individual human

---

[13] *Ibid.*, 188.
[14] *Ibid.*, 191, 192.

autonomy.[15] We discussed this issue extensively in the last chapter with respect to Market freedoms. We have seen that intellectual property rights ensure that only the originator or creator by an act of original acquisition retains this right to transfer, unless he or she expressly transfers or surrenders the copyright or patent to another. As long as the original creator maintains his intellectual property rights, all others who acquire the property through transfer are themselves precluded from performing similar acts of transfer without the consent of the producer. Clearly, if the right to transfer is central to the ownership right, as articulated by Nozick, then the institution of intellectual property is antithetical to individual freedom because in essence these rights abrogate the right of transfer. By enforcing these restrictions, we are treating the individual as a means to other ends, either utilitarian or the narrower objective of rewarding the original creator. From this philosophical perspective it follows that the principle of autonomy and issues of personal integrity cannot be consistently applied to offer a coherent moral defense of intellectual property.

While intellectual property rights fail to find moral support from general Kantian principles, at the same time, there are also critics within the IT community who specifically inveigh against intellectual property rights for similar reasons. In particular, we discussed the 'free software', movement headed by Richard Stallman, one of the principal architects of the GNU/Linux software, who denounces intellectual property rights in software as denial of individual freedom.[16]

Clearly, given the above discussion, if a distinguishable moral defense of intellectual property in software exists, it must rely on some form of utilitarian consequentialism.

Monopolistic Control of Products and Income

One can appreciate that intellectual property rights like copyright and patent rights have become increasingly urgent issues for the software industry where technology has enhanced the facility of duplication. Copies can be rapidly and inexpensively made, and instantly disseminated over vast distances at negligible costs. One could compare this situation with that of the so called old bricks and mortar industries in which patents were primarily used to protect machine design and copyright used to protect works of art such as books. In these cases replication involved considerable production costs and physically challenging issues of transportation and distribution.

---

[15] R. Nozick, *Anarchy, State and Utopia* (New York: Basic Books, 1974).

[16] See also Richard Stallman, "Free Software: Freedom and Cooperation," New York University, New York, 29 May 2001. http://www.mirror5.com/events/rms-nyu-2001-transcript.txt.

This reality should alert us to a possible contradiction between the general stated goals of the institution and the actual consequences of applying intellectual property rights to software. The alleged purpose of copyright and patent rights is to encourage individuals to bring their inventions and creations into the public domain so as to 'promote the progress of science and the useful arts.' They do so by securing for their creators certain exclusive rights to their creations for a limited time. Accordingly, enhancing the wealth of the creators is only ancillary to the goal of promoting the sciences by making these creations available to the public. One can summarize the rationale behind the institution in the following terms: the institution is supposed to stimulate invention in the first place by encouraging individuals to invent with the promise of an exclusive control of profits from the use of the invention. At the same time this encourages the inventor to make the inventions widely available to the public.

Now let us return to issues related to utilitarian consequentialism and look at the issue of increased availability. In non-software markets, copyright and patent rights, while creating an exclusive control, also promote increased supply. This is because with most forms of non-software, increased productivity entails significant increases in production costs. The inventor or author in most cases does not have access to the resources or capital necessary to meet these costs and this places a natural limit on the ability to supply and the availability of the product. However, patent and copyright enable the inventor or author to allow others to assume these costs and produce the item, while the inventor or author retains rights to share in the profitability of the venture through license fees and royalties. In this manner intellectual property rights operate to encourage the increased supply and availability while at the same time ensuring remuneration for the creators. But facility of replication means that production and transportation costs are decidedly negligible in the software industry so that profits have no relation to production or transportation costs but rather are exponentially related to the ability to eliminate or inhibit other suppliers. In the software market there is no incentive to encourage others to produce either under license or subject to royalties, because there really are no significant production costs in replicating the original. Profits, one might say, to a degree depend on restricting availability by enforcing intellectual property rules rather than controlling or sharing the costs of production in order to produce more. In this sense intellectual property rights in the software can be seen to work to restrict availability, rather than encourage increased supply, contrary to legislative intent.

This brings us to an important point, which is that intellectual property rights, when applied to software, function as an important tool in creating and maintaining a monopolistic control. In this respect they secure the same conditions monopolies and cartels strive to create, i.e., controlled scarcities in which prices are a function of management decision rather that the outcome of competition and market forces. Monopolistic conditions associated with higher prices and unconstrained profits are inconsistent with the utilitarian consequentialism, which favors greater availability through lower prices and expanded volume.

Now let us consider if the possibility of spectacular profits is a necessary motivational factor in the realization of software innovation and enhancement. Certainly, as is the case with patented prescription drugs, copyrights and patents on software create a monopolistic control over individual products, which encourages higher prices that don't reflect the production cost. However, one might argue that restricting access to maximize profitability provides the necessary motivation, which ensures that high quality software is produced. Ian Maitland has used this argument to justify profit-taking by large prescription drug companies that rely on patents to protect their interests.[17] This argument depends on the premise that these products would not be available or less available if one removed the possibility to maximize profits through intellectual property rights. Maitland argues that the research and development (R&D) undertaken by drug companies is expensive and often unrewarding. The high cost of drugs, which may appear to be economically produced, in actuality, he says, reflect the 'sunk costs' or costs associated with unsuccessful research projects, which need to be covered if the company is to remain viable. If drug companies were precluded from making substantial profits from their patented successes then they would cut back on R&D. This means fewer life-saving drugs and prescriptions would be available *tout court*, because companies would no longer be willing to undertake the initial financial investment associated with expensive research. Maitland also argues that if society revokes or weakens a company's patent protection then it would have reneged on a commitment. This is because companies undertake expensive research and investment in reliance on the government's policy of granting patents. Weakening patent protection would be like abrogating a contract or breaking a promise.[18]

However, as Maitland states, drug companies spend more on research and development than any other industry.[19] It is for this reason that Maitland's arguments work better in support of intellectual property rights for prescription drugs. Research and development in the software industry are less expensive and time consuming. It is certainly more convincing to argue that innovative drugs and the plethora of new drugs would not be available if not for patent protection because industry would not be prepared to finance risky, expensive research and development without the possibility of reaping healthy profits. The same could not be said as convincingly for the production of new and innovative software. It

---

[17] Ian Maitland, *op. cit.*
[18] *Ibid.*, 464.
[19] *Ibid.*, 466.

is well known that the home computer industry got its start not through massive investment from industry and industrial giants like IBM but through the activities of amateur hobbyists, who met in clubs such as the Homebrew Computer Club in Silicon Valley.[20] Many were motivated to create their innovations by the challenge of invention rather than profit. For example, the creator of the first spread sheet (*Visicalc*), Dan Brickland, never thought of patenting his creation to turn a personal profit.[21] Stallman believes software innovators would continue to invest their creative energies in the production of software, even if the possibilities for profits were vastly reduced, simply because of the desire and commitment to exercise their creative talents.[22] In point of fact he sees copyright and patent law as constraints on the exercise of creative talent, because software engineers are precluded from redeveloping, improving, disseminating, or sharing software that has been copyrighted or patented. Certainly with respect to software it would be much more difficult to claim, as does Maitland for prescription drugs, that the patent system works because it mobilizes scarce resources to create innovations to meet vital human needs. As he states "...the prospect of a "wildly profitable" product mobilizes private resources in the pursuit of a cure for AIDS—rather than a better mouse trap..."[23] In fact, innovative software would probably continue to be produced regardless of the possibility of creating a "wildly profitable" product because software research does not require that that massive sunk costs be covered. And in any case, for many talented individuals, the creation of software is something that it is inherently enjoyable and does not require the same monetary motivation.

Other empirical studies appear to back up this train of thought. It is recognized that so called Silicon Valley outside San Francisco was the locus for much of the pioneering research behind the IT revolution. Richard Gordon argues that the innovative process, especially as occurred in Silicon Valley, is not properly viewed as taking place primarily within individual companies.[24] His studies indicate that small and medium-sized companies were joined together in extended chains of production. These networks effected an innovative capacity that significantly exceeded the sum of the innovative capacities of the component companies. Gordon's thesis is that the flow of information and ideas between companies is the key to innovation. In his study of Silicon Valley he noted three particularly

---

[20] Bob Cringely, *The Triumph of the Nerds: Impressing their Friends*, Volume 1, Ambrose Videos, 1996, recounts the activities of the Homebrew Computer Club in Silicon Valley, which witnessed the first demonstration of the personal computer.

[21] *Ibid.*

[22] Stallman, *op. cit*, note 2.

[23] *Ibid.*, 463.

[24] Richard Gordon, "Innovation, Industrial Networks and High Technology Regions," in R. Camagni ed., *Innovation Networks: Spatial Perspectives* (London: Belhaven, 1991): 121–137.

important information pathways, or interconnections: the professional technical culture of Silicon Valley, in which personnel moved freely between companies, thereby sharing ideas; the interconnections between companies, markets and customers, enabling companies to anticipate and respond effectively to client needs; and strategic business alliances, which promote sharing of technology, research, production, and marketing capabilities between companies. Gordon's model, which sees networks of companies, which share information as crucial to the innovative process, challenges the traditional notion that strong intellectual property rights that prelude sharing are essential to innovation.

Richard Levin's research on spillovers supports Gordon's model of networks of innovation.[25] Levin finds that spillovers of technology between companies may facilitate rapid technological progress. Within certain industries, the more that competing firms can appropriate one another's innovations, the more the industry grows overall, yielding greater returns to even the innovating firms than would have been the case had they been able to keep their innovations to themselves. Spillover increases the competition in the industry, which may increase the number of firms, increase the overall economic surplus, or in other ways improve overall industry performance. Significantly, Levin's data do not support the hypothesis that spillovers discourage R&D investment.

Among other things, Levin investigates the effectiveness of various methods that firms use to acquire one another's technology. These include independent R&D, reverse engineering, licensing, reading patent disclosures, reading publications, attending meetings, hiring away competitors' employees, and talking with competitors' employees. Each of these spillover methods has associated costs. Perhaps not surprisingly, the most effective methods, independent R&D, reverse engineering, and licensing, are also the most costly. The other, less expensive methods, plus reverse engineering, are most effective where a competitor's innovation can be imitated in a relatively short time.

Levin finds the highest levels of spillover in the computer, communications equipment, electronic components, and aircraft industries. One might suppose that in such high-technology, research-intensive industries, spillovers would discourage investment in R&D. In fact, Levin finds no such disincentives. His explanation is that in these industries, innovation is cumulative, with firms building synergistically on each other's achievements. Imitation merges with creation, and spillover R&D enhances, rather than replaces, a firm's own R&D. In these industries, Firm A's spillover may raise rather than lower the marginal productivity of Firm B's own R&D, thus promoting advances and encouraging investment overall. By contrast, in industries such as chemicals or non-genetically

---

[25] Richard C. Levin, "Appropriability, R&D. Spending and Technical Performance," *American Economic Review* 78 (May 1998): 424–450.

engineered pharmaceuticals, innovations tend to be discrete. Firm B's knowledge of Firm A's innovation may not enhance B's R&D and may render us unnecessary further R&D that follows the same research path. In such industries, extensive spillover would lead to R&D disincentives he claims.

Levin believes that uniform strengthening of intellectual property laws can lead to perverse consequences. Changes in law may have different impacts in different industries, and stronger patent laws will not necessarily encourage innovation. In particular, strong intellectual property protection does not necessarily advance cumulative technologies.

Silverman points out our belief in the necessity of patents is often based on mythology that obscures the reality of the innovative process and the innovation itself.[26] We tend to think of a lone inventor like Edison who makes a unique pathbreaking discovery thereby opening up entirely new market possibilities. Most inventions he argues are more mundane that inspired. In modern business the holder of patent is more likely to be a corporation assigned the rights by individual or individual whose name or names are on the patent application. The result will be small incremental advances rather than big breakthroughs and as we pointed out in a previous chapter, the patenting of trivial processes more than anything else will work to trip other inventors.

Microsoft and Market Dominance

However, monopolistic conditions are not simply a function of the ability to restrict supply and ensure that that there are no competitors who could supply more of the good and effect a lower price. There must also be a significant demand for the product. A company must also be able to either control or manipulate demand, or find itself in a market subject to a strong if not inelastic demand that only the producer's product can satisfy.

However, a successful software product can have the potential to create a market dominance which would not be possible, for example, in the prescription drug industry. It is true that in both industries intellectual property rights endow a particular firm with a monopolistic control over the supply of a particular good or service; but in the software industry the requirement of compatibility can enhance the initial success and extend an exclusive control over the supply of related and even future products.

Of course, one might question the alleged tendency of intellectual property to create monopolistic conditions by pointing out that there are no restrictions to

---

[26] Alexander E. Silverman, "Myth, Empiricism, and America's Competitive Edge: The Intellectual Property Antitrust Protection Act," *Stanford Law Review* 43, (July, 1991): 1417–1445.

entering the software market. The existence of software innovators and other software manufacturers should provide the competition that ensures against controlled scarcity and price management, regardless of intellectual property restrictions. However, this argument might have held during the infancy of the personal computer, but no longer, due to certain contingencies that render the industry somewhat unique. Currently the industry consists of two dominant players: Microsoft and Apple, with the former clearly holding the greater share of the market. Microsoft has 95% share of the operating system market, and its current share of the Internet browser market is 90%. Because of the growth of the Internet and the increasing need for computers to communicate with one another a uniform operating system has become a very high priority. Thanks to Microsoft's initial association with IBM, when the giant computer company first entered the PC market, Microsoft was uniquely positioned to become the system of choice and the industry standard. The overwhelming need for compatibility, and Microsoft's initial success through association with IBM created the necessary demand, which helped secure the resulting monopolistic conditions.

In reality, once a given system captures a majority of the market share there can be little or no incentive for consumers to purchase alternative systems and software, as compatibility becomes the overriding concern in selecting a given system. This means that producing a superior, more efficient, securer system will be a negligible factor in consumer choice. For example, if the majority of consumers are buying AZT (the anti-AIDS drug), this does not provide the Burroughs Welcome Co. (the original producers of AZT) with an overwhelming market advantage. If Bristol-Myers produces a superior drug, which is more effective and more competitively priced, then the rational consumer would choose the new product over the AZT regardless. However, in the software industry, even if a start up company produces a better designed, securer, and more efficient operating system than that employed by the majority of users, the rational consumer would still prefer the older system because the key issue is compatibility. The concerns here are the ability to communicate with the majority of users, and also for businesses, the cost of retraining workers to utilize less familiar operating systems.

The reason that most markets, for example, the prescription drug industry or the auto industry, are not susceptible to similar domination is because there is no necessity for different products (for example, drugs or vehicles) to interactively coordinate and communicate with one another. If this were the case in the auto industry, then we might well have one dominant producer of car software and a number of competing manufacturers producing the hardware (the physical vehicles). In any event, the necessity for compatibility drives consumers to prefer a single universal product within the software market. Copyright and patent then give producers a monopoly over the production of their products creating a structured market that in general outlines conforms to monopolistic rather than competitive conditions. Historically it should be remembered that in the 1960s computer manufacturers were required to unbundle their software and offer it separately from the hardware by Anti-Trust legislation.[27]

If you were the major producer of bananas—a giant United Fruit Company type operation—you would certainly have an insurmountable market advantage if you held a copyright or patented license that prevented others producing bananas. Accordingly, while governments give this power to the software giant, at the same time they struggle to stamp out the manifestations of market dominance such as price fixing and innovative packaging that attempt to smother emerging competition and extend dominance into other facets of the IT industry. In fact since the agreement between Microsoft and the American Justice Department in 2001, in which the federal government backed away from breaking up the software giant, Microsoft has maintained its 95% share of the operating system market, and increased its share of the Internet browser market to 90%, up from 60% (see appendix). In effect, governments are continuing to endow the principal supplier with the legal capacity to maintain a monopolistic market in which one can maximize income or economic rent. Overall there should be a rethink of the situation. Simply reacting to the predictable manifestations of Microsoft's market dominance is similar to allowing combustible materials to lie proximate to heated surfaces and reacting only when the inevitable fires break out.

To be fair, a defense of maintaining the intellectual property rights that support a single company's dominance in the marketing of software would need to demonstrate that the current monopolistic situation is in fact beneficial in terms of efficient allocation of resources and the improvement of the human condition. However, most defenses of profit-taking depend on invisible hand arguments that are understood not to apply in less than perfect competition situations. It is difficult to overcome such obvious disutilities such as rent seeking, artificially high prices, restricted supply and the lack of consumer choice that flow from monopolistic conditions, as we have said. One may fall back, however, on the argument that intellectual property rights are necessary to protect the US dominance in world markets as the US market shifts from the old bricks and mortar economy to a new IT economy; and, of course, linking this with the proposition that the global economy depends on a strong US economy. Steven Metalitz, former counsel to the Senate Committee on the Judiciary, reports that congressional debate on intellectual property policy often relies on the argument that that strong intellectual property protection is a key factor in America's technological progress and competitiveness.[28] It is argued that strong intellectual property laws made America

---

[27] A. Branscomb, *Who owns Information: From Privacy to Public Access* (New York: Basic Books, 1994), 138.
[28] Silverman, *op. cit*, 1426.

strong in the past and will continue to do so in the future. The argument is dubious, aside from the obvious issue as to whether this is really a moral argument with any universal application, since the utilities primarily benefit a particular nation state. Moreover, while the link between global prosperity and US prosperity remains an assumption not easily accessible to empirical proof, the conceptualization may itself be highly misleading.

While it is doubtless that information can be a product that can be bought and sold like everything else, it is doubtful that an entire economy can base itself on the buying and selling of information. Adam Smith observed that information and transportation are key factors that allow for the expansion of the market and the possibilities of developing specialties and specializations that generate wealth. However, the economic market must still produce tangible goods and services for the prosperity and survival of mankind. As manufacturing jobs continue to dry up in the US, and future prosperity is threatened, it may be a grand illusion to believe that the IT revolution represents a profound shift for the United States that can replace the old bricks and mortar economy in a way comparable to the shift from the agrarian agricultural based economy to an urban industrialized based economy. Indeed we are not actually revolutionizing production from an industrial to some form of non-industrial base. Computers are simply a technology that enhances industrial productivity, rather than a new form of productivity that can in itself provide tangible goods and services. Industry and agriculture (whether the latter is industrialized or not) provide the essential products that sustain human existence while modern software in itself can only produce a virtual reality of agricultural and manufactured goods. In point of fact, by keeping the price of software artificially high through the mechanism of copyright and patent, we are creating extraordinary concentrations of wealth while diverting scarce resources towards the purchase of overpriced computer technology. Alternatively, such resources could have been used for the purchase of more basic manufactured and agricultural products to alleviate core human needs more immediately relevant to the survival and welfare of humanity.

With respect to patents on prescription drugs, one can argue, as does Maitland, that consumer expenditure on high priced prescription drugs stimulates industry to invest money and energy in the search for innovative life saving medicines. Excessive profits in the prescription drug industry have the effect of marshaling society's resources to meet the most essential of human needs: health and life itself. As we said, it is more difficult to utilize similar arguments for high priced software products. High priced software is not necessary to stimulate the necessary human resources to produce better software. As Stallman argues, it would still be produced even if we significantly reduced potential revenue. Moreover, IP rights work to prevent others from improving and enhancing existing software.

Ultimately intellectual property rights applied to software appear merely to protect the inflated incomes of a small group of successful entrepreneurs without offering compensating benefits to the rest of the human community.

Other societal costs associated with the enforcement of intellectual property rules for software also need to be considered. Libertarians point out that with a *de jure* or legally assisted monopoly there are significant costs incurred by society to regulate the market and enforce the privileges that so called intellectual property sanctions. Society must pay the costs for supporting the institutions that license intellectual property and also those that facilitate the prosecution of those who fail to acknowledge the privileges of the patent or copyright holder.[29] Also a significant component of higher priced software necessarily includes legal fees and related costs of detection undertaken by the producer to ensure that easily replicated software is properly licensed. Indeed, because of the facility with which IT can be copied and disseminated, significant detective work must supplement lawyerly pursuits through the courts to enforce copyrights and patents. For example, in addition to teams of lawyers, Microsoft employs former US law enforcement agents to work as detectives in Europe to discover and prosecute producers of pirated software.[30] Dominance in the software industry requires eternal vigilance on the part of teams of lawyers and investigators. Intimidation or the threats of legal action, and readiness to pursue legal remedies have been essential tools in maintaining control of the software market, even when users dare to use alternative software.[31] While it may be the case that the prescription drug industry spends more on R&D than any other industry, it may also be the case that the software industry spends more on legal and detective fees than any other industry. If software were free, i.e., meaning replication would be unrestricted, societal resources could be allocated to address more basic human needs rather than unnecessary legal and detective services required to ensure compliance with intellectual property legislation.

While patents may have given prescription drug companies monopolies over particular products, for example AZT (the successful anti-AIDS drug), intellectual property rights over software have facilitated an industry wide monopoly. Since monopolies and cartels tend to inflate prices and restrict supply, an intervening authority may be necessary to adjust distribution and reduce these concentrations of wealth. Reasonably priced goods and services could then be accessed by a greater number of consumers. The responsibility to reduce

---

[29] R.M. Stallman, "GNU manifesto," in M.D. Ermann & M.S. Shauf, eds., *Computers, Ethics and Society* (Oxford: Oxford University Press, 2003): 153–161.
[30] BUSINESSWEEK ONLINE: July 26, 1999, http://www.businessweek.com:/1999/99.
[31] *The Gulf Today* (Friday November 17, 2004): 23.

inequalities of wealth may be a responsibility we have not only to the least advantaged class within our own society, but also members of the greater human community, who may exist in dire circumstances. As Peter Singer has explained, it is necessary to recognize a global ethic based on a utilitarian ethics of impartiality. This would mean that we have some overriding duties to foreigners, which trump our duties to fellow citizens. As he states "Reducing the number of human beings living in absolute poverty is surely a more urgent priority than reducing the relative poverty caused by some people living in palaces while others live in houses that are merely adequate."[32]

Indeed this global disparity in wealth can be seen to be increasing through the global trade in intellectual property. As we mentioned previously, according to 1999 IMF figures world wide trade in royalties and licenses primarily for intellectual property realized more than a $ 23 USD billion surplus for the United States. No other country in the world had a net surplus of over $1 billion.[33] This surplus originated from the predominance of copyright-related income. Many third world counties had no calculable intellectual property revenues. These facts have led one researcher to conclude, as we have stated, that "...the main global function of TRIPS is the protection, expansion and longevity of these massive copyright and patent revenue streams".[34]

It is also worth noting that researchers have pointed out that the economic disparity between the Western and non-Western world is also exaggerated by the technological gap in which there has been less participation in the computer and the internet revolutions.[35] In part this has been due to the necessity to repay debts, significant limitation in telephone systems and power grids, and the high cost of computer hardware. But another major factor is the high cost, inaccessibility and the highly restrictive conditions under which schools, universities and individuals users obtain and use computer software. These rules have been enforced universally through the TRIPS agreement, which in the case of software copyright protection is global and mandatory. Thus poor universities in Africa or South America may pay the same licensing costs as a rich university in the US or the UK.

---

[32] Peter Singer, *One World: the Ethics of Globalization* (New Haven and London: Yale University Press, 2002), 175.
[33] Alan Story, "Copyright, TRIPS and International Educational Agenda," in P. Drahos & R. Mayne eds. Global *Intellectual Property Rights: Knowledge Access and Development*, (New York: Palmgrave Macmillan, 2002): 125–143, 131.
[34] *Ibid.*
[35] Alan Story, "Copyright, TRIPS and International Educational Agenda,"; Gary Lea, "Digital Millennium or Digital Dominion? The Effect of IPRs in Software on Developing countries," in P. Drahos and R. Mayne eds., *Global Intellectual Property Rights: Knowledge Access and Development*, (New York: Palmgrave Macmillan, 2002): 144–158.

To summarize, we have argued that the usual moral justifications associated with the institution of property fail to justify intellectual property as applied to software. There are the limitations on personal freedom involved in restricting reproduction and transfer of information. Moreover, intellectual property rights foster a monopolistic market contrary to the utilitarian considerations we have just adumbrated. An overriding concern is to overcome the disutilities of a less than competitive market. One possible solution is to license Microsoft's monopolistic position along the lines of the old Bell Telephone Company, and then impose strict price controls and other forms of monitoring. On the other hand, promoting a more competitive market that operates according to invisible hand principles may be the most efficient mechanism to redress matters. With this in mind, the US government and others such as the EU could still impose the solution that the US backed away from in 2001 and split the company up into two; one that provides the operating system and another that provides applications such as the video players that can be run on the system. This would possibly reduce overall dominance in the software market but would still leave Microsoft, or the operating system wing of Microsoft, a monopoly in the production of the operating system. Because this monopolistic position is only possible through maintaining intellectual property rules, another possibility would involve abandoning copyright and patent as applied to software by legislatively reversing prior court decisions. Governments might then proceed by funding and endowing research institutes to produce and create software that would then be used by industry and education without copyright or patent restrictions attached.[36]

Conclusion:

We began with arguments that provide a moral basis for ownership of tangible physical phenomena, such as land and chattels, and considered whether the same arguments might be used to support intellectual property rights. We identified two principal moral defenses: one based on utilitarian concerns relating to human welfare, the other appeals to issues of individual autonomy and private control. Following Christman's distinction between control and income ownership, we pointed out that intellectual property rights, secured through copyright and patent, really relate to the income right aspect of ownership rather that the control right aspect that includes the right to exclude, use, and alienate. Christman has argued that issues of personal autonomy are to be identified with control rather than income rights. But it would seem that intellectual property rights

---

[36] As advocated by people such as Stallman, *op. cit.*

do have some relevance to issues of individual autonomy and control in so far as they invest in the creator of the property exclusive control over the income that flows from the sale of the inventions or creations. On the other hand, while intellectual property concentrates certain rights in the owner who acquires title through the creative act of original acquisition, it restricts the rights of all those who acquire from him/her through transfer, in so far as they are denied the right to transfer without the consent of the copyright or patent holder. In this sense, intellectual property is at the same time antithetical to individual autonomy in so far as it operates to restrict the right to transfer freely. From the libertarian perspective, which sees ownership as founded on deontological principles relating to the value of individual freedom and autonomy, intellectual property rights, through restrictions on transfer, represent an unnatural interference in the exercise of ownership and personal autonomy. It follows that basing intellectual property rights on the value of autonomy is problematic. Accordingly we concluded that one would be on safer ground if one looks to utilitarian consequentialism.

We considered the utilitarian perspective associated with Locke and more recently H.L.A. Hart. This meant specifically considering the intent of the legislation and other possible positive and negative consequences, which result from creating a monopolistic control of income received from sales. One recognizes that the goal of this special legislation is not to enrich the inventers and authors but to promote the progress of science and the useful arts by encouraging innovators to bring their innovations forward into the public domain and make them available. However, we went on to mention several aspects of the software industry that make it significantly different from most other non-software industries, and which tend to vitiate the role of intellectual property in effecting this goal, and realizing other positive developments.

The first is the fact that replication of software is virtually cost free, which means that there are no significant costs incurred through increased productivity. In contrast, for non-software products, increased productivity means an incremental cost increase and significant capital outlay. In the case of non-software industries, copyright and patent actually encourage increased productivity and thereby increased public access through the mechanisms of royalties and licensing fees. In the software industry they have virtually no function in encouraging increased production because the cost of replication poses no significant barriers that would need to be overcome through these mechanisms. In these circumstances, copyright and patent have a negligible impact on productivity and essentially function as a legal means to restrict supply and close down other reproducers and suppliers, so as to enhance economic rent, given the absence of discernible advantages in terms of mitigating or sharing the increased costs associated with increased productivity.

Another important feature that distinguishes software is the necessity for a single operating system. With the growing importance of the Internet, a single uniform operating system facilitates and allows for communication between machines. The necessity for a uniform operating system creates an overwhelming demand. When linked with intellectual property laws that mandate exclusive control of the income from one's products, we create conditions that encourage a monopolistic market.

Given current realities, it is obvious that intellectual property rights applied to software function not simply to give the producer a monopolistic control over his/her innovation but rather now provide the tools that protect and extend the market dominance of a single producer. The question, subsequently considered, is whether the market monopoly that has emerged through the mechanism of intellectual property rights can be defended on moral grounds. Clearly we answered negatively, as high costs through inflated prices, restrictions on supply and diminished consumer choice can hardly contribute to the increased welfare and well being of humanity. It would seem that society is simply misallocating scarce resources that could be used to address more vital core human needs. Moreover, given that R&D in software is relatively inexpensive, the argument that high priced software is necessary to stimulate and cover the costs of R&D remains unconvincing. If one acknowledges at the same time that intellectual property rights also restrict innovation and improvement by prohibiting others from copying, redesigning and sharing copyrighted or patented software, it would follow that intellectual property rules are doing little to further the progress of science and the useful arts.

As we advised, there are good reasons to reverse the current market structure, and either promote a more competitive industry competitive so that some semblance of an invisible hand mechanism is allowed to work, or officially to recognize the monopoly and license it as such, subject to strict monitoring and price controls. The latter would be a possible solution along the lines of the old Bell Telephone Company. On the other hand, the US government could reconsider the option it rejected in 2001, which would have divided Microsoft into one company that provides the operating system and another that provides applications such as the video players. This would restore a more competitive market although obviously accepting a certain continuing dominance. A third possibility would involve undercutting the commercial character of software engineering altogether through abolition of intellectual property rights as applied to software. This would involve placing software on the same footing as mathematical formulae, scientific laws, and processes of thought by denying the application of copyright and patent. This means legislatively reversing prior court decisions, and then perhaps funding and endowing research institutes to produce and create software that would then be used by industry and education without copyright or patent restrictions.

Appendix

Consider developments over recent years. On April 5, 2004 Judges in the US state of Nebraska re-activated a class-action lawsuit against Microsoft Corp. The action claims Microsoft over-charged customers for Windows 98 by setting the cost artificially high, and seeks $ 425 m in damages. E-mail is likely to form the basis of much evidence in the case, including a 1997 communication reportedly sent by Microsoft group vice president Jeff Raikes to billionaire Warren Buffet, seeking his investment in Microsoft. Raikes told Buffet that some observers had likened Windows to a "toll bridge" adding the company is a "90 % + margin business." Buffet did not then invest in Microsoft.[37] Earlier in March 2004, the European Commission decided to impose a $ 613 million fine and force the software company to market versions of its Windows operating system without its media player. The media player is the software that lets computers play music and videos, something, which has had growing importance as music and video, are widely distributed over the Internet. The Europeans and some of Microsoft's competitors were concerned, as was the US Justice Department when it sued Microsoft in 1998, that Microsoft may use its monopoly over the Windows operating system to limit consumers' ability to choose other products that add functions to Windows. In its editorial commenting on the European case the *New York Times* also said that the Europeans should press Microsoft to be more forthcoming about the code needed for non-Microsoft programmers to write applications that run on Windows.[38] The EC first began investigating Microsoft in the late 1990s at the same time that the US Justice Department was trying to break up the software giant into one company that offers operating systems and another that offers applications. That remedy was rejected by a federal appeals court in 2001 as part of its broader review of the trial judge's ruling that Microsoft was a monopolist. Rather than proceed in a hearing to prove that Microsoft should be split, the Justice Department agreed to settle the case. The decision came shortly after the Sept. 11 attacks, which the court referenced in its plea to the parties to resolve the case without the need for a judicial ruling.[39] As the *New York Times* stated, the agreement reached by the American Justice Department with Microsoft in 2001 left much of the monitoring of Microsoft's actions up to computer manufacturers, which have little stake in policing the giant software company.

---

[37] "US Judges Re-Activate Microsoft Antitrust Case," *ComputerWire*, (March 22, 2004), Issue 4883.
[38] *New York Times*, late edition, New York, N.Y. (Nov 24, 2003): A22.
[39] Jaret Seiberg, "Rules Of The Road," *Daily Deal/The Deal* (April 5, 2004).

Chapter Twelve

A Delicate Balance: The Right to Health Care, IP Rights in Pharmaceuticals and TRIPS Compliance

To this stage we have denied the linkage between intellectual property and the belief in free market values. We also went on to deny that the traditional ethical arguments that have been used to defend non-intellectual property have application to intellectual property. However, with respect to pharmaceuticals, it is necessary to attend to utilitarian arguments that may add counter weight to the suppression of individual freedom and the market intervention associated with the enforcement of IP rights. We discussed the central issue of the possible relationship between IP rights and innovation, including the alleged linkage between research and profits as realized within the software industry. We argued that with respect to pharmaceuticals, it is certainly more convincing to argue that patent protection is necessary for viable research and development. It was alleged that innovative drugs and the plethora of new drugs would not be available if not for patent protection because industry would not be prepared to finance risky, expensive research and development without the possibility of reaping healthy profits, which is not the case with software where innovation does not require the same massive investment.

In this chapter we intend to consider closely this argument, which holds that maintaining strong patent regimes, which impose monopolistic conditions that allow pharmaceutical companies to charge what the market will bear, has been justified by reference to the high cost of research and development. It is claimed that the system works and has provided financial support for the creation of innovative life sustaining medicines, which otherwise would not be available. Thus, the industry and its supporters have promoted the belief that better health care through improved innovative medicines is directly related to strong patent protection.[1] Even the alleged universal right to health and health care that logically entails that medical treatment be more accessible through lower pharmaceutical prices, is denied exigency on the grounds that imposition of this

---

[1] See for example, Ian Maitland, "Priceless Goods: How Should Life-Saving Drugs Be Priced?" *Business Ethics Quarterly* 12, 4 (2002): 451–480, 464.

right would undercut financial support for successful R&D. Indeed multinational pharmaceutical companies that have traditionally benefited from IP regimes within local and national markets have now pushed universal global application for strong patent regimes through the TRIPS agreement.

However, we argue that moral considerations relating to the right to health care impose obligations on the pharmaceutical companies that cannot be avoided by asserting the necessity to impose monopolistic controls over pricing. We will examine closely and question the belief that the relationship between the development of new and effective medicinal products and the assumed necessity to maintain strong intellectual property rights, applies in all circumstances, and therefore should have universal application. We scrutinize closely the TRIPS agreement, which is sponsored by the WTO and seeks to make patent protection for pharmaceuticals mandatory for all members that either lack or weakly enforce patent protection.

In point of fact, we argue that the universal imposition of a strong IP rights regime with global reach (as embodied in the TRIPS agreement) will in the immediate and long term reduce access to life sustaining medicines and most probably in the long term reduce global potential for successful R&D. In conducting this inquiry we give special emphasis to the threat to health care in the developing and less developed world occasioned by the insistence that India be TRIPS compliant.

The Fairness Argument

However, before considering in detail this principal argument based on the relationship between strong IP rights and R&D we should briefly re-visit an argument that defends IP rights in pharmaceuticals on the basis of fairness rather than utility. As discussed by Richard M. De George, this argument holds that within the economic system of free enterprise those who invest effort and or money in the development of ideas that create innovative products useful and beneficial to others, should have the opportunity to recover the investment and possibly make a profit. It would, therefore, be unfair and unjust for others to take the result, market it as their own, and profit from it without having to spend comparable money or time in the development of the product.

This, of course, is a variant of the fairness argument based on the free rider issue. To put the argument in other words, it would be unfair for individuals to benefit from the work and investments of others without having made equivalent contributions to that original work or product. However, Werhane and Gorman have pointed out that knowledge that drives innovation is always to some extent derivative in that all successful inventions and innovation free ride on the earlier work and research of others.[2] This is research and expertise that has accumulated over generations is never simply the reflection of a single researcher or the effort or investment of a team of researchers. The development and marketing of AZT is a case in point. Burroughs Wellcome (now GlaxoSmithKline) claimed the drug as their product, marketed it and profited from it as a successful antiretroviral drug for AIDS sufferers. However, the remedy was first synthesized at the Detroit Institute of Cancer Research as a cancer drug but never patented because it proved to be ineffective for cancer. It also needs to be pointed out that the industry has traditionally benefited from publicly funded research centres, which often supply research and development free of charge. These facts, I believe, seriously vitiate the argument based on fairness that sees other producers of a patented drug free riding on the work and financial investment of the patent holder. In a profound sense all current technology and innovative products have been produced by individuals who have benefited from accumulated stores of human knowledge which they could not possibly have produced or generated. Therefore why should we regard the patent holder as especially unfairly treated?

For these reasons, I believe, the principal argument that needs to be addressed is the utilitarian one, which says that we are better off with a limited availability of innovative drugs rather than their absence altogether, which would result if patent protection were not guaranteed and successful developers and marketers could not generate sufficient profits to cover and finance R& D.

IP Rights and Innovation

Initially, it appears difficult to overcome the argument (if it is reliably the case) that unless the pharmaceutical companies were allowed to charge prices that exceed the actual unit cost of production, the pharmaceutical products that some people desperately need and desire would not be available at all. Empirical studies would appear to support the notion that strong intellectual property rights have a positive relation to innovation in the pharmaceutical industry, which is not the case in the software industry. Edwin Mansfield's studies in the late 1980s indicated that in most industries patents correlate only weakly with innovation. The drug and the chemical industries are the exceptions.[3] These findings are supported by Levin

---

2   P.H. Werhane and M. Gorman "Intellectual Property Rights, Moral Imagination and Access to Life-Enhancing Drugs," *Business Ethics Quarterly* 15, 4 (2005): 595–614.
3   E. Mansfield, "Intellectual Property rights, Technological change and Economic Growth," in C. Walker and M. Bloomfield, eds. *Intellectual Property Rights and Capital Formation in the Next Decade* (New York: University Press of America, 1988).

who argues that innovation in industries such as the chemical and non-genetically engineered pharmaceuticals is discrete rather than cumulative[4] A firm's knowledge of a competitor's innovation renders superfluous any further R&D along the path followed by the competitor. In such industries spillovers, the capture of intellectual property value by competing firms due to imperfect appropriability, would lead to R&D disincentives. On the other hand, in the computer communications equipment, electronic components and the aircraft industries spillovers encourage R&D. This is because in these industries innovation is cumulative with each company building synergistically on the other's achievements.

Patents correlate with innovation in the drug and chemical industries because these products are in fact difficult to develop, easy to copy and have long product life cycles. In other words, a drug such as AZT is a true break through which represents a significant financial and human investment. It can be easily duplicated by means of generic drugs. At the same time there is not much scope for improvement unless one embarks on a promising alternative directed research. In other words imaginative tinkering with the existing product is not very likely to produce a new superior product.

In this case intellectual property rights are seen to make strong sense in terms of enhancing and encouraging innovation which is apparently not the case with IP rights and software, for example. Thus the utilitarian benefits to mankind due to innovative products do apparently provide moral support for strong IP rights applied to pharmaceuticals.

Countervailing Moral Arguments

However, this position is challenged by a moral argument which holds that "one has a duty or obligation to help those in great need whom one can help at little ... cost to oneself". De George holds the obligation to help is not an act of charity. An act of charity would consist in doing more than one is morally obliged to do. If one has a moral obligation to help a fellow human being in need, fulfilling that obligation is not an act of charity. De George goes on to say "... there seems to be at least a prima facie case for saying that they [pharmaceutical companies] have some obligation even though the extent to the obligation may be difficult to

---

[4]   Richard C. Levin, "Appropriability, R&D Spending and Technological Performance," *American Economic Review* 78 (May 1988): 424–450, 427.

specify…"[5] The social responsibility argument based on imperfect obligations is also supported by other positions that hold that individuals have a human right to health care or even more strongly a right to health. The UN Declaration of Human Rights, Article 25 speaks of "a right to a standard of living adequate for health and…medical care".[6] If we accept the application of these moral rights, together with the obligation to help those in great need, then we can say the pharmaceutical companies are subject to both negative and positive obligations. With respect to the negative aspect all relevant parties, governments, businesses and individuals are obliged not to prevent anyone from having access to that which is necessary to sustain life. The positive aspect entails an obligation to take positive steps to ensure that access is available. Clearly no corresponding obligations apply to software producers, for example, absent a general recognition that individuals independent of contractual relations have moral claim rights to software, or that the lack of software creates a great need.

Combining arguments based on the right to health care or health and the obligation to help those in great need, the issue is therefore whether the rights of those in great need trump IP rights in pharmaceuticals which are grounded in the enhancement of the innovative process. It can of course be argued that without IP rights there would be no innovative life sustaining pharmaceuticals *tout court*. Nevertheless, one can reasonably say that the former should take precedence in those instances in which suspension of IP rights in pharmaceuticals would not seriously impair R&D.

Ultimately, one needs to keep in mind that the IP right is essentially an income right.[7] The relationship between strong IP rights and innovation is based on the assumption that exclusive rights to the income from all sales of particular products are justified in so far as income acts as an incentive to innovation by covering the R&D costs in order to allow for a reasonable profit. However, pharmaceutical companies do make spectacular profits that do much more than cover the R&D costs. A Fortune 500 report in 2001 notes that the pharmaceutical industry was the most profitable industry for several years running. In the same year the drug companies channeled 18.5 % of revenue into profits yet spent just 12.5 % of revenue on R&D.[8] The Pharmaceutical Research and Manufacturers Association spent 558

---

[5] De George, "Intellectual Property and Pharmaceutical Drugs: An Ethical Analysis," *Business Ethics Quarterly* 15, 4 (2005): 549–575, 558.

[6] *Ibid.*, 553. See De George for a fuller discussion of this point.

[7] See David Lea, "From the Wright Brothers to Microsoft: Issues in the Moral Grounding of intellectual Property Rights," *Business Ethics Quarterly* 16, 4 (2006): 579–598.

[8] De George, *op. cit.*, 575, note 38.

million in the last decade on political contributions, and between 1993–2000, spent 65 million on fighting legislation that it disliked.[9]

Thus, the picture projected which conceives of drug companies struggling in a competitive environment in which IP rights protect revenues that are desperately needed to cover sunk R&D costs may be far from the actuality. IP rights may well protect profits that are artificially high and well in excess of sunk R&D costs and ordinary operating costs. Altogether this underlines that corporations, as legal persons, have the wealth and means to help those in great need. As de George points out, helping those in need is an imperfect duty and the responsibility and burden falls heavier on the rich than on poor.[10]

As we have argued throughout the text property rights are not ontically independent of the state and the consensual arrangements that form the social contract. *A fortiori*, IP rights represent concessions that the state makes to innovators through the granting of monopolistic controls. Contrary to the natural rights rhetoric that drove the initial TRIPS agreement, IP rights really represent a trade off between the desire for open and competitive markets and the goal of enhancing innovation through the incentive of exclusive rights to income.[11] These are rights that find their justification from a utilitarian approach rather than a deontological perspective in which the denial of the right would represent the violation of some particular human value such as personal autonomy, which is frequently utilized to ground our belief in a particular human or natural right.[12]

Clearly if thinkers such as Ronald Dworkin are correct, this is an instance in which individual rights such as the right to health or the right to health care should trump the monopolistic powers granted to the pharmaceutical industry by means of the authority of the relevant administrative, legislative and international bodies. Individuals and companies have an obligation to help those in need in circumstances in which the effort does not entail a great expense to themselves, and clearly, a heavy responsibility falls on the pharmaceutical companies. These responsibilities would entail both negative and positive duties on the part of the pharmaceuticals.

---

[9] *Ibid.*, 572, note 4.
[10] *Ibid.*, 558.
[11] See A.S. Oddi, "Nature and Scope of the Agreement: Article: TRIPS _ Natural Rights and a Polite Form of Economic Imperialism," *Vanderbilt Journal of Transnational Law* 29 (1996): 415–429.on TRIPS and the natural rights argument.
[12] See David Lea, *op. cit.*

Shared Responsibilities

We should discuss in somewhat more detail the implications of the positive duties which pharmaceutical companies should recognize. As mentioned earlier responsibilities for providing life saving drugs do not fall solely on the shoulders of the pharmaceutical industry. To varying degrees these responsibilities also apply to governments and individuals as well as companies. Article 25 of the UN Declaration on Human rights is primarily addressed to governments. Nevertheless special responsibilities apply to those who are best placed to render service and access. In the case of the pharmaceutical industry, we can say that it is undoubtedly well placed to assist those in great need due to disease or environmental disasters, because their business is health care. As we have said, this means that the pharmaceutical industry not only has a duty not to deny access, it also has a positive obligation to do that which it can do to help those in need. But it needs to be noted that in reality, companies cannot fulfill their obligations through isolated acts of generosity. If pharmaceutical companies abandon their concerns over IP rights and generously give antiretroviral drugs away in the areas populated by impoverished AIDS victims, little will be achieved. As Pat Werhane and Michael Gorman point out, in many impoverished areas of Sub-Sahara Africa where the problem is most acute, there are often no places to send the medicines, no distribution centers, and no competent medical professionals to administer and monitor drug use. In other words, giving the drugs away will be totally ineffective. There needs to be a coordination of government, NGOs, donor agencies and medical professionals to ensure effective use. When drugs are given away as in sub-Sahara Africa, which lacks the necessary infrastructure, pharmaceuticals simply find their way into the black market to be resold at higher prices in more affluent countries. According to one report, 2/3 of the AZT now virtually given away in many African countries finds its way back to Europe through the black market.[13]

Ensuring access to life preserving drugs involves not simply the delivery of a product. It requires coordination between pharmaceutical companies, government, donor agencies, NGOs and medical professionals in order to implement a delivery, medical and monitoring system. This means drug companies need to do more than simply make the product available. They have to be proactive and actually become involved with the above mentioned groups to create alliances and systems. This entails that drug companies need to do more than simply waive their IP rights and allow countries such as South Africa to produce generic copies of patented pharmaceuticals. In many of the worst affected areas in Africa there is complete lack of economic, administrative and medical infrastructure which

---

[13] P.H. Werhane and M. Gorman, *op. cit.*, 605.

completely frustrates the possibilities of the production and delivery of generic drugs. In these circumstances, as Werhane and Gorman point out, drug companies must work to create a cooperative program with the aforementioned groups to ensure a coordinated level of required health care is actually realized. Werhane and Gorman point to the example of the Merck and the Gates Foundation, which is working in Botswana to provide treatment for 40,000 AIDS sufferers.[14]

Pharma Lobbying, legal challenges and the TRIPS Agreement

Negative duties, as we have said, would require non-interference and the obligation not to prevent access to life sustaining medicines, and positive obligations involve actively taking steps to ensure availability. But moving away from the ideal world in which Kantian imperatives universally constrain the actions of rational moral agents, the reality is one in which the pharmaceutical industry not only fails to allow access but vigorously takes positive steps to ensure that access is further reduced.

For example, the pharmaceutical industry has used its resources to lobby Western governments for global enforcement of IP rights in circumstances that in effect reduce world wide access to life saving drugs. A dispute indicative of drug company lobbying involved Brazil's production of anti-retrovirals in pursuance of its national campaign to treat all HIV patents needing such drugs. Brazil initially relied on imported drugs but as the currency fell Brazil manufactured some of the off-patent drugs in its own laboratories greatly reducing costs. In 2001 it threatened to do the same for certain patented drugs through what would have been a compulsory license. This threat ultimately led to negotiated lower costs for the import of these drugs. The United States, responding to pressure from the pharmaceutical companies, threatened Brazil before the WTO, arguing that the country had violated TRIPS agreement, but agreed to put the dispute into bilateral discussions.

The TRIPS agreement (Trade-Related Aspects of Intellectual Property Rights), which came into force in January 1 of 1995, is also a direct result of intensive industry lobbying. This agreement, which was pushed through the WTO by the representatives of Western governments, will have and is having a profound effect, especially upon the Indian pharmaceutical industry, a key producer a generic drugs. The TRIPS agreement concluded in 1995 requires all WTO members to issue patents on medicines. Many countries such as India simply did not recognize patents on medicines. However, TRIPS required that patents be introduced,

---

[14] *Ibid.*, 610.

and India, for example, agreed to introduce theirs on Jan., 1 2005. It should also be pointed out that under the TRIPS agreement, India agreed not only to consider protection for medicines developed after January 1, 2005, it also agreed to consider applications filed during 1995–2005 under the so-called "mailbox" provision (Article 70.8) of TRIPS, which will be discussed later. However, TRIPS does allow a country to implement compulsory licenses. Article 31, following the Doha Declaration of 2001, permits countries to create systems to administer the production or import of generic products from the competitive sector. This approach can be used for emergencies, including health care emergencies (Article 31(b)). Nevertheless despite the fact that TRIPS does allow a country to implement compulsory licenses, the US has, in the recent past, threatened trades sanctions against countries that implemented such licenses. It was only after campaigning by the AIDS activists groups such ACT-UP Philadelphia and the Health GAP Coalition that President Clinton was pressured into issuing an Executive Order in May 2000 stating that the USA would no longer threaten sanctions against Sub-Sahara African countries if they used TRIPS safeguards to gain access to HIV/AIDS medicines.[15]

Earlier the US government had been involved in issuing threats (withdrawal of aid among others) and other forms political pressure to persuade South Africa to annul its 1997 Medicine Act that allowed the government to import cheap versions of patented medicines. Apparently now left to go it alone (after the US government's self constraining commitment to refrain from interfering), the industry in 2001 became involved in a legal challenge to South Africa's development of generic antiviral drugs to combat AIDS. As we mentioned, the TRIPS agreement even specifies that mandatory licensing of necessary drugs is justified in an extreme national emergency.[16] The challenge presented by the pharmaceutical companies was apparently not only a violation of moral principle but also targets allowable policy under the "International Agreement on International Property Rights". A vigorous campaign by NGOs such as Oxfam and MSF (Medecins Sans Frontieres), precipitated intense media coverage of a coordinated effort by thirty nine drug companies to sue the South African government. Due to negative publicity, the pharmaceutical industry withdrew the challenge. The international concern generated by the court case also intensified the price war over anti-retroviral drugs both between the multinational pharmaceutical firms and between them and the generic drug companies. The multinationals were eager to recapture

---

[15] Ruth Mayne, "Global Campaign on Patents: Oxfam Perspective," in P. Drahos & R. Mayne eds., *Global Intellectual Property Rights: Knowledge Access and Development* (New York: Palmgrave Macmillan, 2002): 244–259.

[16] Item 5.1 (c) of the Doha WTO Ministerial "Declaration on the TRIPS agreement and Public Health," 20 November 2001.

public support, to avoid increased scrutiny of global patent rules and mitigate competition from generic drug companies. Prices of HIV/AIDS medicines for triple therapy set by the multinationals fell from the original patent price in the US of around $10,000 per patent per year to the discounted prices offered to African countries of around $900 a year. However, the Indian based generic companies reached prices as low as $289 per year (from Auribindo in August of 2001).[17]

Although the TRIPS agreement applies to all WTO member, the most profound effects of the TRIPS agreement (Trade-Related Aspects of Intellectual Property Rights) with respect to pharmaceuticals, appears to be forthcoming from its implementation in India. Partly due to a 1970 Patent law that excluded drugs from patent protection, Indian drug companies were able to evolve and make and market copies of drugs still under patent in wealthier countries. The Indian patent law was intended to provide low-cost drugs for its people perhaps at the expense of eliminating incentives to create new products. As well as supplying nationally, Indian companies became a major supplier of drugs to countries where these products can be marketed legally because they had not been patented locally.[18] India is the world's fourth-largest drug market in volume, and drugs often cost seven to ten percent of what they do in the USA or Europe. While India's many generic drugs producers, (including such better known brands such as Cipla and Ranbaxy), have thrived in an environment of limited patent protection on pharmaceuticals and exported cheap essential drugs around the world, some argue that the limited protections for intellectual property have kept foreign companies from investing in India. Proponents of TRIPS argued that once patent laws were in place investment in India would increase as India would be a very attractive location for R&D.[19]

The recent saga surrounding the implementation of the TRIPS agreement in India leaves one even less sanguine over the commitment of big Pharma to realize their moral obligations. In this case we are not speaking about the failure of these companies to take positive steps to alleviate a health crisis as in the discussion of shared responsibilities. The Indian case concerns the specific obligation to refrain from enforcing IP rights in circumstances requiring minimal personal loss for the industry and overwhelming benefit to those afflicted with disease. However, from all indices the pharmaceutical companies have been vigorously and unfairly enforcing their 'rights' in just these circumstances.

---

[17] Ruth Mayne, *op. cit.*, 250.
[18] John H. Barton, "TRIPS and the Global Pharmaceutical Market," *Health Affairs* 23, 3 (2004): 146–154.
[19] Jean O. Lanjouw, "The Introduction of Pharmaceutical Product Patents in India: Heartless Exploitation of the Poor and Suffering?" *Center Discussion Paper No. 775* (August 1997): 1–50, 25.

As required by the 1995 TRIPS agreement, in 2005 India embarked on the implementation of the TRIPS agreement. It is yet too early to determine precisely the consequences especially for populations that have had access to cheaper generic drugs both within India and beyond its shores. However, controversy has certainly been generated and some of the criticism does not reflect positively on the pharmaceutical companies. First, there is the fact that pharmaceutical companies initially, through their governments, pushed through the agreement in 1995, an agreement which could potentially deprive millions of people of affordable life saving generic drugs. Some argue that easing intellectual property standards in the interest of generic production and wider access pose no threat to global research and development or to India's industrial policy objectives. Accounting for only 1.3 percent of global sales in dollars, India is still a relatively small consumer of drugs. Although drug companies understandably want strong patent protections in rich country markets where they sell 87 percent of their drugs, the need for such aggressive protections in a relatively poor country like India is certainly questionable. It is doubtful that heightened profits in this tiny portion of the global market will create incentives for research and development, which is one of the main arguments used by drug companies to justify patent protections and higher prices. In fact, major Indian producers like Ranbaxy are looking to the rich markets of North America, Japan and Europe for their future growth.

But we need to re-emphasize that despite the fact that the required full implementation, as of 1 January 2005, of the World Trade Organisation's (WTO) Trade-related Aspects of Intellectual Property Rights (TRIPS) Agreement in India and other developing countries not yet granting pharmaceutical patents, threatens access to affordable new drugs, the TRIPS agreement allows the continuing production of pre-1995 drugs and several "transitional" years to become TRIPS-compliant. As mentioned it also contained important allowances enabling access to lower-priced medicines. These include rights to issue compulsory licenses (involuntary rights to the process and product with payment of a reasonable royalty) and rights to parallel import (unrestricted rights to buy patented medicines previously produced and sold elsewhere at a lower cost). These two flexibilities were clarified and confirmed in the Doha Declaration on the TRIPS Agreement and Public Health of November 2001 and expanded further in the Aug. 30, 2003, WTO decision for countries unable to produce medicines domestically. To a certain extent this has allowed India to prioritize public health and to promote universal access to medicine even while it struggles to comply with TRIPS' mandates.[20]

---

[20] Brook K. Baker, "India's 2005 Patent Act: Death by Patent or Universal Access to Second— and Future—Generation ARVS?" *Health Gap Global Access Project* (Sept 19, 2005), (www. healthgag.org.).

Nevertheless, India was unable to garner sufficient parliamentary support by Jan. 1, 2005 for TRIPS, and passed a temporary patent ordinance in late December 2004. The ordinance, which was clearly a reflection of domestic and international politics and pressure, was in fact more restrictive than TRIPS required. This development can be seen as an expression of the "TRIPS plus" policy, a policy of strong IP rights that goes beyond the basic requirements of TRIPS. The implementation of such a policy apparently reflects the exertion of pressure from developed countries, principally the United States.

An intense period of lobbying and social mobilization by AIDS activists worldwide resulted in the adoption of mitigating amendments in the final patent act enacted in March 2005. These included the tightening of standards for granting patents and restoring procedures for opposing patents, protecting existing producers of 1995–2005 medicines, allowing parallel importation, limiting time periods for negotiating voluntary licenses, and expanding rights to export post-1995 generic medicines produced pursuant to a compulsory license. But according to B.K. Baker of Health Gap Global Access Project these improvements left intact many glaring deficiencies.[21]

1. Instead of limiting patent protection to the newest and most innovative pharmaceutical inventions, i.e. "new chemical entities," the act creates rights to patent certain new uses, formulations, delivery systems, combinations of existing products, and minor variations of existing chemical entities.
2. The act leaves in place India's procedurally laborious and inefficient compulsory licensing scheme.
3. The act fails to specify guidelines for setting modest royalty rates (2–4 percent) for compulsory licenses and, except in a government-declared emergency, it requires applicants for compulsory licenses to wait three-years before applying.
4. The act grants 'patent-like' rights for patent applications between the publication and approval of the patent deterring generic entry even in cases where the patent application may later be denied.

Restricting India's ability to manufacture the newest generations of low-cost essential medicines leaves poor consumers in India and elsewhere in a procedural labyrinth and with long delays in access. Moreover, trade negotiators are seeking a second line of intellectual property protections in the form of new data exclusivity rules. Baker concludes saying Activists must apply pressure on Big Pharma and the U.S. government to relax their pursuit of ever-greater intellectual property

---

[21] *Ibid.*

protections, and on the Indian government to prioritize generic production of second- and third-generation AIDS medicines.

It should also be pointed out that under the TRIPS agreement, India agreed not only to consider protection for medicines developed after January 1, 2005, it also agreed to consider applications filed during 1995–2005 under the so-called "mailbox" provision (Article 70.8) of TRIPS. It is observed that because these applications could cover brand name products for which Indian companies are providing cheaper generic substitutes (e.g., antiretrovirals) it is probable the price of essential drugs will increase considerably when patents are granted. There are 7,000 applications in the mailbox. An initial analysis by the Indian Pharmaceutical Alliance in 2005 suggest that since only 250 of the applications could relate to new chemical entities associated with new drugs that were developed outside India during the 10 year period form 1995–2005, the other 6,750 must be related to something else, for example: minor changes to the structure of molecules.[22] This opened the possibility that Indian generic producers who were manufacturing drugs invented before 1995 could be blocked from producing these older drugs based on these later filed something-else patents.

Determining the Effect of the Implementation of the TRIPS Agreement in India

As mentioned it remains too early to determine the overall effect of the changes to Indian patent law engineered through TRIPS, but experts are already reaching tentative conclusions. A briefing paper for the UK official aid agency DFID, "Updating on China and India and Access to Medicines" concluded that treatment for cancer and diabetes is most likely to be negatively impacted by the implementation of TRIPS since these are treated with relatively new drug classes which have little therapeutic competition/substitution.[23] Classes of drugs that experience a high speed of new product development due to emerging resistance such as antibiotics and anti-infectives (e. g. ARVs, TB drugs and anti-malarials) will also be affected, since newer drugs in this group may have little therapeutic competition, while the older drugs are ineffective. The competition for first-line drugs does not exist in the market for newer drugs because the demand is smaller and the newer medicines are patented, preventing generic manufacturers from making them. The document highlights that lack of access to one drug in a combination therapy (as it is patented) can preclude appropriate treatment,

---

[22] F.M. Abbot, Amy Kapczynski, and T.N. Srinivasan, "The Draft Patent Law," *The Hindu* (Mar. 12, 2005) Online edition of Indian's National Newspaper.

[23] Reported by Sangeeta Shashikant, "Growing Movement Opposing Granting of Drug Patents," (TWN) *Third World Network Geneva*, (2 Aug 2006), (www.tynside.org.sg).

and just a few expensive patented medicines can skew entire health budgets. Taking into account various estimates, the article concludes that 10–15% of the Indian production will initially be affected by product patent protection, and the percentage would increase over time as new, patented medicines become an increasing proportion of the overall market.

Medecins Sans Frontieres (MSF), Australia, also reports similar difficulties, which their programs face following the India's decision to patent pharmaceuticals.[24] The organization points out that changes to the patent rules hamper the development of FDCs: three-in-one pills that helped simplify patients' lives in many MSF programs. Clearly their development is slowed when different companies hold patents on the different compounds in FDCs. MSF already uses FDCs for 70% of its patients on first-line treatment, but patent rules in India will make such combinations difficult to produce, if at all, in the future. In order to understand what this means it is worthwhile noting that The Campaign for Access to Essential Medicines (CAME), a lobbying arm of MSF, has worked to lower drug prices, stimulate research and develop new treatments as well as overcome trade barriers to accessing treatments. MSF reports that the prices of first-line treatments have dropped from over US$10,000 to as little as US$150 a year since 2000—the same year MSF began its first HIV treatment projects in Thailand, Cameroon and South Africa. In light of these current challenges MSF is encouraging the countries that do have manufacturing capacity (e.g. Brazil, Thailand, India and China) to routinely use the safeguards (such as compulsory licenses and government use provisions) affirmed in the 2001 WTO Doha Declaration. The author concludes noting that patents on medicines have an enormous effect on the ability of governments and international organisations to expand treatment to the millions of people living with HIV/AIDS in poor countries around the world, and clearly current restrictions imposed by the TRIPS agreement are only adding to the challenge.

Nevertheless in 2006 there have been significant reactions and challenges to the march toward patent protection. Four new cases of pre-grant opposition to the patenting of the HIV/AIDS medicines have been filed by Indian groups of people living with HIV/AIDS at three separate patent offices in India. These new cases follow two earlier pre-grant oppositions against patent applications pertaining to Combivir and Tenofovir, also filed by groups of people living with HIV/AIDS.[25] The movement by AIDS patients to file pre-grant opposition to patent applications is developing at a moment when serious public apprehension mounts over concerns that Indian generic drug companies will not be able to continue supplying cheaper generic versions of branded products, both to India

---

[24] James Nichols, "Tackling HIV/AIDS in Resource Poor Settings," *Issues* 75 (June 2006): 30–35. (A publication of Medecins Sans Frontieres, Victora, Australia)

[25] Sangeeta Shashikant, *op. cit.*

and to other developing countries. However, the pharmaceutical industry remains relentless in its efforts to maintain strong patent protection. The pharmaceutical company Novartis in 2007 began proceedings with a legal challenge to the Indian government with reference to the "pre-grant opposition" process in the current Indian patent law, which allows any interested party to oppose a patent before it is granted. In this case Novartis was seeking a new patent for Glivec, a brand drug for the treatment of blood cancer, after the original patent of twenty years expired last year. At the same time in January 2007 the Indian Network for People with HIV/AIDS, the People's Health Movement, the Centre for Trade and Development (Centad) and Medecins Sans Frontieres (MSF) all called upon the company to immediately cease its legal action.[26]

Also, it is worth mentioning that on August 6, 2007 the Madras High Court upheld section 6 (d) of the amended patent Act that denies patents to known drugs stipulating that incremental innovations or any type of modification must enhance the therapeutic effectiveness of the drug substantially to qualify for a new patent. Following this decision, Novartis announced that it has decided to move large investments in India elsewhere citing the "culture for investment". International organizations, such as the Geneva-based IFPMA (International Federation of Pharmaceutical Manufacturers and Associations) and the Washington-based PhRMA (Pharmaceutical Research Manufacturers of America) have threatened that their companies may not further invest in India and may deprive its people of their new research products.[27]

There is other bad news for big Pharma in the post TRIPS environment in Thailand and Brazil. The Thai Government issued a compulsory licenses on three drugs in 2007 and has made it clear that it will continue to break patents until prices of AIDS drugs reduce significantly. Brazil has also issued compulsory licenses for HIV drug Efavirenz and India's health minister had also threatened to use the option of compulsory licensing if Novartis won the Glivec case.[28]

Conclusion

In this chapter we argued that moral considerations relating to the right to health care impose obligations on the pharmaceutical companies that cannot be avoided by asserting the necessity to exercise intellectual property rights, maximize profits and recover R&D costs. We pointed out that this moral obligation requires attention to both negative and positive duties. Negative duties require that in certain circumstances pharmaceutical companies must refrain from enforcing IP

[26] *Gulf Today* (Jan 29, 2007): 11.
[27] Virendra Parekh, "Novartis Moving from India," Khaleej Times (August 27, 2007): 39.
[28] *Ibid.*

rights to allow access to life saving drugs where the need is great and the cost to the company would be marginal. Beyond negative duties, the entailed positive duties require more than simply foregoing monopoly profits in certain circumstances involving dire need. Positive duties require drug companies to act positively and work to create and forge alliances with government bodies and NGOs to ensure that a coordinated level of required health care is actually realized. We mentioned as an example the Merck and the Gates Foundation, which is working in Botswana to provide treatment for AIDS sufferers. Nevertheless despite the efforts of some companies to address the health care challenge, the behaviour of large pharmaceutical companies on broader issues relating to global IP policy is far less encouraging. We observe, for example, the uncompromising pressure to assert TRIPS compliance, which has apparently significantly undermined India's generic drug industry. Moreover there is strong evidence that certain companies are unscrupulously attempting Indian patent protection for older products and combinations of older products that according to TRIPS guidelines are exempted from patent protection. These developments seriously threaten many in India and other parts of the developing world where for many health and very survival depend on access to cheaper generic products.

From the above evidence it is easy to subscribe to the assertion that the recent behavior of big Pharma indicates a total disregard for the basic natural rights to health and access to health care in the interests of immediate gain and profit. But this conclusion may not be the whole story. Certainly it accords with the view expressed in a well received article by economist Alan Deardorff written in 1992 following the Uruguay round of Multilateral Trade Negotiations.[29] In the paper he argued the case for the adverse welfare effects of extending intellectual property protection to all countries of the world.[30] Deardorff argued that that the countries in which IP rights currently do not apply would suffer the most significant loss of welfare. In effect the developing countries do gain from this extension but they do so at the expense of the rest of the world. Moreover, although the developed countries would stand to receive some benefit from extending the intellectual property regime beyond their borders, the loss of welfare in the developing world would outweigh the gains realized in the developed world, and thus, the world as a whole would lose from extending the intellectual property regime. However, the Yale economist Jean Lanjouw later commenting on Deardorff's conclusions,

---

[29] The Uruguay round of Multilateral Trade Negotiations sought to bring the protection of intellectual property rights under the auspices of the General Agreement on Tariffs and Trade so as to extend IP protection to countries that do not provide it or only weakly provide it, especially developing countries.

[30] Alan Deardorff, "The Welfare Effects of Global Patent Protection," *Economica* 59 (1992): 35–51.

and considering their application to India, noted the possible adverse effects on the levels of health care in the developing world including Indian, but questioned the possible gains realized by the developed world claiming that at current Indian levels of income, it is unlikely that profits made in India will add substantially to "…profits already available in the world for drugs which are of global interest".[31]

A closer examination of the context in which the so-called 2001 Doha Declaration was realized perhaps reveals a fuller picture of the motivation behind the push for TRIPS compliance. We touched upon allowances in the 2001 Doha Declaration, which sanction rights to parallel import, that is, the right to buy generic drugs produced elsewhere in the event of a compulsory license. This development relates to an anomaly in the original TRIPS agreement that in effect allowed rich countries under a compulsory license to commission a domestic company to produce a generic drug for the domestic market to meet a health crisis, an option that would not be available to the technologically undeveloped. In other words, poor countries would not have the technological capacity to produce such drugs and the provisions under a compulsory license required that the producer of a generic drug only do so for domestic consumption. Traditionally poor countries have depended on India for their generic drugs. However, after 2005 India could no long produce generic drugs unless required to do so under a compulsory license and then only for domestic consumption. The poorer countries understandably protested and underlined the unfairness that necessarily disadvantages them. The pharmaceutical companies vigorously resisted any changes to the existing agreement. However, the Doha agreement of 2001 ultimately provided that countries could import generic versions of patented drugs to treat AIDS/HIV and other diseases that posed an identifiable health crisis. Significantly after the realization of this agreement, the pharmaceutical industry asserted that such programs would have little affect on profits.[32]

The question remains, given the industry's admission that sales in the developing and less developed world were marginal in terms of profits, why did the industry fight so hard to exclude the provision which was finally included in the Doha agreement. The answer can most probably be found in the desire to maintain a long term control of the global market rather than short term or medium run profit maximization. Lanjouw has pointed out that as Indian patents effectively close off the strategy of imitation, this may ultimately force Indian companies to become more innovative.[33] However, others have argued that in reality the multinationals recognized that India, China, Brazil, Argentina, South

---

[31] Jean O. Lanjouw, *op. cit.*, 30.
[32] D.G. Richards, *Intellectual Property Rights and Global Capitalism: the Political Economy of the TRIPs Agreement* (Amonk New York: M.E. Sharpe, 2004), 162.
[33] Lanjouw, *op. cit.*, 29.

Africa and Korea already possessed the capacity to imitate successfully the production process, and produce generic versions of patented drugs, and therefore the powerful multinational pharmaceutical companies recognized that these countries already possessed the potential to realize more sophisticated research and development and ultimately compete with the established Western Industry.[34] Although the promotion of technological transfer from rich countries to technologically poor countries has been an alleged principal rationale for the implementation of TRIPS, the behaviour of the industry in light of the Doha agreement gives strong circumstantial evidence that the real reason driving the promotion of the TRIPS agreement has been an implicit recognition that strengthening the IPR global regime would actually retard the technological development in these countries. Viewed from this perspective, implementing TRIPS and closing off the strategy of imitation, would depress the learning curve, while reducing the available profits from generic Western on-patent drugs, which could be utilized to fund successful R&D. If this is the correct reading of the motivation, then TRIPS is not so much a strategy to secure profits in the short or medium term but rather a vehicle to maintain control of the industry by a small number of pharmaceutical firms.

But even this statement must be understood with qualification. Although sales of patented drugs in the developing world may not be significant sources of revenue for Western companies, India's production of generic on-patent drugs had already indirectly enhanced India's ability to compete for profits in lucrative Western markets. It has been pointed out that a crucial feature of India's lack of protection for pharmaceutical products has been the ability of Indian firms to develop commercial production capacities for on-patent drugs before patent expiry. This acquired expertise has allowed them to move rapidly into the world market as patents lapsed. As the path of imitation becomes closed, these Indian firms also lose the opportunity to acquire the expertise and capability to realize significant revenue at the moment when patents expire. This provides an additional loss of profit for Indian firms and a gain for multinational patent owners. In effect, TRIPS seeks to delay the erosion of profits from sales of patented drugs that result from competition with generic drugs.[35] Also it needs to be recognized that these loses and gains are far from negligible. It has been estimated that just prior to patent expiry Glaxo-Wellcome (now GlaxoSmithKline) was earning around 7 million

---

[34] Richards *op. cit.*, 160. See also Ruth Mayne, "TRIPS and Access to Medicines," in H. Katrak & R. Strange eds., *The WTO and Developing Countries* (New York: Palgrave Macmillan, 2004) 146–165, 156, who similarly concludes that "…if anything the TRIPS Agreement is likely to inhibit technological innovation by restricting the scope to imitate and adapt new technologies".
[35] Lanjouw, *op. cit.*, 6.

profit per day from the sale of Zantac.[36] On the other hand, indications that developing countries, including India, are prepared to use compulsory licensing means generic production of on-patent drugs, although clearly attenuated, may well continue despite the recently introduced patent regime.

Moreover the argument that the introduction of patents for pharmaceuticals would stimulate multinational investment and multinational sponsored R&D in India has proved to be doubtful. This is especially the case following Novartis' announced decision to move large investments from India and threats from International organizations, such as the Geneva-based IFPMA and the Washington-based PhRMA stating their companies may not further invest in India and may deprive its people of their new research products. In any case one source has claimed that that these multinational companies made their maximum investment in India between 1970 (the year in which product patents were abolished) and 1995 (the year in which product patents were re-introduced). The decade thereafter (1995–2005) has witnessed the divestment of manufacturing facilities and decline in fresh investments.[37]

Lanjouw has argued that TRIPS may generate novel R&D from Indian firms by closing off the path of imitation. However, it is reported that even the multinationals are having difficulty realizing innovative research that would result in New Chemical Entities (NECs).[38] Most of the new drugs that have been approved by the US Food and Drug Administration exhibit small modifications of existing drugs with less that significant new benefit to the consumer. Global pharma companies are facing a crisis. With few new drugs to offer and the immanent patent expiry of several important existing drugs, the established industry is depending heavily on the promotion of existing drugs and their modifications rather than spending on new molecular research. One industry journal, *Pharmabiz*, reported that in 2006, the top 15 global companies spent 30.1% of their revenues on marketing, compared with 15.1% on R&D.[39]

One may conclude that circumstantial evidence tells us that the implementation of the global IP regime was intended as a vehicle to ensure the hegemony of a few giant pharmaceutical companies, which the industry clearly regards as an ultimate value in itself that outweighs the human right to health and the access to health care. The argument that a strong patent regime is necessary for maintaining effective programs of R&D is at best only a partial truth. One can say a qualified yes but only if IP protections are applicable to a limited market for a limited time. IP rights create monopolies and IP rights with global application create

---

[36] *Ibid.*
[37] Virendra Parekh, *op. cit.*
[38] *Ibid.*
[39] *Ibid.*

global monopolies. We have presented the argument that the effect of the TRIPS agreement may well result in strangling the growth of R&D potential in the developing and less developed world and there exists the distinct possibility this is the actual motivation behind TRIPS. One cannot discount the implication that the implementation of a strong IP regime has an outcome in which potential R&D in various locales in the developing world is suppressed, which in the long term means a foreseeable possible net loss in the creation of innovative life sustaining pharmaceutical products.

In point of fact, we argue that rather than instituting a regime of universal globally enforced IP rights, patent rights should only be granted where there exists a demonstrative relation between profits that depend on IP protections and the finances necessary to support effective R&D. In markets where profits would not be sufficient or marginally important for the support of effective R&D, IP rights should have no application. Companies such as those in India that can produce lower cost generic drugs (because they don't need to do their own R&D) should then be allowed to be productive and offer their products within markets in which the large firms have little interest while being precluded from the lucrative markets where patents apply. In effect we are arguing for the pre-TRIPS situation. This would better secure the mandate of the UN under the Universal Declaration of Human Rights prescribing the universal the right to health care. At the same time, pharmaceutical multinationals will have to live with the possibility that these companies located in the developing world will elevate their imitative activities and become effective originators of innovative R&D. When this occurs they should also be allowed to enter the lucrative markets in which IP rights are recognized and generic imitations of patented medicines are prohibited.

One needs to recognize that IP rights can be a two edged sword, if used discriminatively they can enhance R&D and the production of innovative medicines, if wheeled indiscriminately, IP rights can undermine future potentially valuable R&D, while denying immediate access to reasonably priced life sustaining medicines. Ultimately there is no moral point in supporting a system whose intent is to eradicate emerging competent competitors, which at the same time results in diminishing a potential future of increased innovative, life sustaining medicines for the greater benefit of mankind, while denying supplies of much needed reasonably priced medicines for marginally profitable markets.

Chapter Thirteen

IP Rights and Genetic Material in Agriculture and Human Research: Two forms of Biopiracy?

This chapter focuses on the application of IP rights to genetic material. We specifically consider the use of such rights in fields of agricultural and human research. We draw attention to the expansion and increased use of these rights within both fields, which threaten deleterious results for both the developing and developed world. Among other things, the developing world has been increasingly concerned about biopiracy. Biopiracy can be roughly described as the manipulation of intellectual property rights laws by corporations to gain exclusive control over genetic resources and local knowledge. It is further understood that these informational resources are appropriated from local communities, based mainly in developing countries, without giving adequate, if any, recognition or remuneration to the original possessors of these resources. In the final section we indicate that Western legal authorities defend the appropriation of genetic material and associated forms of traditional knowledge as Western intellectual property through reliance on a labor theory of original acquisition, which has its philosophical origins in the political philosophy of John Locke. We demonstrate, however, that the apparent legitimization of these forms of acquisition can only be achieved by an extrapolation beyond Locke's intent and an ellipsis that renders Locke's labor theory both incoherent and inconsistent.

The patenting of life forms is a hugely controversial issue. In this chapter I first discuss the extension of intellectual property rights to plants, including their genetic material, and finally to human genes. With respect to the former issue we specifically focus on the patenting of seeds. The patenting of seeds has implications for the traditional farmer's right to save, plant, share, sell and exchange seeds. In our discussion of this topic we describe how intellectual property over germplasm has been given a global reach through international pressure and the TRIPS agreement, as highlighted by recent legal developments in Indian and Iraq. These shifts underline issues associated with "biopiracy", but also include: the vitiation of publicly funded research institutions; monopoly control of the food system by giant agribusiness; loss of biodiversity; ecological risks of genetically engineered seeds, and ultimately loss of autonomy not only for the local farming community but also loss of sovereignty for the developing nation itself.

In the final section of the paper I briefly discuss the human genome project and the human genome diversity project and issues related to the patenting of human genes. The application of IP rights to human genetic material represents a analogous move to transform that which belongs to the wider human community (our common genetic inheritance)—rather than the expertise of a local community of planters and breeders—and attach a private ownership claim. As in the case of issues relating to plant seed, the intent is to privatize genetic information, which ought to be publicly available thereby making it inaccessible in order to maximize revenue claims. We note that this is also undermining the research of public research institutions and the traditions of the research community which involve the sharing and distribution of information in order to maximize and diversify research efforts. By appropriating and withholding information, the IP right holder is ultimately restricting research opportunities and restricting the ultimate benefits because only those with sufficient wealth will be granted access to the benefits

Ultimately people in the developing world may well feel profound resentment over the patenting of seeds and patenting human genetic material. With respect to both cases, that which is essential for existence (agricultural produce) and essentially part of individual existence (genetic makeup) appear to have been illegitimately appropriated by Western corporations. Nevertheless, the more serious issue must be the patenting of plant varieties and their genetic material, which is undermining the traditional farmer's right to save and transfer seeds. This is clearly part of a strategy that threatens to realize a monopolization of agriculture by few giant agribusinesses thus presenting an undeniable threat not only to the food supply of developing nations but also to the world's food supply.

Agribusiness and the Patenting of Genetic material

The absurdity of the intellectual property rights system becomes most apparent when one considers the its use by the agribusinesses. We have made the earlier point that no human inventor or innovator or even artist creates *ex nihlo*. All the great intellectual achievements from the works of Aristotle to Einstein depend upon the researches and achievements of earlier individuals and build upon these materials and tools. In reality, different forms of knowledge, techniques and useful practices depend upon the contributions of countless anonymous individuals. The production of knowledge and information is ultimately a cooperative venture. Nowhere is this more evident than in agriculture and animal husbandry. The various strains of plants and animals developed to provide the staples of the human diet have been evolved and refined over centuries of human effort and toil. But the received notion of Intellectual property rights rests on the assumption that intellectual achievements represent the unique efforts of a single individual or teams of individuals and therefore become the personal property of the individual or a particular corporate body. This view finds expression in the law, which asserts that intellectual property is always the property of a legal person (either a human being or a corporation) and cannot be owned by a community or a particular people, thus denying the contributions of a network of contributors. As a consequence, the law will often regard some relatively minor advance in to an existing corpus of knowledge, which realizes a slight modification in the end product as the basis for an ownership claim that includes this entire line of development.

For example, in the 1990s, American rice growers had been steadily losing market to overseas suppliers of foreign strains of rice. For example, in 1996–1997 India exported nearly 500,000 tonnes of Basmati rice, earning the government $280 million. However, in 1997 an American company, RiceTec Inc, was granted US patent 5,663,484, on Basmati rice and grains, giving it the right to grow and sell a 'new' variety of basmati rice in the Americas, which it claimed to have developed. The variety was developed from 22 Indian and Pakistani basmati lines crossed with semi-dwarf varieties, making it based on varieties developed by Indian and Pakistani farmers. The question is whether RiceTec should have been allowed to patent the variety as their invention. This could be seen as a theft ('biopiracy') from farmers who developed and bred Basmati for centuries and whose export capabilities would now be affected.

The Indian government was pushed to challenge the patent. The Government argued that the specific grain traits listed were already found in over 90 per cent of the basmati germplasm existing in India and Pakistan considerably prior to the filing of the patent. The government offered extensive documentation to establish that the various basmati varieties cultivated over centuries in the subcontinent contained all the 'novel' grain attributes mentioned in the patent. By May 2001 RiceTec had withdrawn all but 5 claims related to the patent. These claims essentially related to three 'novel rice lines', namely Bas867, RT1117 and RT1121, that are capable of producing grains similar or superior to basmati rice. But these are relatively harmless claims pertaining to RiceTec's specific plant varietal breeding efforts and not open-ended claims covering grains per se. Indeed, had the grain-related claims not been withdrawn, RiceTec would have obtained the sole monopoly over the marketing of rice grains possessing the said 'novel' traits in the US. Theoretically, this would have adversely affected the Indian exports of basmati rice to the US as commercial sale of grains with similar attributes would have infringed RiceTec's patent. In fact, the most significant victory for India has been that the USPTO Patent Examiner officially changed the title of RiceTec's patent from the original 'Basmati lines and grains' to 'Rice lines Bas867, RT1117 and RT1121'.

Over all one can say that the manner in which RiceTec established its patent demonstrates a disregard for the contributions of local communities in the production of basmati. As with all such patent claims the intent was to exclude the benefits accruing from the use of their genetic resources. This includes both the informal contributions of farmers who have been growing basmati for hundreds of years in India and Pakistan, as well as the more formal, scientific breeding work that has been done by rice research institutes to evolve better varieties of basmati. RiceTec sought to capitalize on this work by taking out the patent on basmati with the intention of monopolizing the commercial profits of past research, without giving any recognition or remuneration to those who have played key roles in the evolution and breeding of basmati rice in its natural habitat. For many, RiceTec actions represented a form of biopiracy.

Ultimately the RiceTec case was resolved positively in favour of the indigenous farmers through the intervention of the Indian government. This, however, does not in any way prove that system can be made to operate fairly and equitably. This is the case even though some argue that if utilized properly, IP rights can protect indigenous knowledge and innovation. Firstly only legal persons, either corporate or human persons, rather than communities or local people can acquire legal rights. Moreover, there is the ultimate reality, which is the fact that the enjoyment of the IP system depends upon significant if not extraordinary wealth. Ultimately, only those who can afford to enforce and protect their rights reap the benefits.

For example Monsanto, the world's largest genetically modified seed company, has been awarded patents on the wheat used for making chapati—the flat bread staple of northern India. The patents give the US multinational exclusive ownership over Nap Hal, a strain of wheat whose gene sequence makes it particularly suited to producing crisp breads. Another patent, filed in Europe, gives Monsanto rights over the use of Nap Hal wheat to make chapatis, which consist of flour, water and salt. Monsanto inherited a patent application when it bought the cereals division of the Anglo-Dutch food giant Unilever in 1998, and the patent has been granted to the new owner.

As with Basmati rice, Nap Hal's qualities are the result of efforts of generations of farmers in India who spent years crossbreeding crops. It is these collective, not corporate, efforts that should be recognized. Activists clam that Monsanto intends to generate "monopoly profits" from food on which millions depend. There is little hope of the Indian government intervening to prevent the chapati being patented by Monsanto. This is not a possibility because it is reported that the Indian government simply cannot afford the legal fees, having spent hundreds of thousands of dollars fighting the US decision to grant RiceTec a patent on basmati rice in 1997.[1]

The expansion of IP rights, the TRIPS Agreement and Farmers' Rights

Biopiracy has become a very serious issue as a consequence of favorable decisions by the US and European Courts to allow transformation technologies and the introduction of beneficial plant traits to be the subject of intellectual property protection. The result has been an increase in patent applications for DNA sequences. The TRIPS agreement has further exacerbated the problem. Before TRIPS many developing countries did not permit the patenting of life forms, biological processes and knowledge about their use. This changed with TRIPS. Article 27.3 (b) of TRIPS requires the WTO members to provide patent protection or *sui generis* protection for plant verities and some see this as providing the legal infrastructure for the global propertisation of research tools and research products.[2] This possibility of patenting a system of breeder's rights may restrict the right of farmer to save, exchange and use seed. Article 27.3 (b) allows for the exclusion from patentability of plants and animals (but not microorganisms) as well as the exclusion of essentially biological processes for the production of plants and animals (but not for non biological and microbiological processes). This effectively establishes the patentability of microorganisms and genetically modified organisms. Many developing countries in the WTO have argued that 27.3 (b) should be amended.[3] The African group has proposed that the TRIPS review process should make it clear that plants, animals, microorganism and their parts, as well as natural processes are unpatentable. There are signs that TRIPS is opening the floodgates to the patenting of life and to biopiracy. By Nov. 2000 it was reported that patents were pending on or have been granted by 40 patent authorities world wide over 500,000 genes and partial gene sequences in living organisms. Of these there are 9000 patents pending or granted involving 161,195 whole or partial human genes.[4]

These developments and especially article 27.3 of the TRIPS agreement have far reaching consequences for global agriculture. The primary concern is the vitiation

---

[1] Randeep Ramesh, *The Guardian* (January 31, 2004).
[2] Michael Blakeney "Intellectual Property and the CGIAR System," in P. Drahos & R. Mayne eds. *Global Intellectual Property Rights: Knowledge Access and Development*, (New York: Palmgrave Macmillan, 2002): 109–125, 118.
[3] *Ibid.*,120.
[4] Martin Khor, "Rethinking Intellectual Property Rights and TRIPS," in *Global Intellectual Property Rights: Knowledge Access and Development*: 201–214, 208.

of the traditional farmer's right to grow, save, and exchange seeds, thereby creating potential monopoly powers in the corporations that control the seed industry. Within the context of the United States we observe that legislation passed by Congress in the twentieth century encouraged the growth of the private seed industry. Congress enacted legislation in 1924 that ended the Federal distribution of seeds to farmers thereby forcing farmers to rely on varieties offered by private vendors. The Plant Patent Act and the Plant Variety Protection Act provided IP protection for seed developers, which further encouraged the privatization of the seed industry. Genetic engineering has subsequently accelerated the privatization. Plant genomes have been altered by inserting desirable genes from one species into another and increasingly farmers are using genetically engineered seeds. The biotechnical revolution that agriculture is presently experiencing has spawned mergers and acquisitions between firms in separate industries so that the largest chemical corporations are also the largest seed companies with further mergers with the biotechnical firms so that the resulting enterprises are able to control virtually every aspect of the production chain not including the farm labor itself. It is now the case that a small number of large companies now dominate the industry. It has been noted that essentially the same companies: Monsanto, Norvartis, Dow and Dupont, dominate plant breeding, pesticides, veterinary medicine and pharmaceuticals. A further consequent has been the undermining of public research institutions in favor of private commercial entities. These developments have increasingly placed the resources essential to the world's food supply under private commercial control. This may ultimately spell control of the word's food supply by a few multinational corporations. Although the latter statement may appear to be a hyperbole one ought to attend to certain recent legal shifts which have been driven by global agribusiness.

Some argue that in the so called advanced countries such as the United States and Canada colonization of farmers by the biotechnology firms is now complete.[5] As we have noted over the last 80 years a series of legal decisions in the US together with accommodating legislation have removed rights from farmers and enhanced the rights of seed manufacturers and the emerging biotechnology industries culminating finally in 2001 in the court case J.E.M. Ag Supply Inc. v Pioneer Hi-Bred International Inc.[6] Following this decision, any life form can be patented including bacteria, seed and plants (both genetically modified and conventional). Specifically this case has undermined the farmers' right to save and exchange seed, furthering the absolute monopoly of the seed industry by making farmer-

[5] Vandana Shiva, "The Indian Seed Act And Patent Act: Sowing The Seeds Of Dictatorship," (February 14, 2005) <www.zmag.org/content/showarticle.cfm?ItemID=7249>.
[6] 122 S Ct. 593 (2001).

to-farmer exchange and sales illegal for patented varieties. Almost predictably the biotechnology firms have now turned outward toward the non-Western world.

In India, for example, two recent legal shifts are promoting the monopolization of the Indian food supply by the multinational agribusiness: the 2004 Seed Act and amendments to the 1970 Patent Act. Considering the amendments first, one observes the 2nd of the Amendments makes changes in the definition of what is not an invention. This has opened the flood gates for the patenting of genetically engineered seeds.

According to Section 3(j) of the Indian Patent Act, the following is not an invention: Any process for the medical, surgical, creative, prophylactic or other treatment of human beings or any process for a similar treatment of animals or plants or render them free of disease or to increase their economic value or that of their products. In the 2nd Amendment however, the mention of "plants" has been deleted from this section. This deletion implies that a method or process modification of a plant can now be counted as an invention and therefore can be patented. Thus, for example, Monsanto's method of producing Bt. cotton by introducing genes of a bacterium thurengerisis in cotton to produce toxins to kill the bollworm can now be covered by the exclusive rights associated with patents. In other words, Monsanto can now have Bt. cotton patents in India.

The Second Amendment allows for the production or propagation of genetically engineered plants to count as an invention. But this section excludes as inventions "plants and animals including seeds, varieties and species and essentially biological processes for production or propagation of plants and animals". Since plants produced through the use of new biotechnologies are **not** technically considered "essentially biological," section 3(j) has found another way to create room for agribusiness. This loophole, couched in the guise of scientific advancement, thus allows patents on GMOs and hence opens the flood gate for patenting transgenic plants.

Vandana Shiva, a member of the International Forum on Globalization, argues that these amendments are manifest evidence of the influence of the TRIPS agreement.[7] She charges that the language of section 3(j) is a verbatim translation into India law of Article 27.3 (b) of the TRIPS Agreement. Article 27.3 (b) of TRIPS states: Parties may exclude from patentability plants and animals other than micro-organisms, and essentially biological processes for the production of plants or animals other than non-biological and microbiological processes. However, parties shall provide for the protection of plant varieties either by patents or by an effective *sui generis* system or by any combination thereof.

---

[7] *Ibid.*

These amendments should be read together with the 2004 Indian Seed Act which requires farmers to use only registered and patented seeds. In other words seeds used in farming must be purchased from corporations that hold the patent rights to these seeds. The Seed Act 2004 thus effectively prevents farmers from seed saving, seed exchange and seed reproduction. Indeed the objective of the 2004 Act clearly states that it is aimed at replacing farmers saved seeds with seeds from private seed industries. Vandana Shiva argues that the 2004 Seed Act is essential to maintaining a monopolistic patent regime because it precludes the viable alternative of accessing traditional varieties of seeds through seed saving and seed exchange.[8] Clearly farmers are no longer able to rely on their own supply of seeds because compulsory registration thus makes it illegal to plant unlicensed varieties. The overall effect of the legislative changes is to force farmers into dependency on a corporate monopoly of patented seed. It is not unrealistic to interpret this transformation of farmers as breeders and reproducers of their own seed supply to farmers as consumers of propriety seed from the seed industry, as representing a shift from a food economy based on numerous independent autonomous producers to a food system dominated by a handful of transnational corporations, which control both inputs and outputs. She argues this is a recipe for food insecurity, biodiversity erosion and uprooting of farmers from the land.

Although our references to this point have focused on Indian agriculture and its products there is evidence that we are observing an incipient global strategy to implement a IP rights regime that dominates the world's food supply. For example, The former American Administrator of the Iraqi CPA (Coalition Provisional Authority) government, Paul Bremer, while he occupied his position of authority, updated Iraq's intellectual property law to "meet current internationally-recognized standards of protection". Not unsurprisingly for the agricultural sector, the updated law made saving seeds for the following year's harvest, practiced by 97% of Iraqi farmers, and the standard farming practice for thousands of years across human civilizations, illegal.[9] The legislation was designed to force farmers to obtain a yearly license for genetically modified (GM) seeds from American corporations. As with all GM seeds, they have typically been modified from seeds developed over thousands of generations by indigenous farmers like the Iraqis, and shared freely like agricultural 'open source'.

According to Order 81, paragraph 66—[B], issued by L. Paul Bremer [CFR], "Farmers shall be prohibited from re-using seeds of protected varieties or any variety mentioned in items 1 and 2 of paragraph [C] of Article 14 of this chapter." Order 81 directs the reader to Article 14, paragraph 2 [C] to paragraph [B]

---

[8]   *Ibid.*
[9]   "Monsanto Pawn forbids Iraqis to Save Seeds," *St Louis Independent Media* (October 02, 2006), <www.stlimc.org/newswire/display/2276/index.php>.

of Article 4, which states any variety that is different from any other known variety may be registered in any country and become a protected variety of seed—thus defaulting it into the "protected class" of seeds and thus prohibiting the Iraqi farmers from reusing them the following season.[10] Every year, the Iraqis are expected to destroy any seed they have, and repurchase seeds from an authorized supplier, or face fines, penalties and/or imprisonment. Of course, one wonders, given the chaotic lawless character of post invasion Iraq, whether the implementation of such legislation was ever realistic but nevertheless there can be no doubt concerning the intent.

The Effect of IP on Agricultural Research

The increased use of patents on gene sequences in plants has meant that publicly funded international research institutions that provide public goods are now faced with the presence and influence of the private sector. The expense of the IP process is the major reason why agricultural research is shifting from the public to the private sectors.[11] Significant transactional costs and imposed management burdens also result from the necessity to negotiate access to plant varieties subject to IP rights. Secondly, there is a tightening of donor funding due to the fact that donors are unhappy with the authorized privatization of germplasm and research tools, which were created from public monies provided to public research institutes. This has undermined the viability of the public research institution.[12] This in turn has also led to demands that research centers exploit their own research and patent results. But as one researcher points out this proposal fails to address the rights of farmers and local communities who may have contributed germplasm as well as the source countries in which the germplasm might have been collected.[13] Ultimately, the TRIPS agreement, which has spear headed the intrusion of intellectual property into agricultural research has resulted in the concentration of key IP rights in the hands of a small and declining number of private life-science companies. A result of this market concentration has been to lock up key intellectual property rights in the hands of a few powerful entities that are able to raise the barrier to market entry. Thus claims Michael Blakeney, an intellectual property lawyer, by the end of 1998, the top five vegetable seed companies controlled 75% of the global vegetable seed market.[14] There, therefore appears to be an inexorable movement

---

[10] *Ibid.*
[11] Blakeney, *op. cit.*
[12] *Ibid.*, 112, 113.
[13] *Ibid.*, 117.
[14] *Ibid.*, 110.

towards a situation in which agricultural resources no longer belong to the wider public but have become the private property of private entities.

Nevertheless there is resistance to this regime. Some scientists argue that there is no scientific basis for patenting of life forms even if they are genetically modified, and the patent system is an inappropriate method for rewarding innovation in the field of biological science and in relation to biological materials and processes. More to the point perhaps, Tewolde Egziabher, an African scientist and General Manager of the Ethiopian Environmental Authority and Chair of the African Group in the Negotiations Surrounding the Convention of Biodiversity (CBA) argues that the inappropriateness of the patent system with respect to biological processes is due to the fact that living things are not invented. or inventions.[15] Furthermore genetically modified organisms, like all living things reproduce themselves, unlike mechanical things and processes.

As one remembers one of the reasons given for the IP system especially patents is that it allows inventors to make their innovations available through entering into licensing agreements. It is presumed that IP rights enable inventors and inno-vators, who may lack capital, to unite with the possessors of capital to finance production through mutually beneficial arrangements. In exchange for financing production the innovator is able to grant to the producer an exclusive right to pro-duce the product based on the exclusive right the innovator holds through his/her own IP right. Thus, innovative products are made available which might not occur otherwise because one assumes that in most cases creative or inventive individuals would not also have the financial resources to cover production costs, given a significant public demand. With software, as we pointed out, IP rights prove to be extremely lucrative because there are virtually no costs associated with replication of information. Thus the rationale that envisions IP rights as required due to utilitarian advantages associated with increased availability applies marginally to software. In this sense IP rights do nothing to stimulate availability because the innovator can replicate and distribute software (information) without needing to cover any significant associated production costs that would necessitate entering into licensing agreements with a specialized manufacturing sector. As Richard Stallman, the founder of the free software movement, has pointed out, the repro-duction and dissemination of information to an increased number of users requires the allocation of minimal to zero scarce resources as compared to the increased production of ford pickups. As compared with the resource costs of Ford pickups, there is no reason, therefore, why information cannot be distributed freely.[16]

15 Martin Khor, "Rethinking Intellectual Property Rights and TRIPS," in *Global Intellectual Property Rights: Knowledge Access and Development*: 207.
16 See also Richard Stallman, "Free Software: Freedom and Cooperation," New York University, New York, May 29, 2001, <http://www.mirror5.com/events/rms-nyu-2001-transcript.txt>.

A fortiori, the failure of IP rights to secure utilitarian advantages for software applies with renewed vigor to patented life forms in so far as organisms reproduce themselves naturally without having to depend on a human efficient cause. As these organisms spread and proliferate across the globe, anyone who comes to utilize or possess (even inadvertently) one of these patented organisms will owe money to their alleged proprietors, either individuals or corporations. A recent Canadian case (May 21, 2004) illustrates this reality and the problem. Canada's lower courts and finally its highest court ruled that a Canadian farmer infringed Monsanto's legal rights when he harvested and sold his crop of GM canola patented by Monsanto. The court also insisted that infringement occurred regardless of how the plants got there. The Farmer steadfastly maintained that his fields were contaminated by pollen from a neighbor's GM canola (oilseed rape) fields and by seeds that blew off trucks on their way to processing. Strangely enough these are the same set of judges who said in 2002 that higher life forms can't be patented in a decision referenced to a laboratory mouse used in cancer research, known as the Harvard Mouse. With much of the two-million canola hectares in Canada planted with GM varieties from Monsanto and other companies, canola plants with patented genetics can be found growing wild in farmers fields, along roadsides, in schoolyards and parks. Advertisements in Chiapas, Mexico are already warning farmers that if they are found using GM seed illegally, they risk fines and even prison.[17] Although the Canadian case did not penalize the farmer financially the court did recognize the priority of Monsanto's legal claim over modified seeds regardless of source. It is a serious loss, because not only did the court not recognise the fundamental right of farmers to save seeds and use seeds from year to year, but the decision also legitimizes a form of biopiracy because ultimately all crop seeds are the result of thousands of years of seed saving and selection by farmers around the world. Thus allowing a de facto patent, usurps the entire history of that seed.

Obviously, abrogating the farmer's traditional right to save, share, sell and exchange seeds dangerously promotes the monopolization of the food's supply by a few multinational giant agribusinesses such as Monsanto. Like the licensing arrangements IBM imposes on the users of its ubiquitous software, the world's farmers will surrender significant income in the form of licensing fees and royalties as they find themselves required to use germplasm patented by a multinational agribusiness.[18] Not only will the world's farmers be paying government taxes

---

[17] Stephen Leahy, "Canada's Highest Court backs Monsanto Against Farmer," *IPS* Web Page (May 21, 2004).

[18] See Vandana Shiva, *op. cit*. She states that in the 1990s in Britain, holders of plant breeders rights started to issue notices to potato growers through the British Society of Plant Breeders stipulating that the selling of seed potato by farmers to other farmers was illegal. Seed potato growers had to grow varieties under contract to the seed industry, which specified the price

but also they will also be paying taxes to multinational corporations for the privilege of growing produce with privately owned genetic material. These costs will in turn be passed on to the consumers thereby driving up the costs of basic survival on the planet. However, beyond the economic costs there exist the environmental risks. The first is loss of biodiversity. Legal developments in India and Iraq would impose a regime in which a small number of large agribusinesses dominate the market in agricultural seeds. In other words instead of numerous farmers and public research institutions engaged in growing and experimenting with a diversity plant varieties, the possible number of varieties may well reduce, as the number of seed providers is legally and drastically reduced. Control from the centers of agribusiness rather than decentralized control from local communities inevitably spells the loss of biodiversity. Others point out that the introduction of new economically dominant plant varieties developed by agribusinesses could also have the further effect of undermining the gene pool upon which these innovations depend as they have the potential to displace the wild areas that exist in the poor developing world.[19] The second issue involves ecological risks of genetically engineered seeds. Although the Indian legislation, for example, imposes severe constraints on the farmer, it carries no provisions requiring compensation and sanctions in the case of environmental damage due to the introduction of genetically modified plant varieties. Moreover, individual autonomy is undermined. In order to be competitive small farmers must choose production methods dictated by the emerging biotechnology industry. Beyond purchasing seed this involves the adoption of an entire package of capital and chemical intensive complementary inputs. Autonomy is reduced as little discretion is left to the individual farmer because the use of these inputs dictates the timing and intensity of the productive process and the farmer increasingly becomes the provider of raw unskilled labor power.[20] Finally domination of global agricultural activity by giant agribusinesses realizes a transnational form of regulation which undermines not only the sovereignty of the local community and its agricultural producers but also the sovereignty of the nation state itself, as its capacity for self determination, which must include the ability to match policy and the national interest with the basic food and nutritional needs of its population, is vitiated.

---

at which the contracting company would take back the crop and barred growers from selling the crop to anyone. In 1994, seed potato bought from Scottish farmers for £140 was sold for more than double that price to English farmers, whilst the two sets of farmers were prevented from dealing directly with each other.

[19] D.G. Richards, *Intellectual Property Rights and Global Capitalism: the Political Economy of the TRIPs Agreement* (Amonk New York: M.E. Sharpe, 2004), 173.

[20] *Ibid.*, 198.

Intellectual property and the Human Genome

Not only is the patenting of genetic material in non-human organisms contro-versial but equivalent controversy surrounds the patenting of human genes. The Human Genome Project began in 1987 as a public attempt to sequence the entire human DNA. It involved the sequencing of human genes with a genome of 3000 million bases. The intent was to reveal entirely the code of instructions that govern our composition, thus carrying a great potential for future medical benefit with extraordinary financial implications. The HGP was finally completed in April 2003.

In 1996 in the first meeting to discuss genome sequencing it was agreed that the work would be carried out by publicly funded laboratories devoted to large scale human sequencing. All data established would be released immediately as produced without claiming patent rights following the principle that the human genome is common heritage.[21] However in 1998 the Celera company was formed with the aim to sequence the genome "by a method" that would cover most of it rapidly at an accuracy that was limited but sufficient to obtain patent rights to some newly discovered genes and to sell the access to other scientists for their own gene hunting.[22] The reality is that patents on genes are being issued and many more are being applied for. All these patents claim the right of ownership in all uses of the gene even if the patent exhibits a limited understanding of its function. John Sulston, the co-founder of the human genome project, argues that patents did not assist at all in the sharing of the human sequence data. The field was fast moving and at least in the US delays in the release of data after filing meant that patent information was out of date by the time it was made public. The majority of patents are still pending. He points out that a recent survey of US academic laboratories has revealed that a high proportion of researchers are inhibited by patent claims. In addition academic meetings have suffered as well.[23]

Sulston argues that the Human Genome Project is not an end in itself. It should be thought of as a milestone in molecular biology as well as a beginning for biological and medical advances.[24] He points out that the research that is required to patent a gene does not in itself establish that the researcher has invented or devised an application which can be utilized to realize actual medical benefits. He says that in many cases patenting a gene is similar to buying a "genetic lottery ticket". One waits to see if some one else can find a valuable application with real

---

[21] John Sulston, "Intellectual Property and the Human Genome," in *Global Intellectual Property Rights: Knowledge Access and Development*: 61–73.
[22] *Ibid.*, 64.
[23] *Ibid.*
[24] *Ibid.*, 70.

medical benefits, which then allow the original patent holder to claim royalties and licensing fees without having made a real practical innovative contribution.

According to Sulston private ownership rights over genes frustrated the overall project of gene sequencing. Firstly it inhibits the sharing of knowledge between researchers because proprietary rights inhibit redistribution which is destructive of research effort. When signing up to a proprietary database, the researcher must agree only to download that which they need for their use and not to redistribute data thus inhibiting the normal exchanges between researchers—although the policy is essential for the companies business. Secondly the private appropriation of genes is limiting access to non owners who may wish to work on alternative applications using the same gene or genes.[25] He argues that ideally the discovery point and the sequencing of gene functions etc., need to be kept pre-competitive and free of property rights. Developers should have to demonstrate the existence of real applications so that true invention can be rewarded.[26]

Ultimately he argued that keeping the human genome project public rather than allowing the information to be privatized and "owned" by a company is important for the following reasons. Firstly, the sequence would never have been properly finished that way as accepted by all. Secondly, to the extent that the data is fundamental and important, it should be available to all on equal terms and not just the wealthy.[27] For example, he mentions the testing for Beta Thalassaemia which is cheap because it uses low cost labor yet would be impossible if royalties were charged for the test as with Myriad Genetics charges for breast cancer testing.

However, the Human Genome Diversity Project (HGDP) has been even more controversial than the HGP. The former project seeks to preserve the genetic heritage of over 5000 Indigenous groups throughout the world that are threatened with extinction. The goal of the HGDP is to preserve the genes for posterity long after the individuals have died off or the groups have been absorbed into the larger community. This has fostered a hostile reaction from many indigenous groups reminiscent of the Hagahai controversy in the 1990s. In the 1980s it was found that blood samples taken from the Hagahai people of Papua New Guinea possessed a unique property resistant to a type of leukemia. The National Institute of Health in the US filed a patent on the cell line from a member of the tribe. Indigenous groups argued that it was wrong to commodify body parts in this way. In addition it was charged that there was a failure to treat the individual holistically by treating the body and its parts as raw material as distinct from the human person.[28] From the perspective of the patent office the body as raw

[25] *Ibid.*, 71.
[26] *Ibid.*, 72.
[27] *Ibid.*, 70.
[28] Debora Halbert, *Resisting Intellectual Property* (London: Routledge, 2005), 123.

material can be subject to private ownership claims if the material is subsequently manipulated or prepared in such way as to effect some possible positive benefit. For example, private companies that claimed patent rights over human genes in the human genome project successfully argued that they were not patenting the genes per se but a "man-made copy of the coding sequence of a gene", which involves some modification of the original genes.[29] However the use of patents in the HGDP has not been so easily accepted by indigenous groups. From their perspective the actual body of the third world individual is being replaced by the digital body of genetic information, information which has been collected and added to the Western knowledge system.[30] Again indigenous groups have felt that there is an element of biopiracy inherent in the project itself, not to mention a form of neocolonialism in which the genetic inherence of indigenous people is appropriated as has frequently happened with natural resources and labor.

Conclusion

Our discussion of the patenting of genetic material, whether of the plant or human variety, has presented disturbing evidence of an apparent inexorable trend, one in which powerful commercial interests have seized upon the common inheritance of humanity and the particular inheritance of a cultural communities in an attempt to derive income rights from their ownership claims. These are claims based on an intellectual slight of hand, which attempts to convince us that information derived from these sources is the invention of the patent claimant. We have seen, for example, how RiceTec and Monsanto introduced minor modifications into an existing product in order to promote IP claims. In the case of ownership of genes we have seen the acceptance of the dubious argument that a copy of the coding sequence is an invention. Debora Halbert explains that US patent law allows a researcher to patent traditional knowledge, which is already known and obvious to its practitioners by recognizing the labor of the Western patent claimant as an inventive step. Thus, the reduction of a plant or seed to its medicinal properties or a specific color that makes it useful is said to represent the labor which has sufficiently modified the product and justified the patent.[31] The philosophically inclined would attempt to defend this practice through reference to the Lockean theory of original acquisition through labor.

But, ultimately the use of Locke's theory of acquisition through labor to justify IP rights is in actuality an extrapolation of Locke's reasoning beyond acceptable

---

[29] *Ibid.*, 127.
[30] *Ibid.*, 134.
[31] *Ibid.*, 147.

limits. Firstly, labor does not serve as the ultimate justification of the system of ownership, according to Locke.[32] Secondly, Locke's theory applies to material acquisitions, land and its products, Locke never mentions intellectual property; and thirdly, labor was intended to limit ownership claims rather than expand them. *Two Treatises* II: 36) "The measure of Property Nature has well set, by the extent of Mens Labour, and the Convenience of Life: No Mans Labour could subdue or appropriate all…" The labor theory is intended to justify my claims to the particular material products of my labor and Locke would probably be horrified to see it used to justify universal ownership over the products of someone else's labor, as for example, contemporary IP rights may allow Monsanto to claim ownership over the products of the Indian farmer's labor. Finally, for Locke, property claims are always subject to the condition that we leave "enough and as good for others". We have seen that IP rights over seeds have created virtual monopolies in which farmers don't even own the rights to their own produce and the seeds produced through their labor. Locke's social political philosophy cannot be twisted to countenance this result without a convenient ellipsis that omits the "enough and as good" condition.

In *Intellectual Property Rights and Global Capitalism: the Political Economy of the TRIPs Agreement* D.G. Richards attempts to articulate a global context in which intellectual property and the TRIPS agreement have become integral to the changing political economic relationship between the developed and developing world.[33] The author utilizes a method that, he claims, is inspired by a tradition in radical political economy and international relations theory. Accordingly he sees the TRIPS agreement as the outcome of a struggle in which the centers of capitalist activity seek to extend their control and domination of the periphery, the developed and less developed countries. He points out, however, that capitalist centers such as the US are not to be represented as hegemonic states in the spirit of hegemonic stability theory, but as representative of the transnational capitalist class. For example, the biochemical revolution and the growth of huge agribusinesses are cases in point. Accordingly, the author sees the peripheral countries acting as designated repositories and caretakers of an ever diminishing global plant related gene bank. The center countries are expected to have the right to unlimited access and entry allowing transnational companies to convert the preserved raw germ plasm into GMOs that possess a variety of characteristics from a use value perspective. At the same time as groups such as USAID urge

---

[32] *Two Treatises* II: 35 "…God, by commanding to subdue gave authority so far to appropriate. And the condition of Humane Life which requires Labour and Materials to work on, necessarily introduces private possessions." John Locke, *Two treatises of Government*, P. Lazlett, ed., (Cambridge: Cambridge University Press, 1967).

[33] D.G. Richards, *op. cit.*, 173.

open access to globally important food and forage crops, there is no presumption that the benefits that result from the applied R&D on these genetic raw materials will be shared between periphery and center. Thus as possessors of exchange value GMOs are the instruments through which international capital expands its reach into forms of social production that have been foreclosed by the communal nature of knowledge.

While Richards' work is concerned with the dynamics and tendencies of the global forces that have realized the TRIPS agreement, I have emphasized the redefinition of property rights and the arguments that have sought to legitimate the expansion of this novel post colonial form of exploitation. It is the acceptance of this redefinition of property within Western legal theory that ultimately led to the TRIPS agreement as part of a project to actualize a global recognition. My concern has been to enumerate the aspects and ways in which intellectual property that TRIPS and other agreements seek to globalize, differs from tangible forms of property and ownership. Moreover once this is appreciated, one recognizes that one is no longer dealing with a system of property that supports a market system that is fundamentally based on exchange.

Intellectual property establishes rights to income that accrue to the right holder in mere virtue of the fact that another makes use of a particular technique, process or body of knowledge. It is presupposed that the original right holder does not acquire these rights through exchange but through a creative process. In turn the IP right holder does not legally transfer his/her product to the consumer rather he/she retains title throughout the transaction, which ensures he/she retains exclusive rights to all income derived from the use of such processes, techniques or bodies of knowledge. This system is designed to ensure that a portion of benefits actualized by any producer will flow continuously back to the IP right claimant.

Marx argued that relationships based on exploitation enabled the bourgeoisie owners of the means of production to extract surplus value from the labour of the workers without laboring or directly participating in the production process. Exploitation in this sense at the least recognizes the necessity for some form of financial involvement in the productive process even if there is no other contact with the work of the business. The extension and redefining of intellectual property rights creates a growing class of alleged owners of ideas, rather than the physical means of production. These ownership claims offer the possibility of a different form of exploitation in which one realizes access to profits or surplus value from the productive activities of others without having to make even a minimum financial claim or commitment to the means of production. At least with the dominant form of nineteenth century exploitation, of which Marx speaks, there is a greater tendency to wider wealth distribution in so far as increasing profits required increased spending to acquire or create new means of production. In this case, self interest on the part of the bourgeoisie stimulated the production of increased goods and services and their wider distribution to the general public. In contrast, the alleged owner of an idea, once protected as intellectual property, theoretically can increase his/her wealth without redistributing his/her income in order to finance the actual re-production of the tangible embodiment of the patented idea. This allows for the possibility of wealth accumulation that is independent of the necessity for increased investment and the acquisition of attendant costs. It is perhaps no coincidence that the recent cases of unprecedented individual wealth, realized in the last several decades, have been based on intellectual property rights, particularly in the software industry. It is for this reason that we have witnessed the increased efforts by the owners of intellectual property to expand and extend their rights in terms of the increased assertion and registration of such rights, but also in terms of the expanded spatial and temporal application of these rights. Major resources are now devoted to political lobbying and legal fees to enforce and forge agreements that further these ends. In many cases, more resources are spent on acquiring and enhancing these rights as well as marketing (in the case of the pharmaceutical industry) than is spent on R&D.

On Richards' view the emphasis placed on the extension of IP rights is related to the inexorable tendency of capital to extent into the multifarious aspects of human activity and to commodify and endow all compliant phenomena with exchange value. In fact, Richards argues that terms such as "biopiracy" and "bioprospecting" are to be resisted if we are to overcome this competitive culture that seeks to priortize the private domain over the public domain. He argues that the term biopiracy suggests that genetic resources are owned by some interest that has been illegally deprived of them, while bioprospecting implies that resources represent potential exchange value recognized and valued by local communities.[34] He argues that the acceptance of these terms inevitably leads to an orientation that transforms non-capitalist forms of social production in that that which is common inheritance is transformed into "a stream of personal compensation". The extension of intellectual property into this sphere is actually an incursion into the public domain based on cooperation, knowledge sharing and free exchange. The appropriation of this knowledge, and the conversion from the public to the private, involves the imposition of a competitive individualistic culture, which is antithetical to genetic diversity. "Biopiracy" and "bioprospecting", therefore inappropriately suggest the existence of a form of personal ownership when in fact the resources under consideration belong to the public domain that precludes any form of private ownership.

---

[34] Ibid., 197.

However, my point is that these developments need to be recognized as more than the simple movement of capital into forms of social production that have been foreclosed by the communal nature of knowledge. Although it is the case that activities that have been immune to capital are now endowed with exchange value, this statement seems to indicate that we are still referring to a market system based on exchange. In point of fact the owner of ideas does not transfer or convey title in exchange for monetary compensation. Title remains with the right holder who is licensed to extract unlimited compensation without having to alienate or transfer his/her alleged property. As we have stated, the stream of personal income can continue and increase without the necessity to re-invest the acquired profit to create new industrial facilities and corresponding labor opportunities. The same phenomenon occurs on a macro scale as wealth and income drain from the developing world to the developed world and into the hands the holders of intellectual property in the developed world. As revenue continues to flow to the developed world there is no demand to return part of the profit as reinvestment in productive capacities and infrastructure of the developing world. This is a strategy of perpetual dependency based on an economic and legal arrangement in which Western technology and innovation are never actually transferred to the developing world despite the compensation, thus empowering the gatekeepers of the world's so called technological knowledge to deny access if sufficient payment is not forthcoming. This can be interpreted as analogous to the more familiar form of sovereignty over the physical territory. In this instance, this form of arrangement has been extrapolated to include a form of sovereignty over an intellectual territory of ideas and technological innovation. Those who venture onto this intellectual territory will be heavily taxed with no guarantees that a part of these benefits will flow back from the sovereign.

It may be closer to the truth to say that what is being instituted through the IP regime is more akin to taxation in which value is extracted by an authority claiming jurisdiction, without any requirement that the authority share or return benefits. In other words, research and development designed to provide and extend new technological systems are not necessarily intended to create new beneficial products but to create IP rights, whose function is to create new dependents or subjects to be taxed by the authorities claiming legal jurisdiction over these technological systems.

In some respect sovereignty over ideas is superior to sovereignty over physical phenomena because the former is theoretically limitless. In the old days of bricks and mortar industries the bourgeoisie owner of the means of production would find his/her income constrained by the extent of physical holdings: the size of the factory; the accumulated heavy equipment; the acreage enclosed in the industrial farm etc. In contrast, the holder of intellectual property knows no such physical constraint, because ideas are not subject to physical and spatial limitations. With the recent technological revolution ideas move around and disseminate throughout the globe continuously and instantaneously. As information technology becomes inescapable and ubiquitous, ideas, theories and processes of thought also become unavoidable. The heightened attempt to redefine the intellectual as a form of property, and redefine property in this way, is, in reality, an effort to transform ideas and knowledge into legal claims on the exchange value of the ineluctable recipient's holdings. This may be the ultimate irony and subversion of our technological advance, that is, that these advances are no longer intended to improve and ameliorate the human condition but to function as the vehicle through which internationally sanctioned authorities (multi-national companies) make claims on the other's (developing countries') natural wealth, productive activities and the products thereof.

Bibliography

Abbot, F.M., Amy Kapczynski, and T.N. Srinivasan. "The Draft Patent Law." *The Hindu* 12 Mar. 2005 <http://www.hinduonnet.com/2005/03/12/stories/2005031201151000.htm>.

Alchian, A.A. and H. Demsetz. "Production, information costs, and economic organization." *American Economic Review.* 62 (1972): 777–795.

Aldridge, B. *Current Land Situation Report.* Report presented to the Special Parliamentary Committee on Urbanisation and Social Development. Port Moresby: 2000, unpublished;

Altbach, P. "The Subtle Inequalities of Copyright." *Copyright and Development: Inequality in the Exchange.* Ed. P. Altbach. Chestnut Hill Mass.: Bellagio Publishing, Network Research and Information System, 1995. 2–6.

Amarshi, A.K. Good and R. Mortimer. *Development and Dependency: The Political Economy of Papua New Guinea.* Melbourne: Oxford University Press, 1979.

Ambler, T. and A. Wilson, "Problems of Stakeholder Theory." *Business Ethics: A European Review* 4. 1 (1995): 30–35.

Arneil, Barbara. "John Locke, natural law and colonialism." *History of Political Thought* 13. 4 (1992): 587–603

Arthur, W.S. "Towards A Comprehensive Regional Agreement: Torres Strait." *CAEPR Discussion Paper No. 147.* Canberra: Centre for Aboriginal Economic Policy Research, ANU, 1997.

Austen, J. *The Province of Jurisprudence Determined.* Cambridge: Cambridge University Press, 1995.

Baker, Brook K. "India's 2005 Patent Act: Death by Patent or Universal Access to Second— and Future—Generation ARVS?" *Health Gap Global Access Project.* 19 Sept. 2005 <www.healthgag.org>.

Ball, S.J. *Education Reform: A Critique and Post-structural Approach.* Buckingham: Open University Press, 1994.

Ballard, C. "It's the land stupid! The moral economy of resource ownership in Papua New Guinea." *The Governance of Common Property in the Pacific Region.* Ed. P. Larmour. Canberra: ANU, National Centre of Development Studies, 1997. 47–65;

Banfield, Edward. *The Moral Basis of Backward Society.* Gencoe Ill: Freepress, 1958.

Banks, Glen. "Compensation for Mining: Benefit or Time Bomb—The Porgera Case." *Resources, Nations and Indigenous Peoples.* Eds. R. Howatt, J. Connel, and P. Hirsh. Melbourne: Oxford University Press 1995. 59–91.

Barnett, Thomas. *Commission of inquiry into Aspects of the Forest Industry.* Port Moresby: 1989.

Barton, John H. "TRIPS and the Global Pharmaceutical Market." *Health Affairs* 23. 3 (2004): 146–154.

Bauer, P. *Reality and Rhetoric: Studies in the Economics of Development.* London: Weidenfeld Nicholson, 1984.

Benson, B.L. "Enforcement of Private Property Rights in Primitive Societies: Law without Government." *The Journal of Libertarian Studies* IX. 1 (Winter 1989): 1–26

Berg, Scott. *Goldwyn*. New York: Alfred Knopf, 1989.

Berle, A.A. and C. Means. *The Modern Corporation and Private Property*. New York: Macmillan, 1932.

Bethel, T. *The Noblest Triumph: Poverty and Prosperity Through the Ages*. New York: St Martin's Griffin.

Blakeney, Michael. "Intellectual Property and the CGIAR System." *Global Intellectual Property Rights: Knowledge Access and Development*. Eds. P. Drahos and R. Mayne. New York: Palmgrave Macmillan, 2002. 109–125.

Bogle, John. *The Battle for the Soul of Capitalism*. New Haven: Yale University Press, 2005.

Branscomb, A. *Who owns Information: From Privacy to Public Access*. New York: Basic Books, 1994.

Brennan, Frank. *One Land, One Nation: Mabo—Towards 2001*. Brisbane: University of Queensland Press, 1995.

Bruce, J. "Learning from Comparative Experience with Agrarian Reform," Unpublished paper presented at the International Conference on Land Tenure in the Developing World, University of Capetown, Capetown. South Africa, Jan. 27–29, 1998.

Burns Commission. *The Report of the Commission of Inquiry into the Natural Resources and Population Trends of the Colony of Fiji*. Suva: Legislative Council Paper No. 1, 1960.

BUSINESSWEEK ONLINE. 26 July 1999 <http://www.businessweek.com:/1999/99>.

Caldbick, Mary. "Wild Woods and Uncultivated Waste: Aboriginal Versus Lockean Views of Land Ownership." unpublished paper presented to the Canadian Political Science Association, St Catherines, June 1, 1996.

Chand S. and R. Duncan. "Resolving Property Issues as a Precondition for Growth: Access to Land in the Pacific Islands." *The Governance of Common Property in the Pacific Region*. Ed. P. Larmour. Canberra: ANU, National Centre of Development Studies 1997. 33–46.

Chaudhuri, S., P. Goldberg, and P. Jia. "Estimating the Effects of Global Patent Protection in Pharmaceuticals: A Case Study of Quinolones in India." *American Economic Review* 96. 5 (2006): 1477–1491.

Christman, John. *The Myth of Property*. New York: Oxford University Press, 1994.

Christman, John. "Distributive Justice and the Complex Structure of Ownership." *Philosophy and Public Affairs* 23. 3 (Summer 1994): 225–250.

Coase, R.H. "The Nature of the Firm." *Economica* 4 (1937): 386–405.

Codd, John. "Teachers as Managed Professionals in the Global Education Industry: The New Zealand Experience." *Education Review* 57. 2 (May 2005): 193–206.

Cole, Julio H. "Patents and Copyrights: do the Benefits exceed the Costs?" *Journal of Libertarian Studies* 15. 4 (Fall 2001): 79–105.

Comaroff, J. and S. Roberts. *Rules and Processes: the Cultural Logic of Dispute in an African Context*. Chicago: University of Chicago Press, 1981.

Cooter, R. "Kin groups and the common law process, in Papua New Guinea." *Monograph 29 Customary Land Tenure in Papua New Guinea* Ed. P. Larmour. Port Moresby: NRI, 1991. 33–49.

Cragg, W., A. Wellington and A.J. Greenbaum. *Canadian Issues in Environmental Ethics*. Toronto: Broadview Press, 1997.

Cringely, Bob.*The Triumph of the Nerds: Impressing their Friends*, Volume 1, Ambrose Videos, 1996.

Crocombe, Ron. *Land Tenure in the Pacific*. Suva: University of the South Pacific, 1987.

Currie, Jan. "Globalization Practices and the Professoriate in Anglo-Pacific and North American Universities." *Comparative Education Review* 42.1 (Feb. 1998): 15–29.

Curtin, Tim. "Scarcity Amidst Plenty: the Economics of Land Tenure in Papua New Guinea." *Land Registration in Papua New Guinea: Competing Perspectives*. Discussion Paper 2003/1. Eds. T. Curtin, H. Holzknecht, and P. Larmour. Canberra: State Society and Governance in Melanesia, Research School of Pacific and Asian Studies, Australian National University, 2003. 6–17.

Curtin, Tim. "Land Titling and Forestry." unpublished. 2004

Curtin, Tim. "Forestry and economic development in Papua New Guinea." *South Pacific Journal of Philosophy and Culture* 8 (2005): 105–117.

Curtin, Tim. "What Constitutes Illegal logging?" *Pacific Economic Bulletin* 22. 1 (2007): 125–134.

Davis, Richard. "Black Spurs: Aboriginal Pastoralists in the Kimberleys," unpublished paper presented at the North Australia Research Unit, Australian National University, Darwin, Dec, 1, 1999.

De George, Richard. "Intellectual Property and Pharmaceutical Drugs: An Ethical Analysis." *Business Ethics Quarterly* 15. 4 (2005): 549–575.

De Soto, Hernando. *The Mystery of Capital: Why Capitalism Triumphs in the West and Pails Everywhere Else*. Sydney: Random House, 2000.

Deardorff, Alan. "The Welfare Effects of Global Patent Protection." *Economica* 59 (1992): 35–51.

Duncan, Ross. "Mahogany Dreaming." Program transcript from ABC National Radio. 10 Oct. 2004 <www.abc.net.au/talks/bbing/stories/s1218975.htm>.

Dworkin, Ronald. *Taking Rights Seriously*. London: Duckworth, 1977.

Easton, B. *The Whimpering of the State*. Auckland: Auckland University Press, 1999.

Editor Notes. *Harvard Law Review* 107 (1993): 859–876.

Epstein, Richard. *Takings: Private Property and Eminent Domain*. Cambridge Mass.: Harvard University, 1985.

Evan, W.M. and R.E. Freeman. "A Stakeholder theory for of the Modern Corporation: Kantian Capitalism," *Ethical theory and Business*. 4th edition. Eds. T. Beauchamp and N. Bowie. Englewood Cliffs N.J.: Prentice Hall, 1993.

Fallers, Lloyd. *Law without Precedent*. Chicago: University of Chicago Press, 1969.

Fama, E.F. and M.C. Jensen. "Agency Problems and Residual Claims." *Journal of Law and Economics* 26. 2 (1983): 327–349.

Farrell, B.H. and P.E. Murphy. *Ethnic Attitudes Towards Land in Fiji*. Santa Cruz: University of California Press, 1978.

Farrell, B.H. "Fijian Land: A Basis for Intercultural Variance." *Themes on Pacific Lands*. Eds. M.C.R. Edgell and B.H. Farrell. Victoria: University of Victoria Press, 1974. 110–121.

Filer, Colin. "The Bougainville Rebellion, the Mining Industry and the Process of Social Disintegration." *The Bougainville Crisis*. Eds. R. May and M. Sprigs. Bathurst: Crawford House Press, 1990.

Fingleton, J. *Privatising Land in the Pacific: A defense of customary Tenures: Discussion Paper Number 80 June 2005*. Canberra: Australian Institute, 2005.

Flanagan, Thomas. "The Agricultural Argument and Original Appropriation: Indian Lands and Political Philosophy." *Canadian Journal of Political Science* XXII. 3 (Sept 1989): 589–602;

Fletcher, Christine. "Does Federalism Safeguard Indigenous Rights." *Discussion Paper 14*. Darwin: North Australia Research Unit, 1999.

Fletcher, Christine. "Federalism and Civil Societies." *Federalism Studies* 14 (1999): 97–121.

Foucault, Michel *The Birth of the Prison System*. Trans. A. Sheridan. New York: Vintage Books, 1979.

France, Peter. *The Charter of the Land*. Melbourne: Oxford University Press, 1969.

Freeman, R.E. *Strategic Management: a Stakeholder Approach*. Boston: Pitman, 1984.

Freeman, R.E., A.C. Wicks, and B. Parmar. "Stakeholder theory and The Corporate Objective revisited." *Organization Science*. 15. 3 (2004): 364–369.

Friedman, Milton "The Social Responsibility of Business is to Increase its Profits." *New York Times Magazine*. 13 Sept. 1970: 32.

Fukuyama, Francis. *Trust: The Social Virtues and the Creation of Prosperity*. London: Penguin Books, 1995.

Galbraith, John Kenneth. *Money: Whence it Came, Where it Went*. Boston: Houghton Mifflin, 1975.

Garber, Bart K. "1991 Balancing Individual and Group Rights after ANCSA." *Alaska Native News* 2 (January 1985): 21–30.

Garnaut, R. "The Neo-Marxist Paradigm in Papua New Guinea." *Social Stratification in Papua New Guinea*. Ed. R. May. Canberra: Research School of Pacific Studies, 1984. 43–52.

Gautier, David. *Morals by Agreement*. Oxford: Clarendon Press, 1986.

Gordon, Richard. "Innovation, Industrial Networks and High Technology Regions." *Innovation Networks: Spatial Perspectives*. Ed. R. Camagni. London: Belhaven, 1991. 121–137.

Gordon, Rupert. "Kant's Categorical Imperative and Hegel's Conception of the Economic Market." unpublished paper presented for the Canadian Society of Political Science, St Johns Newfoundland, June 1, 1997.

Gorsarevski, S., H. Hughes and S. Windybank "Is Papua New Guinea Viable?" *Pacific Economic Bulletin* 19. 1 (2004): 134–148.

Gorsarevski, S., H. Hughes and S. Windybank. "Is Papua New Guinea Viable with Customary Land Tenure?" *Pacific Economic Bulletin* 19. 3 (2004) 133–136.

Gulf Today 17 Nov. 2004: 23.

Gulf Today 21 June 2005: 23.

Gulf Today 29 Jan. 2007:11.

Halbert, Debora. *Resisting Intellectual Property*. London: Routledge, 2005.

Harrison, David. *The Sociology of Modernization and Development*. London: Unwin Hyman, 1988.

Hart, H.L.A. *The Concept of Law*. Oxford: Oxford University Press, 1961.

Hayek, F.A. *Law, Legislation and Liberty, Rules and Order* Vol. 1. Chicago: University of Chicago Press, 1973.

Hazeldine, T. *Taking New Zealand Seriously*. Auckland: Harpers Collins, 1998.

Henao, Loani "Voluntary Registration of Customary Land." *PNG Post Courier* 10 July 2003: 18.

Holly, Marilyn. "The Persons of Nature Versus the Power Pyramid: Locke, land and American Indians." *International Studies in Philosophy* XXVI. 1 (1994): 14–31.

Holzknecht, Hartmut. *Policy Reform, Customary Tenure and Stakeholder Clashes in Papua New Guinea's Rainforests, Rural Development Forestry Network Paper 19c*. Regents College London: Rural Development Forestry Network, Overseas Development Institute, 1996.

Honore, A.M. Ownership, *Oxford Essays in Jurisprudence*. Ed. A.G. Guest. London: Oxford University Press, 1961. 107–147.

Hume, D. *A Treatise on Human Nature*. London: Dent, 1911 [1740].

Hund, John. "H.L.A. Hart's Contribution to Legal Anthropology." *Journal for The Theory of Social Behaviour* 26. 3 (1996): 275–292.

Jakab, Peter L. and Tom D. Crouch. *Visions of a Flying Machine: The Wright Brothers and the Process of Invention*. Washington: Smithsonian History of Aviation Series, 1990.

James, R.W. *Land law and Policy in Papua New Guinea*. Port Moresby: PNG Land Reform Commission, 1985.

J.E.M A.G. Supply, Inc. v. Pioneer Hi-Bred Int'l Inc. 534 U.S. 124 (2001).

Jensen M.C and W.H. Meckling. "Theory of the Firm: Managerial, Behaviour, Agency Costs and Ownership Structure." *Journal of Financial Economics* 3 (1976): 303–360.

Johnson, D.G. *Computer Ethics*. 3rd Edition. New Jersey: Prentice Hall, 2001.

Johnston, Darlene. "Native Rights as Collective Rights: A Question of Group Self-Preservation." *The Rights of Minority Cultures*. Ed. W. Kymlicka. Oxford: Oxford University Press, 1995. 87–98.

Jones L.T. and A. McGavin. *Land Mobilization in Papua New Guinea*. Canberra: Asia Pacific Press, 2001.

Karper, W. "How to learn Racial Harmony? Fiji would Benefit from a New Game." *Pacific Economic Bulletin* 16. 1, (2001): 136–141.

Kelsen, Hans. *The General Theory of Law and the State*. Trans. Anders Wedberg. Cambridge Mass: Harvard University Press, 1945.

Kemeata, R. "Land Legislation and Practice since Independence." *Land and Churches in Melanesia: Issues and Contexts*. Ed. M. Rynkiewich. Goroka: Melanesian Institute, 2001. 304–334.

Khor, Martin. "Rethinking Intellectual Property Rights and TRIPS." *Global Intellectual Property Rights: Knowledge Access and Development*. Eds. P. Drahos and R. Mayne. New York: Palmgrave Macmillan, 2002. 201–214.

Klemens, Ben. "Software Patents don't Compute." *IEEE Spectrum* (July 2005): 49–50.

Klemens, Ben. "New Legal code: Copyrights should Replace Software Patents." *IEEE Spectrum* (August 2005): 52–53.

Koafman Eleonore and Gillian Youngs. *Globalization: Theory and Practice*. New York: Pinter, 1996.

Kymlicka, Will. "Individual and Community rights." Ed. J. Baker. *Group Rights*. Toronto: University of Toronto Press, 1994.

Kymlicka, Will. *Liberalism, Community and Culture*. Oxford: Clarendon Press, 1989.

Kymlicka, Will. *Multicultural Citizenship*. Oxford: Oxford University Press, 1996.

Ladd, J. "Ethics and the Computer World." *Cyberethics Social and Moral Issues in the Computer Age*. New York: Prometheus Books, 2000.

Land Act of Papua New Guinea, (1982), ch. 185, s. 73.

Land Groups Incorporation Act of Papua New Guinea, (1974) ch. 147, s.1 (e).

Lanjouw, Jean O. "The Introduction of Pharmaceutical Product Patents in India: Heartless Exploitation of the Poor and Suffering?" *Center Discussion Paper No. 775* (New Haven: Economic Growth Center, Yale University, Aug. 1997).

Larmour, P. "Alienated land and Independence in Melanesia." *Pacific Studies* 8. 1 (1984): 1–47.

Lamour, P. "Policy Transfer and Reversal: Customary Land Registration from Africa to the Pacific." Unpublished paper. Canberra: Centre for Development Studies, ANU, 2000.

Lea, David. "Resolving a Complexity of Land Mobilization Issues in Papua New Guinea." *the Pacific Economic Bulletin*. 16. 2 (2001): 36–53.

Lea, David. "From the Wright Brothers to Microsoft: Issues in the Moral Grounding of intellectual Property Rights." *Business Ethics Quarterly* 16. 4 (2006): 579–598.

Lea, David "The PNG Forestry Industry, Incorporated Entities, and Environmental Protection," *Pacific Economic Bulletin* 20. 1 (2005): 168–177.

Lea, David. "The Corporation, Public Responsibility, and Distributive Justice in the Third World." *Business Ethics: A European Review* 8. 3 (July, 1999): 151–162.

Lea, Gary "Digital Millennium or Digital Dominion? The Effect of IPRs in Software on Developing countries." *Global Intellectual Property Rights: Knowledge Access and Development*. Eds. P. Drahos and R. Mayne. New York: Palmgrave Macmillan, 2002.144–158.

Leahy, Stephen. "Canada's Highest Court backs Monsanto Against Farmer." *IPS* Web Page. 21 May 2004 <ipsnews.net/interna.asp?idnews=23862—65k>.

Lebovics, Herman. "The Uses of America in Locke's Second Treatise of Government." *Journal of the History of Ideas* 47. 4 (Oct–Dec 1986): 567–581.

Levin, Richard C. "Appropriability, R&D Spending and Technical Performance." *American Economic Review* 78 (May 1998): 424–450.

Little, I.M.D. *Economic Development: Theory, Policy and International Relations*. New York: Basic Books, 1982.

Locke, John. *Two Treatises of Government*. Ed. Peter Lazlett. Cambridge: Cambridge University Press, 1967.

MacDonald, M, "Defeating Death and Promoting Life: Ancestors among the Enga, Huli, and Kewa of Papua New Guinea." in ed., *Ancestors in Post-Contact Religion: Roots, Ruptures and Modernity's Memory*. Ed. S. Friesen. Cambridge Mass.: Harvard University Press, 2001. 73–91.

Macdonald, Stuart. "Exploring the Hidden Costs of Patents." *Global Intellectual Property Rights: Knowledge Access and Development*. Eds. P. Drahos and R. Mayne. New York: Palmgrave Macmillan, 2002. 13–40.

Machan, Tibo. "Pollution, Collectivism and Capitalism." *Journal Des Economists et Etudes Humaines* 2 (1991): 82–102.

MacIntrye, Alistair. *After Virtue: A Study in Moral Theory*. 2nd edition. London: Duckworth, 1985.

Mack, Eric. "Gautier on Rights and Economic Rent." *Social Philosophy and Policy* 9. 1 (1992): 171–200.

MacWilliams S. and H. Thompson. *The Political Economy of Papua New* Guinea. Woolongong: Journal of Contemporary Asia Publishers, 1992.

Maitland, Ian "Priceless Goods: How Should Life-Saving Drugs Be Priced?" *Business Ethics Quarterly* 12, 4 (2002): 451–480.

Maitland, Ian. "Distributive Justice in Firms: Do the Rules of Corporate Governance Matter?" *Business Ethics Quarterly* 11.1 (2001): 129–145.

Makdisi, George. *The Rise of the Colleges*. Edinburgh: Edinburgh University Press, 1981.

Manning, Mike. "Mid Year Review of the Economy." *PNG Post Courier* 18 July 2003: 11.

Mansfield, E. "Intellectual Property rights, Technological change and Economic Growth." *Intellectual Property Rights and Capital Formation in the Next Decade*. Eds. C. Walker and M. Bloomfield. New York: University Press of America, 1988. 34–48.

Mantovani, E. "Traditional Values and Ethics." *Ethics of Development: The Pacific in the Twentieth Century*. Eds. S. Stratigos and P. Hughes. Port Moresby: UPNG Press, 1987. 102–111.

Margalit, Avishai and Moshe Halbertal. "Liberalism and the Right to Culture." *Social Research* 61. 3 (1990): 491–510;

Margalit, Avishai and Joseph Raz. "National Self-Determination." *The Journal of Philosophy* 87 (Sept 1990): 439–461.

Maritain, Jacques. *The Person and the Common Good.* Trans. John FitzGerald. New York: 1947.

May, R. "Weak States, Collapsed States, Broken-Backed States and Kleptocracies: General Concepts and Political Realities." *New Pacific Review* (2004): 1–10.

Mayne, Ruth. "Global Campaign on Patents: Oxfam Perspective." *Global Intellectual Property Rights: Knowledge Access and Development.* Eds. P. Drahos and R. Mayne. New York: Palmgrave Macmillan, 2002. 244–259.

Mayne, Ruth. "TRIPS and Access to Medicines." *The WTO and Developing Countries.* Ed. H. Katrak & R. Strange. New York: Palgrave Macmillan, 2004. 146–165.

Mc Chesney, Fred. "Government as Defender of Property Rights: Indian Lands, Ethnic Externalities and Bureaucratic Budgets." *The Journal of Legal Studies* 19. 2 (June 1990): 297–335.

McDonald, Michael. "Collective Rights and Tyranny." *University of Ottawa Quarterly* 56 (1986): 115–125.

McDonald, Michael. "Indian Status: Colonialism or Sexism?" *Canadian Community Law Journal* 9 (1986): 23–47.

Meriba Tomakala v Robin Meriba. *PNG Law Reports* (1994): 10–14.

Mill, John Stuart. *On Liberty.* New York: The Liberal Arts Press, 1956.

Millon, David. "Communitarianism in Corporate Law: Foundations and Law Reform Strategies." *Progressive Corporate Law.* Ed. L. E. Mitchell. Boulder CO.: Westview Press, 1995. 115–129.

Millon, David. "Communitarians, Contractarians and the Crisis in Corporate Law." *Washington and Lee Law Review* 50. 4 (1993): 1373–1380.

"Monsanto Pawn forbids Iraqis to Save Seeds." *St Louis Independent Media.* 2 Oct. 2006 <www.stlimc.org/newswire/display/2276/index.php>.

More, Thomas *Utopia.* Trans. C.H. Miller. New Haven: Yale University Press, 2001.

Morito, Bruce. "Aboriginal Right: A Conciliatory Concept." *Journal of Applied Philosophy* 13.2 (1996): 123–140

Mosko, Mark "Customary Land Tenure and Agricultural Success: the Mekeo Case." *Privatising Land in the Pacific. A Defence of Customary Tenures.* Ed. J. Fingleton, Canberra: Australia Institute, 2005. 6–21.

Nesteruk, J. "Law and the Virtues: a Review Article." *Business Ethics Quarterly* 5. 2 (1995): 361–369.

New York Times, late edition. 24 Nov. 2003: A22.

Nichols, James. "Tackling HIV/AIDS in Resource Poor Settings." *Issues* 75 (June 2006): 30–35.

Nizar, Mohamed and Kevin Clark. "Forestry on Customary-owned Land: Some Experiences from the South Pacific." *Rural Forestry Network Paper 19a.* London: Regents College London, Rural Development Forestry Network, Overseas Development Institute, 1996.

Nozick, Robert. *Anarchy, State and Utopia.* New York: Basic Books, 1974.

Oddi, A.S. "Nature and Scope of the Agreement: Article: TRIPS _ Natural Rights and a Polite Form of Economic Imperialism." *Vanderbilt Journal of Transnational Law* 29 (1996): 415–429.

Omari, C.K. *Strategy for Rural Development: The Tanzania Experiment.* Kampala: East African Bureau, 1976.

Omari, C.K. "Traditional African land Ethics." *Ethics of Environment and Development: Global Challenge and International Response.* Eds. R. Engel and I.G. Engel. London: Belhaven Press, 1990.167–175;

Pearson, N. and W. Sanders, "Indigenous Peoples and Reshaping Australian Institutions: Two Perspectives." *AEPR Discussion Paper No. 102.* Canberra: Centre for Aboriginal Economic Policy Research, ANU, 1995.

PNG Forestry Review Team. *Individual Project Report Numbers 12–32: 5 Feb. -5 Mar. 2001.* Port Moresby: Forestry Review Team, 2001.

PNG Forestry Review Team. *Individual Project Reports 2003/2004: Towards Sustainable Timber Production—A Review of Existing Logging Projects Volume I—Main Report, The Review of Current Logging Projects.* Port Moresby: PNG Forestry Review Team, May 2004.

PNG Post Courier 11 July 2003: 11.

Pogue. David. *Macworld,* San Francisco, 14. 10 (Oct. 1997): 190–191.

Pollack, Malla. "Originalism, J.E.M., and the Food Supply or Will the Real Decision Maker Please Stand Up?" *Journal of Environmental Law and Litigation* 19. 2 (2004): 500–538.

Power, A.P. "Resources Development in East Sepic Province." *Ethics of Development: Choices in Development Planning.* Eds. C. Thirwell and P. Hughes. Port Moresby: UPNG Press, 1988. 56–70.

Power, A.P. *Village Guide to Land Group Incorporation Report for Resource Owner Involvement Component, Forest management and Planning Project.* Wewak: World Bank /PNG Forest Authority/Groome Ltd., Irvin Enterprises, Pty Ltd., 1995.

Power, A.P. *Land Group Incorporation.* (three volumes) Port Moresby: Aus Aid, 1999.

Power, A.P. "State Neglect a Major Factor." *PNG National* 19 May 2001: 19.

Prospsil, Leopold. *Anthropology of Law: A Comparative Theory.* New York: Harper and Row, 1971.

Radder, H. "Exploiting the Abstract Possibilities: A Critique of the Concept and Practice of Product Patenting." *Journal of Agriculture and Environmental Ethics* 17. 3 (2004): 275–290.

Randeep, Ramesh. *The Guardian* Jan. 31, 2004: 21.

Ravuvu, A. *The Facade of Democracy.* Suva: Reader Publishing House, 1991.

Rawls, John. *A Theory of Justice.* Cambridge Mass.: Belknap Press, 1971.

Reddy, Mahendra and Padma Lal, "State Land Transfers in Fiji: Issues and Implications." *Pacific Economic Bulletin* 17. 1 (2002): 146–154.

Renato, Cristi. "Waldron on Special Rights *in Rem.*" *Dialogue,* 23. 2 (1994): 183–190.

Reynolds, Henry. *The Law of the Land.* New York: Penguin Books, 1992.

Richards, D.G. *Intellectual Property Rights and Global Capitalism: the Political Economy of the TRIPs Agreement.* Amonk New York: M.E. Sharpe, 2004.

Ricketson, Sam. *Intellectual Property: Cases, Materials and Commentary.* Sydney: Butterworths, 1994.

Roberts, S. *Order and Discipline: An Introduction to Legal Anthropology.* London: Pelican Books, 1979.

Rodman, M. "Breathing Spaces: Customary Land Tenure in Vanuatu." *Land, Custom and Practice in the South Pacific.* Eds. R.G. Ward and E. Kingdon. Melbourne: Cambridge University Press, 1995. 65–109.

Rodman, Margaret. *Masters of Tradition: Consequences of Customary Land Tenure in Longana Vanuatu.* Vancouver: University of BC Press, 1987.

Sandel, Michael. *Liberalism and the Limits of Justice*. Cambridge: Cambridge University Press, 1982.

Sanders, W. "Local Governments and Indigenous Australians: Developments and Dilemmas in Contrasting Power to Sell, Lease, and Dispose of Customary Land Otherwise Than to Natives in Accordance with Custom, and Contract Circumstances." *CAEPR Discussion Paper No. 84*. Canberra: Centre for Aboriginal Economic Policy Research, ANU, 1995.

Saskla Sassen. *Globalization and its Discontents*. New York: New Press, 1998.

Seiberg, Jaret. "Rules Of The Road," *Daily Deal/The Deal* (April 5, 2004): 45.

Shashikant, Sangeeta "Growing Movement Opposing Granting of Drug Patents." (TWN) *Third World Network Geneva*. 2 Aug. 2006 <www.tynside.org.sg.>.

Shaw, Jeff. "Monsanto Looks to Patent Pigs, Breeding Methods." *The NewStandard* (Aug. 18, 2005): 5–7.

Shiva, Vandana "The Indian Seed Act and Patent Act: Sowing the Seeds of Dictatorship." 14 Feb. 2005 <www.zmag.org/content/showarticle.cfm?ItemID=7249>.

Silverman, Alexander E. "Myth, Empiricism, and America's Competitive Edge: The Intellectual Property Antitrust Protection Act." *Stanford Law Review* 43 (July, 1991): 1417–1445.

Singer, Peter. *One World: the Ethics of Globalization*. New Haven and London: Yale University Press, 2002.

Skehan, Craig. "Land of Discontent." *Pacific Islands Monthly* 63. 4 (April 1993): 20–23.

Smith, Adam *The Wealth of Nations*. New York: Random House, 1776.

Smith, G.D. "The Shareholder Primacy Norm." *Journal of Corporate Law* 23 (1998): 277–283.

Stallman, R.M. "Free Software: Freedom and Cooperation." New York University, New York. 29 May 2001 <http://www.mirror5.com/events/rms-nyu-2001-transcript.txt>.

Stallman, R.M. "GNU manifesto." *Computers, Ethics and Society*. Eds. M.D. Ermann & M.S. Shauf. Oxford: Oxford University Press, 2003. 153–161.

Stephenson, Dave. "Tribalizing Alaska's Native Corporations." *Indian Country Today*. 3 June 2003 <http://www.indiancountry.com/content.cfm?id=1054648796>.

Stewart, R. "Autonomy, Dependency, and the State of Papua New Guinea." *Social Stratification in Papua New Guinea*. Ed. R. May. Canberra: Research School of Pacific Studies, 1984. 60–75.

Stobbs Gregory. "Patenting Propagated Data Signals: What Hath God Wrought?" *IEEE Communications Magazine* (July 2000): 12–13.

Stone, Brad. *Newsweek* Aug. 2 2004: 35.

Story, Alan "Copyright, TRIPS and International Educational Agenda," *Global Intellectual Property Rights: Knowledge Access and Development*. Eds. P. Drahos and R. Mayne. New York: Palmgrave Macmillan, 2002.125–143.

Sullivan, Patrick "A Sacred Land, A Sovereign People, An Aboriginal Corporation: Prescribed Bodies and the Native Title Act." *NARU Report Series No. 3*. Darwin: North Australia Research Unit, 1997.

Sulston, John. "Intellectual Property and the Human Genome." *Global Intellectual Property Rights: Knowledge Access and Development*. Eds. P. Drahos and R. Mayne. New York: Palmgrave Macmillan, 2002. 61–73.

Sundaram, A.K and A.C. Inkpen. "The Corporate Objective revisited." *Organization Science* 15. 3 (2004): 350–363.

Svensson, Frances. "Liberal Democracy and Group Rights: The Legacy of Individualism and Its Impact on American Indian Tribes." *Political Studies* 27 (1979): 431–445.

Sweet, Will "Globalization, Philosophy and the Model of Ecumenism." *South Pacific Journal of Philosophy and Culture* 4 (2000): 1–18.

Szekeres, Judy. "General Staff Experiences in the Corporate University." *Journal of Higher Education Policy and Management* 28. 2 (July 2006): 133–145.

Taylor, Rodney. "Sustained Yield Forest Management in Papua New Guinea." *Resources, Development, and Politics in the Pacific Islands*. Eds. Stephen Henningham & R.J. May. Bathurst: Crawford Home Press, 1992. 129–144.

The Chronicle of Higher Education: The Chronicle Review 52, no. 24. 17 Feb. 2006: B20.

Trebilcock, Michael and Jack Knetch. "Land Policy and Economic Development in Papua New Guinea." *Melanesian Law Journal* 9. 1&2 (1981): 102–115.

Tully, James. "Aboriginal property and Western Theory: Rediscovering a Middle Ground." *Social Philosophy and Policy* 11 (1994): 153–180.

Tully, James. "Rediscovering America: the two Treatises and Aboriginal Rights." *Locke's Philosophy: Content and Context*. Ed. G.A. Rogers. Oxford: Clarendon Press, 1994. 165–196.

Tully, James. *A Discourse on Property: John Locke and his Adversaries*. Cambridge: Cambridge University Press, 1980.

Tully, James. *Strange Multiplicity: Constitutionalism in the Age of Diversity*. New York: Cambridge University Press, 1996.

"US Judges Re-Activate Microsoft Antitrust Case." *ComputerWire*. Issue 4883 (22 Mar. 2004): 22–23.

Van Dyke, Vernon. "Justice as fairness; for groups?" *American Political Science Review* 62 (1975): 607–614.

Van Overwalle, G. "From Law to Ethics." *Biotechnology, Patents and Morality.*, 2nd edition. Ed. S. Sterckx. Aldershot: Ashgate, 2000. 197–206.

Varghese, Sam. *Melbourne Age* 12 March 2004: 41.

Vermeersch, E. "Ethical Aspect of Genetic Engineering." *Biotechnology, Patents and Morality*, 2nd edition. Ed. S. Sterckx. Aldershot: Ashgate, 2000. 165–171.

Virendra, Parekh. "Novartis Moving from India." *Khaleej Times* 27 Aug. 2007:39.

Waldron, Jeremy. *The Right to Private Property*. Oxford: Clarendon Press, 1988.

Walker, Brian. "Culturist Dilemmas: On Some Convergences between Kymlicka and the New French Right." Unpublished paper presented at the CPSA Annual Meeting 1995, Montreal, June 2, 1995.

Walsh, J.F. "Settling the Alaska Native Claims Settlement Act." *Stanford Law Review* 38. 1 (Nov. 1985): 227–263.

Ward, A.D. "Agrarian revolution." *New Guinea Quarterly* 6 (1975): 32–40;

Ward, R.G. "Changing forms of communal tenure." *Governance of Common Property in the Pacific Region*. Ed. P. Larmour. Canberra: National Centre for Development Studies, 1997. 19–32.

Ward, R.G. "Land, Law and Custom: Diverging Realities in Fiji." *Land, Custom and Practice in the South Pacific*. Eds. R.G. Ward and E. Kingdon. Melbourne: Cambridge University Press, 2000. 215–226.

Ward, R.G. "Pacific Island Land Tenure: An Overview of Practices and Issues." *Land, Culture and Development in the Aquatic Continent*. Eds. D.G. Malcolm and J. Skog. Kihei, Hawaii: Kapallua Pacific Center, 1992. 29–40.

Weiner, James. "The Incorporate Ground: The Contemporary work of Distribution in the Kutubu Oil Project Area, Papua New Guinea." *Working Paper 1998/1*. Canberra: Resource Management in Asia Pacific, RSPAS, 1998.

Werhane P.H. and M. Gorman. "Intellectual Property Rights, Moral Imagination and Access to Life-Enhancing Drugs." *Business Ethics Quarterly* 15. 4 (2005): 595–614.

Index

Aboriginal Title, 16–18
Agency theory, 57, 64–70
AIDS, 229, 232, 235, 243, 247, 249–257.
Alaskan Indians, 13, 33, 38, 41, 47, 74
Aristotle, 204, 262
Amerindians, 19–20, 78–79, 85, 87
Australia, 5, 7, 13, 17, 28, 33, 36, 37,
38, 41, 42–43, 47, 49, 73–74, 81, 93.
95, 98, 106, 110, 126. 134, 141, 170,
189, 193, 214–215, 254; Australian
Aborigines, 16–18, 36–38, 41–43, 45–
47, 49; Aboriginal Title, 16–18; *Terre
Nullius* doctrine, 49
Australian Aborigines, 16–18, 36–38, 41–
43, 45–47, 49; Aboriginal Title, 16–18;
Terre Nullius doctrine, 49
Autonomy, 2–3, 6, 10, 19, 24–30, 34–38,
46–49, 77–81, 85, 91–93, 134, 159, 170,
173, 184, 201, 205, 207, 211, 225–226,
238, 261, 272

Barnett Report (Forestry, Papua New
Guinea), 143, 149–151
Basmati Rice, 172, 263–265
Berne Convention, 182
Biopiracy, 10, 261–265, 271, 275, 278
Bremer III, Paul, 268
Burns Commission (Fiji), 163

Canadian Indians, 34; Indian Act, 34
Canada, 5, 19, 33–36, 49. 170. 177, 215,
266, 271; Canadian Indians, 34; Indian
Act, 34; Supreme Court of Canada,
277
Capitalism, 4, 9, 16, 30, 59, 71–72, 81–94,
118, 128–129, 152, 160, 167, 170, 173,
189, 194, 196, 203, 257, 272, 276
Communitarians, 32–34, 58–59, 80, 91
Contractarians, 56–59

Control Rights, 5, 26–30, 111–119, 131,
168–173, 225
Copyright, educational Resources, 183,
197, 236; Free rider issue, 187–188; Free
Software Movement, 10, 198, 208–
212, 226, 270; Free Trade Agreements,
214–217, 193; income rights, 9, 26–29,
111–119, 131–132, 168–191, 137, 271–
191; software, 176, 198–201, 213–217,
219–240; TRIPS 182–185, 188–193,
195–198
Corporations, 4, 10, 33, 44, 50, 51–69,
103, 138, 171–172, 175, 185, 190–192,
195–196, 204, 215, 246, 261–262, 266–
268, 271–272; Agency theory, 57, 64–
70; Alaskan Native Corporations,
38–39, 41, 47; Australian Aboriginal
Corporations, 43, 45–47; Incorporated Land Groups in Papua New
Guinea, 38–40, 98, 119, 121, 137–151;
shareholder wealth maximization, 53–
67, 72; stakeholder Theory, 59–63;
universities as corporations, 67
Curtin, Tim, 96–97, 107, 144, 146–148,
151

De George, Richard, 181, 241–246
De Soto, Hernando, 5, 8, 78, 81–93, 95,
106, 118, 128–130, 167–169, 189
Deardorff, Alan, 256
Dependency Theory, 1, 3–4, 214
Doha Declaration, 249, 251, 254, 257–258

Educational Resources, 183, 197, 236
Enron, 72
Europe, 4, 172, 183, 203, 235, 247, 250–
251; European law, 16–21, 43, 49,
81, 181, 183, 201, 214, 240, 264–265:
Europeans in Fiji, 101, 154–157

Fiji, 5, 8–9, 25–26, 28, 85, 96, 101–103, 117, 122, 149–150, 153; Burns Commission, 163; coups, 160–164; Figian Indians, 158–163; history, 155–158; land tenure, 158–165; Land Trust Board 102, 158–159
Filer, Colin, 40. 134
Fingleton, 98–103, 107
Foucault, Michel, 69, 188–190
Free Software Movement, 10, 198, 208–212, 226, 270
Freeman, R.E., 59
Friedman, Milton, 54
Fukuyama, Francis, 45–46, 148, 203–205, 207

Gates, Bill, 171, 175, 220, 248, 256
GATT (General Agreement on Trade and Tariffs), 184
Globalization, 4, 73, 80, 213, 215, 267
GlxoSmithKline, 187, 243, 256
Gordon, Sir Arthur, 156–159
GMOs (Genetically Modified Organisms), 198, 267, 276–277
Group Self-Determination, 31–50

Hart, H.L.A., 188, 224, 238
Hayek, F.A., 98
Hegel, G.W.F., 14, 205
Honore, A.M. 84, 88–91
Human Genome Project, 10, 187, 262, 273–274
Human Genome Diversity Project, 274–275
Human Rights, 199, 245–247, 260; *see also* natural rights

IBM, 91, 174–176, 183, 189, 217, 232, 272
Income rights, 9, 26–29, 111–119, 131–132, 168–191, 137, 275
Incorporated Land Groups in Papua New Guinea, 38–40, 98, 119, 121, 137–151
India, 10, 13, 154, 172, 196–199, 242, agribusiness, 263–265, 267–268, 272; Fijian Indians, 158–163; pharmaceuticals, 248–250; pharmaceuticals and TRIPS, 251–260;
Iraq, 268–269

Jamestown Colony, 153–154, 158, 161, 165
Japan, 2, 46, 61, 203, 251
J.E.M. Ag Supply Inc. v Pioneer Hi-Bred International Inc.(USSC), 266

Kant, Immanuel, 15, 59, 129, 205–206, 216, 225–226, 248
Kymlicka, Will, 6, 23–26, 30, 34–36, 48, 77–78, 207

Land Trust Board (Fiji) 102, 158–159
Lanjouw, Jean, 256–257
Libertarianism 135, 150–151, 175, 205–206, 211–213, 235, 238; *see also* Nozick
Locke, John, 5, 11, 13, 15–22, 30, 79, 92–93, 101, 105, 108, 116, 152, 174, 184, 206, 222–225, 262, 276

Mabo Decision (Australia), 17, 36–38
Managerialism, 62–76
Maitland, Ian, 61, 222, 228, 241
Maritain. Jacques, 204–205
Marxism, 3, 115, 195, 277
MacIntyre, Alastair, 67, 70–71
Melanesia, 110, 141, 163
Microsoft Corp., 171, 175–176, 193, 201, 210, 215, 219, 231–234, 237, 239–240
Mill, John Stuart, 9, 202–204, 207, 212, 216
Modern Constitutionalism, 19–21, 77–80
Modernization Theory, 1
Monsanto, 172, 178, 195–196, 264, 266–268, 271–272, 275–276
More, Sir Thomas, 79
Morse, Samuel, 276–277
MSF (Medecins Sans Frontieres), 249, 254–255

Natural Rights, 5–6, 13, 19, 183–185, 223, 246–257 *se also* human rights
Novartis, 255, 259
Nozick, Robert, 10, 13–30, 173, 194–195, 205–208, 211–212, 216, 225–226

Open Source Software, 189, 193, 214–215, 208
Oxfam, 249

Papua New Guinea, 2–10, 28, 38–
   40, 42, 62, 74, 85, 89, 91, 153, 214;
   Bougainville Crisis, 132–135; custom
   121–130; customary land tenure,
   95–120, 131–132; forestry sector,
   142–152; Hagahai controversy 274;
   Incorporated Land Groups, 38–40, 98,
   119, 121, 137–151; Southern Highlands,
   135–142
Patents, aeronautics, 219–220; enforcement and TRIPS, 188–193, 195–200;
   farming techniques, 177–178; genetic
   material 177–178, 261–280; history 173;
   innovation, 243–244; income rights,
   171–191; laws of nature, 3, 177–179;
   medicine 176; pharmaceuticals, 196–
   199, 182, 222–223, 228–231, 234, 241,
   241–260; Plant Patent Act (US), 266;
   plant patents, 177; process patents,
   179; product patents 179–181; software,
   175–176, 201, 212–216, 226–228, 231,
   236; specification, 177–181, 191
Performativity Indexing, 68–69
Plant patents, 177
Plant Patent Act (US), 266
Plant Variety Protection Act (US), 266
Plato, 78, 87, 99
Pharmaceuticals, 10; patent rights 222–
   223, 228–231, 234, 242–244; TRIPS
   compliance 196–199, 182, 241, 248–
   255; drug company responsibilities,
   241–248, 255–260
Plymouth Colony, 153–155, 158, 161, 164,
   203
Point Four Program of Development
   Aid, 1
Polynesia, 110
Process patents, 179
Property Rights, customary land tenure
   in Papua New Guinea, 95–120, 131–
   132; de Soto, Hernando, on Western
   ownership rights, 5, 8, 78, 81–93, 95,
   106, 118, 128–130, 167–169, 189; Fijian
   land tenure, 158–165; intellectual
   property rights and agriculture,
   261–272; intellectual property rights
   and human genetic material 271–
   275; intellectual property rights in

general, 167–200; intellectual property
   rights and pharmaceuticals, 241–
   260; intellectual property rights and
   software, 201–240; Mabo Decision
   (Australia), 17, 36–38; *Terre Nullius*
   doctrine (Australia), 49

Rabuka, Sitiveni, 160–163
Rawls, John, 14–15, 32, 80, 116, 207
Reynolds, Henry, 16–21, 30, 81
RiceTec, 172, 264–265, 275
Richards, D.G., 4, 196, 257, 272, 276–278

Shareholder Wealth Maximization, 53–
   67, 72
Shiva, Vandana, 266–268, 271
Somare, Sir Michael, 2–3
Smith, Adam, 71, 130, 134
Socialism, 2
Speight, George, 162–164
Stakeholder Theory, 59–63
Stallman, Richard, 10, 188, 199, 207–210,
   213, 216, 220, 226, 229, 234–235, 237,
   270
Supreme Court of Canada, 277

Tanzania, 2, 85–86, 97, 104
Terre Nullius doctrine (Australia), 49
Torres Strait Islanders, 37–38, 93
TRIPS (compliance), 3–4, 6, 9–10, 182–
   199, 217, 237, 242; copyright 182–185,
   188–193, 195–198; genetic material,
   261–280; patents 188–193, 195–200;
   pharmaceuticals, 196–199, 182, 241,
   248–255; software, 185; TRIPS Plus, 9,
   182, 195, 252
TRIPS Plus, 9, 182, 195, 252
Tully, James, 5–8 18–26, 30, 49, 77–81,
   84–85, 92, 100, 107, 170

United Nations, 96; UN Conference
   on Trade and Development, 191; UN
   Declaration of Human Rights, 245
United States, 1, 4–5, 7, 31, 33, 36, 45–46,
   49, 60, 63, 71, 74, 177, 182–183, 188,
   203, 220, 234, 236, 248, 252, 266–267;
   J.E.M. Ag Supply Inc. v Pioneer Hi-
   Bred International Inc.(USSC), 266;

US Court of Appeals of the Federal
Circuit, 188–189; USAID, 276
Universities, 45, 65–73, 202, 236
Uruguay Round of Multilateral Trade
Negotiations, 256
US Court of Appeals of the Federal
Circuit, 188–189
USAID, 276

Vanuatu, 49, 95–97, 122, 159

Werhane, Patricia, 186, 243, 247–248
World Intellectual Property Organization
(WIPO), 183–184
World Trade Organization, 182–183, 190,
215–217